Buying Your Self on the Internet

Future Law

Series Editors
Lilian Edwards, Professor of Law, Innovation and Society,
Newcastle University
Burkhard Schafer, Professor of Computational Legal Theory,
University of Edinburgh
Edina Harbinja Senior Lecturer in Media/Privacy Law, Aston University

Books in the series are critical and topic-led, reflecting the global
jurisdiction of technology and culture interacting with law. Each title
responds to cutting-edge debates in the field where technology interacts
with culture to challenge the ability of law to react to frequently
unprecedented scenarios.

Available or forthcoming titles

Buying Your Self on the Internet: Wrap Contracts and Personal Genomics
Andelka M Phillips

Future Law: Emerging Technology, Regulation and Ethics
Lilian Edwards, Burkhard Schafer and Edina Harbinja (eds)

edinburghuniversitypress.com/series/ful

Buying Your Self on the Internet

Wrap Contracts and Personal Genomics

Andelka M Phillips

EDINBURGH
University Press

To my husband Kent and to my parents,
Michelle and Petar,
and to my grandmother Dorothy
and to my friend Bernard Brown

Edinburgh University Press is one of the leading university presses in the UK. We publish academic books and journals in our selected subject areas across the humanities and social sciences, combining cutting-edge scholarship with high editorial and production values to produce academic works of lasting importance. For more information visit our website: edinburghuniversitypress.com

Edinburgh University Press Ltd
The Tun – Holyrood Road
12 (2f) Jackson's Entry
Edinburgh EH8 8PJ

First published in hardback by Edinburgh University Press 2019

Typeset in 11/13pt Adobe Garamond by
Servis Filmsetting Ltd, Stockport, Cheshire, and
printed and bound by CPI Group (UK) Ltd,
Croydon, CR0 4YY

A CIP record for this book is available from the British Library

ISBN 978 1 4744 2259 8 (hardback)
ISBN 978 1 4744 8430 5 (paperback)
ISBN 978 1 4744 2260 4 (webready PDF)
ISBN 978 1 4744 2261 1 (epub)

Contents

Expanded Table of Contents

Box Text

Foreword

The original work upon which this book is based began almost a decade ago and as with many other new technologies, the personal genomics industry is still developing at a rapid pace. This is also a period of change for the law and so this book captures the industry and the state of the law at a particular moment. I intend to be able to update this volume in the future, but as this manuscript was submitted in late 2018 and will be published in mid-2019, some things may change in the interim and I will only be able account for these changes in the future. I ask readers to bear this in mind and to please note that this book is intended to provide an introduction to a complex area and provide some suggestions for reform, which it is hoped will contribute to stimulating a wider discussion of regulation of personal genomics and of technology more generally and the ways in which we all interact with contracts and privacy policies online.

The Table of Abbreviations for DTC Contracts provides links to the Wayback Machine wherever possible. Efforts have also been made to provide archived links throughout.

Preface

There are many people I wish to thank for their help, friendship and guidance along the way. This work began in Oxford and it has been written in three countries: the UK; Ireland; and finally, New Zealand (Aotearoa), which is my original home. It is ongoing work and I plan to do other things with my existing datasets and build upon them in the future. It is hoped that this book will provide an introduction to this complex area, but it is just that: an introduction. The references provided in the footnotes and bibliography should allow readers to explore issues they are interested in further.

I should firstly like to express my gratitude to Lilian Edwards, Burkhard Schafer and Edina Harbinja, the editors of the Future Law series for Edinburgh University Press. This is my first book and I am delighted to be able to contribute to such an interesting and timely series. I should also like to thank Laura Williamson, David Lonergan, Eddie Clark, Naomi Farmer, Zuzana Ihnátová, Rebecca Mackenzie and everyone at Edinburgh University Press, and my copy-editor Helen Johnston and my indexer Lesley Wilson.

I wish to particularly thank Jonathan Herring for his guidance and invaluable feedback on earlier drafts of this book. I also wish to particularly thank Stuart Newman for his comments at a much later stage. A special thank you also to my friend Saira Mian. From my time at Oxford, I also wish to thank my doctoral supervisor Jane Kaye and everyone at Oxford's HeLEX Centre, and thank you as well to my friends and colleagues, Charles Foster, Marina Jirotka, Sigrid Sterckx, Julian Cockbain, Donna Dickenson, Thana de Campos, Teresa Finlay, Michael Morrison, and Fiona Coldwell.

I also wish to say a special thank you to my earliest academic mentors. To Doug Sutton, who first recommended pursuing doctoral study. To Bernard Brown, my friend and mentor, who supervised my LLM thesis and who is a constant source of inspiration. I also wish to thank David Vaver, George Mousourakis, Cam Kyle, Andrew Allan, and the late Nin Tomas.

Also from my time at Oxford, I wish to thank Ian Brown, Michelle Lanzoni, Heather Bradshaw-Martin, David Erdos, David Goldberg, Helena Webb, Imogen Goold, Kate Greasley, Jesse Wall, Pip Coore, Heloise

Robinson, Marija Jovanovic, Poorna Mysoor, Tobias Lutzi, Krishnaprasad KV, Kunal Sharma, Santa Slokenberga, Tamara Hervey, Rachel Wechsler, Bendert Zevenbergen, Elo Luik, Andrew Dwyer, Greg and Jen Dubbin, Alice Schneider, and Katherine Fletcher at Oxford Cyber Security Network. I also want to thank my friends and colleagues Emiliano De Cristofaro, Marina Chang, Claudio Lombardi, Jan Charbonneau, Tina Stevens, Trudo Lemmens (Toronto), Pascale Chapdelaine, Graham Reynolds (UBC), Meghan Murtha, Karmela Krleža-Jerić, Stuart Hogarth, Helen Wallace (GeneWatch UK), Jesus Niebla Zatarain, Misha Angrist (Duke), Brad Malin, James Hazel, Chris Slobogin and Ellen Wright Clayton (Vanderbilt), Catherine Tucker (MIT), Liz Steiner, Miranda Mowbray, and Geoff Ginsburg (Duke). I also wish to thank Stewart Dresner and everyone at Privacy Laws and Business and Mary Chitty at Cambridge Healthtech Institute.

From Ireland I wish to thank my friends and colleagues Blanaid Clarke, Deirdre Ahern, Mark Bell, Oran Doyle, Helen Dixon (and the Office of the Irish Data Protection Commissioner), Eoin O'Dell, David Fennelly, Liz Heffernan, Andrea Mulligan, Kouroch Bellis, Surya Roy, Anne Flanagan, Martina Kirchberger and Maureen Junker-Kenny. I also wish to thank John Kyle and Riemke Ensing for their support.

I have completed my final revisions for this book by the sea and am extremely grateful to my husband Kent, my parents, Michelle and Petar, and my grandmother Dorothy and my aunt Fleur for their patience during this period of writing.

Acknowledgements

This book is based upon research which began in 2011 and draws upon my related work in a number of published papers and presentations. I would like to begin by thanking the universities where I have studied and worked during this time: the University of Oxford; and Trinity College Dublin, the University of Dublin.

At Trinity, I wish to particularly thank my friends and colleagues Blanaid Clarke, Deirdre Ahern, Eoin O'Dell, David Fennelly, Andrea Mulligan and Martina Kirchberger. Also a special thank you to Helen Dixon (the Irish Data Protection Commissioner) and all the staff at the Office of the Irish Data Protection Commissioner.

I wish to thank my colleagues at Te Piringa – Faculty of Law, University of Waikato, but especially to the Dean, Wayne Rumbles, and Nicky Parsons-Roberts. Also in New Zealand I should like to thank Tim McBride, Katrine Evans and Gehan Gunasekara for their support.

I wish to thank the universities and conferences where I have presented my work, particularly the University of Oxford's Medical Law and Ethics Discussion Group, Peter A. Allard School of Law (University of British Columbia), the Information Security Group (Department of Computer Science, University College London), the University of Toronto, Lund University, the National University of Singapore, the University of Ghent, the GikII conference, the Privacy Laws and Business 2018 conference 'Navigating GDPR: The art of the possible', and the GenoPri workshops.

Please note that some of the links provided to websites in the footnotes may be out of date, but records of these are on file and for those who are interested in exploring this further archived content can often be accessed through the Internet Archive's Wayback Machine (https://archive.org). The Table of Abbreviations for DTC Contracts provides links to the Wayback Machine wherever possible. Efforts have also been made to provide archived links throughout.

This book specifically draws upon the following works:

Andelka M Phillips, 'Will my genes really help me fit into those jeans? Personal genomics and wrap contracts', in B. Schafer, L. Edwards and E. Harbinja (eds), *Future Law: Emerging Technology, Ethics and Regulation* (forthcoming Edinburgh University Press, 2019).

Andelka M Phillips (2018), 'Genetics goes online – privacy in the world of personal genomics', *Privacy Laws & Business International*, October <https://www.privacylaws.com/Publications/int/PLB_International_Issues/PLB-International-Issue-155/>

Andelka M Phillips (2017), 'Reading the fine print when buying your genetic self online: Direct-to-consumer genetic testing terms and conditions' *New Genetics and Society*, 36(3) 273–95 <http://dx.doi.org/10.1080/14636778.2017.1352468>

Andelka M Phillips (2016), 'Only a click away – DTC genetics for ancestry, health, love . . . and more: A view of the business and regulatory landscape', *Applied & Translational Genomics* 16–22 <https://doi.org/10.1016/j.atg.2016.01.001>

Andelka M Phillips, 'Genomic privacy and direct-to-consumer genetics – big consumer genetic data – what's in that contract?' (presented at GenoPri'15 [The 2nd Workshop on Genome Privacy and Security] and published as part of IEEE Conference Proceedings 2015).

Andelka M Phillips (2016), 'Take an online DNA test and you could be revealing far more than you realise', *The Conversation*, 12 January <https://theconversation.com/take-an-online-dna-test-and-you-could-be-revealing-far-more-than-you-realise-52734>

Andelka M Phillips, 'Think before you click', republished as part of the American Bar Association's 'The Best of ABA Sections' in its *GPSolo* magazine, July/August 2015 <http://www.americanbar.org/publications/gp_solo/2015/july-august/science_and_technology_law_think_you_click_ordering_genetic_test_online.html>

Andelka M Phillips (2015), 'Think before you click: Ordering a genetic test online', *The SciTech Lawyer*, Winter 11(2) <http://www.americanbar.org/publications/scitech_lawyer/2015/winter/think_before_you_click_ordering_genetic_test_online.html>

Some of my data has also been publicly released. Please refer to: Data on Direct-to-Consumer Genetic Testing and DNA Testing Companies Version 1.3 (Open Access Dataset, Zenodo, February 2018). doi: 10.5281/zenodo.1175799 <https://zenodo.org/record/1183565#.WunK6y-ZNp8>

Statutes

US Legislation

International

Cases

Abbreviations

ACCC	Australian Competition and Consumer Commission
Additional Protocol	Additional Protocol to the Convention on Human Rights and Biomedicine, concerning Genetic Testing for Health Purposes
AIMD	Directive 90/385/EEC regarding active implantable medical devices
AMP	Association for Molecular Pathology
ASHG	American Society of Human Genetics
Brussels I-Regulation (recast)	Regulation (EU) No 1215/2012 of the European Parliament and of the Council of 12 December 2012 on jurisdiction and the recognition and enforcement of judgments in civil and commercial matters (recast) OJ 2012, L 251/1
CCMG	Canadian College of Medical Geneticists
CLHIA	Canadian Life and Health Insurance Association
CMA	Competition & Markets Authority
CPUTR	Consumer Protection from Unfair Trading Regulations 2008
CRA	Consumer Rights Act 2015
DPA	Data Protection Act 1998
DPA18	Data Protection Act 2018
DTC	Direct-to-consumer genetic testing
EASAC	European Academies of Science Advisory Council
ECJ	European Court of Justice
ESHG	European Society of Human Genetics
FCA	Financial Conduct Authority
FEAM	Federation of European Academies of Medicine
Framework of Principles	A Common Framework of Principles for direct-to-consumer genetic testing services
GAO	Government Accountability Office

GDPR	Regulation (EU) 2016/679 of the European Parliament and of the Council of 27 April 2016 on the protection of natural persons with regard to the processing of personal data and on the free movement of such data, and repealing Directive 95/46/EC (General Data Protection Regulation) [2016] OJ 2 119/1
GINA	Genetic Information Nondisrimination Act 2008
GNA	Genetic Non-Discrimination Act 2017
GPPC	Genetics and Public Policy Center
GPSD	Directive 2001/95/EC of the European Parliament and of the Council of 3 December 2001 on general product safety
HGC	Human Genetics Commission
HIPAA	Health Insurance Portability and Accountability Act
HRA	Human Rights Act 1998
HTA	Human Tissue Authority
ICO	Information Commissioner's Office (UK)
IVD Directive	Directive 98/79/EC on in vitro diagnostic medical devices
Draft IVD Regulation	Proposal for a Regulation 9770/15 of the European Parliament and of the Council on in vitro diagnostic medical devices of 12 June 2015. Interinstitutional File: 2012/0267 (COD)
IVD Regulation	Regulation (EU) 2017/746 of the European Parliament and of the Council of 5 April 2017 on in vitro diagnostic medical devices and repealing Directive 98/79/EC and Commission Decision 2010/227/EU
LDTs	Laboratory developed tests
MDD	Directive 93/42/EEC of 14 June 1993 concerning medical devices
MHRA	Medicines and Healthcare Products Regulatory Agency
NCC	Norwegian Consumer Council
OFT	Office of Fair Trading
OPC	Office of the Canadian Privacy Commissioner

Oviedo Convention	Convention for the Protection of Human Rights and Dignity of the Human Being with regard to the Application of Biology and Medicine: Convention on Human Rights and Biomedicine
PIPEDA	Personal Information Protection and Electronic Documents Act 2000
Rome I	Regulation (EC) No 593/2008 of the European Parliament and of the Council of 17 June 2008 on the law applicable to contractual obligations (Rome I)
RUO	Research use only
SACGHS	The Secretary's Advisory Committee on Genetics, Health, and Society
SNPs	Single nucleotide polymorphisms
Unfair Terms Directive	Directive 93/13/EEC of 5 April 1993 on unfair terms in consumer contracts
UTCCR	The Unfair Terms in Consumer Contracts Regulations 1999

Abbreviations for Direct-to-Consumer Company Contract Documents

Company	Title of Contract or Privacy Policy	URL	Date Saved	Abbreviated Document Name
1. 23andMe	Terms of Service Privacy Statement Consent Document	<www.23andme.com/about/tos/>[1] Archived content available at <http://web.archive.org/web/20130807140525/www.23andme.com/about/tos/> https://www.23andme.com/about/consent/	21 July 2013 10 August 2013 31 October 2018	TOS Privacy Consent
2. 23DNA	Privacy Policy	<http://www.23dna.co/privacy.html> Archived content available at <http://web.archive.org/web/20150811094824/http://23dna.co/privacy.html>	28 August 2013 31 October 2018	Privacy
3. Accu-metrics Viaguard	No document available	<http://accu-metrics.com> Archived content available at <http://web.archive.org/web/20180823141450/http://www.accu-metrics.com/>	28 August 2013 31 October 2018	
4. American International Biotechnology, LLC (AIBioTech)	Privacy Practices	<www.alphabiolabs.com> Archived content available at <https://web.archive.org/web/20140619211625/http://www.alphabiolabs.co.uk/terms-conditions/>	2 October 2014	Privacy

	Document	URL	Dates	Category
5. Any Lab Test Now®	PayPal User Agreement PayPal Privacy Policy	<http://www.mylabsa.com/index.html>	28 August 2013 13 August 2013	Agreement Privacy
6. Any Time Lab	Privacy Policy	<http://anytimelab.com/index.html> Archived content available at <http://web.archive.org/web/20180824111528/http://anytimelab.com/index.html>	8 April 2014 31 October 2018	Privacy
7. ARUP Lab	Disclaimer Online Privacy Policy (last updated 21 September 2008)	<http://www.aruplab.com/genetics/tests> Archived content available at <http://web.archive.org/web/20180402091542/http://www.aruplab.com:80/genetics/tests>	14 January 2014 31 October 2018	Disclaimer Privacy
8. Asper Biotech	Terms and conditions Genetic Testing Terms and Conditions	<http://www.asperbio.com/genetic-tests> Archived content available at <http://web.archive.org/web/20131102112725/http://www.asperbio.com:80/genetic-testing-process/terms-and-conditions>	5 October 2014 13 August 2013 31 October 2018	T&C
9. Athleticode	No document available	<http://athleticode.com> Archived content available at <http://web.archive.org/web/20141216200403/http://athleticode.com/>	10 August 2013 Checked again 22 January 2014 and still operating. Checked again 9 April 2014. 31 October 2018	

(Continued)

Company	Title of Contract or Privacy Policy	URL	Date Saved	Abbreviated Document Name
10. BalanceDiet™	No document available	<http://www.gobalancediet.com/about/about-balancediet/> Archived content available at <http://web.archive.org/web/20150727030039/http://www.gobalancediet.com:80/about/about-balancediet/>	Accessed 28 August 2013. Checked again 28 January 2014 and still operating. Checked again 30 April 2014. 31 October 2018	
11. Beyond Nutrition	No document available	<http://www.beyond-nutrition.co.uk/dna-diet/> Archived content available at <http://web.archive.org/web/20140219093727/http://www.beyond-nutrition.co.uk:80/dna-diet>	Accessed 28 August 2013. Checked again 28 January 2014 and still operating. Checked again 10 April 2014. 31 October 2018	
12. BioClinics (Genetic Health Management)	Client Privacy Policy	<http://www.weightloss-dnatesting.co.uk/about> Not available in the Internet Archive	5 October 2014 31 October 2018	Privacy
13. Bio Logis	Terms of Service Privacy	<https://pgsbox.com> Archived content available at <http://web.archive.org/web/20180824200345/https://pgsbox.com/>	14 January 2014 14 January 2014 31 October 2018	TOS Privacy
14. Biotechnology Group Inc	No document available	<http://www.biotechnologygroup.com/index.html>	Accessed 22 January 2014.	

		Archived content available at	Checked again 28 January 2014 and still operating. Checked again 10 April 2014.	
		<http://web.archive.org/web/20130806225802/http://biotechnologygroup.com/index.html>	31 October 2018	
15. Cancer Genetics Inc	Legal Notice and Terms of Use	<http://www.cancergenetics.com>	2 October 2014	TOS
	Privacy Policy	Archived content available at <http://web.archive.org/web/20180824212352/http://www.cancergenetics.com/>	5 January 2014 31 October 2018	Privacy
16. CD Genomics	Terms & Conditions	<http://www.cd-genomics.com>	5 October 2014	T&C
	Privacy Policy	Archived content available at <http://web.archive.org/web/20180823185559/https://www.cd-genomics.com/>	5 October 2014 31 October 2018	Privacy
17. C2DNA (Canadian Centre for DNA Diagnostics)	Terms of Use	<http://www.c2dna.com/index.html>	13 August 2013	TOU
	Return Policy	Archived content available at <http://web.archive.org/web/20151218045017/http://www.c2dna.com:80/index.html>	13 August 2013	Return
	Privacy Policy		13 August 2013 31 October 2018	Privacy
18. Center for Medical Genetics	Privacy Statement	<http://www.geneticstesting.com>	15 January 2014	Privacy
		Archived content available at <http://web.archive.org/web/20180605044120/https://www.geneticstesting.com/?>	31 October 2018	

(*Continued*)

Company	Title of Contract or Privacy Policy	URL	Date Saved	Abbreviated Document Name
19. Counsyl	Terms of Service Informed Consent	\<https://www.counsyl.com> Archived content available at \<http://web.archive.org/web/20181026095129/http://www.counsyl.com/>	15 January 2014 5 October 2014 31 October 2018	TOS IC
20. Cygene Direct	Cygene Direct Privacy Policy CyGene DNA Testing Security Policy	\<http://cygene.infinityarts.com> Archived content available at \<http://web.archive.org/web/20160403100041/http://cygene.infinityarts.com:80/>	2 October 2014 22 August 2013 31 October 2018	Privacy Security
21. Darwin Dieticians	No document available	\<http://www.darwindietitians.com.au> Archived content available at \<http://web.archive.org/web/2/http://www.darwindietitians.com.au>	Accessed 22 August 2013. Checked again 28 January 2014 and still operating. Checked again 10 April 2014. 31 October 2018	
22. DDC, DNA Diagnostics Center	Privacy Statement	\<http://www.dnacenter.com> Archived content available at \<http://web.archive.org/web/20180923010104/https://dnacenter.com/>	3 October 2014 31 October 2018	Privacy

Name	Document	URL	Date	Type
23. DDC, DNA Diagnostics Centre	Terms and Conditions for Use of this Site	<http://www.dna-bioscience.co.uk>	16 August 2013	T&C
24. DeCODEme	Terms of Use Privacy Policy	Not available in Internet Archive <http://www.decodeme.com> Archived content available at <http://web.archive.org/web/20130110122214/http://www.decodeme.com>	31 October 2018 22 August 2013 22 August 2013 31 October 2018	TOU Privacy
25. Diagnomics	No document available	<http://www.diagnomics.com> Archived content available at <http://web.archive.org/web/*/http://www.diagnomics.com>	27 January 2014 31 October 2018	
26. DNALYSIS Biotechnology	Privacy Policy	<http://www.dnalysis.co.za/About-us.aspx> Archived content available at <http://web.archive.org/web/*/http://www.dnalysis.co.za/About-us.aspx>	22 August 2013 31 October 2018	Privacy
27. DNAFit	Terms of Use Privacy Policy	<http://www.dnafit.com/uk/> Archived content available at <http://web.archive.org/web/*/http://www.dnafit.com/uk/>	20 January 2014 20 January 2014 31 October 2018	TOU Privacy
28. DNA Dimensions	No document available	<http://detroitdna.com> Archived content available at <http://web.archive.org/web/*/http://detroitdna.com>	Accessed 11 April 2014. Checked again accessed 13 May 2014. 31 October 2018	

(Continued)

Company	Title of Contract or Privacy Policy	URL	Date Saved	Abbreviated Document Name
29. DNA Direct	Terms of Use Privacy Policy	<http://www.dnadirect.com> Archived content available at <http://web.archive.org/web/*/http://www.dnadirect.com>	22 August 2013 10 August 2013 31 October 2018	TOU Privacy
30. DNA DTC	DNADTC.com –Terms and Conditions – Individual Customer Privacy Policy Consent Document for Individual Research Use	<http://www.dnadtc.com/about.aspx> Archived content available at <http://web.archive.org/web/20130501000000*/http://www.dnadtc.com/about.aspx>	10 August 2013 10 August 2013 10 August 2013 31 October 2018	T&C Privacy Consent
31. DNA Genie	Terms & Conditions Privacy Policy	<http://www.dna-genie.com> Archived content available at <http://web.archive.org/web/*/http://www.dna-genie.com>	29 January 2014 29 January 2014 31 October 2018	TOC Privacy
32. DNA Plus	Terms of Use	<http://www.dnaplus.de/en/products/> Archived content available at <http://web.archive.org/web/*/http://www.dnaplus.de/en/products/>	20 January 2014 31 October 2018	TOU
33. DNA Slim	No document available	<https://www.dnaslim.org> Archived content available at <http://web.archive.org/web/*/https://www.dnaslim.org>	29 April 2014 31 October 2018	

34. DNA Spectrum	Terms of Use (Terms of Service)	<http://www.dnaspectrum.com>	9 September 2013	TOU
		Archived content available at <http://web.archive.org/web/*/http://www.dnaspectrum.com>	31 October 2018	
35. DNA Testing Centres of Canada	Disclaimer Privacy Policy	<http://dnatestingcanada.com/about-us/>	1 October 2014 1 October 2014	Disclaimer Privacy
		Archived content available at <http://web.archive.org/web/*/http://dnatestingcanada.com/about-us/>	31 October 2018	
36. DNA Traits	Terms and Conditions	<http://www.dnatraits.com/about.aspx>	10 August 2013	T&C
		Archived content available at <http://web.archive.org/web/*/http://www.dnatraits.com/about.aspx>	31 October 2018	
37. easyDNA	Terms and Conditions (Australia) Terms and Conditions (UK) Terms and Conditions (USA) Privacy Policy (USA)	<http://www.easydna.com.au> <http://www.easydna.co.uk> <http://www.easy-dna.com/>	15 August 2013 15 August 2013 10 August 2013 15 August 2013	T&C (Auz) T&C (UK) T&C (USA) Privacy (USA)
		Archived content available at <http://web.archive.org/web/*/http://www.easydna.com.au> <http://web.archive.org/web/*/http://www.easy-dna.com/>	31 October 2018	
38. EnteroLab	About Privacy	<https://www.enterolab.com>	15 August 2013	Privacy
		Archived content available at <http://web.archive.org/web/*/https://www.enterolab.com>	31 October 2018	

(Continued)

Company	Title of Contract or Privacy Policy	URL	Date Saved	Abbreviated Document Name
39. FitGenes	Privacy	\<http://www.fitgenes.com\>	3 October 2014	Privacy
		Archived content available at \<http://web.archive.org/web/*/http://www.fitgenes.com\>	31 October 2018	
40. ForuMed Biotechnology	Not available	\<http://www.forumed.eu/επικοινωνία\>	30 April 2014	
		Archived content available at \<http://web.archive.org/web/*/http://www.forumed.eu/επικοινωνία\>	31 October 2018	
41. Foundation Medicine Inc	Legal Notice and Terms of Use	\<http://www.foundationmedicine.com\>	19 January 2014	TOU
		Archived content available at \<http://web.archive.org/web/*/http://www.foundationmedicine.com\>	31 October 2018	
42. Gene By Gene	Terms and Conditions	\<https://www.genebygene.com\>	1 October 2014	T&C
		Archived content available at \<http://web.archive.org/web/*/https://www.genebygene.com\>	31 October 2018	
43. GenePeeks	GenePeeks, Inc. Terms of Use	\<http://www.genepeeks.com\>	3 October 2014	TOU
	GenePeeks Privacy Policy		3 October 2014	Privacy
		Archived content available at \<http://web.archive.org/web/*/http://www.genepeeks.com\>	31 October 2018	

44. GenePlanet	Terms and Conditions Privacy Statement	<http://www.geneplanet.com> Archived content available at <http://web.archive.org/web/*/http://www.geneplanet.com>	10 August 2013 10 August 2013 31 October 2018	T&C Privacy
45. Geneticom	No document available	<http://www.geneticom.nl> Archived content available at <http://web.archive.org/web/*/http://www.geneticom.nl>	10 September 2013. Checked again 28 January 2014 31 October 2018	
46. Genetic Center Company Limited	Terms and Conditions for Use of Website Privacy Statement	<http://www.genetic-center.com> Archived content available at <http://web.archive.org/web/*/http://www.genetic-center.com >	13 August 2013 13 August 2013 31 October 2018	T&C Privacy
47. Genetic Health	No Terms and Conditions Privacy Policy	<http://www.genetic-health.co.uk> Archived content available at <http://web.archive.org/web/*/http://www.genetic-health.co.uk>	10 August 2013 31 October 2018	T&C Privacy
48. Genetic Healthcare Group (geneLAB)	No terms and Conditions	<http://genetic-healthcare.com/gh_about_us.html> Archived content available at <http://web.archive.org/web/*/http://genetic-healthcare.com/gh_about_us.html>	30 April 2014 31 October 2018	

(Continued)

Company	Title of Contract or Privacy Policy	URL	Date Saved	Abbreviated Document Name
49. Genetic Performance	Genetic Performance – Terms and Conditions	<http://geneticperformance.com> Archived content available at <http://web.archive.org/web/*/http://www.gtldna.com>	29 April 2014 7 October 2014 31 October 2018	T&C
50. Genetic Testing Laboratories Inc (GTL)	Genetic Testing Lab: Terms of Use Disclaimer GTL DNA Testing Privacy Policy	<http://www.gtldna.com> Archived content available at <http://web.archive.org/web/*/http://www.gtldna.com>	10 August 2013 10 August 2013 31 October 2018	TOU Privacy
51. Genewiz	GENEWIZ Intellectual Property GENEWIZ Confidentiality	<http://www.genewiz.com> Archived content available at <http://web.archive.org/web/*/http://www.genewiz.com>	19 January 2014 3 October 2014 31 October 2018	IP Confidentiality
52. Genex Diagnostics Inc	Terms and Conditions Security and Privacy	<http://www.genexdiagnostics.com> Archived content available at <http://web.archive.org/web/*/http://www.genexdiagnostics.com>	2 October 2014 2 October 2014 31 October 2018	T&C Security
53. Genomic Express Inc	Privacy Policy	<https://secure.genomicexpress.com/home.html> Archived content available at <https://secure.genomicexpress.com/home.html>	19 January 2014 31 October 2018	Privacy

#	Company	Description	URL	Date	Category
54.	Genomic Health Inc	Legal	<http://www.genomichealth.com/en-US.aspx#.UuuKSv07S44>	7 October 2014	Legal
		Archived content available at <http://web.archive.org/web/*/http://www.genomichealth.com/en-US.aspx#.UuuKSv07S44>	31 October 2018	
55.	Genosense	Standard terms of business	<http://www.dnaplus.de/en/products/>	20 January 2014	Terms
		Archived content available at <http://web.archive.org/web/*/http://www.dnaplus.de/en/products/> <http://web.archive.org/web/2018090 2090058/http://www.genosense.com/us>	31 October 2018	
56.	GenoVive	GenoVive Website Terms & Conditions of Use Privacy & Usage Policy	<https://www.genovive.com>	3 October 2014 3 October 2014	TOC Privacy
		Archived content available at <http://web.archive.org/web/*/https://www.genovive.com>	31 October 2018	
57.	Gentle	Terms of service Informed consent information	<https://gentlelabs.com>	7 April 2014 7 April 2014	TOS Consent
		Archived content available at <http://web.archive.org/web/*/https://gentlelabs.com>	31 October 2018	
58.	Gonidio	Terms of Use Privacy Policy Security	<http://www.gonidio.com>	13 August 2013 13 August 2013 13 August 2013	TOS Privacy Security
		Archived content available at <http://web.archive.org/web/20180824 214638/http://www.gonidio.com/>	31 October 2018	

(Continued)

Company	Title of Contract or Privacy Policy	URL	Date Saved	Abbreviated Document Name
59. Graceful Earth	No document	\<http://gracefulearth.com\> Archived content available at \<http://web.archive.org/web/201806 24132423/https://www.gracefulearth.net/\>	2 January 2013. Checked again 29 January 2014 and still operating. Checked again 15 April 2014. 31 October 2018	
60. Halo Health	Website Terms of Service Privacy Policy	\<http://halohealth.com/item/home-4/\> Archived content available at \<http://web.archive.org/web/20130927 000927/http://halohealth.com/item/ home-4/\>	13 August 2013 13 August 2013 31 October 2018	TOS Privacy
61. Holistic Health International	No document available	\<http://www.holisticheal.com/dna-oxidative-damage.html\> Archived content available at \<http://web.archive.org/web/201801 31191514/http://www.holisticheal. com:80/dna-oxidative-damage.html\>	3 February 2013 Checked again 29 January 2014 and still operating. Checked again 15 April 2014 31 October 2018	
62. Indian Biosciences	General Terms and Conditions Privacy Policy	\<http://www.inbdna.com\> Archived content available at \<http://web.archive.org/web/2018080 5154653/http://inbdna.com/\>	9 September 2013 9 September 2013 31 October 2018	T&C Privacy

				TOU
63. Inherent Health	Terms of Use	<http://www.inherenthealth.com/our-tests.aspx>	3 October 2013	TOU
		Archived content available at <http://web.archive.org/web/20170621223234/http://www.inherenthealth.com/our-tests.aspx>	31 October 2018	
	Privacy Policy	<http://web.archive.org/web/20130512083806/http://www.inherenthealth.com/privacy-policy.aspx>	29 January 2019	
64. Interleukin Genetics, Inc		<http://ilgenetics.com/content/products-services>	15 April 2014	
		Archived content available at <http://web.archive.org/web/20160731112823/http://ilgenetics.com/content/products-services>	31 October 2018	
	Privacy Policy	<http://web.archive.org/web/20141005190220/http://www.ilgenetics.com/content/products-services/privacy>	11 September 2013	
65. International Biosciences	Terms of Use Terms and conditions Privacy Policy	<http://www.ibdna.com/regions/UK/EN/>	14 August 2013 14 August 2013 14 August 2013	
		Archived content available at <http://web.archive.org/web/20151031125623/https://www.ibdna.com/regions/UK/EN/>	31 October 2018	

(Continued)

Company	Title of Contract or Privacy Policy	URL	Date Saved	Abbreviated Document Name
66. ION (Institute for Optimal Nutrition)	Website usage terms and conditions Privacy Policy	\<http://www.ion.ac.uk/performance/dna_testing\> Archived content available at \<http://web.archive.org/web/201604032 22017/http://www.ion.ac.uk/performance/dna_testing\>	3 October 2014 3 October 2014 31 October 2018	T&C Privacy
67. Kimball	No terms and conditions.	\<http://www.kimballgenetics.com/tests.html\> Archived content available at \<http://web.archive.org/web/201808272 10337/http://kimballgenetics.com/tests.html\>	2 January 2013. Checked again 16 April 2014 31 October 2018	
68. Knome	No terms and conditions.	\<http://www.knome.com/knome-blog/direct-to-consumer-genomics-reinvents-itself/\> Archived content available at \<http://web.archive.org/web/2014011 7160519/http://www.knome.com:80/knome-blog/direct-to-consumer-genomics-reinvents-itself/\>	accessed 10 August 2013. Checked again 16 April 2014 31 October 2018	

69.	LifeGenetics	General Terms of Business	<http://lifegenetics.net/terms-of-business/> <http://lifegenetis.net/legal-notice-privacy-statement/>	13 August 2013 13 August 2013	T&C Privacy
		Privacy And Personal Data Protection Statement	Archived content available at <http://web.archive.org/web/20180917062138/http://lifegenetics.net/terms-of-business/>	31 October 2018	
70.	Lumigenix	No terms and conditions.	<www.lumigenix.com> No longer operating	5 January 2013. Checked again 16 April 2014	
			Archived content available at <http://web.archive.org/web/201808 09081311/http://lumigenix.com/>	31 October 2018	
71.	Map My Gene	Terms & Conditions Privacy Policy	<http://www.mapmygene.com/terms.htm> <http://www.mapmygene.com/privacy.htm>	7 October 2014 7 October 2014	T&C Privacy
			Archived content available at <http://web.archive.org/web/2014102120 0202/http://www.mapmygene.com:80/terms.htm>	31 October 2018	
			<http://web.archive.org/web/20141021200157/http://www.mapmygene.com:80/privacy.htm>		

(Continued)

Company	Title of Contract or Privacy Policy	URL	Date Saved	Abbreviated Document Name
72. Map My Genome	No terms and conditions.	<http://www.mapmygenome.in> Archived content available at <http://web.archive.org/web/20180921133400/https://mapmygenome.in/>	27 January 2014. Checked again 29 January 2014 and still operating. Checked again 22 April 2014 31 October 2018	
73. Matrix Genomics	Terms and Conditions Privacy Policy	<http://www.matrixgenomics.com/aboutourlabCRL.php> Archived content available at <http://web.archive.org/web/20141120182459/http://matrixgenomics.com/cgi-sys/suspendedpage.cgi>	14 August 2013 20 January 2014 Checked again 29 January 2014 and still operating. Checked again 22 April 2014 31 October 2018	T&C Privacy
74. Matt Roberts	Matt Roberts Disclaimer Matt Roberts Privacy Policy	<http://www.mattroberts.co.uk/legal/> <http://www.mattroberts.co.uk/privacy/> <http://www.mattroberts.co.uk/disclaimer/> Archived content available at <http://web.archive.org/web/20180916094909/https://mattroberts.co.uk/> <http://web.archive.org/web/20150214195025/http://www.mattroberts.co.uk/disclaimer/>	8 April 2014 8 April 2014 31 October 2018	Disclaimer Privacy

75. MEDomics	No terms and conditions.	<http://www.medomics.com> Archived content available at <http://web.archive.org/web/201808 18111332/https://medomics.com/>	29 January 2014 and still operating. Checked again 22 April 2014 / 31 October 2018	
76. Molecular Diagnostic Services (PTY) LTD	Legal	<http://www.mdsafrica.net/site/default.asp> Archived content available at <http://web.archive.org/ web/20180616114639/https://www.mdsafrica.net/>	19 January 2014 / 31 October 2018	Legal
77. Myriad	Terms of Use Safe Harbor Policy Privacy Policy	<http://www.myriad.com/terms-of-use/> <http://myriad.com/safe-harbor-policy/> <http://myriad.com/privacy-policy/> Archived content available at <http://web.archive.org/ web/20180909033747/https://myriad. com/terms-of-use/> <http://web.archive.org/ web/20161219042759/https://www. myriad.com/safe-harbor-policy/> <http://web.archive.org/ web/20180908213420/https://myriad. com/privacy-policy/>	3 October 2014 3 October 2014 3 October 2014 / 31 October 2018	TOU Safe Privacy

(Continued)

Company	Title of Contract or Privacy Policy	URL	Date Saved	Abbreviated Document Name
78. myDNA	myDNA Terms of Service myDNA Privacy Policy	\<http://mydna.co.in/Terms%20of%20 Service.html\> \<http://mydna.co.in/Privacy%20Policy. html\> Archived content available at \<http://web.archive.org/ web/20150805115732/http://www. mydna.co.in:80/Terms%20of%20Service. html\> \<http://web.archive.org/ web/20150805115727/http://www. mydna.co.in:80/Privacy%20Policy.html\>	3 October 2014 3 October 2014	TOS Privacy
79. MyGene	No terms and conditions.	\<http://www.mygene.com.au\> Archived content available at \<http://web.archive.org/web/2/http:// www.mygene.com.au\>	13 August 2013. Checked again 29 January 2014 and website suspended. Checked again 22 April 2014	
80. My Gene Diet (Natures Remedies Ltd)	Website Terms and Conditions and Privacy Policy	\<http://www.my-gene-diet.com/terms. php?\>	31 October 2018 13 August 2013 Checked again 29 31 October 2018	T&C Privacy

81. Navigenics	Navigenics Terms and Conditions Navigenics Privacy Policy	Archived content available at <http://web.archive.org/web/2018081604 2515/http://my-gene-diet.com/terms.php> <http://www.navigenics.com> Archived content available at <http://web.archive.org/web/2/http://www.navigenics.com>	January 2014. Checked again 23 April 2014 13 August 2013 13 August 2013 Checked again 29 January 2014. Checked again 24 April 2014	T&C Privacy
82. Nimble Diagnostics	No terms and conditions	<http://www.nimblediagnostics.co.uk> Archived content available at <http://web.archive.org/ web/20180809024440/http:// nimblediagnostics.co.uk/>	31 October 2018 8 September 2013 Checked again 29 January 2014 Checked again 24 April 2014	
83. Pathway Genomics	Terms and Conditions Privacy Statement	<www.pathway.com/about-us/terms-and-conditions> <www.pathway.com/about-us/privacy-policy> Archived content available at <http://web.archive.org/web/2016020 4235715/https://www.pathway.com/ about-us/terms-and-conditions> <http://web.archive.org/web/2016020 5121141/https://www.pathway.com/ about-us/privacy-policy>	31 October 2018 13 August 2013 13 August 2013 Checked again 24 April 2014 31 October 2018	T&C Privacy

(Continued)

Company	Title of Contract or Privacy Policy	URL	Date Saved	Abbreviated Document Name
84. Perkin Elmer Genetics	Terms and Conditions Privacy Policy	\<http://www.perkinelmer.com/Our Company/AboutUs/Legal/TermsAnd Conditions/default.xhtml> \<http://www.perkinelmer.com/Our Company/AboutUs/Legal/PrivacyPolicy/ default.xhtml> Archived content available at \<http://web.archive.org/web/201801142 00152/http://www.perkinelmer.com:80/ corporate/error/404.html?aspxerrorpath=/ OurCompany/AboutUs/Legal/ TermsAndConditions/default.xhtml> \<http://web.archive.org/web/201801 14193606/http://www.perkinelmer. com:80/OurCompany/AboutUs/Legal/ PrivacyPolicy/default.xhtml>	10 August 2013 10 August 2013 31 October 2018	T&C Privacy
85. PerioPredict™ Genetic Risk Test	No terms and conditions	\<http://periopredict.com/patient/about. php> Archived content available at \<http://web.archive.org/web/20140514 235604/http://periopredict.com:80/ patient/about.php>	15 April 2014 31 October 2018	
86. Personal Genome Diagnostics Inc	Legal/Privacy	\<http://www.personalgenome.com/legal- privacy>	19 January 2014 Checked again 24 April 2014	Privacy

87. PHENOM Biosciences Inc	Terms of Service Privacy Policy	Archived content available at <http://web.archive.org/web/20140526011107/http://www.personalgenome.com:80/legal-privacy> <www.phenombio.com/about-us>	31 October 2018 6 October 2014 6 October 2014	TOS Privacy
		Archived content available at <http://web.archive.org/web/20180829031657/http://www.phenombio.com/>	31 October 2018	
88. Progenika Inc	Legal Disclaimer Privacy Policy	<www.progenika.com/us/index.php>	19 January 2014 19 January 2014 Checked again 24 April 2014	Disclaimer Privacy
		Archived content available at <http://web.archive.org/web/2018080711 4021/http://progenika.com/>	31 October 2018	
89. Remede	No terms and conditions.	<http://remede.com.au/dna-profiles-nutrigenomics/>	7 April 2014 Checked again 24 April 2014	
		Archived content available at <http://web.archive.org/web/201804 26000251/http://www.remede.com.au/dna-profiles-nutrigenomics/>	31 October 2018	
90. Signal Genetics Inc	No terms and conditions.	<http://www.signalgenetics.com>	27 January 2014. Checked again 29 January 2014 and still operating. Checked again 24 April 2014	
		Archived content available at <http://web.archive.org/web/20180902214136/http://ww31.signalgenetics.com/>	31 October 2018	

(Continued)

Company	Title of Contract or Privacy Policy	URL	Date Saved	Abbreviated Document Name
91. Smart DNA	Smart Terms	\<http://www.smartdna.net.au/howitworks.htm\>	14 August 2013	T&C
		Archived content available at \<http://web.archive.org/web/20160306022336/http://smartdna.net.au/\>	31 October 2018	
92. Test Country	Terms & Conditions Privacy Policy	\<http://www.testcountry.com\>	10 August 2013 10 August 2013	T&C PP
		Archived content available at \<http://web.archive.org/web/20181027232159/https://testcountry.com/\>	31 October 2018	
93. Test Diagnostics	Terms of Use Privacy and Cookies Policy	\<http://www.testdiagnostics.com/uk/\>	5 February 2014 5 February 2014	TOU PP
		Archived content available at \<http://web.archive.org/web/20171002173400/http://www.testdiagnostics.com:80/uk\>	31 October 2018	
94. Theranostics Lab	Terms and Conditions	\<www.theranostics.co.nz/afawcs0143120/tn-products.html\>	13 August 2013	T&C
		Archived content available at \<http://web.archive.org/web/20120424025240/http://www.theranostics.co.nz:80/afawcs0143120/tn-products.html\>	31 October 2018	

				TOU Agreement Privacy
95. The Makings of Me	Terms of Use (dated 29 November 2011) Service Agreement (dated 29 November 2011) Privacy Policy (dated 29 November 2011)	<www.themakingsofme.com/terms-of-use.html> <www.themakingsofme.com/service-agreement.html> <www.themakingsofme.com/privacy-policy.html> Archived content available at <http://web.archive.org/web/20180219031607/http://www.themakingsofme.com:80/terms-of-use.html> <http://web.archive.org/web/20180219031401/http://www.themakingsofme.com:80/service-agreement.html> <http://web.archive.org/web/20180219031357/http://www.themakingsofme.com:80/privacy-policy.html>	3 October 2014 3 October 2014 3 October 2014 31 October 2018	
96. The Wellness Brothers	No terms and conditions.	<http://thewellnessbrothers.com/dna-diet.htm> Archived content available at <http://web.archive.org/web/2015080911 3101/http://thewellnessbrothers.com:80/dna-diet.htm>	7 April 2014. Checked again 24 April 2014 31 October 2018	
97. Toldot Genetics	No document available, although the website says there are terms. However, these are not accessible when the links are clicked upon.	<www.toldot-dna.com/> Archived content available at <http://web.archive.org/web/2018082304 3401/http://www.toldot-dna.com/>	28 January 2014. Checked again 24 April 2014 31 October 2018	

(Continued)

Company	Title of Contract or Privacy Policy	URL	Date Saved	Abbreviated Document Name
98. vuGene	Important Notices and Disclaimers Privacy Policy	<http://www.mygenesdirect.com> Archived content available at <http://web.archive.org/web/20180800 5192832/http://mygenesdirect.com/>	13 August 2013 13 August 2013 31 October 2018	Disclaimer Privacy
99. The Wellness Gene	No terms and conditions	<http://www.wellnessgene.com/DNA-Test.html> Archived content available at <http://web.archive.org/web/20180825 000512/http://wellnessgene.com/DNA-Test.html>	29 April 2014 31 October 2018	
100. WellPro	No terms and conditions	<http://www.wellpro.co.za/tests-landing/> Archived content available at <http://web.archive.org/web/201707060 82112/http://www.wellpro.co.za/tests-landing/>	27 January 2014. Checked again 22 April 2014 31 October 2018	
101. YOUology	No terms and conditions	<http://www.youology.com/about-youology.html> Archived content available at <http://web.archive.org/web/201305010 91052/http://www.youology.com:80/about-youology-html>	7 April 2014. Checked again 24 April 2014 31 October 2018	

¹ Please note that all documents are on file both in soft- and hard-copy form and the websites have also been checked more recently, but for the purposes of the analysis of contracts herein these are the relevant dates.

1

Direct-to-Consumer Genetic Testing and Regulating Disruptive Technology

1.1 Introduction

We are all made up of DNA (deoxyribonucleic acid). We all have our own unique genetic code. When any one of us gives up a physical sample for the purpose of a genetic test, that code becomes decipherable. Through genetic testing, information that is contained in our bodies is encapsulated in digital form. This genetic data has the potential to be stored indefinitely and it can serve not only as a unique identifier for you, but also to identify family members. The shared nature of genetic data also means that data collected for one purpose can be used for a variety of secondary purposes, including criminal investigations and tracing family members.

Our DNA is part of each of us as individuals and we might assume that we own it in the same way that many of us might assume we own our bodies. Yet in many places the law does not actually provide for property rights in samples of DNA, once they are extracted from us or in our own bodies.[1] While we might often feel that we in some sense own our bodies and their parts, this is not the case for the most part at present. For example, in the United States of America, tissue samples such as skin and saliva that we leave behind us are often treated as abandoned and can be used by law enforcement in criminal investigations.[2] This has been exemplified by the recent involvement of the geneology database GEDmatch in the

---

[1] For contrasting views on this see Donna Dickenson, 'Alternatives to a corporate commons: Biobanking, genetics and property in the body', in Goold, Greasley, Herring and Skene, *Persons, Parts and Property*, 177–95; and Jonathan Herring, 'Why we need a statute regime to regulate bodily material', in ibid. 214–29; also see generally Donna Dickenson, *Body Shopping The Economy Fuelled by Flesh and Blood* and Donna Dickenson, *Property in the Body Feminist Perspectives*, chapters 1, 2 and 6.

[2] Available at <https://www.bloomberg.com/news/features/2018-10-27/your-dna-is-out-there-do-you-want-law-enforcement-using-it> accessed 31 October 2018; <https://med.stanford.edu/content/dam/sm/cirge/documents/activities/journalclubs/Joh%202006.pdf> accessed 31 October 2018.

investigation of the Golden State Killer case, which will be discussed in Chapter 4.

While we often will not have property rights in our own DNA or our bodies, our rights in genetic data are protected in various jurisdictions in different ways, but significantly genetic data is included within the definition of personal data in the European Union's (EU) General Data Protection Regulation (GDPR).[3] This means that entities that collect and process genetic data should be complying with the provisions of the GDPR. One of the most significant requirements of the GDPR in this context is the standard of consent required. Consent as specified in Article 4(11) of the GDPR must be 'freely given, specific, informed and unambiguous indication of the data subject's wishes by which he or she, by a statement or by a clear affirmative action, signifies agreement to the processing of personal data relating to him or her'.

While the GDPR is EU law, it is having a siginicant influence on privacy and data protection law worldwide, with many countries outside the EU seeking to reform their laws, so that they are still able to do business with the EU, where it involves personal data. This includes: Brazil; Japan; New Zealand; and Singapore.[4]

Many of us access new types of service online and in particular there are many new and emerging technologies, which are directed at the consumer market. This means that other areas of law also have a role to play in governing industries and in protecting consumer rights. Most significant here for present purposes are consumer protection and contract law. In the UK and EU there are a number of Directives that protect consumer rights

---

[3] Council Regulation (EU) 2016/679 of 27 April 2016 on the protection of natural persons with regard to the processing of personal data and on the free movement of such data, and repealing Directive 95/46/EC (General Data Protection Regulation) [2016] OJ 2 119/1 <http://eur-lex.europa.eu/legal-content/EN/TXT/?qid=1525272154893&uri=CELEX:32 016R0679> last accessed 29 July 2018.

[4] Melanie Ramey, 'Brazil's new general data privacy law follows GDPR provisions' *Inside Privacy* (20 August 2018) <https://www.insideprivacy.com/international/brazils-new-general-data-privacy-law-follows-gdpr-provisions/> accessed 31 October 2018 – the English version of the new Brazilian legislation is available here <https://www.pnm. adv.br/wp-content/uploads/2018/08/Brazilian-General-Data-Protection-Law.pdf>; Hogan Lovells, 'Changes in Japan privacy law to take effect in mid-2017' *LEXOLOGY* (1 February 2017) <https://www.lexology.com/library/detail.aspx?g=efa0a2b0-b73e-456c-b4fa-26a268e9e751> accessed 31 October 2018; Key Regulator Provides Compliance Insights, New Zealand Privacy Commissioner, 'Privacy law reform' <https://www. privacy.org.nz/the-privacy-act-and-codes/privacy-law-reform/> accessed 31 October 2018; 'Singapore personal data protection reforms in force from next year' *Out-Law* (3 September 2018) <https://www.out-law.com/en/articles/2018/september/singapore-personal-data-protection-reforms/> accessed 31 October 2018.

and also provide for fairness in consumer contracts. The most significant in this context are the Directive on Consumer Rights and the Unfair Contract Terms Directive (although the Unfair Commercial Practices Directive also has relevance).[5]

We are also living in an age when our lives are increasingly becoming digital and many services we engage with do collect, store, share and sell data about us. This is the era of Big Data, dataveillance, self-tracking and connectivity. Dataveillance is 'the systematic use of personal data systems in the investigation or monitoring of the actions or communications of one or more persons'.[6] Dataveillance occurs in many different contexts and a wide range of businesses use dataveillance in some form. The Internet of Things (IoT), which essentially involves equipping an ever-increasing array of every-day objects with sensors and Internet connectivity is rapidly expanding the variety of entities engaging in dataveillance.[7] IoT is estimated to grow significantly in the coming years.[8] Many online services make money through

---

[5] Council Directive 93/13/EEC of 5 April 1993 on unfair terms in consumer contracts <https://eur-lex.europa.eu/legal-content/EN/TXT/?uri=CELEX%3A31993L0013> accessed 18 October 2018; and Directive 2011/83/EU of the European Parliament and of the Council of 25 October 2011 on consumer rights, amending Council Directive 93/13/EEC and Directive 1999/44/EC of the European Parliament and of the Council and repealing Council Directive 85/577/EEC and Directive 97/7/EC of the European Parliament and of the Council <http://eur-lex.europa.eu/legalcontent/EN/TXT/?qid=1525272546102&uri=CELEX:32011L0083> accessed 18 October 2018; Directive 2005/29/EC of the European Parliament and of the Council of 11 May 2005 concerning unfair business-to-consumer commercial practices in the internal market and amending Council Directive 84/450/EEC, Directives 97/7/EC, 98/27/EC and 2002/65/EC of the European Parliament and of the Council and Regulation (EC) No 2006/2004 of the European Parliament and of the Council ('Unfair Commercial Practices Directive') <https://eur-lex.europa.eu/legal-content/en/ALL/?uri=CELEX%3A32005L0029> accessed 18 October 2018.

[6] Roger Clarke, 'Introduction to dataveillance and information privacy, and definitions of terms' (2018) <http://www.rogerclarke.com/DV/#SurvD> accessed 18 October 2018.

[7] Ian Brown, *GSR Discussion Paper: Regulation and the Internet of Things* (ITU 2015) <https://www.itu.int/en/ITU-D/Conferences/GSR/Documents/GSR2015/Discussion_papers_and_Presentations/GSR_DiscussionPaper_IoT.pdf> accessed 18 October 2018.

[8] Tanmay, 'Internet of Things (IoT) market is projected to grow at CAGR 30% during the forecast period' Business Tactics (30 July 2018) <https://thebusinesstactics.com/423736/internet-of-things-iot-market-is-projected-to-grow-at-cagr-30-during-the-forecast-period/> accessed 22 October 2018; see Goldstein Research, 'Global Internet Of Things (IoT) Outlook 2024: Global Opportunity And Demand Analysis, Market Forecast, 2016–2024' (July 2018). <https://www.marketinsightsreports.com/reports/120484853/global-internet-of-things-iot-outlook-2024-global-opportunity-and-demand-analysis-market-forecast-2016-2024?source=thebusinesstactics&mode=24> accessed 18 October 2018.

advertising[9] and the European Commission's European Data Market study found that 'the overall value of the data economy grew from the €247 billion in 2013 to almost reaching €300 billion in 2016' and it estimates that 'by 2020, the EU data economy is expected to increase to €739 billion'.[10] This data-driven age is also an age increasingly of data breaches. Symantec's 2017 Threat Report estimated that over the previous eight years, 'more than seven billion online identities have been stolen in data breaches, which is almost the equivalent of one for every person on the planet'.[11] The last few years have also seen growth in mega-breaches, with 15 occurring in 2016 alone.[12] Yahoo's breach is one of the most prominent and in December of 2016 it was revealed that this breach affected more than 1 billion users. Breaches can now affect almost any kind of organisation and so businesses that offer new types of commercial services that rely on personal data and sensitive data need to have sound and reliable security infrastructure.

So, what is this book about? Are you interested in learning about your genetic origins? Have you recently noticed advertisements for commercial genetic tests? Do you regularly read website terms and conditions or privacy policies? Would knowing the content of a company's online terms and conditions or privacy policy influence your decision to engage with a particular service or product?

Let's be honest. Most of us are active online today, regardless of our interests or profession. Most of us have an email account. Most of us use a particular search engine. Most of us have personal data about us collected and stored somewhere by others we do not know. Most of us will give up some personal data in order to use a free service and most of us have entered into contractual arrangements with businesses through their website without reading the lengthy terms and conditions, terms of service or privacy policy documents. Although laws such as the Consumer Rights Directive and the GDPR aim to enhance our rights as consumers and data subjects, most of us

---

[9] Yonas Mitike Kassa et al., 'Your data in the eyes of the beholders: Design of a unified data valuation portal to estimate value of personal information from market perspective', 11th International Conference on Availability, Reliability and Security (ARES 2016), 31 August–2 September 2016, Salzburg, Austria <http://eprints.networks.imdea.org/1510/> accessed 18 October 2018.

[10] European Commission, 'Final results of the European data market study measuring the size and trends of the EU data economy' (2 May 2017) <https://ec.europa.eu/digital-single-market/en/news/final-results-european-data-market-study-measuring-size-and-trends-eu-data-economy> accessed 18 October 2018.

[11] Symantec, *Internet Security Threat Report* (2017) Vol 22, 45. <https://www.symantec.com/content/dam/symantec/docs/reports/istr-22-2017-en.pdf>

[12] Ibid. 45.

do not really know what those rights are in full and we do not really know or understand the content of all these documents. Remember: every website you visit has some form of contractual document or policy, whether or not we actually notice it.

What does all this mean? It means that if you are like me, you have entered into contractual relationships without pausing to read the fine print. This book will take you on a journey to explore the content of the terms and conditions of personal genomics – of direct-to-consumer genetic testing (DTC) companies. It will also discuss privacy and data protection issues drawing upon other recent studies.[13]

It should be noted at the outset that DTC contracts are of a specific type. These documents are wrap contracts, which are either framed as clickwrap or browsewrap agreements. These are contractual forms that have evolved from shrink-wrap agreements or licences. Shrink-wrap agreements were originally conceived in order to protect the rights of software developers. Shrink-wrap contracts are included on the packaging of software products and a person normally signals their assent to be bound by these contracts by ripping open the packaging.[14] They are also a form of adhesion contract and may also be viewed as mass consumer standard form contracts (that is, boilerplates). In this book, 'wrap contract' is used in the same manner as in Nancy Kim's leading text *Wrap Contracts: Foundations and Ramifications*. Accordingly, the term 'wrap contract' is used as:

> a blanket term to refer to a unilaterally imposed set of terms which the drafter purports to be legally binding and which is presented to the non-drafting party in a nontraditional format. Nontraditional in this context means that the contracting form wasn't commonly used prior to 1980 and includes electronic media and offline mediums. The single common characteristic is that the adhering party does not have to use a pen in order to accept the terms.[15]

---

[13] LI Laestadius, Jennifer R Rich and Paul L Auer, 'All rour data (effectively) belong to us: Data practices among direct-to-consumer genetic testing firms' (2016) 19 *Genetics in Medicine* 513–20 doi:10.1038/gim.2016.136; James Hazel and Christopher Slobogin, 'Who knows what, and when?: A survey of the privacy policies proffered by U.S. direct-to-consumer genetic testing companies' (19 April 2018, last revised 18 October 2018) *Cornell Journal of Law and Public Policy* and Vanderbilt Law Research Paper No 18 <https://ssrn.com/abstract=3165765> accessed 24 October 2018.; E Christofides and K O'Doherty, 'Company disclosure and consumer perceptions of the privacy implications of direct-to-consumer genetic testing' (2016) *New Genetics and Society* 35(2): 101–23 doi: 10.1080/14636778.2016.1162092.

[14] Nancy S Kim, Wrap Contracts: Foundations and Ramifications (OUP 2014) 2–3.

[15] Ibid. 2.

Both clickwrap and browsewrap are contractual forms common to all types of e-commerce and many DTC contracts strongly resemble the contracts used by Google, iTunes, Twitter and Amazon. Such contracts are normally extremely lengthy. For instance, a recent article compared the lengths of iTunes' and Amazon's contracts to the length of *Macbeth* and *Hamlet*[16] respectively and both contracts are longer than these plays. So now people can choose whether to read wrap contracts or Shakespeare.

This book is based on research which originally began in 2011.[17] This research involved the compilation of a database containing data concerning the DTC industry, including the location of companies, the types of service they offered, screen shots, electronic contracts and privacy policies, where these were publicly available. Several versions of the dataset were publicly released via Zenodo in 2018 and updated versions will be released over the coming years.[18] A significant part of this project involved the review of 71 wrap contracts of DTC companies that provide tests for health purposes.[19] The book also draws upon more recent studies of privacy policies and electronic contracts[20] of DTC companies and other digital services. In conducting this research, screen shots were saved and the content of DTC websites explored. However, it has not been possible to provide an in-depth analysis of DTC marketing claims herein and so reference will be made to other studies that have examined DTC website content and marketing claims.[21]

---

[16] Wigley + Company Solicitors, 'To read or not to read . . . Online Ts and Cs. Or Hamlet' (Wigley + Company Solicitors 2015) <http://www.wigleylaw.com/assets/Uploads/To-read-or-not-to-read.pdf > accessed 18 October 2018.

[17] Please see the related papers: Andelka M Phillips, 'Reading the fine print when buying your genetic self online: Direct-to-consumer genetic testing terms and conditions' (2017) *New Genetics and Society* 36(3) 273–295, 285–6 <http://dx.doi.org/10.1080/14636778.2017.135 2468>; Andelka M Phillips, 'Only a click away – DTC genetics for ancestry, health, love . . . and more: A view of the business and regulatory landscape' (2016) 8 *Applied and Translational Genomics* 16–22 <https://doi.org/10.1016/j.atg.2016.01.001>; and Andelka M Phillips, 'Genomic privacy and direct-to-consumer genetics – Big consumer genetic data – What's in that contract?' (presented at GenoPri'15 [The 2nd Workshop on Genome Privacy and Security] and published as part of IEEE Conference Proceedings 2015) <https://www.computer.org/csdl/proceedings/spw/2015/9933/00/9933a060.pdf> accessed 23 October 2018.

[18] Please see Andelka M Phillips, 'Data on direct-to-consumer genetic testing and DNA testing companies' Version 1.3 (Open Access Dataset, Zenodo, February 2018) doi: 10.5281/zenodo.1175799 <https://zenodo.org/record/1183565#.WunK6y-ZNp8> accessed 23 October 2018.

[19] Phillips, 'Reading the fine print' (n 17).

[20] Laestadius et al. (n 13); Hazel and Slobogin (n 13).

[21] Rose Geransar and Edna Einsiedel, 'Evaluating online direct-to-consumer marketing of genetic tests: Informed choices or buyers beware?' (2008) 12(1) *Genetic Testing* 13. <https://doi.org/10.1089/gte.2007.0024> accessed 18 October 2018; Gregory Kutz,

How many contracts have you entered today? The Norwegian Consumer Council (NCC) in its APPFAIL campaign[22] estimated that on average one smartphone contains approximately 250,000 words of application terms and conditions and privacy policies. Furthermore, if you own five Apple devices, it is likely that you have entered into 'at least 30 contracts, totalling more than 100,000 words'.[23] Most of these documents are lengthy and written in complex legalese which the layperson would struggle to understand. A recent study by Conklin and Hyde investigating the readability of seven insurance policies found that all policies 'required a very high level of education to be understood' with the easiest requiring 14 years of education and the most difficult requiring a PhD-level education.[24]

The Australian consumer group CHOICE carried out a study of e-reader terms and conditions in 2017.[25] They hired an actor to read the terms

Direct-to-Consumer Genetic Tests: Misleading Test Results are Further Complicated by Deceptive Marketing and Other Questionable Practices: Congressional Testimony (GAO 10 847T, 2010) <https://www.gao.gov/assets/130/125079.pdf> accessed 18 October 2018; P Saukko, M Reed, N Britten, and S Hogarth, 'Negotiating the boundary between medicine and consumer culture: Online marketing of nutrigenetic tests' (2010) 70(5) *Social Science & Medicine* 744–53 <https://doi.org/10.1016/j.socscimed.2009.10.066>; P Saukko, 'State of play in direct-to-consumer genetic testing for lifestyle-related diseases: Market, marketing content, user experiences and regulation' (2013) 72 *The Proceedings of the Nutrition Society* 53 <https://doi.org/10.1017/S0029665112002960> accessed 18 October 2018.

22   Norwegian Consumer Council, '250,000 words of app terms and conditions' (24 May 2016). <https://www.forbrukerradet.no/side/250000-words-of-app-terms-and-conditions/> accessed 18 October 2018; Norwegian Consumer Council, *APPFAIL Threats to Consumers in Mobile Apps* (March 2016) <https://www.forbrukerradet.no/undersokelse/2015/appfail-threats-to-consumers-in-mobile-apps/> accessed 18 October 2018.

23   Christopher Groskopf, 'CLICK "I AGREE" Apple fans have click-signed more than 100,000 words of legal contracts' *Quartz* (5 November 2016) <https://qz.com/797 928/apple-fans-have-click-signed-more-than-100000-words-of-legal-contracts/> accessed 9 August 2018. This is also mentioned in the chapter Andelka M Phillips, 'Will my genes really help me fit into those jeans? Personal genomics and wrap contracts' in Lilian Edwards, Burkhard Schafer, and Edina Harbinja (eds), *Future Law: Emerging Technology, Ethics and Regulation* (forthcoming Edinburgh University Press 2019).

24   K Conklin and R Hyde, 'If small print 'terms and conditions' require a PhD to read, should they be legally binding?' *The Conversation* (10 May 2018) <https://theconver sation.com/if-small-print-terms-and-conditions-require-a-phd-to-read-should-they-be-legally-binding-75101> accessed 18 October 2018; see also K Conklin, R Hyde, and F Parente, 'Assessing plain and intelligible language in the Consumer Rights Act: a role for reading scores?' (2018) *Legal Studies* ISSN 1748-121X (in Press) <http://eprints.notting ham.ac.uk/51073/> accessed 18 October 2018.

25   Elle Hunt, 'Amazon Kindle's terms "unreasonable" and would take nine hours to read, Choice says' *The Guardian* (15 March 2017) <https://www.theguardian.com/australia-news/2017/mar/15/amazon-kindles-terms-unreasonable-and-would-take-nine-hours-

aloud.[26] For Amazon's Kindle there were at least eight documents in total, which together exceeded 73,000 words[27] – approaching the length of this book. As well as not being easy to read, many wrap contracts used in e-commerce more generally may contain terms that are challengeable on the grounds of unfairness and they may also include terms that give businesses additional advantages. This practice has been dubbed by Kim as the inclusion of 'crook' provisions.[28] In the last few years there have been a number of experiments centred around including clauses of this type. These range from GameStation's inclusion of an immortal soul clause[29] to the more recent example of Purple's community service clause. In the Purple example, they added the clause for a two-week period. Under the clause 'over 22,000 people agreed to carry out 1,000 hours of community service', which included agreeing to clean public toilets, hug stray animals and paint snails' shells.[30] 'All users were given the chance to flag up the questionable clause in return for a prize, but remarkably only one individual, which is 0.000045% of all Wi-Fi users throughout the whole two weeks, managed to spot it'.[31]

This is not a contract law textbook; it deals with regulation of technology, focusing on the specific example of DTC and the use of electronic wrap contracts in that context. As wrap contracts play a significant role in industry self-regulation in this context, this book does address wrap contracts and comes at this from a critical perspective. It takes a practical rather than theoretical approach, seeking to draw attention to the ways

to-read-choice-says> accessed 18 October 2018; CHOICE, 'Nine hours of "conditions apply"' <https://www.choice.com.au/about-us/media-releases/2017/march/nine-hours-of-conditions-apply> accessed 18 October 2018.

26 Ibid.; The videos are available here <https://www.youtube.com/watch?v=6QZml7sPbVU& feature=youtu.be> accessed 18 October 2018.

27 Hunt (n 25).

28 Kim, *Wrap Contracts* (n 14) 51–2; Nancy S Kim, 'Contract's adaptation and the online bargain' (2011) 79 *University of Cincinnati Law Review* 1327–70.

29 Marc Perton, 'Read fine print or GameStation may own your soul' *Consumerist* (16 April 2010) <http://consumerist.com/2010/04/16/read-fine-print-or-gamestation-may-own-your-soul/> accessed 28 October 2018; Brendon Behesti, 'Cross-jurisdictional variation in Internet contract regulation' (2013) 8(1) *Journal of International Commercial Law and Technology* 49, 51.

30 Purple, '22,000 people willingly agree to community service in return for free WiFi' (13 July 2017) <https://purple.ai/blogs/purple-community-service/> accessed 18 October 2018.

31 D Tuffley, 'How not to agree to clean public toilets when you accept any online terms and conditions' *The Conversation* (23 July 2017) <https://theconversation.com/how-not-to-agree-to-clean-public-toilets-when-you-accept-any-online-terms-and-conditions-81169> accessed 18 October 2018.

in which we all as consumers and data subjects engage with wrap contracts and privacy policies, and the issues which this raises for our society and the law. In relation to the designed environment of websites, contracts and privacy settings it draws upon the work of Frischmann and Selinger, Obar and Oeldorf-Hirsch,[32] and the Norwegian Consumer Council.[33] Frischmann and Selinger's work[34] (which draws upon Radin's *Boilerplate*) argues that the architecture of electronic contracts can mean that 'it is completely rational for a user to blindly accept the terms of use'.[35] They suggest that the designed environment of websites encourages people to behave as automatons and this in turn has negative consequences for autonomy and sociality.[36] In its *Deceived by Design* report the Norwegian Consumer Council identified a number of dark patterns in user-interface design, which they argue nudge users away from privacy-friendly options.[37] This book also draws upon a number of more recent studies of wrap contracts and privacy policies, by Hazel and Slobogin,[38] Laestadius et al.,[39] Obar and Oeldorf-Hirsch,[40] Elshout et al.,[41] and the Norwegian Consumer Council.[42]

---

[32] Jonathan A Obar and Anne Oeldorf-Hirsch, 'The biggest lie on the Internet: Ignoring the privacy policies and terms of service policies of social networking services' (2018) *Information, Communication and Society* 1–20 <https://doi.org/10.1080/1369118X.2018.1486870> accessed 22 October 2018.

[33] See Norwegian Consumer Council (n 19) and Norwegian Consumer Council, *Deceived by Design* (June 2018) <https://www.forbrukerradet.no/undersokelse/no-undersokelsekategori/deceived-by-design/> accessed 26 July 2018.

[34] BM Frischmann and E Selinger, 'Engineering humans with contracts' (September 2016) Cardozo Legal Studies Research Paper No. 493. <https://papers.ssrn.com/sol3/papers.cfm?abstract_id=2834011>; BM Frischmann and E Selinger, *Re-Engineering Humanity* (Cambridge University Press 2018).

[35] Ibid. at 5.

[36] Ibid. at 2–3.

[37] NCC, *Deceived by Design* (n 33)

[38] Hazel and Slobogin (n 13)

[39] Laestadius (n 13)

[40] Obar & Oeldorf-Hirsch, 'The biggest lie on the Internet . . .' (n 32)

[41] Maartje Elshout, Millie Elsen, Jorna Leenheer, Marco Loos, and Joasia Luzak, *Study on Consumers' Attitudes Towards Terms Conditions (T&Cs) Final Report* (Report for the European Commission, Consumers, Health, Agriculture and Food Executive Agency (CHAFEA) on behalf of Directorate-General for Justice and Consumers, 22 September) <https://ssrn.com/abstract=2847546>; Marco Loos and Joasia Luzak, 'Wanted: A bigger stick. On unfair terms in consumer contracts with online service providers' (2015) 39 J Consum Policy 63–90 <https://doi.org/10.1007/s10603-015-9303-7> accessed 18 October 2018.

[42] NCC, *Deceived by Design* (n 33); NCC, *APPFAIL* (n 22)

1.2 Aims of this Book

This book has a number of aims. It provides an overview of the rise of the DTC industry and the challenges and issues that these services raise for the law and society and the regulation of technology. DTC can be viewed as an example of both an emerging technology and disruptive innovation. It is also an example of consumer-centred healthcare services and raises issues similar to those of wearable fitness monitors and other innovations considered as part of the quantified self (or lifelogging) movement.[43] A useful definition of what constitutes the 'quantified self' is 'any individual engaged in the self-tracking of any kind of biological, physical, behavioural or environmental information'.[44] This book uses the DTC industry as an example to allow discussion of broader issues related to technology governance in this context, focusing on wrap contracts and privacy policies. As the DTC industry has largely been unregulated to date, companies have tended to rely on electronic wrap contracts and privacy policies to govern relationships with consumers. A further aim is to highlight problems with current industry practice in relation to both wrap contracts and privacy policies and suggest possible reform.

Chapter 2 provides a brief introduction to the science behind DTC, while Chapter 3 gives an overview of the industry and the types of service it offers. Chapter 4 will then address the privacy, data protection and security issues raised by the DTC industry, drawing upon the more recent study by Hazel and Slobogin of DTC privacy policies and the Norwegian Consumer Council's *Deceived by Design* and *APPFAIL* reports.[45] The second part of the book discusses the contracts of DTC companies, drawing upon the review conducted between 2011 and 2016 looking at this primarily from the perspective of consumer protection. The Conclusion suggests some possibilities for improving regulation.

1.3 Guidance for Readers

It is hoped that this book will be of interest to a variety of readers. Those with a background in medicine may not need to read Chapter 2, while those with in an interest in contract may find Chapter 5 most relevant to their interests. Those from a computer science background may find Chapter 4 useful, and finally those with an interest in reform may find Chapter 6 most useful.

---

[43] Melanie Swan, 'The quantified self: Fundamental disruption in big data science and biological discovery' (2013) 1(2) *Big Data* 85–99, 85.

[44] Ibid. 85.

[45] Hazel and Slobogin (n 13); NCC, *APPFAIL* (n 22)

1.4 What is Personal Genomics or Direct-to-Consumer Genetic Testing?

A 2018 report from GenomeWeb states that:

> An average of 14 new genetic tests are launched on the market each day, and by the end of 2017, the number of consumers who purchased genetic testing online to learn their ancestry or genetic risks for diseases more than doubled to 12 million. Meanwhile, the US Food and Drug Administration last year approved a record of 16 new personalized drugs.[46]

The DTC industry has developed within the last two decades, essentially beginning with the launch of University Diagnostics' mail order service in 1996.[47] This was followed by the launch of 23andMe and deCODEme's services[48] in 2007. The industry has experienced considerable growth in the last two years, with 23andMe's database exceeding 5 million customers and AncestryDNA exceeding 10 million.[49] 23andMe has also been valued at a 'market cap of over $1 billion, making it Silicon Valley's first "unicorn" mega-company in the field of biotechnology'.[50] A recent study by Research and Markets suggests that the 'global predictive genetic testing and consumer/wellness genomics market is anticipated to reach USD 4.6 billion

---

[46] Turna Ray, 'Public awareness of personalized medicine not growing in step with industry, survey shows' *GenomeWeb* (23 May 2018) <https://www.genomeweb.com/molecular-diagnostics/public-awareness-personalized-medicine-not-growing-step-industry-survey-shows?destination=node/398087> accessed 27 October 2018.

[47] Stuart Hogarth and Paula Saukko, 'A market in the making: The past, present and future of direct-to-consumer genomics' (2017) 36(3) *New Genetics and Society*, 197–208, 197 <https://doi.org/10.1080/14636778.2017.1354692> accessed 23 October 2018.

[48] SA Leachman, DG MacArthur, M Angrist, SW Gray, AR Bradbury, and DB Vorhaus, 'Direct-to-consumer genetic testing: Personalized medicine in evolution' (2011) *American Society of Clinical Oncology* 34–40, 36 <https://theprivacyreport.com/wp-content/uploads/2011/06/ASCO-DTC-Abstract.pdf> accessed 22 October 2018; Pascal Su, 'Direct-to-consumer genetic testing: A comprehensive view' (2013) 86(3) *The Yale Journal of Biology and Medicine* 359–65 <https://www.ncbi.nlm.nih.gov/pmc/articles/PMC3767220/> accessed 22 October 2018.

[49] 23andMe, 'About Us' <https://mediacenter.23andme.com/company/about-us/> accessed 18 October 2018; AncestryDNA, <https://www.ancestry.co.uk/cs/ireland-dna> accessed 13 July 2018.

[50] Aaron Krol, 'What comes next for direct-to-consumer genetics?' (Bio IT World, 2015) <http://www.bio-itworld.com/2015/7/16/what-comes-next-direct-consumer-genetics.html> accessed 18 October 2018.

by 2025'.[51] The most current version of my list of DTC companies includes 289 companies.[52]

The industry can be viewed as an example of disruptive innovation, as it has created a new market for genetic testing services as consumer services. 'Disruptive innovation' is a term coined by Clayton Christensen and it can be defined as 'a process by which a product or service takes root initially in simple applications at the bottom of a market and then relentlessly moves up market, eventually displacing established competitors'.[53] Disruptive innovations often create markets that did not exist previously, which is true of DTC. One of the leading DTC companies, 23andMe, has been described as 'an example of what we call a "Big Bang Disruption" – a product or service innovation that undermines existing markets and industries seemingly overnight by being simultaneously better and cheaper than the competition'.[54]

The industry allows people to purchase genetic tests online for a variety of purposes, ranging from health-related tests to ancestry and child talent. Previously genetic tests for health purposes were provided in a face-to-face medical setting and whether to have the test was determined by medical professionals. Non-health-related tests would normally only be performed as part of legal proceedings or a criminal investigation, but again the tests were performed in person and according to strict standards. By bringing genetic tests outside these structures and into people's homes, the nature of the industry poses challenges for regulation.

At present, it is not subject to specific regulation and as with many other web-based industries, companies have tended to rely on their wrap contracts (which may appear as terms and conditions, terms of service or terms of use) as well as privacy policies to govern their relationship with their purchasers. However, DTC companies providing services to UK consumers ought to be complying with the UK's Human Tissue Act, which sets requirements for consent and has made it an offence to analyse DNA without appropriate consent. In the EU, the GDPR, which will be discussed further in

---

[51] Research and Markets, 'Predictive genetic testing and consumer/wellness genomics market by application and trend analysis from 2013 to 2025' (January 2017). <http://www.researchandmarkets.com/research/26mxz4/predictive> accessed 22 October 2018.

[52] Phillips, 'Only a click away' (n 17).

[53] Clayton Christensen, 'Disruptive Innovation' <http://www.claytonchristensen.com/key-concepts/> accessed 18 October 2018.

[54] Larry Downes and Paul Nunes, 'Regulating 23andMe won't stop the new age of genetic tTesting' *Wired* (1 January 2014) <https://www.wired.com/2014/01/the-fda-may-win-the-battle-this-holiday-season-but-23andme-will-win-the-war/> accessed 18 October 2018.

Chapter 4, also includes genetic data within its definition of personal data and sets a high standard of consent for the processing of personal data, requiring 'explicit consent'. As all DTC companies that provide genetic testing services are processing both genetic data and other forms of personal data, they should also be complying with the provisions of the GDPR in relation to EU-based consumers. As European data protection law also exerts a global influence, with many countries outside the EU wanting to adapt their own laws in order to continue trading with EU Member States, it would be in many DTC companies' best interests to comply with the provisions of the GDPR.

1.5 Summary of How DTC Services Operate

DTC companies offer a variety of services, but their normal procedure is to allow people to purchase a genetic test kit through their website. The customer then receives a kit in the post and uses the kit to take a sample of their DNA, normally in the form of saliva.[55] The customer will then send this sample back to the company for analysis.[56] After the sample has been analysed the company will convey the results of the test to the consumer and sometimes provide on-going updates on their health information. These results and on-going updates are normally accessible through an IT interface. Web-based return of results is the primary mode of delivering results to consumers and this is often done without recourse to genetic counselling, although the state of California requires DTC companies to offer genetic counselling.[57]

1.6 Bringing Disruptive Technology to the Public

The current genetic testing technologies used by DTC companies have their origins in the methods developed by Sanger and the Human Genome Project.[58] The scientific background will be covered in Chapter 2, but it is

---

[55] 23andMe, 'How it works' <https://www.23andme.com/howitworks/> accessed 7 January 2013, accessed 22 October 2018. Please note, archived content from this website is accessible here <https://web.archive.org/web/20180111022316/https://www.23andme.com/howitworks/> accessed 22 October 2018.

[56] Anna Harris, Sally Wyatt and Susan E Kelly, 'The gift of spit (and the obligation to return it): How consumers of online genetic testing services participate in research' (2013) 16(2) *Information, Communication and Society* 236–57 <https://doi.org/10.1080/1369118X.2012.701656>

[57] J Kaye, 'The regulation of direct-to-consumer genetic tests' (2008) 17(R2) *Human Molecular Genetics* R180–83 <https://doi.org/10.1093/hmg/ddn253> accessed 18 October 2018.

[58] Human Genome Project, 'History of the human genome project' <https://web.ornl.gov/sci/techresources/Human_Genome/project/hgp.shtml> accessed 18 October 2018; G Laurie,

useful to touch upon it here. Many DTC companies use next-generation sequencing methods to conduct their tests, but the technology is continuing to change rapidly. The majority of DTC companies only sequence part of a person's genome, focusing on testing for specific single nucleotide polymorphisms (SNPs) and not the whole genome.

Although much progress has been made, scientific understanding of how genes function and their role especially in the development of complex diseases is still developing. Understanding of how epigenetic factors contribute to health is also continuing to develop. There is also growing interest in the impact of the microbiome on human health. Consequently, some of the information that DTC companies offer to their consumers may currently have little practical application for the individuals tested.[59]

Where companies offer health-related tests without proven utility or validity, there is a need to consider the nature of the product they are selling. There is evidence suggesting that some consumers believe that the test results they receive from DTC companies constitute a medical diagnosis. This is problematic because while many companies do offer health-related tests, they also commonly have exemption clauses including quite broad disclaimers indicating that these tests should not be viewed as medical tests.[60] In line with Caulfield and the views expressed by Javitt, Hudson, Su and the various policymakers that have released guidance (which will be discussed in Chapter 3), it seems desirable that information provided by DTC companies needs to at least be accurate.[61] If it is possible to regulate the industry in such a manner

---

Genetic Privacy: A Challenge To Medico-Legal Norms (reprint edn, Cambridge University Press 2002) 86–7.

[59] JM Dreyfuss, D Levner, JE Galagan, GM Church, and MF Ramoni, 'How accurate can genetic predictions be?' (2012) 13 BMC *Genomics* 340 <https://doi.org/10.1186/1471-2164-13-340>; Peter Kraft and David J Hunter, 'Genetic risk prediction: Are we there yet?' (2009) 360 *New England Journal of Medicine* 1701–3 doi: 10.1056/NEJMp0810107; Peter Kraft et al., 'Beyond odds ratios—communicating disease risk based on genetic profiles' (2009) 10 *Nature Reviews Genetics* 264–9 <https://www.nature.com/articles/nrg2516> accessed 22 October 2018; Sabrina Prudente, B Dallapiccola, F Pellegrini, A Doria, and V Trischitta, 'Genetic prediction of common diseases. Still no help for the clinical diabetologist!' (2012) 22 *Nutrition, Metabolism and Cardiovascular Diseases* 929–36 <https://doi.org/10.1016/j.numecd.2012.04.010> accessed 22 October 2018.

[60] HC Howard and P Borry, 'Personal genome testing: Do you know what you are buying?' (2009) 9(6–7) *American Journal of Bioethics* 11–34 <https://doi.org/10.1080/15265160902894005> accessed 22 October 2018.

[61] Timothy Caulfield, 'Predictive or preposterous? The marketing of DTC genetic testing' (2011) 10(3) *Journal of Science Communication* C02 doi: 10.22323/2.10030302; Su (n 48); Gail H Javitt and Kathy Hudson, 'Federal neglect: Regulation of genetic testing – government needs to ensure that genetic tests provide useful medical information and that

as to improve the quality of services offered, this will be beneficial for both consumers and scientific progress.

1.7 Data Deluge

The DTC industry fits into broader trends both in personalised medicine and the growth of information technology. The cost of genetic sequencing has fallen drastically in large part due to further advances in information technology. Increasing use of the Internet is generating vast amounts of data and similarly,[62] sequencing technology is allowing for the generation of significant amounts of genetic data.[63] However, the cost of interpretation and analysis of genetic data has not decreased at the same rate and it may take a significant period of time before this gap can be ameliorated.[64]

1.8 Methodology

A major component of the second part of this book draws upon a document review of DTC companies' contracts, which appear on websites as terms of use, terms of service, privacy policies, and disclaimers of liability. In order to do this, a list of companies currently operating in this field was compiled, which contains information on the types of test offered by particular companies and their location. The majority of this research was carried out between 2011 and 2016, but it is continuing to be updated.[65] This work builds upon work conducted by the Human Genetics Commission (HGC), the Government Accountability Office (GAO) and the Genetics and Public Policy Center (GPPC) at Johns Hopkins University, which have all

---

the test results are reliable' (2006) 22(3) *Issues in Science and Technology* 59–66 <https://www.jstor.org/stable/43314223> accessed 22 October 2018.

[62] McKay Cunningham, 'Next generation privacy: The Internet of Things, data exhaust, and reforming regulation by risk of harm' (2015) 2(2) *Groningen Journal of International Law* 115–44; D Greenbaum and M Gerstein, 'The role of cloud computing in managing the deluge of potentially private genetic data' (2011) 11(11) *The American Journal of Bioethics* 39–41 <https://doi.org/10.1080/15265161.2011.608242> accessed 22 October 2018.

[63] A Pollack, 'DNA sequencing caught in deluge of data' *The New York Times* (30 June 2011) <https://beacon-center.org/wp-content/uploads/2010/10/NYT113011_DNASeqDelugeData.pdf> accessed 29 July 2018.

[64] Muhammad Naveed, Erman Ayday, Ellen W Clayton, Jacques Fellay, Carl A Gunter, Jean-Pierre Hubaux, Bradley A Malin, and XiaoFeng Wang, 'Privacy and security in the genomic era' (2014) arXiv:1405.1891v3 <https://arxiv.org/abs/1405.1891> accessed 22 October 2018.

[65] Phillips, 'Reading the fine print' (n 17); I am also grateful to Mary Chitty of Cambridge Healthtech Institute, as in 2013 I had the benefit of comparing her list of companies with my own.

compiled lists of DTC companies.[66] This data was compiled with the long-term intention of creating a publicly available database which listed relevant information about these companies.

In order to compile this catalogue of companies, searches were performed using an Internet search engine (Google) and the following terms were entered: order genetic test online; order disease risk genetic test; genetic test diet; order genetic predisposition test; genetic test for athletic ability; genetic paternity test; genetic test for drug response; genetic test nutrition; genetic test metabolism; DNA diet test; DNA health risk test; infidelity DNA test; genetic test for Warfarin; genetic test for statin; genetic test for prostate cancer; genetic test for breast cancer risk; genetic carrier test; ancestry DNA test; genetic ancestry test. These searches were used to identify English-language websites for potential DTC companies (229 companies). This procedure was repeated on a semi-regular basis. In conducting these searches, reference was also made to the work conducted by the HGC, the GAO and the GPPC and all websites of companies listed in the work of these organisations were examined.

Chapter 3 draws upon this dataset and discusses the different types of test available and the issues each category of tests raises. Several versions of the dataset have now been released via Zenodo. Version 1.3 is the most up to date, but updated versions will be released over the coming years. My most current version on file lists 289 companies (as of October 2018).[67] However, the figures presented in this book will necessarily not be current by the time the book is published, so the discussion of different categories of tests is meant to provide a general introduction to these types of test. For those who

---

[66] The Genetics and Public Policy Center, 'Table – Tests listed by disease category' (11 August 2011) archived content available through the Internet Archive <http://www.dnapolicy.org/news.release.php?action=detail&pressrelease_id=145> accessed 22 October 2018 – link to the 'Table – Tests listed by disease category'. <https://web.archive.org/web/20120124144407/http://www.dnapolicy.org/resources/DTCAug2011byDiseasecategory.pdf> accessed 22 October 2018; Human Genetics Commission, *Genes Direct: Ensuring The Effective Oversight Of Genetic Tests Supplied Directly To The Public* (Department of Health, 2003) <http://webarchive.nationalarchives.gov.uk/20120504102222/http://www.hgc.gov.uk/Client/document.asp?DocId=34&CAtegoryId=10> accessed 30 October 2018; Human Genetics Commission, *More Genes Direct* (Department of Health, 2007) <http://sites.nationalacademies.org/cs/groups/pgasite/documents/webpage/pga_053238.pdf> accessed 22 October 2018; Human Genetics Commission, *A Common Framework of Principles for Direct-to-Consumer Genetic Testing Services* (Department of Health, 2010) <https://ukgtn.nhs.uk/resources/library/article/human-genetics-commission-a-common-framework-of-principles-for-direct-to-consumer-genetic-testing-services-70/> accessed 22 October 2018.

[67] Phillips, 'Data on direct-to-consumer genetic testing' (n 18).

want to explore the most current figures, please refer to the datasets released through Zenodo.

Each candidate website was inspected manually to confirm that it was for a DTC company (229 companies). Each DTC company was assigned to one of the following categories: health (subdivisions of pharmacogenetic; predisposition; pre-symptomatic; nutrigenetic; carrier testing; and testing available through physicians) – 102 companies in total; ancestry – 68 companies; paternity – 85 companies; surreptitious ('infidelity') – 34 companies; DNA dating – 4 companies; and child talent and athletic ability – 29 companies. All companies identified were tabulated with one master table (229 companies) and then tables of the various categories, running to 481 pages. The tables briefly summarise the services offered by each company and also classify the companies into groups based on the type of service they offer.[68] If a company's website was no longer functioning or the company ceased to operate this was also recorded.

In compiling the list of health-related testing companies, those companies which market their services to physicians and/or allow consumers to order through physicians were also included for the sake of comprehensiveness. The websites of DTC companies in the health category (102 companies) were examined to identify those whose terms and conditions were available to the public (71 companies).

The online contracts and privacy policies of health-related DTC companies were saved as electronic documents (PDF files). Where available the contracts and privacy policies were also saved for all other categories of testing and these will be examined in future research. Common clauses have then been tabulated and the tabulation runs to 468 pages. Chapter 5 provides an overview of the typical DTC contract, describing the types of term commonly found in the contracts. This discusses the effect of particular terms from a consumer protection perspective.

1.9 How Should the DTC Industry be Regulated? The Policy Response to Date

The nature and mode of sale of DTC tests do not fit clearly into existing legal regulation in the UK, EU, USA or elsewhere. The industry has developed rapidly. As a web-based industry, it poses challenges for regulation which are not unique, but which are common to many web-based industries and

---

[68] Andelka M Phillips, 'Think before you click: Ordering a genetic test online' (2015) 11 *SciTech Lawyer* 8 <https://www.americanbar.org/publications/scitech_lawyer/2015/winter/think_before_you_click_ordering_genetic_test_online/> accessed 22 October 2018.

also wearable and mobile health technology. By offering their services online companies can sell tests to consumers globally, rather than nationally. This also means that if a dispute were to arise between the company and a consumer, jurisdictional issues arise.

The industry has developed as a consequence of recent advances in genetic and genomic sciences together with advances in computing technology. The cost of sequencing technology is dropping extremely rapidly and that has meant that what is new about DTC genetics is the speed at which advances can be made.[69] Thus, what is new about the DTC industry is the speed at which advances can be made. This changes the context considerably and makes it more difficult for law to keep up with the times. Of course, this problem is not unique to genetics and is a feature in the digital sphere more generally. Advances in genetics have also been facilitated by the rapid advances made in computing technology. Computing technology has been tremendously influential in improving the ability and speed with which large quantities of data can be processed.[70] Without computers, much of modern genomic science would not be possible. The rapidity of scientific progress in this area does give rise to new problems, not only for scientists or medical researchers, but also for lawyers and laypeople.

In the context of companies that provide testing for health purposes, testing which has previously been considered as medical is being provided in a new space – a consumer space. The consumer space differs significantly from the medical space, but in the context of health-related testing it is also not clear that DTC services ought to be viewed as consumer services and not medical services.[71] This shift is emblematic of the industry's disruptive nature.

To date, much of the regulatory response has been a policy response rather than a legislative one and this also is reflective of the industry's disruptive nature, as regulators have not been able to keep up with the pace of technological change and have found it difficult to fit the industry into existing regulation. However, as with several other new technologies, such as wearable technology and the various devices that form the Internet of Things, there

---

[69] Erica Check Hayden, 'The $1,000 genome' (2014) 507 *Nature* 294 <https://www.nature.com/polopoly_fs/1.14901!/menu/main/topColumns/topLeftColumn/pdf/507294a.pdf> accessed 22 October 2018.

[70] Pollack (n 63); Greenbaum and Gerstein (n 62); G Timp et al., 'Third generation DNA sequencing with a Nanopore' in SM Iqbal and R Bashir (eds), *Nanopores: Sensing and Fundamental Biological Interactions* (Springer 2011) 287.

[71] K Offit, 'Genomic profiles for disease risk: Predictive or premature?' (2008) 299(11) JAMA 1353–55 doi: 10.1001/jama.299.11.1353.

is a need for a wider discussion including all stakeholders and the public, so that existing law can be adapted and enforced, and new law cognisant of the various issues raised by new technologies can be developed.

It seems that the most likely area of existing law which has direct applicability to DTC is the regulation of medical devices. In both the EU and the USA, DTC genetic tests have been viewed as capable of coming under this branch of regulation.[72] To date in the EU, many DTC tests, as 'laboratory developed tests' (LDTs), have been considered to be medical devices,[73] but they have not been subject to pre-market review, as they were classified as being low risk.[74] However, the new In Vitro Diagnostics Regulation may have an impact on improved industry governance once all of its provisions come into force.[75]

(a) Policy Guidance to Date

Various policymakers have released guidance on the appropriate regulation of the industry. These include: the reports and principles developed by the Human Genetics Commission (HGC);[76] the European Council's 2008 Additional Protocol to the Convention on Human Rights and Biomedicine concerning Genetic Testing for Health Purposes; the European Society of Human Genetics' (ESHG) statement on direct-to-consumer genetic testing for health purposes;[77] a report by the European Academies of Science Advisory Council and Federation of European Academies of Medicine';[78]

---

[72] S Hogarth, G Javitt, and D Melzer, 'The current landscape for direct-to-consumer genetic testing: Legal, ethical, and policy issues' (2008) 9 *Annual Review of Genomics and Human Genetics* 161–82 <https://doi.org/10.1146/annurev.genom.9.081307.164319> accessed 22 October 2018.

[73] Ibid. 173.

[74] Hogarth et al., 'Current Landscape . . .' (n 72) 173.

[75] Council Regulation (EU) 2017/746 of 5 April 2017 on in vitro diagnostic medical devices and repealing Directive 98/79/EC and Commission Decision 2010/227/EU <https://eur-lex.europa.eu/legal-content/EN/TXT/?uri=CELEX%3A32017R0746> accessed 22 October 2018.

[76] HGC, *Genes Direct* (n 66); HGC, *More Genes Direct* (n 66); HGC, *Common Framework* (n 66).

[77] European Society of Human Genetics, 'Statement of the ESHG on direct-to-consumer genetic testing for health-related purposes' (2010) 18(12) *European Journal of Human Genetics* 1271–3 doi: 10.1038/ejhg.2010.129.

[78] European Academies Science Advisory Council (EASAC) and the Federation of European Academies of Medicine (FEAM), *Direct-to-Consumer Genetic Testing: Summary Document* (EASAC-FEAM Project on Direct-to-Consumer Genetic Testing, October 2012) <https://www.easac.eu/fileadmin/PDF_s/reports_statements/Easac_12_DTCGT-Lay_Web.pdf> accessed 22 October 2018.

the Association for Molecular Pathology's two statements;[79] OECD guidelines;[80] the Canadian College of Medical Geneticists (CCMG), which in 2012 released its statement on direct-to-consumer genetic testing[81]; and the Office of the Canadian Privacy Commissioner's (OPC) statement on the use of genetic test results by life and health insurance companies, released in 2014[82], and its more recent guidance on direct-to-consumer genetic testing and privacy[83] and its policy statement on the collection, use and disclosure of genetic test results.[84]

Work of the UK's Human Genetics Commission (HGC)
In the UK, the HGC did some very significant work in relation to governance of the DTC industry. The HGC was established in 1999 as an independent advisory body dealing with genetic issues.[85] It took over from the Advisory Committee on Genetic Testing (ACGT), which was established in 1996.[86] The ACGT developed a 'code of practice' for

---

[79] Association for Molecular Pathology, *Association for Molecular Pathology Position Statement: On Direct Access Genetic Testing (Direct to Consumer Genetic Testing)* (Association for Molecular Pathology, 2007) <https://www.amp.org/AMP/assets/File/position-statements/2007/AMPDTCPositionStatement_Final.pdf> accessed 22 October 2018; Association for Molecular Pathology, *Position Statement: Direct Access Genetic Testing (Direct to Consumer Genetic Testing)* (Association for Molecular Pathology, 2015) <https://www.amp.org/AMP/assets/File/position-statements/2015/AMPpositionstatementDTCtesting-FINAL_002.pdf> accessed 22 October 2018.

[80] OECD, *OECD Guidelines for Quality Assurance in Molecular Genetic Testing* (Organisation For Economic Co-Operation 2007) <http://www.oecd.org/science/emerging-tech/38839788.pdf> accessed 22 October 2018.

[81] Canadian College of Medical Geneticists, 'CCMG statement on direct-to-consumer genetic testing' (2012) 81 Clin Genet 1 <https://www.ccmg-ccgm.org/documents/Policies_etc/Pos_Statements/PosStmt_EPP_DTC_FINAL_20Jan2011.pdf> accessed 25 October 2018.

[82] Office of the Privacy Commissioner, *Statement on the use of genetic test results by life and health insurance companies* (OPC, 2014) <https://www.priv.gc.ca/en/opc-news/news-and-announcements/2014/s-d_140709/> accessed 30 July 2018.

[83] OPC, 'Direct-to-consumer genetic testing and privacy' (OPC, updated December 2017) <https://www.priv.gc.ca/en/privacy-topics/health-genetic-and-other-body-information/02_05_d_69_gen/> accessed 27 October 2018.

[84] OPC, *Policy Statement on the Collection, Use and Disclosure of Genetic Test Results* (OPC, updated December 2017) <https://www.priv.gc.ca/en/privacy-topics/health-genetic-and-other-body-information/s-d_140710/> accessed 27 October 2018.

[85] Deirdre Janson-Smith, 'The Human Genetics Commission' <genome.wellcome.ac.uk/doc_WTD021009.html> accessed 24 July 2015; Rebecca Hill, 'Human Genetics Commission publish final report' (BioNews 7 July 2012) <http://www.bionews.org.uk/page_149450.asp> accessed 24 July 2015.

[86] HGC, *More Genes Direct* (n 66) paras 1.3–5.

DTC. It also established a voluntary system to encourage and monitor compliance, which did have some degree of success, but has since ceased to be used.[87]

The HGC was disbanded in 2012, although its work was to be continued by the Emerging Science and Bioethics Advisory Committee (ESBAC). However, ESBAC was in turn disbanded, on 31 May 2014.[88] During its lifetime, the HGC released two important reports on DTC: *Genes Direct*;[89] and *More Genes Direct*.[90] It also released a set of principles: *A Common Framework of Principles for Direct-to-Consumer Genetic Testing Services*, intended to provide guidance on the regulation of DTC. After the initial *Genes Direct* report in 2003, *More Genes Direct* was the result of a meeting held in 2007 and prompted by rapid growth of the DTC industry. This meeting considered the developments that had occurred since the original report and 'focussed on three key areas: pre-market review of tests; quality assurance of testing services; advertising and promotion, and the provision of independent, impartial advice.'[91]

The HGC recommended stricter regulation of DTC, that 'most genetic tests that provide health information should not be offered as direct genetic tests', and that the Medicines and Healthcare Products Regulatory Agency (MHRA) should have an important role in 'developing an appropriate regulatory framework' for DTC.[92] However, this role was rejected by the UK Government in its response to the *Genes Direct* report.[93]

The Policy Response in the United States of America
In the USA, a number of organisations have released policy statements and guidance on the DTC industry. These include: the Government Accountability Office (GAO); the Secretary's Advisory Committee on Genetics, Health, and Society (SACGHS); the American Society of Human Genetics (ASHG); the

---

[87] Hogarth et al., 'Current Landscape . . .' (n 72) 169; S Hogarth, D Melzer, and R Zimmern, 'The regulation of commercial genetic testing services in the UK' (briefing for the Human Genetics Commission, Cambridge, 2005) <https://www.kcl.ac.uk/sspp/departments/politicaleconomy/research/biopolitics/publications/Regulationofcommercialgenetictestingservices HGCbriefing.pdf> accessed 22 October 2018.

[88] Emerging Science and Bioethics Advisory Committee, 'Emerging Science and Bioethics Advisory Committee (closed)' <https://www.gov.uk/government/groups/emerging-science-and-bioethics-advisory-committee> accessed 22 October 2018.

[89] HGC, *Genes Direct* (n 66).

[90] HGC, *More Genes Direct* (n 66).

[91] OPC (n 82).

[92] Ibid.; HGC, *Genes Direct* (n 66).

[93] HGC, *Genes Direct* (n 66) 39–40.

Association for Molecular Pathology (AMP); and the American Academy of Pediatrics (AAP). In 2012, the National Institutes of Health (NIH) created the Genetic Testing Registry (GTR), which is 'a public database of test information submitted voluntarily by genetic test providers'.[94] While the GTR is a voluntary register and is primarily intended for use by medical practitioners and researchers, it may prove to be useful tool in improving standards across the industry.

In terms of improving regulation of DTC within the USA, ASHG's statement on direct-to-consumer genetic testing in the United States[95] recommended that the Centers for Medicare and Medicaid Services (CMS) 'create a genetic-testing specialty under CLIA, to ensure the analytic validity of tests and the quality of genetic testing laboratories' and also that 'CMS should ensure that all DTC genetic-testing laboratories are certified under CLIA and should maintain a publicly accessible list containing the certification status of laboratories'.[96] It went on to recommend that 'FDA and the FTC should work together to develop guidelines for DTC testing companies to follow, to ensure that their claims are truthful and not misleading and that they adequately convey the scientific limitations for particular tests'.[97] Although at present the FDA has taken a different approach, these ideas could provide useful guidance for both the FTC and FDA in considering governance of the industry.

The Work of the Canadian Privacy Commissioner and the Genetic Non-Discrimination Act

The work of the Canadian Privacy Commissioner (OPC)[98] is also noteworthy, as it has issued a number of relevant policy statements and also commissioned several studies as part of its ongoing work 'examining the privacy implications arising from the collection and use of genetic information as one of its four policy priorities'.[99] In 2014, it released a statement on the

---

[94] WS Rubinstein et al., 'The NIH genetic testing registry: A new, centralized database of genetic tests to enable access to comprehensive information and improve transparency' (2013) 41 Nucleic Acids Research D925–35 <https://doi.org/10.1093/nar/gks1173> accessed 28 October 2018.

[95] K Hudson, G Javitt, W Burke, P Byers, and ASHG Social Issus Committee, 'ASHG statement on direct-to-consumer genetic testing in the United States' (2007) 81(3) *American Journal of Human Genetics* 635–7 <https://www.ncbi.nlm.nih.gov/pmc/articles/PMC1950839/> accessed 24 October 2018.

[96] Hudson et al. (n 92) 637.

[97] Ibid. 637.

[98] HGC, *Genes Direct* (n 66).

[99] OPC (n 82).

use of genetic test results by life and health insurance companies. This drew upon two papers it had commissioned, which explored the impact on the Canadian insurance industry if that industry did not have access to genetic test results. Both papers found that 'at the present time and in the near future, the impact of a ban on the use of genetic test results by the life and health insurance industry would not have a significant impact on insurers or the efficient operation of insurance markets'.[100] In preparing its statement, the Commissioner considers that 'where the personal information collected is perceived to be of a particularly sensitive nature (such as a genetic test result) the need to consider less privacy invasive alternatives is particularly strong'.[101] It concluded that 'it is not clear that the collection and use of genetic test results by insurance companies is demonstrably necessary, effective, proportionate or the least intrusive means of achieving the industry's objectives at this time'.[102]

More recently, the OPC has released further guidance for the public in relation to DTC with its policy statement on the collection, use and disclosure of genetic test results[103] and a guidance document that lists a number of questions which individuals should consider before purchasing a DTC test.[104] These were both linked with the passing of new legislation, the Genetic Non-Discrimination Act 2017 (GNA).[105] This Act significantly enhances the privacy rights of Canadians in their genetic data. It creates a number of offences and specifically prohibits requiring an individual to undergo genetic tests or requiring an individual to disclose results of a genetic test, and also sets a high standard for consent.

Common Themes of Policy Response
Overall, there is much commonality amongst the different policy documents to date. It is possible to identify key points that might in turn provide the basis for either new legislation or an industry code of conduct. Many organisations emphasize the importance of test quality, which should entail

---

[100] OPC (n 82) 3.

[101] (n 82) 4.

[102] (n 82) 5.

[103] OPC, *Policy Statement on the Collection, Use and Disclosure of Genetic Test Results* (OPC, updated December 2017) <https://www.priv.gc.ca/en/privacy-topics/health-genetic-and-other-body-information/s-d_140710/> accessed 27 October 2018.

[104] OPC, 'Direct-to-consumer genetic testing and privacy' (OPC, updated December 2017) <https://www.priv.gc.ca/en/privacy-topics/health-genetic-and-other-body-information/02_05_d_69_gen/> accessed 27 October 2018.

[105] Genetic Non-Discrimination Act 2017 (CA) <https://laws-lois.justice.gc.ca/eng/acts/G-2.5/page-1.html#h-3>

consideration of both analytical validity and also the quality of interpretation of test results. Tests should be medically relevant. Generally, tests should not be offered to minors, pregnant women or third parties who have not consented to testing. Certain types of test such as what the Association for Molecular Pathology dubs 'business interest' tests should actually be prohibited. Also, many tests that lack clinical validity and utility should also be prohibited. As of October 2018, the AAP has also reaffirmed its previous policy statement of 2013 highlighting that DTC tests should not be performed on newborns.[106]

Furthermore, tests should only be provided when companies have received a person's informed consent, which should be free and voluntary. Further specific consent should also be obtained where companies intend to perform secondary tests or engage in research involving consumers' genetic information. This is also in line with the requirements of the EU's GDPR. Companies ought to provide genetic counselling services or make information about genetic counselling available. Companies should provide consumers with adequate information regarding the respective risks, benefits and limitations of testing and also implications or consequences of undergoing testing, such as how this might relate to obtaining insurance. Companies should also consider the potential impact of tests can on families and give consideration to the personal circumstances of consumers.

Policy guidance also often emphasizes the importance of protection of an individual's privacy rights together with the importance of secure storage of biological samples and genomic data.[107] They also stress the need for maintaining confidentiality in this context. More mechanisms for enforcing compliance are required. There are lots of potential problems here. These include: possible secondary uses which the information may be put to by the testing entities; circumstances in which these uses may

---

[106] 'Not for the littlest' *GenomeWeb* (24 October 2018) <https://www.genomeweb.com/scan/not-littlest> accessed 27 October 2018 – this cites Alyson Sulaski Wyckoff, 'Lack of reliability, privacy plague DTC genetic tests for newborns' *AAP News* (24 October 2018) <http://www.aappublications.org/news/2018/10/24/genetictesting102418> accessed 27 October 2018; this cites the Committee On Bioethics, Committee On Genetics, The American College Of Medical Genetics and Genomics Social, Ethical, and Legal Issues Committee, 'Ethical and policy issues in genetic testing and screening of children' (2013) 131(3) from the American Academy of Pediatrics Policy Statement – A Statement of Reaffirmation for this policy was pPublished at e20181836 <http://pediatrics.aap publications.org/content/131/3/620.short> accessed 27 October 2018.

[107] HGC, *Genes Direct* (n 66) and HGC, *More Genes Direct* (n 66); ESHG, 'Statement of the ESHG . . .' (n 77).

be justified, for example in cases of medical emergency where stored data may be useful in the treatment of the person tested; the effect of consent including a waiver of any rights to the benefit of research derived from these uses; the possibility of data mining and using stored data to make money from research interests; and should the money derived from such a use be held for the benefit of the individual contributors or their heirs? It is hoped that this book will serve to stimulate discussion of improved industry governance.

Overall, many of these documents highlight the importance of unbiased marketing of tests and promote the need for greater transparency in both marketing and the provision of information regarding testing and the use, storage and processing of genetic information. As a number of studies have shown, many companies are not being sufficiently transparent in their marketing[108] and may also not be providing sufficient information to consumers about the respective risks and benefits of testing.

As will be shown in Chapter 5, companies are often seeking to avoid liability and are using wrap contracts to avoid obligations imposed by statute, such as the requirements to supply services with reasonable care and skill and that services and digital information be fit for purpose, as set out in the UK's Supply of Goods and Services Act and the Consumer Rights Act. While policy guidance stresses the importance of clinical validity, companies often state that their services are provided on an 'as is' basis and also attempt to avoid liability for tests being fit for purpose.

1.10 Sources of Law which might be Applicable to DTC in the UK and EU

In its discussion of legislation, this book is primarily focused on the applicable law in the UK, but it also makes reference to EU, US and Canadian law. This section will briefly consider the areas of existing law which might be drawn upon to regulate DTC, namely medical devices legislation, consumer protection legislation and data protection. In the EU, many DTC tests are not subject to pre-market review, as they are classified as being low risk.[109] In

---

[108] Geransar and Einsiedel (n 21); Christofides and O'Doherty (n 13); AK Datta et al., 'Quality of information accompanying on-line marketing of home diagnostic tests' (2008) 101 *J R Soc Med* 34–8; Amanda Singleton, Lori Hamby Erby, Kathryn V Foisie, and Kimberly A Kaphingst, 'Informed choice in direct-to-consumer genetic testing (DTCGT) websites: A content analysis of the benefits, risks, and limitations' (2012) 21(3) *Journal of Genetic Counseling* 433–9 <https://www.ncbi.nlm.nih.gov/pmc/articles/PMC3348288/pdf/nihms353182.pdf> accessed 22 October 2018.

[109] Hogarth et al. (n 87) 12.

the UK, the DTC industry is growing, but the majority of companies offering services to UK consumers are based in the USA. 23andMe's recent entry into Superdrug has received much media attention[110] and while it does have a UK website, tests on UK consumers are still in fact carried out in laboratories in the USA.

As a large number of DTC companies currently offering services to UK consumers are in fact based in the USA it is desirable that the USA does play a role in developing effective governance of the industry. In the USA, the majority of DTC tests have also not been subject to pre-market review. However, since 2010 the FDA has taken a varied stance towards regulating DTC. It issued a warning letter to 23andMe in 2013,[111] but has since granted 23andMe approval for carrier testing[112] and in 2017 created a new pathway for approval for health-related DTC testing.[113]

---

[110] I was interviewed by the *Newsnight* programme organisers in preparation for their episode on the launch of 23andMe in the UK (2nd December 2014). James Meikle, 'Superdrug criticised by doctors for stocking genetic self-testing kits' *The Guardian* Genetics (31 March 2015) <https://www.theguardian.com/science/2015/mar/31/superdrug-criticised-doctors-genetic-self-testing-kits> accessed 22 October 2018; Samuel Gibbs, 'DNA-screening test 23andMe launches in UK after US ban' *The Guardian* (2 December 2014) <https://www.theguardian.com/technology/2014/dec/02/google-genetic-testing-23andme-uk-launch> accessed 22 October 2018; H Wallace, 'GeneWatch UK PR: Shoppers warned not to buy gene tests from Superdrug' (*GeneWatch UK*, 30 March 2015) <http://genewatch.org/article.shtml?als%5Bcid%5D=406259&als%5Bitemid%5D=575612> accessed 22 October 2018.

[111] B Patsner, 'New "home brew" predictive genetic tests present significant regulatory problems' (2009) 9 *Houston Journal of Health Law and Policy* 237–77 <https://www.law.uh.edu/hjhlp/volumes/Vol_9_2/Patsner.pdf> accessed 22 October 2018; Dan Vorhaus, Daniel MacArthur, and Luke Jostins, 'DTC genetic testing and the FDA: Is there an end in sight to the regulatory uncertainty?' (Genomes Unzipped, 16th June 2011) <http://genomesunzipped.org/2011/06/dtc-genetic-testing-and-the-fda-is-there-an-end-in-sight-to-the-regulatory-uncertainty.php> accessed 22 October 2018; Felix W Frueh, Henry T Greely, Robert C Green, Stuart Hogarth, and Sue Siegel, 'The future of direct-to-consumer clinical genetic tests' (2011) 12 *Nature Reviews Genetics* 511–15 <https://www.nature.com/articles/nrg3026> accessed 22 October 2018; PJ Zettler, JS Sherkow, and HT Greely, '23andMe, the Food and Drug Administration, and the future of genetic testing' (2014) 174(4) JAMA Intern Med 493–4 doi: 10.1001/jamainternmed.2013.14706.

[112] Warning letter from US Food and Drug Administration to 23andMe (22 November 2013) <http://www.fda.gov/iceci/enforcementactions/warningletters/2013/ucm376296.htm> accessed 22 October 2018.

[113] US Food and Drug Administration, 'FDA allows marketing of first direct-to-consumer tests that provide genetic risk information for certain conditions' (FDA, press release, 6 April 2017) <https://www.fda.gov/newsevents/newsroom/pressannouncements/ucm551185.htm> accessed 30 July 2018.

Overall there is a general lack of specific regulation for DTC globally.[114] DTC as an industry challenges legal regulation. It is challenging as an example of disruptive innovation which does not fit neatly into existing legal categories.[115] It is challenging because it provides genetic tests framed as consumer services. Such tests were previously restricted to a medical setting and subject to governance mechanisms, which sought to protect individuals undergoing such testing and also ensure standards in both clinics and scientific research.[116] Now DTC companies often offer these services outside the clinic and tests are often offered that have not been clinically validated; even where they are validated, they will often lack clinical utility, meaning that there are no treatment options which a person can take on the basis of such results.

Consequently, it is questionable and also quite probable that for disease predisposition testing especially and also nutrigenetic testing, consumers will derive no real benefit from such testing or at least that any benefit that might be derived by the consumer is likely to occur only at some undetermined future date when the effects of genetics on human health are better understood. Although the $1,000 genome sequencing service is now a reality,[117] the cost of interpretation of that genome is still much higher than $1,000 and unlikely to come close to that figure in the near future.[118]

DTC is also challenging because of the features of the DTC service, in the sense that they do not qualify solely as services or products. The way that DTC services are provided means that consumers purchase a test online, but in order for the test to be carried out there are several steps which must

---

[114] Pascal Borry, Rachel E van Hellemondt, Dominique Sprumont, Camilla Fittipaldi Duarte Jales, Emmanuelle Rial-Sebbag, Tade Matthias Spranger, Liam Curren, Jane Kaye, Herman Nys, and Heidi Howard, 'Legislation on direct-to-consumer genetic testing in seven European countries' (2012) 20 *European Journal of Human Genetics* 715–21 <https://www.nature.com/articles/ejhg2011278> accessed 22 October 2018; Hogarth et al., 'Current Landscape . . .' (n 72).

[115] Hogarth et al. (n 72); SJ Schlanger, 'Filling in the cracks: Improving the regulation of direct-to-consumer genetic tests' (2011) 14 *Journal of Health Care Law and Policy* S1 <https://digitalcommons.law.umaryland.edu/cgi/viewcontent.cgi?article=1003&context=appendix> accessed 22 October 2018; Paula Boddington, 'The ethics and regulation of direct-to-consumer genetic testing' (2009) 1 *Genome Medicine* 71 <https://doi.org/10.1186/gm71> accessed 22 October 2018; Hogarth et al., 'The regulation of commercial genetic testing services in the UK' (n 87).

[116] Hogarth et al., 'Current Landscape . . .' (n 72).

[117] Ajai Raj, 'Soon, it will cost less to sequence a genome than to flush a toilet – and that will change medicine forever' (*Business Insider*, 2014) <https://www.businessinsider.com/super-cheap-genome-sequencing-by-2020-2014-10?IR=T> accessed 22 October 2018.

[118] Naveed et al. (n 64) 7.

be taken. The consumer will receive a test kit (which might be construed as a medical device or consumer product). This kit is used to collect the consumer's DNA, normally in the form of saliva. The consumer collects their sample and then sends the kit back to the company. The company then carries out the sequencing service (which can be construed as either a medical or consumer service). The company then provides the consumer with test results, either in the form of raw data or data with interpretation (which can be considered digital content). Finally, if the company is engaged in ongoing research they may also provide the consumer with ongoing updates on their genetic information, also in digital form. These points are all significant because in law they trigger the application of different legislation or governance mechanisms.

(a) The Wrap Contract as a Governance Mechanism

As DTC is framed as a consumer service offered and marketed via the Internet, DTC companies are using wrap contracts to govern the transaction between the company and the consumer.[119] This contrasts with the provision of genetic tests in a clinical setting, where there are a variety of governance mechanisms applicable including institutional review boards, genetic counselling requirements, consent requirements and the guidance released by professional bodies. These contracts are used to govern several matters, including the sale of tests, participation in research activities, use, sharing and storage of genetic and other types of personal information, and use of their websites. The use of wrap contracts in this context can be viewed as a form of private legislation and industry self-regulation, which is heavily biased in favour of companies. These contracts are a form of adhesion contract and are common in online commerce more generally and their use in the DTC context is representative of the shift from patient or research participant to consumer. It is also representative of this being a web-based industry.

Such contracts often are much longer than more traditional paper contracts and may include provisions relating to assent or consent, both of which are often conflated and might be deemed from a consumer's use or viewing of a website. Kim argues that assent in adhesion contracts and wrap contracts has generally been understood 'to mean acquiescence rather than agreement, devoid of any requirement of voluntariness or volition'.[120] This conception is in opposition to the traditional conception of mutual assent in contract

---

[119] See generally Kim, *Wrap Contracts* (n 14).

[120] Kim, *Wrap Contracts* (n 14) 193 citing Karl N Llwellyn, 'What price contract? An essay in perspective' (1931) 40 *Yale Law Journal* 704, 728 n 49.

law and the normal requirements of consent in a medical context under UK law. In the medical context, an individual undergoing medical treatment in the UK must provide valid consent in order to undergo treatment. In order to provide valid consent there are three elements that must be shown: that the person is competent; that the person is sufficiently informed; and that the person is not subject to coercion or undue influence.[121]

In other words, consent needs to be 'voluntary and informed'.[122] The UK Supreme Court decision of *Montgomery* v *Lanarkshire Health Board*[123] reinforces the importance of providing patients with adequate information,[124] so that they are able to make informed decisions about treatment options. This may suggest that were a dispute to arise involving a DTC company providing health testing to a UK consumer, a court might hold that the company is required to provide consumers with more information.

As in the DTC context, wrap contracts together with privacy policies are often used to govern the purchase of a genetic test. Also, to participate in companies' research, these contracts often cover assent or consent. The assent or consent is often intended to cover the transaction, participation in research and general use of personal data. This raises issues regarding the validity of both consent and assent and it also highlights the issue of whether DTC companies are in fact obtaining adequate consent from their consumers in line with the requirements of the Human Tissue Act, as might be expected in a clinical setting, especially given the lack of voluntariness.

In the digital environment, which has allowed for the proliferation of wrap contracts, consumers have also become habituated to clicking, which means that obtaining valid assent or consent may be challenging.[125] While wrap contracts are often treated as valid contracts, the complex nature of the services offered by DTC companies, especially those providing health tests, might mean that it could be argued that it is not in the best interests of consumers to rely solely on contracts to govern the range of activities in which DTC companies engage. Note too that DTC companies should also be complying with data protection law when offering services to UK or EU consumers and current practice may not be sufficient to meet the requirements of

---

[121] J Herring, *Medical Law and Ethics* (4th edn, Oxford University Press 2012) 155.
[122] NHS Choices, 'Consent to treatment' (NHS Choices) <https://www.nhs.uk/conditions/consent-to-treatment/> accessed 22 October 2018.
[123] (Scotland) [2015] UKSC 11.
[124] Mark Campbell, 'Montgomery v Lanarkshire Health Board' (2015) 44(3) Common Law World Review 222–8 <https://doi.org/10.1177/1473779515592118> accessed 22 October 2018.
[125] Kim, *Wrap Contracts* (n 14) 59.

the new GDPR. Data protection authorities may also have a role to play in assessing and enforcing compliance.

(b) Consent: From the Clinic to the Home

The DTC industry provides genetic tests in a new setting: a domestic setting. Individuals are now able to order a large variety of tests online without the involvement of the medical profession. This is challenging for legal regulation and also for professional organisations that have traditionally played a role in regulating the provision of these tests, as such tests were previously confined primarily to a medical setting.[126] The provision of such tests in clinics has been subject to governance mechanisms, which were designed to protect those tested and ensure testing standards. A vital aspect to this governance was the requirement that the participants being tested, whether patients or research participants, provided adequate consent to testing. Such consent needed to be voluntary and informed. As already mentioned, the *Montgomery*[127] decision also stresses the need for the provision of adequate information to enable informed decision-making. Consent in the clinic normally involves genetic counsellors who will meet patients or research participants in person and provide them with information regarding testing. This means that undergoing testing in a clinic involved personal interaction with trained experts who were able to explain the complex nature of test results. More recently, initiatives such as the HeLEX Centre's Dynamic Consent Project have been working to enhance consent mechanisms and allow individuals to have better understanding of the respective risks and benefits of testing while also enabling them to have a greater role in determining how their data is used in the context of medical research, including a right to withdraw consent.[128]

---

[126] Geransar and Einsiedel (n 21); Liam Curren and Jane Kaye, 'Revoking consent: A 'blind spot'in data protection law?' (2010) 26(3) *Computer Law and Security Review* 273–83; D Kishore, 'Test at Your Own Risk: Your Genetic Report Card and the Direct-to-Consumer Duty to Secure Informed Consent' (2009) 59 Emory LJ 1553; Eline M Bunnik, ACJW Janssens, and Maartje HN Schermer, 'Informed consent in direct-to-consumer personal genome testing: The outline of a model between specific and generic consent' (2014) 28(7) *Bioethics* 343–51 <https://doi.org/10.1111/bioe.12004> accessed 22 October 2018; Jay Katz, 'Informed consent: A fairy tale-law's vision' (1977) 39(2) *University of Pittsburgh Law Review* 137; Megan Allyse, '23 and Me, We, and You: direct-to-consumer genetics, intellectual property, and informed consent' (2013) 31(2) Trends in Biotechnology 68–9.

[127] (Scotland) [2015] UKSC 11; Campbell (n 124).

[128] J Kaye, Edgar A Whitley, David Lund, Michael Morrison, Harriet Teare, and Karen Melham, 'Dynamic consent: A patient interface for twenty-first century research networks' (2015) 23 *European Journal of Human Genetics* 141–6 <https://www.nature.com/articles/ejhg201471> accessed 22 October 2018.

In contrast, at present the mechanisms for consent in the DTC context are not as rigorous as might be desired. Currently, DTC companies normally use wrap contracts to govern all matters pertaining to the purchase of a genetic test, including consent. Some may now have additional consent documents either publicly available on their websites or provided with test kits, but current practices may not meet the requirements for consent in a medical context, transparency requirements under consumer protection and data protection law or the standard of consent required by the GDPR. Furthermore, documents often deem consent through use or viewing of a website, which means that the adequacy of consumer consent more broadly is challengeable.

DTC companies should also think carefully about their user interfaces and how things might be improved for the consumer to help them with making an informed decision. This could involve slowing down the transaction process with the provision of informational resources. As Frischmann and Selinger argue, the designed environment of many websites may have the effect of reducing an individual's autonomy as it can be viewed as rational to completely ignore contracts[129] and this is problematic when a product or service is complex in nature. It is desirable that user interfaces do not nudge consumers towards making a decision, rather allow them to make an informed choice.

(c) Consumer Protection Legislation

As DTC is currently framed as a consumer industry, rather than a medical service, consumer protection legislation may be a useful mechanism to draw upon in order to improve regulation. While the UK has enacted the Consumer Rights Act, which will be discussed in Chapter 4, there are several other pieces of legislation which may be relevant to DTC. The relevant regulatory authority is the Competition & Markets Authority (CMA), which has taken on the consumer protection functions of the now disbanded Office of Fair Trading.

UK consumer protection law has been influenced by EU legislation and case law. 'It is commonly recognized that EU law and the law of the Member States do not have a unique definition of the consumer.'[130] Through comparing a number of consumer protection directives, though, it is possible to identify common features and thereby 'delineate a common notion of the consumer'.[131] The European Court of Justice (ECJ) has also developed

---

[129] Frischmann and Selinger, 'Engineering Humans with Contracts' (n 34) and Frischmann and Selinger, *Re-Engineering Humanity* (n 34) chapter 5.
[130] Iris Benöhr, EU Consumer Law and Human Rights (OUP 2013) 16.
[131] Ibid. (n 130) 17.

ideas about consumers. The conception of consumers promulgated by the Court depicts the consumer as 'a natural person, who, in transactions is acting for purposes which can be regarded as being outside his or her trade or profession.'[132] The Court also frequently makes reference to 'the average consumer', who is 'reasonably well informed and reasonably observant and circumspect'.[133]

The ECJ has also 'recognised the "vulnerable consumer", who requires a higher level of protection in particular circumstances'.[134] There is growing recognition that vulnerability should be viewed as a spectrum. It is also possible for a person to become vulnerable in a particular context,[135] but 'some personal characteristics can imply that vulnerability remains an enduring characteristic for particular groups of consumers'.[136]

The Directive on Consumer Rights

The Consumer Rights Directive[137] is significant in this context. This Directive on Consumer Rights (2011/83/EC) came into force on 13 June 2014 and replaces the previous Directives (97/7/EC) and (85/577/EEC). It is aimed at harmonising consumer protection across the internal market while also maintaining 'the competitiveness of enterprises'.[138]

The Directive defines consumer in Article 2(1) to mean 'any natural person who, in contracts covered by this Directive, is acting for purposes which are outside his trade, business, craft or profession'. This definition has influenced the definitions of consumer used in both the Consumer Rights Act and the previous Unfair Terms in Consumer Contracts Regulations 1999, which will both be discussed in Chapter 5. The Directive is intended to apply to all contracts between consumers and traders (Article 3(1)).

The Directive provides for certain requirements in relation to distance and off-premises contracts. It is likely that these requirements are applicable to DTC contracts, which seem to meet the definition for Distance contracts set out in Article 2. Chapter III of the Directive in Article 6 requires traders

---

[132] Ibid. (n 130) 17 citing Case C-269/95 *Francesco Benincasa v Dentalkit Srl* [1997] ECR I-3767.

[133] Ibid. (n 130) 17.

[134] Ibid. (n 130) 17.

[135] European Commission, *Consumer Vulnerability across Key Markets in the European Union* (2016) xvii–xviii and 39 <https://ec.europa.eu/info/publications/understanding-consumer-vulnerability-eus-key-markets_en> accessed 30 July 2018.

[136] Ibid. (n 135) xviii.

[137] Consumer Rights Directive (n 5).

[138] See recital 4 of the Consumer Rights Directive (n 5).

to provide consumers with information regarding a number of matters. DTC companies ought to be complying with these information requirements and currently.

Sections of the Consumer Rights Directive (Article 6[1]) most relevant to DTC contracts

(a) 'The main characteristics of the goods or services, to the extent appropriate to the medium and to the goods or services':

(b) 'the identity of the trader, such as his trading name'

(c) 'the geographical address at which the trader is established' and other contact information

(e) 'the total price of the goods or services inclusive of taxes [. . .]'

(h) 'where a right of withdrawal exists, the conditions, time limit and procedures for exercising that right in accordance with Article 11(1), as well as the model withdrawal form set out in Annex I(B)'

(k) 'where a right of withdrawal is not provided for in accordance with Article 16, the information that the consumer will not benefit from a right of withdrawal or, where applicable, the circumstances under which the consumer loses his right of withdrawal'

(t) 'where applicable, the possibility of having recourse to an out-of-court complaint and redress mechanism, to which the trader is subject, and the methods for having access to it'[139]

Consumer Protection from Unfair Trading Regulations 2008 (CPUTR)
Meanwhile, the CPUTR[140] could be drawn upon and used to improve regulation of DTC companies' advertising practices. In line with these regulations, it seems desirable to develop an industry code of conduct for DTC services offered in the UK. This could involve collaboration with DTC companies and public consultation. Such a code could also draw upon the principles set out in the HGC's *Framework of Principles*. If the CPUTR were to be extended to apply to DTC, then the most relevant provisions are:

- Regulation 3, which prohibits 'unfair commercial practices';
- Regulation 5, which sets out the matters relevant to ascertaining whether there has been a constitute misleading action;

---

[139] Consumer Rights Directive (n 5).
[140] Consumer Protection from Unfair Trading Regulations 2008, SI 2008/1277.

- Part 3, which creates offences relating to unfair commercial practices; and
- Part 4 which deals with enforcement.

Regulation 5 sets out the matters which will constitute misleading actions. In the context of DTC, the most relevant provisions of Regulation 5 are 5(5) and 5 (4). In examining the contracts of DTC companies and reviewing their websites, it is possible that many DTC companies may potentially be engaging in practices that would qualify as misleading actions. As will be shown in Chapter 4, companies often make exaggerated claims about the benefits of their tests, but their contracts often include broad disclaimers of liability, including disclaiming liability for fitness for purpose.

Part 3 establishes offences relating to unfair commercial practice. Regulation 8 deals with the criteria for establishing when an offence has been committed. Accordingly under 8(1), a trader will be guilty of an offence if (a) 'he knowingly or recklessly engages in a commercial practice which contravenes the requirements of professional diligence under regulation 3(3)(a)' and (b) 'the practice materially distorts or is likely to materially distort the economic behaviour of the average consumer with regard to the product under regulation 3(3)(b)'. Under 8(2) a trader can be guilty of an offence where they engage in a practice 'without regard to whether the practice contravenes the requirements of professional diligence'. The penalty for such offences is set in Regulation 13 and allows for those found guilty of an offence to be liable to a fine or imprisonment.

Part 4 deals with enforcement and it allows regulators certain enforcement powers, which would include the CMA and under Regulation 20 an 'enforcement authority' is provided with a power to make test purchases. This could mean that the CMA could make sample purchases of DTC tests. Schedule 1 of the Regulations lists commercial practices which should always be considered as unfair. Most relevant in this context are points 17 and 18. It is possible that the website content of some DTC companies might at present be deemed as an unfair commercial practice under these provisions.

(d) Medical Devices Legislation

European Union Medical Devices Legislation[141]
One approach to regulating DTC relying on existing legislation is to draw upon the regulatory mechanisms governing medical devices and this is the area of existing regulation, which seems most likely to be used to regulate DTC. This relies on one aspect of how DTC services are provided, namely

---

[141] IVD Regulation (n 75).

the test kit, which is normally sent to consumers in order for them to collect their DNA sample in the form of saliva. Test kits as such are collection devices and 23andMe has been allowed to market through Superdrug in the UK because it obtained a Conformité Européenne (CE) mark for its test kit, which means essentially that the kit has been approved as safe for the purposes of collecting saliva.[142] This also means that the kit can be marketed throughout the EU, as CE certification is recognised reciprocally, so that if a company receives a CE mark in one Member State, the mark will be recognised by others. This certification, though, does not provide for any additional assessment of the reliability or safety of the sequencing service itself or the interpretation or analysis performed.

In the EU, the medical devices legislation is undergoing a period of transition and at the time of writing there are two new regulations.[143] The In Vitro Diagnostics Regulation (IVD Regulation) is most relevant to regulation of DTC testing. The IVD Regulation may prove useful in improving industry governance, as genetic tests that have a medical purpose will be classified as medical devices and companies will have to provide clinical evidence to demonstrate the safety and effectiveness of their product.[144] However, although it came into force in 2017,[145] most of its provisions will not come effect until

---

[142] Turna Ray, '23andMe gets CE Mark, launches PGS offering in UK for £125' *GenomeWeb* (1 December 2014) <https://www.genomeweb.com/microarrays-multiplexing/23andme-gets-ce-mark-launches-pgs-offering-uk-1255> accessed 22 October 2018; Samuel Gibbs, 'DNA-screening test 23andMe launches in UK after US ban' *The Guardian* (2 December 2014) <https://www.theguardian.com/technology/2014/dec/02/google-genetic-testing-23andme-uk-launch> accessed 22 October 2018.

[143] Medicines and Healthcare Products Regulatory Agency, 'New legislation on medical devices' <http://webarchive.nationalarchives.gov.uk/20141206092023/http://www.mhra.gov.uk/Howweregulate/Devices/Legislation/NewLegislationonMedicalDevices/index.htm> accessed 18 October 2018.

[144] L Kalokairinou, HC Howard, S Slokenberga, E Fisher, M Flatscher-Thöni, M Hartlev, R van Hellemondt, J Juškevičius, J Kapelenska-Pregowska, P Kováč, L Lovrečić, H Nys, A de Paor, AM Phillips, L Prudil, E Rial-Sebbag, CM Romeo Casabona, J Sándor, A Schuster, S Soini, KH Søvig, D Stoffel, T Titma, T Trokanas, and P Borry, 'Legislation of direct-to-consumer genetic testing in Europe: A fragmented regulatory landscape' (2018) 9(2) *Journal Of Community Genetics* 117–32, 118 <https://link.springer.com/article/10.1007/s12687-017-0344-2>

[145] J Summerfield and J Fraser, 'UK MHRA publishes guide to the new EU Medical Device and IVD Regulations' *Focus on Regulation* (7 September 2017) <https://www.hlregulation.com/2017/09/06/uk-mhra-publishes-guide-to-the-new-eu-medical-device-and-ivd-regulations/> accessed 30 July 2018; MHRA, 'Medical devices: EU regulations for MDR and IVDR' (Guidance, 29 August 2017, last updated 5 February 2018) <https://www.gov.uk/guidance/medical-devices-eu-regulations-for-mdr-and-ivdr> accessed 30 July 2018; GeneWatch UK, 'The EU's In Vitro Diagnostics (IVD) Regulation: a summary

2022 and many DTC tests will still fall outside the Regulation's remit.[146] Also at the time of writing, negotiations regarding Brexit are ongoing, which may have an impact on exactly how the EU regulatory framework applies in the UK. If an agreement is reached, the Regulations will be applicable to the UK.[147]

The HGC did advocate for an increased role of the MHRA in regulating DTC,[148] although this was rejected by the UK Government.[149] The MHRA enforces the European medical devices legislation within the UK. The older directives are: Directive 93/42/EEC regarding medical devices (MDD); Directive 90/385/EEC regarding active implantable medical devices (AIMD); and Directive 98/79/EC on in vitro diagnostic medical devices (IVD Directive).[150] The current domestic Regulations enforced by the MHRA are: the Medical Devices Regulations 2002 (SI 2002 No 618, as amended); and the General Product Safety Regulations 2005 (SI 2005 No 1803).

The IVD Regulation replaces the IVD Directive. The Directive's scope, as set out in section 2 (a) was intended to apply to all medical devices 'intended by the manufacturer to be used for human beings for the purpose of: diagnosis, prevention, monitoring, treatment or alleviation of disease'.[151]

Much genetic testing for health purposes should be covered by such a definition, and it seems arguable that all test kits which are to be used for

---

of the regulatory requirements for software and genetic tests' (GeneWatch UK Briefing, December 2017) <http://www.genewatch.org/uploads/f03c6d66a9b354535738483c1c 3d49e4/IVDReg_GWbrief_fin.pdf> accessed 18 October 2018.

[146] Kalokairinou et al. (n 144) 118.

[147] Ronald Boumans, 'Brexit Update: New UK MHRA Guidance for Medical Device Companies' (EMERGO 15 August 2018) <https://www.emergobyul.com/blog/2018/08/ brexit-update-new-uk-mhra-guidance-medical-device-companies> accessed 28 October 2018.

[148] HGC, *More Genes* (n 66) 16.

[149] Ibid. Appendix 3 'UK Government response to the HGC's Genes Direct report' 39–40 – this sets out the Letter from From Andy Burnham, the Minister of State to Baroness Helena Kennedy QC (10 July 2006).

[150] Directive 93/42/EEC of 14 June 1993 concerning medical devices <https://eur-lex.europa. eu/legal-content/EN/TXT/HTML/?uri=CELEX:31993L0042&from=EN> accessed 22 October 2018; Directive 90/385/EEC of 20 June 1990 on the approximation of the laws of the Member States relating to active implantable medical devices <https:// eur-lex.europa.eu/legal-content/EN/TXT/?uri=CELEX:31990L0385> accessed 22 October 2018; Directive 98/79/EC of the European Parliament and of the Council of 27 October 1998 on in vitro diagnostic medical devices <https://eur-lex.europa.eu/legal- content/en/TXT/?uri=CELEX:31998L0079> accessed 22 October 2018.

[151] D Stynen, 'Revision of Europe's IVD Directive 98/79/EC: Lessons and results from the Public Consultation document' *IVD Technology* June 2011 <https://www.qarad.com/ data/acms/docs/f1f68f41f74041848885fcf741a39d70/1_revision_of_europes_ivd_direc tive.pdf > accessed 22 October 2018.

health-related purposes, and especially those that are used for tests which are classed as either predictive, predisposition, carrier or pharmacogenetic, ought to be considered as medical devices and regulated as such in both the UK and throughout the EU.

However, many predictive tests, which have an unclear medical purpose, and lifestyle tests have previously fallen outside the Directive's remit. This has meant that most lifestyle tests carried out in the EU have not required pre-market review. Furthermore, as most tests that have been deemed as within the Directive's remit have been classified as low risk, they have also escaped pre-market review, as 'manufacturers usually self-certificate' and the regulation of medical devices is generally less rigorous than the regulatory regime governing medicinal products.[152]

While the primary focus herein is with DTC providers of health-related testing, it is suggested here that in light of the overlap between different categories of testing and the tendency of companies to offer testing of more than one type, broadening the scope for pre-market review of a significant number of lifestyle tests could significantly improve the quality of services offered to consumers and reduce the risks of harm. As the HGC noted in their *More Genes Direct* report, 'the Australian device regulators have recently issued guidance that states that nutrigenetic tests' (regarded as 'lifestyle' tests in the UK) 'will be regulated as IVDDs' (that is, in vitro diagnostic devices).[153] Thus, it might be possible to draw upon the Australian guidance in developing regulation in the UK and EU.

The IVD Regulation defines medical devices broadly in Article 2 and it is likely that DTC test kits will be included within the scope of Article 2, especially in relation to the definition in article 2(5) which relates to a 'device for self-testing'. It seems likely that this will cover test kits provided by DTC companies:

> 'informed consent' means a subject's free and voluntary expression of his or her willingness to participate in a particular performance study, after having been informed of all aspects of the performance study that are relevant to the subject's decision to participate or, in the case of minors and of incapacitated subjects, an authorisation or agreement from their legally designated representative to include them in the performance study

---

[152] Nassim Parvizi and Kent Woods, 'Regulation of medicines and medical devices: Contrasts and similarities' (2014) 14(1) *Clinical Medicine* 6–12 doi: 10.7861/clinmedicine.14-1-6; Proposal for a Regulation 9770/15 of 12 June 2015. Interinstitutional File: 2012/0267 (COD).

[153] HGC, *More Genes* (n 66) 16, para 3.8.

Although this definition is given in relation to performance studies of medical devices, it also deals with genetic information, counselling and informed consent in Article 4, which also allows for Member States to adopt or maintain measures that are more protective for patients than the requirements of the IVD Regulation.

Article 6 covers distance sales, which should include DTC services given that they are offered online. Article 7, which relates to claims made in labeling, instructions and advertising is also relevant and DTC companies providing tests for health purposes would need to comply with this.

Under the Regulation, devices would need to be fit for purpose – and as such tests would be classified as class C, they would be subject to more pre-market review and manufacturers would need to provide clinical evidence for their tests.[154] The requirements for clinical evidence are set out in article chapter VI.

The Regulation makes genetic counselling mandatory for genetic tests for health purposes and should also improve 'post-marketing surveillance and tracing of medical devices'.[155] However, as Borry et al. have noted in relation to the requirement to provide clinical evidence, such evidence need 'only be limited to uses stated by the manufacturer' meaning that if a company claimed to test one gene variant for one purpose, but that variant might also reveal information regarding another disease, it would not be caught by the Regulation.[156]

Finally, as the EU does not have a centralised regulatory authority equivalent to the Food and Drug Administration (FDA), enforcement would rely on national regulators and consequently there may still be problems with enforcement, and the issue of enforcement should not be underestimated. The potential impact of the Regulation will be dependent on whether regulatory bodies in EU Member States, such as the UK's MHRA, have sufficient resources to devote to enforcement. Due to the international character of the industry it may also be difficult for nationally based regulators to take action against companies located in other jurisdictions.

American Medical Devices Legislation

In the USA, there has been a division in regulation between diagnostic tests developed by manufacturers and sold on to other companies, which must undergo pre-market review, and Laboratory Developed Tests (LDTs or

---

[154] Louiza Kalokairinou, Heidi Carmen Howard, and Pascal Borry, 'Changes on the horizon for consumer genomics in the EU' (2014) 346(6207) *Science* 296–8 doi: 10.1126/science.1256396.

[155] Parvizi and Woods (n 152) 9.

[156] Louiza Kalokairinou and Heidi Carmen, 'INSIGHTS' (2014)

'home brews').[157] LDTs are tests that have been 'developed by individual laboratories'.[158] Many DTC tests have escaped pre-market review due to their classification as LDTs.[159] In July 2014, US senators wrote to the FDA requesting that they release Draft Guidance on the Regulation of LDTs, which they had had on file for some time. This Guidance has since been released, but in relation to the regulation of DTC it has not been as helpful as anticipated. Specifically, according to footnote 4 of the *Anticipated Details of the Draft Guidance for Industry, Food and Drug Administration Staff, and Clinical Laboratories,* the FDA is not going to regulate DTC tests. This is unfortunate in terms of improving regulation of DTC tests provided for health-related purposes, and sits uncomfortably with the FDA's previous actions, as it has not previously produced specific regulation for DTC. In 2015, the US House of Representatives passed the 21st Century Cures Act (HR 6). Although during the hearings related to the passing of this legislation, the issue of 'whether or not the FDA should take a more active role in the regulation of laboratory developed testing' was considered by 'the House and Senate', it was not included in the Act. If it had been included within the ct's remit, then the Act would have potentially applied to more DTC tests.[160]

More recently, in 2017 the FDA created a new pathway for approval for health-related DTC testing.[161] Very few companies operating in the US have gained approval as yet. 23andMe was the first to receive approval under this Pathway, for its BRCA cancer disease risk tests, although this approval did impose a number of controls. Specifically, in its authorisation the FDA states that: 'Consumers and health care professionals should not use the test results to determine any treatments, including anti-hormone therapies and

---

[157] This section is very similar to my presentation at the Society for Computers & Law's (SCL) Technology Law Futures Forum in 2014. I also had a short article published in SCL's magazine and on their website based on my presentation entitled 'Direct-to-Consumer Genetic Testing – A Brief Introduction', this is available at <https://www.scl.org/articles/3160-direct-to-consumer-genetic-testing-a-brief-introduction> accessed 22 October 2018.

[158] *Nature* editorial 'Home-brew tests need regulation' (2014) 512 *Nature* 5 doi:10.1038/512005a <https://www.nature.com/news/home-brew-tests-need-regulation-1.15669>; see also Jonathan R Genzen et al., 'Laboratory-developed tests: A legislative and regulatory review' (2017) 63(10) Clinical Chemistry 1575-84 DOI: 10.1373/clinchem.2017.275164.

[159] Patsner (n 111)

[160] N Myers, CE Steding, and P Mikolaj, 'Competing policy windows in biotechnology: The FDA, the 21st Century Cures Act, and laboratory-developed Tests' (2018) 35(1) Review of Policy Research 89–199, 93 <https://doi.org/10.1111/ropr.12262> accessed 22 October 2018.

[161] FDA, 'FDA allows marketing of first direct-to-consumer tests that provide genetic risk information for certain conditions' (FDA, press release, 6 April 2017) <https://www.fda.gov/newsevents/newsroom/pressannouncements/ucm551185.htm> accessed 30 July 2018.

prophylactic removal of the breasts or ovaries. Such decisions require confirmatory testing and genetic counselling.[162]

It should also be noted, though, that the FDA currently treats DTC tests quite differently depending on whether or not they are available for order directly by a consumer – or are advertised as DTC but must be ordered via a physician. While companies that allow people to order directly from their website must obtain approval from the FDA, companies such as Veritas, Color Genomics and Helix, which make their tests available for order via a physician, have not yet had their tests approved.[163] This is problematic, as the involvement of a physician may not actually be direct, as DTC companies may connect the consumer with a doctor to order the test, but the consumer may not in fact meet them.

October 2018 approval of pharmacogenetic tests

At the end of October 2018, the FDA announced[164] that it had granted permission for 23andMe to market pharmacogenetic tests for 33 genetic variants.[165] This authorisation was granted with six controls, 'including a labeling requirement that a warning statement must be included noting

---

162 23andMe, '23andMe granted first FDA authorization for direct-to-consumer genetic test on cancer risk' (press release, 6 March 2018) <https://mediacenter.23andme.com/press-releases/23andme-granted-first-fda-authorization-direct-consumer-genetic-test-cancer-risk/> accessed 30 July 2018; FDA, 'FDA authorizes, with special controls, direct-to-consumer test that reports three mutations in the BRCA breast cancer genes' (FDA, press release, 6 March 2018) <https://www.fda.gov/newsevents/newsroom/pressannoun cements/ucm599560.htm> accessed 7 April 2019.

163 Ike Swetlitz, 'Genetic tests ordered by doctors race to market, while 'direct-to-consumer' tests hinge on FDA approval' *STAT* (16 March 2018) <https://www.statnews.com/2018/03/16/genetic-tests-fda-regulation/> accessed 27 October 2018.

164 FDA, 'FDA authorizes first direct-to-consumer test for detecting genetic variants that may be associated with medication metabolism' (FDA, press release, 31 October 2018) <https://www.fda.gov/NewsEvents/Newsroom/PressAnnouncements/ucm624753.htm> accessed 6 November 2018.

165 Staff Reporter, '23andMe gains FDA market authorization to sell PGx test reports directly to consumers' *GenomeWeb* (31 October 2018) <https://www.genomeweb.com/regulatory-news/23andme-gains-fda-market-authorization-sell-pgx-test-reports-directly-consumers> accessed 6 November 2018; Kulraj Singh Bhangra, 'FDA approves DNA test for predicting drug effectiveness – if it carries warnings' *BioNews* (5 November 2018) <https://www.bionews.org.uk/page_139392> accessed 6 November 2018; see also 23andMe, '23andMe granted the first and only FDA authorization for direct-to-consumer pharmacogenetic reports' (press release, 31 October 2018, updated 1 November 2018) <https://mediacenter.23andme.com/press-releases/23andme-granted-the-first-and-only-fda-autho rization-for-direct-to-consumer-pharmacogenetic-reports/> accessed 6 November 2018.

that the consumer should not use the test results to stop or change any medication. These special controls, when met along with general controls, provide reasonable assurance of safety and effectiveness for this test.'[166]

This move is controversial, as although research in pharmacogenomics is promising, it has not yet advanced to a point where it is possible to make medication choices based on testing of this type.[167] Bousman and Dunlop's study of four pharmacogenetic tests provided by 'CNSDose, Genecept, GeneSight, and Neuropharmagen' found that the test providers made different medical recommendations.[168] In an interview with *The Verge*, Dunlop explains that 'There's a lot of supposition, and the companies have their own algorithms that are proprietary, and that's where you get the most variation in recommendations.'[169]

Furthermore, in its press release regarding the 23andMe approval, the FDA recommends that consumers should not consider changing their dosage of a drug without having further genetic testing in a clinic. The day after announcing the approval, the FDA also issued an alert regarding pharmacogenetic testing, cautioning the public and physicians regarding accessing these tests and indicating that it may take enforcement action against companies providing unapproved tests.[170] The approval and

---

[166] FDA (n 163).

[167] Angela Chen, '23andMe's genetic test for how you'll react to medication is ahead of its time' *The Verge* (2 November 2018) <https://www.theverge.com/2018/11/2/18 055544/23andme-fda-approval-pharmacogenetic-testing-drugs-health-science> accessed 6 November 2018 – this cites the following study: CA Bousman and BW Dunlop, 'Genotype, phenotype, and medication recommendation agreement among commercial pharmacogenetic-based decision support tools' (2018) 18 *The Pharmacogenomics Journal* 613–22 <https://doi.org/10.1038/s41397-018-0027-3> accessed 6 November 2018; see also Jamie Ducharme, '23andMe can now tell you how you may respond to some drugs. But experts are wary' *Time* (1 November 2018) <http://time.com/5441955/23andme-pharmacogenetics/> accessed 6 November 2018.

[168] Bousman and Dunlop (n 166); and Z Zeier et al., 'Clinical implementation of pharmacogenetic decision support tools for antidepressant drug prescribing' (2018) 175(9) *The American Journal of Psychiatry* 873–86 <https://doi.org/10.1176/appi.ajp.2018.17111282> accessed 6 November 2018.

[169] Chen (n 166).

[170] 'FDA tells patients, docs to take caution when using unapproved PGx tests to make treatment decisions' *GenomeWeb* (1 November 2018) <https://www.genomeweb.com/regulatory-news/fda-tells-patients-docs-take-caution-when-using-unapproved-pgx-tests-make-treatment> accessed 6 November 2018; FDA, 'The FDA warns against the use of many genetic tests with unapproved claims to predict patient response to specific medications: FDA safety communication' (FDA, Safety Communication, 1 November 2018) <https://www.fda.gov/MedicalDevices/Safety/AlertsandNotices/ucm624725.htm> accessed 6 November 2018; see also FDA, 'Jeffrey Shuren, M.D., J.D., director

subsequent alert have caused some confusion regarding the regulator's position in relation to tests of this type.[171]

(e) The UK Human Tissue Act 2004

The Human Tissue Act (HTA) governs the use of human tissue and organs in the UK. The Human Tissue Authority enforces the Act. The Act sets requirements for consent and makes it a criminal offence under section 45 to analyse DNA without appropriate consent. It would appear that the Act has direct application to the DTC industry. Although to date it would appear that DTC companies may not be complying with the Act, it might be possible for the Human Tissue Authority to work with the industry to create a code of conduct and improved consent mechanisms. This could draw upon the previous work of the Human Genetics Commission.

(f) Privacy, Data Protection and Security

Central to all categories of DTC testing are the related issues of data privacy and data security. These issues will be explored in Chapter 4, but it should be noted here that in the DTC context this necessitates a balancing of interests. While in the context of health research it might be easier to justify limitations on participants' privacy on the basis that such research is for the benefit of the public, the situation is not as straightforward for DTC companies carrying out research. DTC companies' research endeavours should not automatically be treated in the same manner as medical research carried out in the public and academic sectors.

(g) Genetic Discrimination and Human Rights

Another area of law which may be applicable to DTC is that of human rights. There has been concern regarding possible genetic discrimination,[172] especially

---

of the FDA's Center for Devices and Radiological Health and Janet Woodcock, M.D., director of the FDA's Center for Drug Evaluation and Research on agency's warning to consumers about genetic tests that claim to predict patients' responses to specific medications' (FDA, Statement, 1 Novemer 2018) <https://www.fda.gov/NewsEvents/Newsroom/PressAnnouncements/ucm624794.htm> accessed 6 November 2018.

[171] Turna Ray, 'FDA actions on PGx testing confuse genetic industry players' *GenomeWeb* (5 November 2018) <https://www.genomeweb.com/regulatory-news/fda-actions-pgx-testing-confuse-genetic-industry-players> accessed 6 November 2018.

[172] Iulia Voina Motoc, 'The international law of genetic discrimination' in Thérèse Murphy (ed.) *New Technologies and Human Rights* (Oxford Scholarship Online 2009) <http://www.oxfordscholarship.com/view/10.1093/acprof:oso/9780199562572.001.0001/acprof-9780199562572>

in the context of insurance and employment. There is also increasingly some degree of overlap between human rights and consumer protection law.[173] It has been argued that some consumer rights can now be viewed as part of a third generation of human rights, which while not yet universally recognised have been 'approved by various organisations of the United Nations. These include the right to development and to peace, environmental rights, and cultural rights.'[174] There is also overlap with privacy and data protection law, so this section is more concerned with the law in this context that directly relates to genetic tests and genetic discrimination.

The UK's Human Genetics Commission produced a report on a seminar they held on the topic of genetic discrimination, and this provides some helpful guidance on the topic.[175] The report shows that there is no universal definition of genetic discrimination, but it identifies two main views on it. The first view is:

> that genetic discrimination is best thought of as an extension of discrimination on grounds of disability or illness: it is discrimination on the grounds of a genetic predisposition to a disability or illness. Extending disability legislation, if such an extension is required, to include 'presumed' or 'predicted' genetic predispositions, would offer protection against the majority of instances of genetic discrimination that are currently occurring.[176]

This view does have flaws, though, as it 'probably does not capture the full range of contexts in which genetic discrimination is liable to occur, especially in the future.'[177] Consequently, the HGC favours a second, broader conception of genetic discrimination, which would 'include unfair treatment as a result of genetic tests which indicate that an individual has a predisposition to a condition or to a behaviour which could be used as a basis for selection'. They viewed this broader approach as 'prudent, given the ever-increasing analytical capabilities of genomic technologies which makes it difficult to anticipate the contexts in which genetic discrimination might arise in the future.'[178] If we follow this broader view, they suggested that new

---

[173] Benöhr (n 130) 45–9.

[174] Ibid. (n 130) 47.

[175] HGC, *The Concept of Genetic Discrimination: A Seminar Report and Reflections and Recommendations* (HGC, report, April 2011) archived content available at <http://webarchive.nationalarchives.gov.uk/20120504102747/http://www.hgc.gov.uk/UploadDocs/DocPub/Document/The%20concept%20of%20genetic%20discrimination%20-%20final.pdf> accessed 30 October 2018.

[176] Ibid. 19 para. 72.

[177] Ibid. 19, paras 73–4.

[178] Ibid. 19, para. 75.

legislation would be needed to address this and this would need to prohibit 'discrimination on genetic grounds'.[179] It would also need:

> to include protection from discrimination on all genetic grounds, as it would be difficult, or even impossible, to draw a line between conditions and traits where the onset can be accurately predicted by genetic factors and those whose onset cannot be accurately predicted by genetic factors.[180]

Canada's Genetic Non-Discrimination Act 2017 provides one of the most promising examples of legislation prohibiting genetic discrimination.

Another view of genetic discrimination is offered by Mark Taylor, who suggests that genetic discrimination can be divided into three different categories – primary, secondary and tertiary. Primary discrimination can be described as 'discrimination that is informed by interpreted genetic data'.[181] Secondary discrimination is where assumptions can be made about a person's genetic makeup based on other types of information, that are not genetic.[182] Finally, tertiary discrimination involves 'the act of expressing a preference for a characteristic that is disproportionately associated with a particular genetic variation' and can occur 'when a decision-making process is informed by the presence or absence of a property that is not uniformly shared across all genetic variations'.[183]

While it has been suggested that genetic discrimination is not a significant problem at present,[184] it is possible that as the science continues to progress and as the industry grows, insurers might require disclosure of DTC test results. As the Golden State Killer investigation demonstrates, there is also broad potential for genetic data to be used for secondary research by third parties, which may not be in the interests of the individuals to whom the data relates.[185] Human history in the last two centuries has demonstrated why we should take a cautious approach to how we use genetic data. One

---

[179] Ibid. 20 para. 77.

[180] Ibid. 20 para. 77.

[181] Mark Taylor, Genetic Data and the Law: A Critical Perspective on Privacy Protection (Cambridge University Press 2012) vol. 16, 185.

[182] Ibid. 187.

[183] Ibid. 187.

[184] Timothy Caulfield, 'Direct-to-consumer testing: If consumers are not anxious, why are policymakers?' (2011) 130(1) Human Genetics 23–5.

[185] Peter Aldhous, 'Cops forced a company to share a customer's identity for the golden state killer investigation' BuzzFeed News (1 May 2018) <https://www.buzzfeednews.com/article/peteraldhous/family-tree-dna-subpoena-golden-state-killer#.klPB3w6vpm> accessed 31 October 2018; Drake Bennett and Kristen V Brown, 'Your DNA is out there. Do you want law enforcement using it?' Bloomberg (27 October 2018)

only need think of the eugenics experiments carried out by Nazi scientists or the Tuskagee Syphilis study,[186] or the HeLa cell line developed from the cancer cells of Henrietta Lacks.[187] Other examples of studies in behavioural genetics, which have often served racist agendas and generally not been validated by further research, highlight the need to treat genetic data with care.[188] As will be discussed in Chapter 3, some DTC companies are offering tests for child talent, which purport to tell parents about their child's abilities based on their genes, but testing of this type is not well validated and as previously mentioned much policy guidance to date recommends that DTC testing should not be performed on children.

Currently there is a lack of data and there are limitations on existing surveys, but genetic discrimination does seem a realistic possibility. Given the data-sharing practices of several prominent DTC companies (for example, 23andMe's partnerships with pharmaceutical companies), the risks of genetic discrimination on the basis of access to DTC companies' databases should not be underestimated.[189]

There is also a real possibility of genetic discrimination for indigenous peoples and other isolated population groups who may already be marginalised. The example of one DTC company providing First Nations ancestry estimates for dog DNA samples is discussed in Chapter 3.[190] As DTC

<https://www.bloomberg.com/news/features/2018-10-27/your-dna-is-out-there-do-you-want-law-enforcement-using-it> accessed 31 October 2018.

[186] Sarah Toy, '45 years ago, the nation learned about the Tuskegee Syphilis Study. Its repercussions are still felt today' *USA Today* (25 July 2017, updated 26 July 2017) <https://www.usatoday.com/story/news/2017/07/25/tuskegee-syphilis-study-its-repercussions-still-felt-today/506507001/> accessed 31 October 2018; VL Shavers, CF Lynch, and LF Burmeister 'Knowledge of the Tuskegee study and its impact on the willingness to participate in medical research studies' (2000) 92(12) *Journal of the National Medical Association* 563–72.

[187] See Johns Hopkins Medicine, 'The legacy of Henrietta Lacks' <https://www.hopkinsmedicine.org/henriettalacks/index.html> accessed 31 October 2018; also see generally Rebecca Skloot, *The Immortal Life of Henrietta Lacks* (Broadway 2011).

[188] See John Horgan, 'My problem with "taboo" behavioral genetics? The science stinks!' *Scientific American* (4 October 2013) <https://blogs.scientificamerican.com/cross-check/my-problem-with-e2809ctabooe2809d-behavioral-genetics-the-science-stinks/> accessed 31 October 2018.

[189] Laura Geggel, '23andMe is sharing its 5 million clients' genetic data with drug giant GlaxoSmithKline' (*Livescience,* 26 July 2018) <https://www.livescience.com/63173-23andme-partnership-glaxosmithkline.html> accessed 22 October 2018; GlaxoSmithKline, 'GSK and 23andMe sign agreement to leverage genetic insights for the development of novel medicines' (25 July 2018) <https://www.gsk.com/en-gb/media/press-releases/gsk-and-23andme-sign-agreement-to-leverage-genetic-insights-for-the-development-of-novel-medicines/> accessed 2 August 2018.

[190] See Chapter 3, section 3.4 of this book.

companies have already begun to merge and partner with other entities, there is broad potential here too for stored genetic data to be sold on and used for a wide range of secondary research purposes, which might not be in the interests of the individuals to whom the data relates. Allowing such information to be shared with insurers, pharmaceutical companies, law enforcement, and others, which is already beginning to happen, could lead to unforeseen harms, which we cannot fully predict.[191]

Convention for the Protection of Human Rights and Dignity of the Human Being with Regard to the Application of Biology and Medicine: Convention on Human Rights and Biomedicine (Oviedo Convention)
Article 11 of the Council of Europe's Oviedo Convention prohibits 'discrimination against a person on grounds of his or her genetic heritage' and article 12 of the Convention sets requirements for predictive tests. It reads:

> Tests which are predictive of genetic diseases or which serve either to identify the subject as a carrier of a gene responsible for a disease or to detect a genetic predisposition or susceptibility to a disease may be performed only for health purposes or for scientific research linked to health purposes, and subject to appropriate genetic counselling.[192]

---

[191] AL Morrison, 'A research revolution: Genetic testing consumers become research (and privacy) guinea pigs' (2011) 9 *Journal on Telecommunications and High Technology Law* 573; MM Mello and LE Wolf, 'The Havasupai Indian Tribe case: Lessons for research involving stored biologic samples' (2010) 363 *The New England Journal of Medicine* 204–7 doi: 10.1056/NEJMp1005203; Elizabeth Adjin-Tettey, 'Potential for genetic discrimination in access to insurance: Is there a dark side to increased availability of genetic information?' (2013) 50 *Alberta Law Review* 577–614; AM Goh, E Chiu, O Yastrubetskaya, C Erwin, JK Williams, AR Juhl, JS Paulsen, and the I-RESPOND-HD Investigators of the Huntington Study Group, 'Perception, experience, and response to genetic discrimination in Huntington's disease: The Australian results of The International RESPOND-HD study'; Y Joly, I Ngueng Feze and J Simard, 'Genetic discrimination and life insurance: A systematic review of the evidence' (2013) 11(25) *BMC Medicine* 1–15 <https://doi.org/10.1186/1741-7015-11-25> accessed 23 October 2018; study (2013) 17(2) *Genetic Testing and Molecular Biomarkers* 115–21 doi: 10.1089/gtmb.2012.0288; M Otlowski, S Taylor and Y Bombard, 'Genetic discrimination: International perspectives' (2012) 13 *Annual Review of Genomics and Human Genetics* 433–54 <https://doi.org/10.1146/annurev-genom-090711-163800> accessed 23 October 2018; L Slaughter, 'Genetic Information Non-Discrimination Act' (2013) 50(1) *Harvard Journal on Legislation* 41–66; MJ Taylor, 'Problems of practice and principle if centring law reform on the concept of genetic discrimination' (2004) 11(4) *European Journal of Health Law* 365–80 doi: 10.1163/1571809043418379.

[192] Convention for the Protection of Human Rights and Dignity of the Human Being with regard to the Application of Biology and Medicine: Convention on Human Rights

The UK is not yet a signatory to the Convention, but if it were to become a signatory, the Convention might be drawn upon in developing new regulation for the industry together with its Additional Protocol, mentioned below.

Additional Protocol to the Convention on Human Rights and Biomedicine
As the UK is not yet a signatory to the Oviedo Convention, it is not yet bound by the Additional Protocol to the Convention on Human Rights and Biomedicine concerning Genetic Testing for Health Purposes.[193] However, if the UK does sign and ratify the Oviedo Treaty and the Additional Protocol, this could provide a useful tool in assisting with regulation of the DTC industry, at least in the context of the companies offering tests for health-related purposes.

Additional Protocol to the Convention on Human Rights and Biomedicine (Oviedo Convention)

The following are most significant provisions of the Additional Protocol to the Convention on Human Rights and Biomedicine, concerning Genetic Testing for Health Purposes:

Article 2 sets out the scope of the Protocol.
Article 6 states that 'Clinical utility of a genetic test shall be an essential criterion for deciding to offer this test to a person or a group of persons'.
Article 7(1) requires individualised supervision for all genetic tests that are performed for health purposes.
Article 7(2) provides for some exceptions 'subject to appropriate measures being provided, taking into account the way the test will be carried out, to give effect to the other provisions of this Protocol'.

However, exceptions are not permitted 'with regard to genetic tests with important implications for the health of the persons concerned or members of their family or with important implications concerning procreation choices'. The Protocol would therefore restrict many tests currently

---

and Biomedicine (ETS No 164) <https://www.coe.int/web/conventions/full-list/-/conventions/treaty/164> accessed 23 October 2018.

[193] Additional Protocol to the Convention on Human Rights and Biomedicine concerning Genetic Testing for Health Purposes CETS No.203 <https://www.coe.int/en/web/conventions/full-list/-/conventions/treaty/203> accessed 23 October 2018.

offered by DTC companies, including carrier testing and predisposition testing.

Article 8 sets out information requirements for people undergoing genetic testing.

Article 8(1) states that individuals undergoing tests 'shall be provided with prior appropriate information in particular on the purpose and the nature of the test, as well as the implications of its results.

Article 8(2) specifies that individuals undergoing 'predictive genetic tests' should receive genetic counselling. If applied to the DTC industry this would require companies to provide genetic counselling to consumer.

Article 9(1) sets out requirements for consent, specifying that a genetic test can only be carried out 'after the person concerned has given free and informed consent to it'.

Article 16 affords protection for privacy and the right to information while also acknowledging a person's right to choose not to be informed of test results. It specifies in 16(2) that 'Everyone undergoing a genetic test is entitled to know any information collected about his or her health derived from this test. The conclusions drawn from the test shall be accessible to the person concerned in a comprehensible form.'

Relying on the Protocol could lend support to banning DTC tests for health purposes without clinical utility in the UK. It could also serve to improve governance mechanisms for tests that are permitted to be sold and help to improve standards and supervision of such tests.

Universal Declaration on the Human Genome and Human Rights

The Universal Declaration on the Human Genome[194] is an important document in this context. It affords special protection to the human genome and human dignity. Article 1 states that 'The human genome underlies the fundamental unity of all members of the human family, as well as the recognition of their inherent dignity and diversity. In a symbolic sense, it is the heritage of humanity.'

Article 2 of the Declaration highlights the importance of freedom from discrimination on the basis of genetic characteristics, stating that

---

[194] Universal Declaration on the Human Genome and Human Rights (adopted 11 November 1997) UNGA Res. 27 C/5.15 <http://www.unesco.org/new/en/social-and-human-sciences/themes/bioethics/human-genome-and-human-rights/> accessed 23 October 2018.

'dignity makes it imperative not to reduce individuals to their genetic characteristics and to respect their uniqueness and diversity'. Articles 5 to 7 set out certain rights, including the requirements for research and the right not to be discriminated against (Article 6). These also stress the importance of informed consent and protection of the confidentiality of genetic information, as well as the right to choose whether or not to be informed of test results.

Article 5(b) requires that 'In all cases, the prior, free and informed consent of the person concerned shall be obtained. If the latter is not in a position to consent, consent or authorization shall be obtained in the manner prescribed by law, guided by the person's best interest.' Article 5(d) requires that, where research is performed, 'protocols shall, in addition, be submitted for prior review in accordance with relevant national and international research standards or guidelines'. If applicable to DTC this should mean that DTC research projects should also follow this requirement.

Article 7 then specifies that 'Genetic data associated with an identifiable person and stored or processed for the purposes of research or any other purpose must be held confidential in the conditions set by law'.

These provisions clearly have direct applicability to genetic tests offered by DTC companies and could be used to support suggestions for improving the protection of consumers' privacy and confidentiality in this context.

European Convention on Human Rights (ECHR)

The ECHR is a very important source for human rights protection in the EU.[195] The Human Rights Act 1998 implements the Convention in the UK. Schedule 1 of the Act sets out the rights and freedoms provided for in the Convention. In the context of the current discussion, the most relevant rights protected under the ECHR and the HRA are the right to privacy and the prohibition against discrimination. Article 8 of the ECHR as set out in Schedule 1 of the HRA provides that 'Everyone has the right to respect for his private and family life, his home and his correspondence'.

This area of law has direct applicability to the DTC industry in relation to protecting consumers' rights in this context. Regardless of the suggestions herein relating to challenging terms on the grounds of unfairness, DTC companies should also be complying with these laws and should be affording

---

[195] Convention for the Protection of Human Rights and Fundamental Freedoms (European Convention on Human Rights, as amended) (ECHR) <https://www.echr.coe.int/Documents/Convention_ENG.pdf> accessed 30 October 2018.

sufficient protection to consumers' privacy rights. Current business practice does not seem to be doing this and there is a real need for improvement.[196]

1.11 What Can Go Wrong ?

Various commentators have raised concerns about the DTC industry and the need for improving regulation of the industry.[197] This is primarily due to concerns over the lack of clinical validity and utility of many tests currently offered, the ambiguous nature of test results and legal and ethical issues raised by the industry, and the potential risks that the industry poses to consumers. Given the ambiguous nature of many genetic tests results, Howard and Borry have suggested that:

> most DTC genetic tests being sold at the present time can be seen as an uninformative waste of consumers' money and time. Moreover, they have the potential to cause concrete and extensive harm to consumers' health and wellbeing.[198]

Two of the most significant areas of concern in this context are genetic privacy (as well as general concern over privacy of personal data) and information security. Briefly, when a person orders a genetic test online she is giving up both a physical sample of herself and personally identifiable and potentially sensitive information. Once the physical sample is processed by the DTC company, the genetic data can serve as a unique identifier for the individual tested and can also be used to identify related individuals. This has implications where a company might sell or share the information with third parties including law enforcement agencies. While it was previously believed that complete anonymisation of personal data was possible, there is growing recognition that it is not possible to truly anonymise genetic data. Even the best encryption of data can only be guaranteed for between 30 and 50 years.[199] There have been several recent efforts by researchers which have demonstrated that it is possible to re-identify research participants in large

---

196 Hsiao-Ying Huang and Masooda Bashir, 'Direct-to-consumer genetic testing: Contextual privacy predicament' Proceedings of the 78th ASIS&T Annual Meeting: Information Science with Impact: Research In and For the Community (2015) *American Society for Information Science* 50 <https://onlinelibrary.wiley.com/doi/pdf/10.1002/pra2.2015.145052010050> accessed 23 October 2018.

197 HC Howard and P Borry, 'Direct-to-consumer genetic testing: More questions than benefits?' (2008) 5(4) *Personalised Medicine* 317–20 <https://doi.org/10.2217/17410541.5.4.317>; ESHG, 'Statement of the ESHG . . .' (n 77).

198 Howard and Borry (n 196) 319–20.

199 This is based on discussion with Professor Emiliano De Cristofaro at UCL, who is an expert in cryptography.

genetic studies. Two examples are the work of Gymrek et al.[200] and Erlich and Narayanan.[201] It has even been demonstrated that identification is possible through reliance on research statistics.[202]

In relation to the potential for discrimination in this context, although the US Genetic Information Nondiscrimination Act (GINA)[203] affords some level of protection against discrimination in the context of employment and insurance, it does not cover all types of insurance. Meanwhile, in the UK, there has been a Concordat and Moratorium between the British Association of Insurers (ABI) and the Government on the use of predictive genetic tests in insurance. This is an agreement, which has taken a number of iterations, the most recent being a voluntary code of practice released in October 2018. It should be noted that this is still voluntary and not a law, but whereas the previous versions of the Concordat had to be renewed after three years, the Code is open ended and provide some ongoing level of protection to UK consumers.[204]

However, as previously mentioned, Canada has introduced stronger protection for genetic privacy with the Genetic Non-Discrimination Act, which makes it an offence to require individuals to undergo genetic testing and also prohibits requiring the disclosure of test results for those who do have genetic tests. This can be viewed as a positive example, which other countries could follow.

As the dominant method of DTC companies involves self-sample collection by consumers, there is also 'no way of controlling for the identity of the sample provider'.[205] What this means is that consumers can use DTC

---

[200] M Gymrek, AL McGuire, D Golan, E Halperin, and Y Erlich, 'Identifying personal genomes by Ssurname inference' (2013) 339(6117) *Science* 321–4 doi:10.1126/science.1229566.

[201] Yaniv Erlich and Arvind Narayanan, 'Routes for breaching and protecting genetic privacy' (2014) 15 *Nature Reviews Genetics* 409–21.

[202] R Wang, Y Li, XF Wang, H Tang, and X Zhou 'Learning your identity and disease from research papers: Information leaks in genome wide association study' in Proceedings of the 16th ACM conference on Computer and Communications Security, 534–44 (ACM 2009) <https://www.cs.indiana.edu/pub/techreports/TR680.pdf> accessed 23 October 2018.

[203] Genetic Information Nondiscrimination Act 2008

[204] ABI, 'ABI and Government publish updated Code on Genetic Testing & Insurance' (23 October 2018) <https://www.abi.org.uk/news/news-articles/2018/10/abi-and-government-publish-updated-code-on-genetic-testing--insurance/> accessed 5 April 2019; ABI and HM Government, Code on Genetic Testing and Insurance (October 2018) <https://www.abi.org.uk/globalassets/files/publications/public/genetics/code-on-genetic-testing-and-insurance_embargoed.pdf> accessed 5 April 2019.

[205] Howard and Borry (n 196) 319.

for fraudulent or criminal purposes. Consumers may choose to send in the samples of third parties without their consent. They may also send in samples belonging to their children or the samples of third parties who have agreed to help them engage in some form of identity fraud, such as sending in another person's sample in order to receive test results indicating the individual is not the father when in fact he is, in order to avoid maintenance payments.

There is also the possibility that companies will provide inaccurate test results. An older example of Cellmark Diagnostics illustrates this point, as the company provided a man with an inaccurate test result, indicating he was not the father of the child in question, when in fact he was.[206] Such errors can result in serious harm to family relationships.

As the DTC industry grows, companies will accumulate more data and it is vital that such data is stored securely, as potential attackers could target DTC companies in order to engage in identity theft or perhaps create synthetic DNA, which might be planted at a crime scene. As Ayday et al. note, due to the shared nature of genetic data, potential data leakage is not a matter that will only affect the individual concerned, but also their family. Genetic data stored in DTC databases if leaked could actually impact upon a large family group. As biometric identifiers are increasingly used in banking security and home security systems, there may be an increased incentive for criminal organisations to attempt to gain access to both DTC databases and biobanks. Fingerprint recognition is a good example of the use of biometrics. Apple Pay's Touch ID is the most prominent example, although Samsung and banks such as Royal Bank of Scotland and NatWest are using similar technology, while EyeLock has developed an iris scanner.[207] Apple Pay's Touch ID was successfully hacked one day after its launch.[208] A German hacking group has claimed to be able to recreate fingerprints based on photographs. While a number of banks have also introduced voice recognition software into their security systems, it has also been demonstrated that it is possible to fool these systems as well. A good example is the work of BBC

[206] Macer Hall, 'False DNA test led father to reject daughter' *The Telegraph* (11 February 2001) <https://www.telegraph.co.uk/news/uknews/1322077/False-DNA-test-led-father-to-reject-daughter.html> accessed 23 October 2018.

[207] P Belton, 'In your irises: The new rise of biometric banking' *BBC News Business* (20 March 2015) <https://www.bbc.com/news/business-31968642> accessed 23 October 2018; Nicholas Yeap, 'Your finger is about to replace your bank password' *CCN Money* (9 June 2015) <https://money.cnn.com/2015/06/05/technology/bank-fingerprint-reader/index.html> accessed 23 October 2018.

[208] Ibid. Belton.

Click reporter Dan Simmons, following an experiment in which his account was accessed by his non-identical twin, Joe.[209]

If genetic data is not stored securely, this may lead to as yet unforeseen harm. It is therefore desirable that companies use encryption technology and also have rigorous policies in place on data storage, sharing, access, and destruction of data. It has also been demonstrated that hacking medical devices is a real possibility, with the FDA publishing an alert regarding the Hospira drug pump.[210] Here, security experts demonstrated that it would be possible for a person with access to the hospital network to alter drug dosage remotely, meaning that it would be possible for a hacker with malicious intent to cause a patient's death.[211]

Another area of concern is in the context of pharmacogenetic testing, as consumers may self-manage their dosage of particular medications without appropriate medical advice. While pharmacogenetic testing is probably one of the most promising areas of genetic research for personalised medicine, it also entails the greatest potential risk of real harm. It is important that consumers accessing pharmacogenetic testing are provided with sufficient information to understand the test results and the potential risks of altering dosage. Furthermore, as many tests currently offered lack clinical validity and utility, concern has also been expressed regarding the possibility of people undertaking unnecessary medical treatment and putting unnecessary strain on public health resources.[212]

---

[209] Dan Simmons, 'BBC fools HSBC voice recognition security system' *BBC News Technology* (19 May 2017) <https://www.bbc.com/news/technology-39965545> accessed 23 October 2018.

[210] FDA, 'Cybersecurity vulnerabilities of Hospira Symbiq Infusion System' (FDA Safety Communication, 31 July 2015) <https://www.fda.gov/medicaldevices/digitalhealth/ucm 373213.htm> – archived content available at <http://wayback.archive-it.org/7993/2017 0722144742/https://www.fda.gov/MedicalDevices/Safety/AlertsandNotices/ucm4468 09.htm> accessed 23 October 2018.

[211] Guneet Bhatia, 'FDA fears hacking risks in medical devices: Says Hospira pump should not be used' *International Business Times* (Technology) (5 August 2015) <https://www.ibtimes.com/fda-fears-hacking-risks-medical-devices-says-hospira-pump-should-not-be-used-2039898> accessed 23 October 2018; William Brady and Emma Glazer, 'Cybersecurity in hospitals: Protecting electronic patient devices from the risk of hacking' *MD News* (Legal Technology) (7 August 2015). <http://lowerhudsonbronx.mdnews. com/cybersecurity-hospitals-protecting-electronic-patient-devices-risk-hacking> accessed 11 August 2018; Darlene Storm, 'MEDJACK: Hackers hijacking medical devices to create backdoors in hospital networks' *Computerworld* (8 June 2015) <computerworld. com/article/2932371/cybercrime-hacking/medjack-hackers-hijacking-medical-devices-to-create-backdoors-in-hospital-networks.html> accessed 9 August 2018.

[212] Su (n 48).

Social networking functions of DTC websites also pose potential risks to consumers, as they are encouraged to share potentially sensitive health information, which could be used against their interests. Sharing functions also pose risks when it comes to account deletion, as it may not be possible to fully ensure that all content has been deleted if other users have already downloaded it. Furthermore, as some companies, such as 23andMe, AncestryDNA and Gene By Gene, are partnering with third parties, it is possible that user content may be shared more widely than consumers might anticipate.

When thinking about consumer vulnerability in this context, it should be noted that vulnerability is something that can affect everyone. It is also not a constant state and people can move in and out of it. It may also vary according to the nature of goods and services purchased. Consumers are more likely to be vulnerable or experience detriment when they are dealing with products and services that are either complex in nature or unfamiliar to them.[213] In the context of DTC for health purposes, the information provided in test results is of a complex nature. While some consumers may have sufficient competence to understand these results if DTC becomes widespread, as it will reach a larger proportion of the population this in turn will mean that a larger number of ordinary consumers will access these services. This may then increase the likelihood of issues arising regarding consumers' levels of understanding and it is also possible that specific vulnerable groups of consumers are more likely to access these services and experience detriment.

Much of the research conducted to date on the experiences, motivations and overall behaviour of DTC consumers has been focused on early adopters.[214] If DTC is to become more widely accessible, the potential for it to negatively impact upon vulnerable consumers will increase and as Lachance et al. have noted, 'there is no evidence that even the early adopters of these services understand the information being given to them by [DTC websites].'[215]

---

[213] Financial Conduct Authority, *Consumer Vulnerability* (FCA, Occasional Paper No 8, 2015) 22, citing Office of Fair Trading, *Vulnerable Consumer Groups: Quantification and Analysis* (Office of Fair Trading, Research Paper 15 1998, 1998) <https://www.fca.org.uk/publications/occasional-papers/occasional-paper-no-8-consumer-vulnerability> accessed 23 October 2018.

[214] J Scott Roberts and Jenny Ostergren, 'Direct-to-consumer genetic testing and personal genomics services: A review of recent empirical studies' (2013) 1(3) *Current Genetic Medicine Reports* 182–200 doi: 10.1007/s40142-013-0018-2; TMD Finlay, 'UK Users' and Genetics Clinicians' Experiences of Direct-to-Consumer Genetic Testing' (PhD thesis, Cardiff University 2015); P Saukko, 'State of play . . .' (n 18)

[215] Lachance (n 82) 311.

1.12 Conclusion

This book discusses the DTC industry and its regulation, focusing on wrap contracts as the dominant governance mechanisms for the industry. It also draws upon other studies of wrap contracts, privacy policies[216] and personal data practices of DTC companies,[217] as well as studies of contracts and privacy policies used by other types of business.[218] Chapter 5 explores the effects such contracts have on the rights of consumers in the context of DTC services. It suggests that at present these contracts often do not appropriately balance the respective rights of companies and consumers and that reform is needed.

This book makes a number of arguments, including that certain terms commonly included in DTC contracts could be construed as unfair terms under English and EU law. Specifically, the following terms are likely to be deemed to be unfair: terms allowing for unilateral alteration of terms; clauses forcing a consumer to resolve disputes in another jurisdiction; indemnity clauses; exclusion clauses disclaiming liability for fitness for purpose or personal injury caused by the company's negligence; scope of purpose clauses; and clauses deeming consent or assent.

The book also argues that the CMA should seek to improve DTC contracts and discontinue the use of problematic terms; that the use of wrap contracts in this context can be viewed as a form of private legislation which is effectively industry self-regulation that is skewed heavily in favour of companies and does not afford sufficient protection to the rights of consumers; and improved legal regulation of the industry is desirable.[219]

The contractual review did use particular versions of these contracts, but more recent studies support its findings[220] and the need for reform. This review looked at common terms and how these could be challenged on the basis of their potential unfairness and how this might be achieved through the intervention of the CMA. It is possible to compare DTC services with other web-based industries and a useful comparison can be made with cloud storage providers. Given that the CMA has only recently completed a review of compliance of cloud storage providers, which has already resulted in a number of companies agreeing to improve their terms,[221] the possibility of the

[216] Laestadius et al. (n 13).

[217] Christofides and O'Doherty (n 13).

[218] Obar and Oeldorf-Hirsch, 'The on the Internet' (n 32); Elshout et al. (n 41); NCC, *APPFAIL* (n 22); and NCC, *Deceived by Design* (n 33).

[219] Kim, *Wrap Contracts* (n 14) 71–6.

[220] Hazel and Slobogin (n 13); *APPFAIL* (n 22); Laestadius et al. (n 13)

[221] CMA, *Consumer Law Compliance Review: Cloud Storage* (CMA, Findings Report, 2016)

CMA conducting a similar compliance review of DTC companies does seem a workable solution to improving consumer protection in this context. In the long term further reform is needed and this could include specific legislation to regulate the industry and enforcement action from the UK's Human Tissue Authority, Information Commissioner's Office (ICO) and MHRA are necessary. At present, there are several options that might be taken to improving the regulation of the industry and it is hoped that the discussion herein will serve to assist regulators and policymakers in thinking about regulation of the industry and that it can highlight any current industry practices which are problematic. It is also hoped that this discussion will aid others interested in the DTC industry and in wrap contracts and privacy policies on how these might be improved.

<https://assets.digital.cabinet-office.gov.uk/media/57472953e5274a037500000d/cloud-storage-findings-report.pdf> accessed 23 October 2018.

2

The Science Behind that Click of the Mouse

2.1 Introduction

The DTC industry is centred around the online sale of genetic tests. The industry has emerged and has been able to develop because of rapid advances made in two technological areas: genetic and genomic science; and computing. The rate of technological advances in genetics and genomics is continuing on an almost unprecedented scale. This chapter provides a brief introduction to the scientific advances that have enabled the DTC industry to develop and an overview of the types of service currently available.

2.2 The Nature of Genetic Information and Genetic Exceptionalism

(a) What is Genetic Information?

Genetic information can be defined as 'the information carried in a sequence of nucleotides in a molecule of DNA or RNA'.[1] For present purposes, genomic sequence data can be understood as the data generated by sequencing technology. It has recently been suggested by Raymond McAuley that the cost of sequencing a genome will be less than the cost of flushing a toilet by 2020.[2] 'As of January 2014, sequencing a human genome cost just under $1,000 – less than the cost of a chest X-ray' and 'genome scanning is dropping in cost faster than computers can keep up. Moore's Law observes that computing power doubles every two years, but the cost of sequencing a genome drops by 5 or 10 times per year.'[3]

DTC services normally only sequence a portion of an individual's

---

[1] Richard Cammack et al. (eds), *Oxford Dictionary of Biochemistry and Molecular Biology* (2nd edn, Oxford University Press 2006) 476.

[2] A Raj, 'Soon, It Will Cost Less To Sequence A Genome Than To Flush A Toilet — And That Will Change Medicine Forever' (*Business Insider*, 2014) <https://www.businessinsider.com/super-cheap-genome-sequencing-by-2020-2014-10?IR=T> accessed 22 October 2018.

[3] Ibid.

genome, rather than the entire genome sequence. However, this may change, as more companies begin to offer whole genome sequencing. Currently Dante Labs, Gene By Gene and Sure Genomics[4] are the most prominent examples of this. Dante Labs now offers whole genome sequencing (€849 as of 3 August 2018) and appears to allow consumers to order this directly from their website,[5] while Sure Genomics and Gene By Gene (1,095 US dollars as of 3 August 2018) offers this for order through a physician.

In the context of DTC, the focus herein is on sequenced data, which is generated by analysing an individual's DNA sample. This is normally a saliva sample or cheek swab collected by the consumer and sent to the company. In the context of DTC, the sample gains value for the company once it has been sequenced and interpreted, although it is also possible that some companies may also conduct research on the stored physical sample, especially in metabolics. Some companies offer data-only services, which means that they only provide their customers with the raw sequenced data, which they have not subjected to interpretation. Gene By Gene's DNA DTC and the service 23andMe offered its American consumers after the warning letter from the FDA are good examples of this. Other companies supply their customers with results that have been interpreted. It should be noted that 23andMe continued to offer interpretation services for its UK and Canadian consumers when it had halted such services for its American customers. If these tests were to carried out in a clinical setting, there would normally be pre- and post-test genetic counselling, but while some DTC companies offer counselling, the majority do not and there are questions around the adequacy of genetic counselling services offered by these companies.[6]

(b) Is Genetic Information Special?

DTC companies provide genetic sequencing services and through the provision of these services they are collecting and often storing sequenced genetic data from consumers. Several of the most prominent DTC companies also have research branches and are using consumers' data for a variety of purposes. There is debate over whether or not genetic information should be

---

[4] Dante Labs <https://www.dantelabs.com/collections/our-tests> accessed 3 August 2018; Gene By Gene <https://genebygene.com/pages/research?goto=exome-sequencing> accessed 3 August 2018; Sure Genomics <http://www.suregenomics.com/full-dna-sequence/> accessed 3 August 2018.

[5] Dante Labs, 'Whole genome sequencing (WGS) – Full DNA analysis for rare diseases' <https://www.dantelabs.com/products/whole-genome-sequencing> accessed 27 July 2018.

[6] HC Howard and P Borry, 'Survey of European clinical geneticists on awareness, experiences and attitudes towards direct-to-consumer genetic testing' (2013) 5(45) *Genome Medicine* 1–11 doi: https://doi.org/10.1186/gm449.

treated differently from other types of personal information.[7] It is possible to argue that genomic sequence data should be treated as special on the grounds that it can reveal important information on a variety of matters. Most significant here is its ability to serve as an unique identifier for the individual tested, which means that where companies store genetic information and share it with third parties, such information has the potential to be used against an individual's interests. This is largely due to other features of genetic information. For instance, genetic information can be used to reveal an individual's level of risk of developing a particular disease or condition or their carrier status. In the DTC context, when consumers purchase genetic tests, they may find information of this type personally useful, but when shared it could be used by insurance companies or employers in a discriminatory manner.

It should be noted that genetic information is also to a large extent immutable and can be preserved for a significant period of time, meaning that secure storage is not an issue that decreases in importance over time. A person can change her passwords and even her name. However, she cannot change her genome and as genetic information can also be used to identify family members, the issue of privacy in this context continues after death.[8]

Other features of genetic information include: revelations about traits that are not health-related, but which might be fun, such as eye colour or bitter taste perception; and information about a person's family, ancestry and personal identity. While learning about eye colour and ancestry information might seem relatively innocuous, ancestry testing can be used to reinforce notions of race,[9] which could result in an individual being discriminated against. Furthermore, as this information can also be used to identify family members, there is the potential for DTC databases to be used against consumers' interests through sharing of data with government agencies and law enforcement, which as mentioned in chapter 1 is already beginning to happen. (The example of the Golden State Killer investigation will be discussed in chapter 4.) It could also be used for targeted marketing of family

---

[7] ELSI Contributor Alan E Dow, 'Genetic exceptionalism and the precautionary principle' (*Genomics Law Report*, 6 October 2009) <https://web.archive.org/web/20120720104101/genomicslawreport.com/index.php/2009/10/06/genetic-exceptionalism-and-the-precautionary-principle/> last accesed 23 October 2018; James P Evans and Wylie Burke, 'Genetic exceptionalism. Too much of a good thing?' (2008) 10 Genet Med 500–1.

[8] E Ayday, E De Cristofaro, J-P Hubaux, and G Tsudik, 'Whole genome sequencing: Revolutionary medicine or privacy nightmare?' (2015) 48(2) *Computer* 58–66 doi: 10.1109/MC.2015.59.

[9] Kim TallBear, 'The emergence, politics, and marketplace of Native American' in Daniel Lee Kleinman and Kelly Moore (eds), *Routledge Handbook of Science, Technology and Science* (Routledge 2014) 21 doi: 10.4324/9780203101827.ch1.

or large population groups that possess certain genetic traits. For instance, a pharmaceutical company might develop a particular drug for a specific group and then market directly to consumers through a DTC company's website. As there is growing recognition that it is not possible to completely de-identify or anonymise genetic data, the risks of misuse due to data-sharing should not be underestimated.[10] Two of the most prominent early DTC companies, DeCODE and Navigenics, have since been sold on to life sciences research companies and while they are no longer offering DTC services, their stored consumer data is being used in ongoing research.[11]

Genetic exceptionalism 'is the concept that genetic information is inherently unique and should be treated differently in law than other forms of personal or medical information'.[12] The term was coined by Thomas Murray.[13] Some argue strongly for the special treatment of genetic and genomic sequence data, as it can be connected with notions of personal identity. There are several important international documents supporting the special treatment of genetic information. The International Declaration on Human Genetic Data sets out the 'special status' of human genetic data in Article 4.[14]

---

[10] M Naveed et al., 'Privacy and security in the genomic era' (2014) arXiv:1405.1891v3 <https://arxiv.org/abs/1405.1891> accessed 22 October 2018; M Gymrek et al., 'Identifying personal genomes by surname inference' (2013) 339(6117) *Science* 321–4 doi:10.1126/science.1229566.

[11] D Vorhaus, 'Implications of Amgen/deCODE deal for genetic testing consumers' *Genomics Law Report* (10 December 2012) <https://theprivacyreport.com/2012/12/10/implications-of-amgendecode-deal-for-genetic-testing-consumers/> accessed 23 October 2018; T Ray, 'With decode purchase, Amgen gains genetics expertise, consumers lose DTC testing option' *GenomeWeb* (12 December 2012) <https://www.genomeweb.com/clinical-genomics/decode-purchase-amgen-gains-genetics-expertise-consumers-lose-dtc-testing-option> accessed 23 October 2018; Navigenics, 'How it works' <navigenics.com/visitor/what_we_offer/how_it_works/international_orders/> accessed 2 April 2012 on file with author, please see <https://web.archive.org/web/20120814190220/navigenics.com/visitor/what_we_offer/how_it_works/international_orders/> accessed 23 October 2018; Navigenics, 'Our acquisition by life technologies' <navigenics.com> accessed 10 December 2012; Navigenics, 'Find a physician' <navigenics.com/visitor/about_us/find_a_physician/> accessed 5 April 2012.

[12] Dow (n 7).

[13] Mark A Rothstein, 'Epigenetic Exceptionalism' (2013) 41 *The Journal of Law Medicine and Ethics* 733 citing TH Murray, 'Genetic exceptionalism and "future diaries": Is genetic information different from other medical information?' in MA Rothstein (ed.), *Genetic Secrets: Protecting Privacy and Confidentiality in the Genetic Era* (Yale University Press 1997).

[14] Health Law Institute, Analysis of Privacy Policies and Practices of Direct-to-Consumer Genetic Testing Companies: Private Sector Databanks and Privacy Protection Norms (Report funded by the Office of the Privacy Commissioner of Canada, 2010) 11 <https://www.priv.gc.ca/en/opc-actions-and-decisions/research/funding-for-privacy-

UNESCO's Declaration on the Human Genome and Human Rights states in Article 1 that 'The human genome underlies the fundamental unity of all members of the human family, as well as the recognition of their inherent dignity and diversity. In a symbolic sense, it is the heritage of humanity.' It also prohibits genetic discrimination, in Article 6. Meanwhile, the Council of Europe's Convention on Biomedicine prohibits 'discrimination against a person on grounds of his or her genetic heritage'. The provisions of some of these documents will be considered in Chapter 4 in the context of discussion of genetic discrimination and human rights.

The genetic exceptionalist approach has been criticised. One of the main criticisms levelled at the genetic exceptionalist approach is that genetic information differs from other forms of personal data in that much of it is shared between people.[15] For example, if Mary has a test for the gene variants associated with Huntington's disease and has a positive test result, it does significantly increase the likelihood that other family members will also possess this mutation. With Huntington's and some other monogenic conditions, if one possesses the specific gene variant associated with the condition, they will actually develop the disease. At present, Huntington's is untreatable and so tests of this kind often do not have clinical utility in the sense that physicians cannot offer the individual treatment options. Because of this, sometimes a person may choose not to be tested, where they have a known family history of this type of disease.[16] Where individuals are tested for diseases of this type, they may suffer psychological harm and where some family members choose to be tested, while others do not, this can cause division within families and also the question of how to balance rights. How should one person's right to be tested (or right to know) be balanced against another's right not to know. The answer is still unclear at present. Some individuals choose to take the test and use the knowledge they gain to make life choices.

An interesting suggestion is that it might be desirable to protect genetic information more strongly where it has limited clinical utility, and afford it

---

research-and-knowledge-translation/completed-contributions-program-projects/2009-2010/p_200910_07/> accessed 23 October 2018; UNESCO, International Declaration on Human Genetic Data <http://portal.unesco.org/en/ev.php-URL_ID=17720&URL_DO=DO_TOPIC&URL_SECTION=201.html> accessed 23 October 2018.

[15] Trevor Woodage, 'Relative futility: Limits to genetic privacy protection because of the inability to prevent disclosure of genetic information by relatives' (2010) 95 *Minnesota Law Review* 682–713.

[16] Rhona MacLeod, Anna Beach, Sasha Henriques, Jasmin Knopp, Katie Nelson, and Lauren Kerzin-Storrar, 'Experiences of predictive testing in young people at risk of Huntington's disease, familial cardiomyopathy or hereditary breast and ovarian cancer' (2014) 22 *European Journal of Human Genetics* 396–401 doi: 10.1038/ejhg.2013.143.

less where it has strong clinical utility.[17] This approach seems to deal with competing interests quite well.

However, even if one accepts that genetic information is not essentially different from any other type of personal information, the fact that it can be used to identify individuals and also give insights about their family members should urge caution. In the business context, many companies will do whatever they think is permissible under the law and will often take this to the limits of what the law allows. Given that in other contexts where information is less sensitive there is regulation of how companies use it, it might be advisable to improve regulation of DTC. An analogy could be made with the financial services industry, which often has industry-specific regulators in different countries (the UK's regulator is the Financial Conduct Authority)[18] and it may be advisable that if the DTC industry continues to develop, such an industry-specific regulator might be created.

2.3 Recent Advances in Genetic and Genomic Science

The DTC industry has developed as a direct consequence of recent advances in genetics and genomics combined with the exponential decrease in the cost of genetic sequencing.[19] This section will outline the recent advances in genetics and genomics that have made DTC possible and in so doing will define some key terminology.

Over the course of the twentieth century and now at the dawn of the twenty-first, scientific understanding of the nature of the human body and genetics has greatly improved. Watson and Crick identified the structure of DNA (deoxyribonucleic acid) in 1953 and it is their model that has facilitated developments in genetic and subsequently genomic science.[20] The Human Genome Project began in 1990 and by 2003 the first complete genome had

[17] James P Evans and Wylie Burke, 'Genetic exceptionalism. Too much of a good thing?' (2008) 10 *Genetic Medicine* 500–1; James P Evans, Wylie Burke and Muin Khoury, 'The rules remain the same for genomic medicine: The case against "reverse genetic exceptionalism"' (2010) 12 *Genetics in Medicine* 342–3.

[18] Financial Conduct Authority, *FCA Mission: Approach to Consumers* (Financial Conduct Authority, July 2018) <https://www.fca.org.uk/publication/corporate/approach-to-consumers.pdf> accessed 29 October 2018; and Financial Conduct Authority, Discussion Paper on a duty of care and potential alternative approaches (FCA, Discussion Paper 18/5, July 2018) <https://www.fca.org.uk/publication/discussion/dp-18-05.pdf> accessed 29 October 2018.

[19] Raj (n 2).

[20] AJF Griffiths et al., *Introduction to Genetic Analysis* (10th edn, GH Freeman and Company 2012) 279–80, 84–89.

been sequenced.[21] Since that time, major technological advances have been made and the cost of sequencing has been drastically reduced. What used to take months can now be done in a fraction of the time and at a greatly reduced cost. Since 2003, technology has evolved so rapidly and the cost of sequencing has reduced so much that there has been a shift from genetic testing to whole genome scanning.

The current genetic testing technologies used by DTC companies have their origins in the methods developed by Sanger and the Human Genome Project. Many DTC companies use next-generation sequencing methods to conduct their tests, but the technology is continuing to change rapidly. The majority of DTC companies only sequence part of a person's genome, focusing on testing for specific single nucleotide polymorphisms (SNPs) and not the whole genome. While this may change in the near future, sequencing only part of the genome means that some of the tests offered, especially those for predictive purposes, may in fact have limited predictive value.[22]

Furthermore, scientific understanding of the human genome is still progressing and the implications that a person's genomic data have on their health and well-being are still being deciphered. Although much progress has been made, scientific understanding of how genes function and their role, especially in the development of complex diseases, has not advanced as rapidly as once hoped. Our understanding of how epigenetic factors contribute to health is also continuing to develop. There is also growing interest in the impact of the microbiome on human and animal health and researchers have also found that a person's genetic makeup may in fact vary in different organs of their body, a phenomenon known as mosaicism.[23] This is more common in individuals suffering from cancer, but there are examples of women and men who are chimeras and have more than one genome. For instance, 'a woman needing a kidney transplant did not genetically match her children' and a

---

[21] Human Genome Project, 'History of the Human Genome Project' <https://web.ornl.gov/sci/techresources/Human_Genome/project/hgp.shtml> accessed 27 July 2018; G Laurie, *Genetic Privacy: A Challenge To Medico-Legal Norms* (reprint edn, Cambridge University Press 2002) 86–7.

[22] Luke Jostins and Jeffrey C Barrett, 'Genetic risk prediction in complex disease' (2011) 20 *Human Molecular Genetics* R182–R188 <https://doi.org/10.1093/hmg/ddr378> accessed 23 October 2018.

[23] Maeve O'Huallachain, Konrad J Karczewski, Sherman M Weissman, Alexander Eckehart Urban, and Michael P Snyder, 'Extensive genetic variation in somatic human tissues' (2012) 109(44) PNAS 18018–18023 <https://doi.org/10.1073/pnas.1213736109> accessed 23 October 2018; Carl Zimmer, 'DNA double take' *The New York Times* (16 September 2013) <https://www.nytimes.com/2013/09/17/science/dna-double-take.html> accessed 23 October 2018.

kidney was grown for her 'from the cells of her lost twin brother'.[24] As Field and Davies write, the new dogma could be 'one human, multiple genomes'.[25]

Consequently some of the information that DTC companies offer to their consumers may currently have little practical application for the individuals tested.[26] Where companies offer health-related tests without proven utility or validity, the nature of the product they are in fact selling is worthy of consideration. As noted in Chapter 1, there is some evidence suggesting that some consumers believe that the test results they receive from DTC companies constitute a medical diagnosis.[27] This is problematic because while many companies do offer health-related tests, they also commonly have quite broad exemption clauses indicating that these tests should not be viewed as medical tests.[28] Whether such disclaimers are enforceable will be considered in subsequent chapters.

(a) Genetics and Genomics

The terms genetics, genome, gene and genomics are used widely and sometimes interchangeably without strong definitions. Genetics as a science can be defined as:

the scientific discipline dealing with

1. the study of inheritance and variation of biological traits, and
2. the study of genes, including their structure, function, variation, and transmission.[29]

---

[24] Dawn Field and Neil Davies, *Biocode The New Age of Genomics* (Oxford University Press 2015) 33.

[25] Ibid. 33.

[26] JM Dreyfuss et al., 'How accurate can genetic predictions be?' (2012) 13 *BMC Genomics* 340 <https://doi.org/10.1186/1471-2164-13-340>; Peter Kraft and David J Hunter, 'Genetic risk prediction: Are we there yet?' (2009) 360 *New England Journal of Medicine* 1701–3 doi: 10.1056/NEJMp0810107; Peter Kraft et al., 'Beyond odds ratios: Communicating disease risk based on genetic profiles' (2009) 10 *Nature Reviews Genetics* 264–9 <https://www.nature.com/articles/nrg2516> accessed 22 October 2018; Sabrina Prudente et al., 'Genetic prediction of common diseases. Still no help for the clinical diabetologist!' (2012) 22 *Nutrition, Metabolism and Cardiovascular Diseases* 929, 929–36 <https://doi.org/10.1016/j.numecd.2012.04.010> accessed 22 October 2018.

[27] AL McGuire, CM Diaz, T Wang, and SG Hilsenbeck, 'Social networkers' attitudes toward direct-to-consumer personal genome testing' (2009) 9 (6–7) *American Journal of Bioethics* 3–10 doi:10.1080/15265160902928209.

[28] HC Howard and P Borry, 'Personal genome testing: Do you know what you are buying?' (2009) 9 (6–7) *American Journal of Bioethics* 11–34 <https://doi.org/10.1080/15265160902894005> accessed 22 October 2018.

[29] Robert C King, Pamela Mulligan and William Stansfield (eds), *A Dictionary of Genetics* (8th edn, OUP 2013) 189.

The genome can be defined as 'an organism's complete set of genetic information, encoded in its DNA'.[30] Thus the human genome is the species' as well as an individual's, complete set of genetic data. The genome consists of units known as genes. A more comprehensive definition of the genome sequence is that it is:

> the linear order of nucleotide sequences in a genome. The genome sequence is a sequence map with the highest resolution, in which each nucleotide is a landmark. Determining the sequence of a genome is important for many reasons, including identifying genes and regulatory regions, deciphering gene function, understanding genome structure, and determining the degree of sequence similarity between species.[31]

The definition of the term 'gene'[32] has been changing over time, but for present purposes, it can best be understood as both 'a unit of heredity' and 'a segment of DNA encoding a protein'.[33] The exact number of genes that exist in humans is not yet known, but current estimates vary between 20,000 and 25,000. The human genetic code at its simplest is a series of four nucleotide bases. These are Adenine (A), Cytosine (C), Guanine (G) and Thymine (T). These bases form pairs of T and A and C and G. There are around 3 billion base pairs in the human genome. The genome DNA is contained in 46 chromosomes, which also normally form pairs, but in this case usually only 23 pairs.

Meanwhile, genomics can be defined as the:

> field of genetics concerned with the study of the structure, function and evolution of whole genomes. This field has its origins in recombinant DNA technology [. . .] and has evolved rapidly due to significant technical advances in large-scale cloning, sequencing, and analyses of sequence data using computational means. Genomics represents a major advance in genetics, shifting the focus from identifying and studying single genes and genetic elements to discovering and studying coding and noncoding genetic components on a much larger, genome-wide scale. The term is often used broadly to include not only the study of genomes, but also transcriptomes and proteomes.[34]

---

[30] Griffiths et al. (n 20) 4.

[31] King et al. (n 29) 189.

[32] Ibid. 182.

[33] WG Feero, AE Guttmacher, and FS Collins, 'Genomic medicine: An updated primer' (2010) 362 *New England Journal of Medicine* 2001–11, 2002 doi: 10.1056/NEJMra0907175.

[34] King et al. (n 29) 190.

Another definition of genomics is that 'it is the study of all of a person's genes (the genome), including interactions of those genes with each other and with the person's environment'.[35]

(b) Causes of Genetic Variation

There are three main categories relating to the main causes of genomic variation and the reason why one person will be different to another, even though so much of our DNA is shared. These categories are: single nucleotide polymorphisms (SNPs); insertions and deletions of nucleotides from the DNA; and 'structural rearrangements that reshuffle the DNA'.[36] When an SNP occurs in a person's genomic sequence, there is an alteration in the base sequence at a single site, so for example a person may have a guanine base present at a particular point in their genome where many other people have a cytosine base. These small genetic variations can sometimes result in significant changes in an individual's phenotype (or visible trait).[37] Scientific understanding of these categories and their effects on human health has changed over time and should improve with more research and emerging technologies.

(c) Genetic Sequencing

Sequencing technology allows for the analysis and deciphering of the human genetic code. This code plays an important role in causing individuals to possess certain traits (or phenotypes) and in whether or not they may develop particular diseases or conditions, or possess particular abilities, but it is not the only determining factor. Some conditions, which are monogenic, are particularly heritable and if a person possesses the gene associated with that particular condition, they will normally develop that disease. A good example is Huntington's disease.[38] However, there are many conditions to which individuals might have a genetic predisposition, but which they may avoid if they take precautionary measures. The environment in which people live, their lifestyle choices (for instance whether they smoke or exercise regularly) and their family history will often also play an influential role in determining

---

[35] National Human Genome Research Institute, 'Frequently asked questions about genetic and genomic science' <https://www.genome.gov/19016904/> accessed 23 October 2018.

[36] Ibid. 2003.

[37] Griffiths (n 20) 610–12.

[38] SB Haga, WT Barry, R Mills, GS Ginsburg, L Svetkey, J Sullivan, and HT Willard, 'Public knowledge of and attitudes toward genetics and genetic testing' (2013) 17 *Genetic Testing and Molecular Biomarkers* 327 <https://doi.org/10.1089/gtmb.2012.0350> accessed 23 October 2018.

whether or not they develop breast cancer or heart disease.[39] There is also growing interest in the role of the microbiome and its impact on human health, so while genetics may be important to an individual's health it is very important that the benefits of testing are not overstated.[40] 'The microbiome comprises all of the genetic material within a microbiota (the entire collection of microorganisms in a specific niche, such as the human gut)'.[41]

First-generation sequencing technology was developed by Sanger in 1977 and was the technique used predominantly for the next 30 years. Then in 2005, second-generation sequencing technology (or next-generation) was introduced. Today there is third- and fourth-generation sequencing technology with the very recent developments, which include the use of nanopores, and it may be possible soon to sequence a whole genome in less than an hour.[42] While each generation of technology brings significant improvements, second-, third- and fourth-generation techniques have not superseded each other and all techniques continue to be used in different contexts.[43]

Next-generation sequencing technologies allow for the sequencing of 'millions of fragments in parallel' and the generation of more than 100Gb of data in days or hours. Traditional sequencing prior to this could only 'sequence about 100 fragments in parallel' and generate 0.1Mb of data per 'run'.[44] The advents of exome sequencing and genome-wide association studies (GWAS) are causing further improvements in researchers' ability

---

[39] Feero et al. (n 33) 2002–6.

[40] TR Sampson and SK Mazmanian, 'Control of brain development, function, and behavior by the microbiome' (2015) 17(5) *Cell Host & Microbe* 565–76 <https://doi.org/10.1016/j.chom.2015.04.011> accessed 23 October 2018; S Khanna and PK Tosh, 'A clinician's primer on the role of the microbiome in human health and disease' (2014) 89(1) Mayo Clinic Proceedings 107–14 <https://doi.org/10.1016/j.mayocp.2013.10.011> accessed 23 October 2018; P Kramer and P Bressan, 'Humans as superorganisms: How microbes, viruses, imprinted genes, and other selfish entities shape our behavior' (2015) 10(4) *Perspectives on Psychological Science* 464–81 <https://doi.org/10.1177/1745691615583131> accessed 23 October 2018.

[41] Nature, Microbiome <https://www.nature.com/subjects/microbiome> accessed 16 October 2018.

[42] S McGinn and IG Gut, 'DNA sequencing – spanning the generations' (2013) 30(4) *New Biotechnology* 366–72 <https://doi.org/10.1016/j.nbt.2012.11.012> accessed 23 October 2018; PL Ståhl and J Lundeberg, 'Toward the single-hour high-quality genome' (2012) 81 *Annual Review of Biochemistry* 359–78 <https://doi.org/10.1146/annurev-biochem-060410-094158> accessed 23 October 2018; GF Schneider and C Dekker, 'DNA sequencing with nanopores' (2012) 30 *Nature Biotechnology* 326–28; Sboner et al. (n 10) 1.

[43] McGinn and Gut (n 42) 366–72.

[44] Feero et al. (n 33) 2010.

to analyse and process data.[45] Both these new technologies should help lead to improvement in understanding heritability and the development of complex diseases and traits. Furthermore, the cost of sequencing the whole genome or the whole exome (which can be understood as the functional part of the genome – it is also the protein coding part of the genome) is continuing to fall rapidly. Gene By Gene's DNA DTC previously offered whole exome sequencing for 795 US dollars and whole genome sequencing for 5,495 US dollars on a direct-to-consumer basis (these were the prices as of 2012).[46] The company continues to offer whole genome and exome sequencing for order through a physician. Its whole genome and whole exome services currently cost 2,895 and 1,095 US dollars respectively (as of October 2018).[47]

Scientific understanding of how individuals differ from one another genetically has been greatly improved through research in population genetics and genome-wide association studies (GWAS). Roughly 99.6 per cent of the human genome is the same from one person to another[48] and an individual may share even more of their genome with their blood relatives.[49] Population genetics 'analyses the amount and distribution of genetic variation in populations and the forces that control this variation',[50] and GWAS:

---

[45] MJ Bamshad, SB Ng, AW Bigham, HK Tabor, MJ Emond, DA Nickerson, and J Shendure, 'Exome sequencing as a tool for Mendelian disease gene discovery' (2011) 12 *Nature Reviews Genetics* 745–55.

[46] DNA DTC, 'Products' <dnadtc.com/products.aspx> accessed 11 December 2012 – archived content available <https://web.archive.org/web/20121203025126/dnadtc.com/products.aspx> accessed 23 October 2018; D Vorhaus, 'DNA DTC: The return of direct to consumer whole genome sequencing' *Genomics Law Report*, 29 November 2012 <https://web.archive.org/web/20171229050514/https://www.genomicslawreport.com/index.php/2012/11/29/dna-dtc-the-return-of-direct-to-consumer-whole-genome-sequencing/> accessed 23 October 2018.

[47] Gene By Gene, 'Whole genome sequencing' <https://genebygene.com/pages/research?goto=exome-sequencing> accessed 18 October 2018; Gene By Gene, 'Whole exome sequencing' <https://genebygene.com/pages/research?goto=exome-sequencing> accessed 18 October 2018.

[48] Feero et al. (n 33); Hon-Cheong So et al., 'Risk prediction of complex diseases from family history and known susceptibility loci, with applications for cancer screening' (2011) 88(5) *American Journal of Human Genetics* 548–65 <https://doi.org/10.1016/j.ajhg.2011.04.001>; P Barry, 'Seeking genetic fate: personal genomics companies offer forecasts of disease risk, but the science behind the packaging is still evolving' (2009) 176 *Science News* 17 <www.sciencenews.org/view/feature/id/44786/description/Seeking_genetic_fate> accessed 18 October 2018.

[49] Woodage (n 15) 683.

[50] Griffiths (n 20) 610.

is an approach that involves rapidly scanning markers across the complete sets of DNA, or genomes, of many people to find genetic variations associated with a particular disease. Once new genetic associations are identified, researchers can use the information to develop better strategies to detect, treat and prevent the disease.[51]

It is GWAS in particular that has contributed greatly to the development of the DTC industry, as many companies rely on published GWAS studies. These studies have identified 'hundreds of gene variants that contribute to disease', but research has shown that many common genetic variations 'in the majority of studies confer only very small relative risks (ranging from 1.1 per cent to 1.5 per cent) and account for only a small part of the known inheritability of the condition studied'.[52] Also, while GWAS has been very useful, many GWAS studies have concentrated on 'common variants with modest effect size in a scenario where a large proportion of disease risk is under the control of environmental factors', although further study may improve this.[53]

In the context of DTC, one problem with GWAS testing is that while the person tested may receive a great deal of information as a result of such analysis, much of that information is currently of little practical use. While many companies use the promise of empowerment through knowledge of a person's genome in their marketing, much information offered by testing companies may not be truly empowering for the ordinary consumer at this point.

(d) From SNP-based Sequencing to Whole Genome Sequencing

It was primarily the work of the Human Genome Project that showed that whole genome sequencing (WGS) was possible, although advances since that time have greatly reduced its cost. In fact the speed of technological change is almost unprecedented. The dramatic reduction in the cost of sequencing technologies means that large numbers of the population in developed countries are likely to have their genomes sequenced in the near future. In the research and clinical context, interest is shifting from SNP-based tests to whole genome scans. It is the promise of the availability of whole genome sequencing at an affordable price which may ultimately revolutionise

---

[51] National Human Genome Research Institute, 'Genome-Wide Association Studies' <https://www.genome.gov/20019523/> accessed 23 October 2018.

[52] UA Meyer, 'Personalized medicine: A personal view' (2012) 91(3) *Clinical Pharmacology & Therapeutics* 373–5, 374 <https://doi.org/10.1038/clpt.2011.238> accessed 23 October 2018; Kraft and Hunter, 'Genetic risk prediction . . .' (n 20).

[53] Prudente et al. (n 26) 934.

healthcare,[54] but at present as most DTC companies are not providing whole genome sequences, much of the information they provide to consumers may have little value for the individual tested.

(e) Analytical Validity, Clinical Validity and Clinical Utility

In order for a test to become part of clinical practice, it ultimately needs to have analytical validity, clinical validity and clinical utility.[55] A test will have analytical validity where its results are 'positive when a particular sequence is present and negative when it is absent'.[56] It will have clinical validity where the test results in a positive finding 'in people with the disease and negative in those without'.[57] Finally, it will have clinical utility where its 'benefits outweigh its risks'.[58] At present many tests offered by DTC companies lack clinical validity and utility and this means that the nature of the product that DTC companies are selling is questionable. Given the growing trend of companies entering into partnerships with third parties or merging with other companies and the growth in the research activities of these companies, it is becoming clear that while companies are selling a service to consumers, the main source of value for the company is not the sale of tests, but the use to which sequenced genetic data from consumers can be put.

2.4 Conclusion

This chapter has provided an overview of the scientific developments that have allowed the DTC industry to develop and is intended to provide background for those unfamiliar with genetic and genomic science. The next chapter will provide an overview of the DTC industry itself, the different types of tests offered by companies, and the issues which testing for different purposes raise for consumers.

---

[54] Ayday et al. (n 8).

[55] HGC, *More Genes Direct* (Department of Health, 2007) 23, para 2.1 <http://sites. nationalacademies.org/cs/groups/pgasite/documents/webpage/pga_053238.pdf> accessed 22 October 2018,

[56] Justin P Annes, Monica A Giovanni and Michael F Murray, 'Risks of presymptomatic direct-to-consumer genetic testing' (2010) 363 *New England Journal of Medicine* 1100–1 doi: 10.1056/NEJMp1006029.

[57] Ibid. (n 56) 1100–1.

[58] Ibid. 1100; Martina C Cornel, Carla G van El, and P Borry, 'The challenge of implementing genetic tests with clinical utility while avoiding unsound applications' (2014) 5(1) *Journal of Community Genetics* 7–12.

3

The Rise of Personal Genomics:
An Overview of the Direct-to-Consumer
Genetic Testing Industry

3.1 Introduction

As discussed in Chapter 1, this chapter draws upon research originally conducted between 2011 and 2016 and which involved the compilation of a list of companies offering DNA testing services online. This included data regarding companies, including their location and the type of test offered as well as screen shots, wrap contracts and privacy policies, where these were available. All companies identified were tabulated with one master table and then tables of the various sub-categories were created, with each company being assigned to a particular category. The categories were: health (subdivisions of pharmacogenetic; predisposition; pre-symptomatic; nutrigenetic; carrier testing; and testing available through physicians); ancestry; paternity; surreptitious ('infidelity'); DNA match making; child talent; and athletic ability.[1] In 2018, several versions of the master table were released via Zenodo[2] and further updates will be released over the coming years. Version 1.3 lists 287 companies that offer some form of DNA testing online, but at October 2018, 289 companies are on file.

It is important to recognise that as most companies only perform tests on a portion of an individual's genome, their utility for individual consumers is

---

[1] Andelka M Phillips, 'Genomic privacy and direct-to-consumer genetics – Big consumer genetic data – What's in that contract?' (presented at GenoPri'15 [The 2nd Workshop on Genome Privacy and Security] and published as part of IEEE Conference Proceedings 2015) <https://www.computer.org/csdl/proceedings/spw/2015/9933/00/9933a060.pdf> accessed 23 October 2018.

[2] Andelka M Phillips, 'Data on direct-to-consumer genetic testing and DNA testing companies' Version 1.3 (Open Access Dataset, Zenodo, February 2018) doi: 10.5281/zenodo.1175799 <https://zenodo.org/record/1183565#.WunK6y-ZNp8> accessed 23 October 2018.

inherently limited. This idea has been highlighted again in an op-ed piece by Sarah C. Hopkins for the *Los Angeles Times*.[3] Sarah is training to be a genetic counsellor and the article is based on her experience purchasing a DTC test. As she has previously undergone genetic testing and genetic counselling in a clinical setting, having been diagnosed with bilateral breast cancer she was particularly interested in 23andMe's BRCA testing. Her description of the work of a genetic counselor provides helpful background for the experience of an individual undergoing a genetic test in a clinical setting:

> A genetic counselor takes a family history of three generations, explains treatment guidelines and, if the patient chooses, tests her for thousands of mutations in several genes related to breast cancer and other cancers. The sessions are in-depth. A first visit with a cancer genetics specialist might take as long as 90 minutes. If the patient's results show an inherited mutation, a second visit is typically scheduled to discuss screening and management options as well as risk to other family members.[4]

The experience of taking a health test with a DTC company is often quite different and Sarah notes that the test results provided for BRCA1 and 2 are incomplete, as 23andMe's report focuses only on 'three mutations common among Jewish women' and while this is explained in their printed materials, there are a number of 'other genes that can have mutations that substantially increase one's risk for breast cancer, including PALB2, CHEK2, PTEN, CDH1, TP53 and STK11' that are not considered in 23andMe's test.[5] As she explains, these limitations were a factor in the FDA's previous decision to request that 23andMe stop selling its health tests in 2013. Although 23andMe's BRCA test has now been approved by the FDA, this has involved a reclassification of the device from Class III to Class II, which requires less scrutiny, rather than making the test more complete.

It is recommended herein that all DTC services should be viewed with caution due to the ambiguous and complex nature of many genetic test results and the lack of clinical validity and utility of many tests. Furthermore, as genetic information can serve as an identifier not only for the individual

---

[3] Sarah C Hopkins, 'Take it from a genetic counselor: 23andMe's health reports are dangerously incomplete' *Los Angeles Times* (26 October 2018) <http://www.latimes.com/opinion/op-ed/la-oe-hopkins-23andme-genetic-testing-health-20181026-story.html> accessed 30 October 2018.

[4] Ibid.

[5] Ibid.

tested but also for their family, the importance of protection of privacy and security in this context should not be underestimated.[6]

In the space of less than two decades there has been a dramatic fall in the cost of this technology and the 'price of sequencing an average human genome has plummeted from about US$10 million to a few thousand dollars in just six years'[7] with the price of sequencing an individual genome dropping below $1,000 in 2014. However, the process of sequencing while vital is only one part of the genetic testing process. Sequencing allows for the generation of an individual's genetic data, but the value of such data to individuals and to scientific research is dependent on the quality of interpretation and analysis of the data. At present, while costs of sequencing continue to fall, the cost of interpretation and analysis is not dropping at the same rate.[8] Largely due to the gap between the power to generate data and the challenges of analysis and interpretation there is still more uncertainty in the field of genomic research than was previously expected.[9] This gap means

---

[6] James Hazel and Christopher Slobogin, 'Who knows what, and when? A survey of the privacy policies proffered by U.S. direct-to-consumer genetic testing companies' 19 April 2018 *Cornell Journal of Law and Public Policy* and Vanderbilt Law Research Paper No 18–18 <https://ssrn.com/abstract=3165765> accessed 18 October 2018.

[7] Erica Check Hayden, 'The $1,000 genome' (2014) 507 *Nature* 294 <https://www.nature.com/polopoly_fs/1.14901!/menu/main/topColumns/topLeftColumn/pdf/507294a.pdf> accessed 22 October 2018; A Raj, 'Soon, it will cost less to sequence a genome than to flush a toilet — and that will change medicine forever' (2014) *Business Insider* <https://www.businessinsider.com/super-cheap-genome-sequencing-by-2020-2014-10?IR=T> accessed 22 October 2018.

[8] Ibid. Raj (n 7); M Naveed et al., 'Privacy and security in the genomic era' (2014) arXiv:1405.1891v3 <https://arxiv.org/abs/1405.1891> accessed 22 October 2018; Andrew Pollack, 'DNA sequencing caught in deluge of data' *The New York Times* (30 June 2011) <https://www.nytimes.com/2011/12/01/business/dna-sequencing-caught-in-deluge-of-data.html?_r=1&ref=technology> accessed 27 July 2018.

[9] A Nordgren, 'Neither as harmful as feared by critics nor as empowering as promised by providers: Risk information offered direct to consumer by personal genomics companies' (2014) 5(1) Journal of Community Genetics 59–68 doi: 10.1007/s12687-012-0094-0; RR Kalf, R Mihaescu, S Kundu, P De Knijff, RC Green, A Cecile, and JW Janssens, 'Variations in predicted risks in personal genome testing for common complex diseases' (2014) 16 *Genetics in Medicine* 85–91; A Lindblom and PN Robinson, 'Bioinformatics for human genetics: Promises and challenges' (2011) 32(5) *Human Mutation* 495–500 <https://doi.org/10.1002/humu.21468> accessed 23 October 2018; T Caulfield, NM Ries, PN Ray, C Shuman, and B Wilson, 'Direct-to-consumer genetic testing: Good, bad or benign?' (2010) 77(2) *Clinical Genetics* 101–5 <https://doi.org/10.1111/j.1399-0004.2009.01291.x> accessed 23 October 2018.

that many tests currently offered by DTC companies may at present offer consumers little benefit.[10]

Even without the issues posed by interpretation and analysis of genomic data, DTC services are also challenging merely because they do allow individuals to purchase genetic tests without medical involvement and prior to the advent of this industry genetic tests were not available in this manner.

Note that some of the links provided to websites in the footnotes may be out of date, but records of these are on file and for those who are interested in exploring this further, archived content can often be accessed through the Internet Archive's Wayback Machine.[11] Efforts have been made to provide archived links where possible.

3.2 Overview of the DTC Industry

The nature of sequenced genetic information means that it can be used for a wide variety of genetic testing purposes. The DTC industry is a novel industry as it is web-based and centred on the sale of genetic tests as consumer services internationally, which represents an important shift, as previously these tests have been confined to a medical setting.[12] The present chapter provides an overview of the industry, discussing the various categories of test available and the issues which different types of testing raise for consumers. It will begin with a description of some of the most prominent companies in the industry. As has been discussed previously, at present the industry is in a volatile state with companies entering the market and merging or partnering with others.[13] This chapter will highlight the issues posed by the availability of such a wide variety of tests and suggest that there is a general need for greater oversight of the industry. Advertising on some websites is also potentially

---

[10] Andrea Sboner, XJ Mu, D Greenbaum, RK Auerback, and MB Gerstein, 'The real cost of sequencing: Higher than you think!' (2011) 12(125) *Genome Biology* 1–10 <https://doi.org/10.1186/gb-2011-12-8-125> accessed 23 October 2018.

[11] Internet Archive, Wayback Machine <https://archive.org> – consistent error messages when trying to access this in October 2018.

[12] Margaret Curnutte and Giuseppe Testa, 'Consuming genomes: Scientific and social innovation in direct-to-consumer genetic testing' (2012) 31(2) *New Genetics and Society* 159–81 <https://doi.org/10.1080/14636778.2012.662032> accessed 23 October 2018; Kayte Spector-Bagdady and Elizabeth R Pike, 'Consuming genomics: Regulating direct-to-consumer genetic and genomic information' (2014) 92(4) *Nebraska Law Review* 677–745.

[13] M Sullivan, '23andMe has signed 12 other genetic data partnerships beyond Pfizer and Genentech' (14 January 2015) *VentureBeat* <https://venturebeat.com/2015/01/14/23andme-has-signed-12-other-genetic-data-partnerships-beyond-pfizer-and-genentech/> accessed 17 August 2018; Christine Lagorio-Chafkin, '23andMe Exec: You Ain't Seen Nothing Yet' (7 January 2015) *Inc* <http://www.inc.com/christine-lagorio/23andMe-new-partnerships.html> accessed 17 August 2018.

misleading, although this is outside the scope of this book. Generally, companies engage in practices which are at odds with most policy guidance to date, such as encouraging consumers to send in samples belonging to children, or encouraging consumers to send in the samples of other third parties without appropriate consent.[14] It is hoped that this book will demonstrate the need for more oversight of the industry as a whole.

At the outset, it should be noted that in the UK, the Human Tissue Act 2004 (HTA) sets requirements for consent for tests involving the use of human tissue and DNA. (The DTC industry should also be complying with applicable data protection law and this will be discussed in chapter four.) DNA tests prior to the rise of DTC were previously only performed in a medical setting, as part of medical research, as part of legal proceedings for identification purposes (including to establish paternity) or by law enforcement agencies for identification purposes. Under the HTA, it is an offence to conduct a DNA test without 'qualifying consent', with very few exceptions. It would appear from the guidance documents and information provided by the Human Tissue Authority (which enforces the HTA) that companies providing DNA test kits to UK-based consumers come within the Act's remit. The Human Tissue Authority's 'Analysis of DNA under the HT Act FAQs' states that 'All companies providing DNA testing kits or DNA testing services must comply with the provisions of the Human Tissue Act 2004 relating to consent and the holding of bodily material with the intent to analyse DNA.'[15]

Consequently, it seems that any DTC company regardless of the type of test they offer should be complying with the HTA. The offence of non-consensual DNA analysis under section 45 of the HTA carries with it penalties of fines or imprisonment, so it would be wise for DTC companies to work on improving their consent mechanisms and for the Human Tissue Authority to investigate compliance. (The requirements for what constitutes 'qualifying consent' are set out in Schedule 4 of the HTA.) Furthermore, the recent Supreme Court ruling in *Montgomery* v *Lanarkshire Health Board*[16] might indicate that some DTC companies providing tests of a certain type, most especially health-related tests, may need to provide their consumers with more information about the respective risks and

---

[14] Hazel and Slobogin (n 6).

[15] Human Tissue Authority, 'Analysis of DNA under the HT Act FAQs', <https://www.hta.gov.uk/faqs/analysis-dna-under-ht-act-faqs> accessed 12 May 2016, accessed 27 October 2018 – note that the Human Tissue Authority has not altered its stance on this.

[16] (Scotland) [2015] UKSC 11; Mark Campbell, 'Montgomery v Lanarkshire Health Board' (2015) 44(3) *Common Law World Review* 222–228.

benefits of undergoing testing and possible risks relating to potential misuse of data, especially in the context of ongoing health research using consumers' data.[17]

(a) Overview of Prominent Companies

As part of this research, a list was compiled of all the companies operating in the last three years with English-language websites which offered some form of genetic testing via the Internet. In total 229 companies were identified (289 as of October 2018). The list categorised the companies according to services type: health-related testing; ancestry; genetic relatedness (primarily paternity); athletic ability; child talent; and non-consensual testing.

Chapter 5 discusses the actual terms included in DTC contracts used by companies providing testing for health purposes. It should be noted however that the contracts of companies providing other types of testing were also saved, but it was not possible to analyse all the data herein. However, in a preliminary analysis of the contracts of ancestry testing companies it was found that overall these contracts tended to be very similar to those of companies providing health testing. The choice was made to focus on testing for health purposes for the contractual analysis as a case study, because this category of testing is most representative of the challenges that DTC in general poses to regulation. It is also the category of testing which if it proliferates is more likely to have an impact on a larger range of consumers and may also impact upon health service providers, such as general practitioners.

The DTC industry essentially began in 2007, when:

> deCODEme and 23andMe began offering consumers genome scans. For a price of approximately $1,000, one could spit into a tube and mail the tube to a genetic analysis laboratory, which would genotype the sample at

---

[17] Jane Kaye, Jessica Bell, Linda Briceno, and Colin Mitchell, 'Biobank Report: United Kingdom' (2016) 44(1) *The Journal of Law, Medicine & Ethics* 96–105, 102; note: the recent case of *Spencer* v *Anderson* (Paternity Testing) [2016] EWHC 851 (Fam) suggested that the Human Tissue Act did not apply to DNA because 'DNA does not contain human cells' – see Rosalind English, 'Judge allows paternity test for DNA disease analysis' (*UK Human Rights Blog*, 20 April 2016), <https://ukhumanrightsblog.com/2016/04/20/judge-allows-paternity-test-for-dna-disease-analysis/> accessed 11 May 2016; However, if this is correct it is limited to the very narrow situation of applying for post-mortem scientific testing and consequently does not seem likely to have bearing on whether or not DTC companies should be complying with the consent requirements set out in Schedule 4 of the Human Tissue Act and the code of practice issued by the Human Tissue Authority.

somewhere between 500,000 and 1 million SNPs, or approximately 0.03% of the genome.[18]

Since then the industry has continued to grow and due to the decrease in the cost of sequencing technology, the prices offered by DTC companies are continuing to fall and a UK-based consumer can now purchase a health and ancestry test from 23andMe for £149 or an ancestry test for £79.[19] At present there are several leading companies that offer specific tests and have amassed quite significant databases, which are being or are likely to be used for on-going health research.[20] Such databases might also be used for targeted marketing and broader surveillance. The industry has thus developed in the space of less than a decade as a direct consequence of advances in genetic and genomic science. This section will describe the activities of the most prominent companies identified. These are the companies which have received the most attention from academics and the media and also have established the largest databases to date.

The most prominent companies originally were: DeCODE (which became DeCODEme); 23andMe; Navigenics; Pathway Genomics; and Knome.[21] However, Gene By Gene and Ancestry.com's AncestryDNA are also now very significant in this area. Each of these companies has been the focus of the majority of academic attention in this context and most early studies of DTC companies have focused primarily on the activities of DeCODE, 23andMe, Navigenics and Pathway.

DeCODE was really the first company to emerge, beginning its operations in 1996, and it gained the contract to conduct testing on the Icelandic population. It made a lot of advances in genetic research. However, deCODE's Icelandic research was done on the basis of people automatically

---

[18] SA Leachman, DG MacArthur, M Angrist, SW Gray, AR Bradbury, and DB Vorhaus, 'Direct-to-consumer genetic testing: Personalized medicine in evolution' (2011) *American Society of Clinical Oncology* 34–40, 36 <https://theprivacyreport.com/wp-content/uploads/2011/06/ASCO-DTC-Abstract.pdf> accessed 22 October 2018.

[19] This price is accurate as of October 2018.

[20] Jessica Cussins, 'Direct-to-consumer genetic tests should come with a health warning' (15 January 2015) *The Pharmaceutical Journal* <https://www.pharmaceutical-journal.com/opinion/comment/direct-to-consumer-genetic-tests-should-come-with-a-health-warning/20067564.article?firstPass=false> last accessed 23 October 2018.

[21] S Hogarth, G Javitt, and D Melzer, 'The current landscape for direct-to-consumer genetic testing: Legal, ethical, and policy issues' (2008) 9 *Annual Review of Genomics and Human Genetics* 161–82 <https://doi.org/10.1146/annurev.genom.9.081307.164319> last accessed 22 October 2018; Kalf et al., 'Variations in predicted risks ...' (n 9).

being opted in to the project, which was not uncontroversial, with 20,000 people choosing to opt out from participation in the project.[22]

DeCODE subsequently declared bankruptcy in 2009, was purchased by another entity and continued to operate under the name DeCODEme. It launched its direct-to-consumer service in 2007. Then in December 2012, DeCODEme was sold again, to Amgen.[23] This led to it ceasing to offer DTC services, but at present it continues to operate[24]; in 2014 they resumed operations in Iceland, going door to door and offering free T-shirts in exchange for an individual's DNA sample.[25] It previously offered a variety of services but they specifically described their activity as a 'genetic health scan'. Their Complete Scan service (which it should be noted was not a whole genome scan) tested an individual's risk-susceptibility for 47 specific traits and conditions, including gout, pancreatic cancer, breast cancer and chronic kidney disease.[26] They offered the Complete Scan service for the price of $1,100 (USD). DeCODEme's website claimed that 'the total number of SNPs or genetic variants analyzed is the key to scientific accuracy. In analyzing nearly twice as many SNPs as any of its competitors, the deCODEme Complete Scan is by far the most comprehensive genetic health scan available today'.[27]

23andMe was founded in 2006 and is probably the DTC testing company with the most prominent public profile, partly due to its co-founder Anne

22 A Abbott, 'Icelandic database shelved as court judges privacy in peril' (13 May 2004) 429 *Nature* 118 <https://www.nature.com/articles/429118b.pdf> last accessed 1 October 2018.

23 Vorhaus, 'Implications of Amgen . . .' (n 11); Ray, 'With Decode Purchase . . .' (n 11).

24 Pete Shanks, 'Genomic controversy in Iceland: Déja vu all over again' (Center for Genetics and Society, 28 May 2014) <http://www.biopoliticaltimes.org/article.php?id=7778> last accessed 23 October 2018; Alda Sigmundsdóttir, 'Privacy on ice: This company wants to collect DNA from one-third of Iceland's population' (21 May 2014) *Slate* <http://www.slate.com/articles/technology/future_tense/2014/05/decode_genetics_wants_to_collect_dna_from_one_third_of_icelanders.html> last accessed 23 October 2018; ALDA, 'Why I won't give a sample of my DNA to Decode Genetics' (11 May 2014) *The Iceland Weather Report* <http://icelandweatherreport.com/why-i-wont-give-a-sample-of-my-dna-to-decode-genetics/> last accessed 23 October 2018.

25 They were continuing to offer DTC services in January 2013.

26 DeCODEme, 'Conditions covered' <decodeme.com/conditions-covered> 19 October 2012 – archived content available at <http://web.archive.org/web/20121019213723/http://www.decodeme.com:80/> last accessed 23 October 2018.

27 DeCODEme, 'deCODEme Complete Scan' (DeCODEme, June 2011) <decodeme.com/complete-genetic-scan> last accessed 20 October 2012 – archived content available at <https://web.archive.org/web/20121006062317/decodeme.com/complete-genetic-scan> last accessed 23 October 2018.

Wojcicki's link with Google. Wojcicki was married to Google co-founder Sergey Brin, who has also invested in 23andMe (their divorce was finalised in June 2015).[28] From November 2013 to October 2015, 23andMe only offered ancestry testing in the USA. They ceased to offer health-related testing services in the US after the FDA sent the company a letter requiring it to cease marketing their health-related testing service. The letter also classed 23andMe's test kit as a medical device.[29] They have faced multiple class action lawsuits. Prior to the FDA's action, 23andMe had offered a single service, Journey Through Your DNA, at the reduced price of $99 (USD) with no subscriptions[30] (as of 11 December 2012). Its website claimed that its company has: 'over 200 online health and traits reports'; 'the largest genealogical DNA database in the world'; [and will provide] 'updates on new genetic discoveries that are personalized for your DNA by our experts'.[31] Prior to this, it had offered two services, both of which involved a one-year subscription where you would receive updates on your genomic information throughout the year. The price of its US-based international service as of October 2018 remains at $99 (USD),[32] while its UK website offers ancestry testing for £79 and an ancestry and health package for £149.[33]

However, although after the FDA's warning letter 23andMe stopped selling health tests to US customers, it continued to sell health tests internationally. In December 2014 it launched a UK website and has been marketing health-related testing services to UK customers for £125. It was also selling tests in Canada. Its UK service offered reports for more than 100 health conditions and traits, as well as ancestry testing.[34] In March 2015, 23andMe

---

[28] 23andMe, '23andMe raises more than $50 million in new financing' (23andMe, Press Release, 11 December 2012) <https://mediacenter.23andme.com/press-releases/23andme-raises-more-than-50-million-in-new-financing/> last accessed 23 October 2018; M Lewis, 'Sergey Brin's wife runs a genetics startup, 23AndMe, and it just raised $50 million' (*Business Insider,* 12 December 2012). <http://www.businessinsider.com/sergey-brins-wife-runs-a-genetics-startup-23andme-and-it-just-raised-50-million-2012-12> last accessed 23 October 2018.

[29] Warning letter from US Food and Drug Administration to 23andMe (22 November 2013) <http://www.fda.gov/iceci/enforcementactions/warningletters/2013/ucm376296.htm> last accessed 22 October 2018.

[30] 23andMe, <www.23andme.com/store/cart/> accessed 10 October and then 13 December 2012.

[31] 23andMe, <www.23andme.com/store/cart/> accessed 10 March 2013.

[32] 23andMe, <https://www.23andme.com/en-int/> last accessed 30 October 2018.

[33] 23andMe, <https://www.23andme.com/en-gb/> last accessed 30 October 2018 – as of October 2018, the UK website continues to offer health reports for more than 90 conditions.

[34] 23andMe, <23andme.com/en-gb/> accessed 11 March 2015.

was selling its test kits through Superdrug via the Superdrug website and in-store.[35] It should be noted that 23andMe was allowed to market its services in the UK because their test kits have a Conformité Européenne (CE) mark meaning that the kit has been approved as safe for the purposes of collecting saliva. This certification, though, is only an assessment of the test kit's safety as a collection device. It does not provide an assessment of the quality of the sequencing service provided or of any accompanying analysis or interpretation services.

More recently, 23andMe has received approval in the US to market a test for Bloom syndrome, and in October 2015 it resumed health testing for US customers, although this was restricted to carrier testing.[36] Its database now contains the data of more than 5 million customers.[37] In 2018, it became the first DTC company to obtain approval for testing for its disease risk tests for the BRCA1 and 2 variants, which are associated with breast and ovarian cancer.[38]

Navigenics was also founded in 2006 and provided DTC services originally without the involvement of medical practitioners. It then shifted to a model which required tests to be ordered via physicians.[39] In 2012 it was sold to Life Technologies and ceased offering DTC services, although the database it developed based on consumer data is being used in on-going research.

---

[35] H Wallace, 'GeneWatch UK PR: Shoppers warned not to buy gene tests from Superdrug' (30 March 2015) *GeneWatch UK* <http://www.genewatch.org/article.shtml?als[cid]=4062 59&als[itemid]=575612> last accessed 23 October 2018; James Meikle, 'Superdrug criticised by doctors for stocking genetic self-testing kits' *The Guardian* Genetics (31 March 2015) <https://www.theguardian.com/science/2015/mar/31/superdrug-criticised-doctors-genetic-self-testing-kits> last accessed 23 October 2018.

[36] 23andMe, '23andMe granted authorization by FDA to market first direct-to-consumer genetic test under regulatory pathway for novel devices' (23andMe, Press Release, 19 February 2015) <https://mediacenter.23andme.com/press-releases/fdabloomupdate/> last accessed 23 October 2018; Caroline Humer and Julie Steenhuysen, '23andME launches new consumer test service to check for genetic disorders' (2015) *Scientific American* <http://www.scientificamerican.com/article/23andme-launches-new-consumer-test-service-to-check-for-genetic-disorders/> last accessed 23 October 2018.

[37] 23andMe, 'About Us' <https://mediacenter.23andme.com/company/about-us/> last accessed 30 October 2018; and Anne Wojcicki, 'Power of one million' (23andMeBlog, 2015) <https://blog.23andme.com/news/one-in-a-million/> last accessed 17 October 2018.

[38] 23andMe, '23andMe granted first FDA authorization for direct-to-consumer genetic test on cancer risk' (Press Release, 6 March 2018) <https://mediacenter.23andme.com/press-releases/23andme-granted-first-fda-authorization-direct-consumer-genetic-test-cancer-risk/> last accessed 30 July 2018; FDA, 'FDA authorizes, with special controls, direct-to-consumer test that reports three mutations in the BRCA breast cancer genes' (FDA, Press Release, 6 March 2018). <https://www.fda.gov/newsevents/newsroom/press announcements/ucm599560.htm> last accessed 30 July 2018.

[39] HC Howard and P Borry, 'Personal genome testing: Do you know what you are

Knome was co-founded by George Church in 2007 as an offshoot of the Personal Genome Project and provided whole genome sequencing at a much higher cost than the other early companies' services. It charged $350,000 for a whole genome sequence.[40] It has since stopped offering DTC services.

Pathway Genomics was founded in 2008 and moved to a model requiring orders through physicians. It is still operating and provides a wide variety of testing services including pharmacogenomics, cancer, general health and wellness, and carrier testing.[41] It also now provides a mobile healthcare application for smartphones.

One of the other earliest companies, which has received less attention to date, is Gene By Gene, a Texas-based company founded in 2000 as FamilyTreeDNA. It initially specialised in ancestry testing and has a partnership with National Geographic to provide the testing for National Geographic's Genographic Project.[42] As of 2016, Illumina's Helix provides DNA testing services for the Genographic Project for US consumers, while Family Tree DNA continues to provide tests for international customers.[43] In 2011, Gene By Gene launched DNA Traits and DNA DTC,[44] which provide health testing and whole genome and whole exome sequencing.[45] These two have now been amalgamated under the one name: Gene By Gene. They have also purchased other smaller ancestry companies including DNA Heritage[46]

---

buying?' (2009) 9(6–7) *American Journal of Bioethics* 11–34 <https://doi.org/10.1080/15265160902894005> last accessed 22 October 2018.

[40] Misha Angrist, *Here Is a Human Being* (Harper Perennial 2011) 75–6; Personal Genome Project: Harvard, 'Sharing personal genomes' <personalgenomes.org/harvard> accessed 3 August 2015 – archived content available at <https://web.archive.org/web/20151117032037/personalgenomes.org/harvard> last accessed 23 October 2018.

[41] Pathway Genomics, <https://www.pathway.com> accessed 21 July 2015 – last accessed 23 October 2018.

[42] FamilyTreeDNA, 'Surname & geographical projects' <https://www.familytreedna.com/projects.aspx> accessed 3 August 2015 – last accessed 23 October 2018.

[43] International Society of Genetic Genealogy Wiki, 'FamilyTreeDNA' <https://isogg.org/wiki/Family_Tree_DNA#cite_note-12> last accessed 23 October 2018 – citing National Geographic, Geno 2.0 'FAQ: Participation, testing, and results' <https://genographic.nationalgeographic.com/faq/participation-testing-results/#where-are-the-dna-samples-processed> last accessed 23 October 2018.

[44] Vorhaus, 'DNA DTC: The return of direct to consumer whole genome sequencing'

[45] Gene By Gene, 'The Gene By Gene story' <https://genebygene.com/pages/company> last accessed 23 October 2018.

[46] International Society of Genetic Genealogy Wiki, 'DNA Heritage' <https://isogg.org/wiki/DNA_Heritage> last accessed 23 October 2018.

and DNA-Fingerprint.[47] To date, it has received less attention than the other leading companies, but it is worthy of greater attention due to its involvement in several different categories of genetic testing and its acquirement of other companies. Its database is growing and it seems likely to rival that of 23andMe in the near future.

Ancestry.com's AncestryDNA is one of the newest entries into the DTC space. Ancestry.com began as a genealogy company, which has been operating for several decades. It allows its customers to compile family trees and search for related family members and also search archival documents. However, in 2012 it launched its AncestryDNA service and has now exceeded 10 million customers.[48] In 2015, the company announced its intention to transition into the field of medical research[49] and as of July 2015 they have begun their AncestryHealth division, which is as yet not using genetic information; rather it is collecting consumers' health information via surveys. While AncestryHealth and AncestryDNA are currently separate entities, consumers who use AncestryHealth 'are asked upon accessing the service to consent to take part in an internal Ancestry project'. However:

> [although] the information stored by customers in both is not currently accessible simultaneously to customers, the company in its privacy statement notes that by consenting to take part in its research project, a customer gives Ancestry permission to upload his or her AncestryDNA data for use in Ancestry's internal research.[50]

AncestryDNA has also acquired other ancestry companies, including Relative Genetics, GeneTree and Sorenson Molecular Geneology Foundation.[51]

47 FamilyTreeDNA, 'DNA-Fingerprint joins forces with FamilyTreeDNA'<http://www.dna-fingerprint.com/static/Press-release-2006-07-22.pdf> last accessed 23 October 2018.

48 AncestryDNA, <https://www.ancestry.co.uk/cs/ireland-dna> last accessed 27 July 2018; Justin Petrone, 'AncestryDNA aims to have 1.3m genotyped by year end' *GenomeWeb* (28 April 2015) <https://www.genomeweb.com/microarrays-multiplexing/ancestrydna-aims-have-13m-genotyped-year-end> last accessed 23 October 2018.

49 Justin Petrone, 'Ancestry sees AncestryHealth offering as first step in new health-focused strategy' *GenomeWeb* (17 July 2015) <https://www.genomeweb.com/microarrays-multiplexing/ancestry-sees-ancestryhealth-offering-first-step-new-health-focused> last accessed 23 October 2018.

50 Ibid. (n 49).

51 Sorenson Molecular Geneology Foundation, <http://www.smgf.org> accessed 22 July 2015 <http://www.smgf.org> last accessed 23 October 2018 – the company is no longer operating and its assets were purchased by AncestryDNA; International Society of Genetic Genealogy, 'Welcome to ISOGG!' <https://isogg.org> 3 August 2015, last accessed 23 October 2018.

Brief note: privacy-friendly options – the example of Guardiome

In thinking about privacy friendly options, Guardiome is an interesting example. This is another California based company. However, it differs from the other DTC companies mentioned above, as it has a privacy-centred focus. It provides a full genome sequencing service, which consumers receive on a device. The current price of this is $3,100.00 (USD, as of 17 April 2019). In its alpha testing it originally sent its consumers a device accompanied by a hammer, which was meant to emphasise its commitment to protecting privacy.[52] It now provides a whole genome sequencing service called Omics Lab, which consumers receive on a 'Lenovo Yoga touchscreen 2-in-1 laptop running Ubuntu'. Guardiome states on its website that:

> We don't keep any of your genomic data, or give anyone access to it – except you. In fact your Omics Lab, and accompanying external hard drive, will safely store the only copies of your Guardiome genome sequence in existence.[53]

The company has also developed a number of applications, which its consumers can use to analyse their genomes. This example is highlighted, as it demonstrates that businesses can try to do things differently. While the industry still needs better regulation and oversight, if more companies consider alternative approaches such as this, it will help to better protect consumers' privacy rights.

As can be seen, several of the leading companies have entered partnerships, merged with others or have been sold on to other entities. This highlights the need for appropriate regulation of the industry, especially in relation to the protection of consumers' privacy, as often consumers' genetic data and other types of personal information are being shared more widely then consumers might anticipate. Given the privacy and data protection issues here, it may be beneficial for the ICO, other European data protection authorities, the European Data Protection Board and privacy regulators elsewhere to take on a more active role in regulating the industry and assessing compliance.

[52] Turna Ray and Uduak Grace Thomas, 'Startup Guardiome Emphasizes Privacy in New WGS Consumer Offering' GenomeWeb (29 December 2015) <https://www.genomeweb.com/sequencing-technology/startup-guardiome-emphasizes-privacy-new-wgs-consumer-offering#.XLZXo3ZR1PU> last accessed 17 April 2019.
[53] Guardiome, <https://www.guardiome.com/omics-lab> accessed 17 April 2019.

(b) Summary of the Different Types of Test Available

The DTC industry is notable for its diverse variety of services with companies offering tests for a wide variety of purposes, most of which have not been validated in the research community. It should be stressed that the vast majority of tests currently available have not been well validated in the research community. Furthermore, as there is debate within the research community regarding the impact of particular genetic variants on human health, the wide availability of these tests should cause some degree of concern.[54] Some types of DTC testing may be in breach of UK and EU law already and it would be beneficial for UK consumers if the Human Tissue Authority, the Medicines and Healthcare Products Regulatory Agency (MHRA), the Competition & Markets Authority (CMA) and the Information Commissioner's Office (ICO) were to take a more active role in regulating this industry. There is also scope for consumer regulators, medical devices regulators and data protection authorities in other European Member States to also play a role in improving industry regulation.

Central to all categories of DTC testing are the related issues of data privacy and data security. These issues will be considered in Chapter 4. However, it should be noted here that in the DTC context this necessitates a balancing of interests. While in the context of health research it might be easier to justify limitations on participants' privacy on the basis that such research is for the benefit of the public, the situation is not as straightforward for DTC companies carrying out research and DTC companies' research endeavours should not automatically be treated in the same manner as medical research carried out in the public and academic sectors.

(c) Why do People Purchase DTC Tests?

While there has been much concern expressed about the availability of DTC, it is useful to consider the motivations of individuals in ordering these tests.[55]

---

[54] Howard and Borry, 'Personal genome testing . . .' (n 39).

[55] Pascal Su, 'Direct-to-consumer genetic testing: A comprehensive view' (2013) 86(3) *The Yale Journal of Biology and Medicine* 359–65 <https://www.ncbi.nlm.nih.gov/pmc/articles/PMC3767220/> last accessed 22 October 2018; Juli Murphy Bollinger, Robert C Green and David Kaufman, 'Attitudes about regulation among direct-to-consumer genetic testing customers' (2013) 17 *Genetic Testing And Molecular Biomarkers* 424–8 doi: 10.1089/gtmb.2012.0453; Jessica S Ancker, Michael Silver, Melissa C Miller, and Rainu Kaushal, 'Consumer experience with and attitudes toward health information technology: A nation-

These do vary. Consumers may choose to have a DTC test because it enables them to learn information about their physical and genetic characteristics, about predispositions to disease[56] which they may possess, whether they are carriers for particular diseases or conditions,[57] and also about their familial heritage.[58] Thus some people may purchase a test to satisfy personal curiosity, while others may have genuine medical concerns.[59] They may also choose to have a test with a company rather than through a clinic because they do not want the test to be included in their health records.[60] It seems doubtful that customers would in fact purchase tests for disease risk, such as tests for breast cancer susceptibility, 'for fun'. Consumers were not interviewed for this book. However, consumers' perceptions of DTC are touched upon with reference to secondary sources.[61]

wide survey' (2013) 20(1) *Journal of the American Medical Informatics Association* 152–6 <https://doi.org/10.1136/amiajnl-2012-001062> last accessed 23 October 2018.

[56] AL McGuire, CM Diaz, T Wang, and SG Hilsenbeck, 'Social networkers' attitudes towards direct-to-consumer personal genome testing' (2009) 9 (6–7) *American Journal of Bioethics* 3–10 doi:10.1080/15265160902928209; Sandra Soo-Jin Lee, Simone L Vernez, KE Ormond, and Mark Granovetter, 'Attitudes towards social networking and sharing behaviors among consumers of direct-to-consumer personal genomics' (2013) 3(4) *Journal of Personalized Medicine* 275–87 doi: 10.3390/jpm3040275; SB Trinidad, Stephanie M Fullerton, Julie M Bares, Gail P Jarvik, Eric B Larson, and Wylie Burke, 'Genomic research and wide data sharing: Views of prospective participants' (2010) 12(8) *Genetics in Medicine* 486–95 doi: 10.1097/GIM.0b013e3181e38f9e.

[57] A Frumkin, AE Raz, M Plesser-Duvdevani, and S Lierberman, '"The most important test you'll ever take"? Attitudes toward confidential carrier matching and open individual testing among modern-religious Jews in Israel' (2011) 73(12) *Social Science & Medicine* 1741–7 <https://doi.org/10.1016/j.socscimed.2011.09.031> last accessed 23 October 2018; KL Edwards et al., 'Genetics researchers' and IRB professionals' attitudes toward genetic research review: A comparative analysis' (2012) 14 *Genetics in Medicine* 236–42; Alex Wilde et al., 'Public interest in predictive genetic testing, including direct-to-consumer testing, for susceptibility to major depression: Preliminary findings' (2010) 18 *European Journal of Human Genetics* 47–51.

[58] LA Daley et al., 'Personal DNA testing in college classrooms: Perspectives of students and professors' (2013) 17 *Genetic Testing and Molecular Biomarkers* 446 <http://doi.org/10.1089/gtmb.2012.0404> last accessed 23 October 2018; JK Wagner and KM Weiss, 'Attitudes on DNA ancestry tests' (2012) 131(1) *Human Genetics* 41–56 <https://link.springer.com/article/10.1007/s00439-011-1034-5> last accessed 25 October 2018.

[59] Ancker et al. (n 54) 152; Daley et al. (n 57) 446.

[60] Health Law Institute (n 14) 5.

[61] Lee et al., 'Attitudes towards social networking and sharing behaviours among consumers of direct-to-consumer personal genomics' (n 55) 275; Daley et al. (n 57) 3; Trinidad et al., 'Genomic research and wide data sharing: Views of prospective participants' (n 55); Eric Vermeulen et al., 'Public attitudes towards preventive genomics and personal interest in genetic testing to prevent disease: Asurvey study' (2013) 24(5) *The European Journal of*

Consumer perceptions of DTC

Borry and Howard in referring to McGuire's study noted:

> Survey results from McGuire and colleagues (2009) imply that a portion of social networkers who responded to their questionnaire believe that personal genome testing (PGT) offers diagnostic information. They report that 34% (374/1087) of all survey respondents (including a majority who have not used PGT) believe the information provided by PGT to be a medical diagnosis, and 74% (549/745) would consider using PGT for themselves "to see if a specific disease runs in family or is in DNA". This is of particular interest for many reasons, one of which being that many companies, including those mentioned in McGuire and colleagues' survey (2009) in fact, have statements or disclaimers on their websites stating that their services are not meant to have a medical purpose.[62]

It should be noted that colleagues conducting research on consumer experiences with DTC have found that consumers generally trust companies not to share data inappropriately.[63] Yet 23andMe and AncestryDNA's partnerships with pharmaceutical companies show that data-sharing is a real probability and some consumer trust may be misplaced. There is at present a disconnect between consumer perception and business practice.[64]

3.3 Health Tests

In total 102 companies were identified which offer (or have offered these services between 2011 and 2016) some form of health-related testing service. Of

---

Public Health 768–75 <https://doi.org/10.1093/eurpub/ckt143> last accessed 24 October 2018; Wagner and Weiss (n 57) 41–56.

[62] Howard and Borry, 'Personal genome testing . . .' (n 39).

[63] Two colleagues (Teresa Finlay and Jan Charbonneau) have engaged in research projects investigating consumer understanding of genetic test results and consumers' perceptions of the DTC industry. In interviews some consumers likened DCTGT contracts to their iTunes agreements and admitted that they did not read these documents. Andelka M Phillips and TMD Finlay, '"DNA a click away" – Workshop on "agreements" in DTC' (Translation in Healthcare – Exploring the Impact of Emerging Technologies, Oxford, 23–5 June 2015); Teresa Finlay, 'Testing the NHS: The tensions between personalized and collective medicine produced by personal genomics in the UK' (2017) 36(3) New Genetics and Society 227–49 doi: 10.1080/14636778.2017.1351873.

[64] Jan Charbonneau, 'Straight from the lab to the market: General public engagement with direct-to-consumer genetic testing (conference slides)' (DTC genetics – consumers, contracts and complexities, King's College London, 19 June 2015).

these, 55 were located in the USA. The category of health-related testing itself covers a broad range of services and it is possible to further classify companies within this category into subcategories, namely: predisposition; pre-symptomatic; pharmacogenetics or pharmacogenomics; nutrigenetics or nutrigenomics; susceptibility; and carrier testing. At present, the majority of tests offered by DTC companies lack clinical validity and utility. Nutrigenetics is the area of health genetic testing with the least validation so far.[65] DTC companies providing genetic tests for health purposes can more readily be likened to clinical laboratories and research institutions, especially where they engage in health research using consumers' data.

The Human Tissue Authority has released several versions of its Code of Practice on Consent. In the most recent version it sets out that 'it must be given voluntarily, by an appropriately informed person who has the capacity to agree to the activity in question'.[66]

It further states that '[t]he person should understand what the activity involves, any reasonable or variant treatment and, where appropriate, what

---

[65] P Saukko, M Reed, N Britten, and S Hogarth, 'Negotiating the boundary between medicine and consumer culture: Online marketing of nutrigenetic tests' (2010) 70(5) *Social Science & Medicine* 744–53 <https://doi.org/10.1016/j.socscimed.2009.10.066>; Nola M Ries and David Castle, 'Nutrigenomics and ethics interface: Direct-to-consumer services and commercial aspects' (2008) 12(4) OMICS *A Journal of Integrative Biology* 245 <https://doi.org/10.1089/omi.2008.0049> last accessed 25 October 2018; Cynthia Marietta and Amy L McGuire, 'Direct-to-consumer genetic testing: Is it the practice of medicine?' (2009) 37(2) *The Journal of Law, Medicine & Ethics* 369–74 doi:10.1111/j.1748-720X.2009.00380.x; Sboner et al. (n 10); A Adeyemo and C Rotimi, 'Genetic variants associated with complex human diseases show wide variation across multiple populations' (2010) 13 *Public Health Genomics* 72–9 <https://doi.org/10.1159/000218711> last accessed 25 October 2018; Kalf et al. (n 9); Marilynn Marchione AP Chief Medical Writer, 'Study reveals shortcomings in gene testing; results on estimating disease risk often conflict' The Associated Press – in *US News* (27 May 2015) <https://www.usnews.com/news/business/articles/2015/05/27/study-reveals-flaws-in-gene-testing-results-often-conflict> last accessed 25 October 2018 – the original study is reported in Heidi L Rehm et al., 'ClinGen The Clinical Genome Resource' (2015) 372(23) *New England Journal of Medicine* 2235–42 doi:10.1056/NEJMsr1406261.

[66] Human Tissue Authority, *Code A: Guiding Principles and The Fundamental Principle of Consent* (version updated 3 April 2017) 11 para 40 <https://www.hta.gov.uk/hta-codes-practice-and-standards-0> last accessed 25 October 2018; The previous version of this code was substantially similar. Please see Human Tissue Authority, *Code of Practice 1 – Consent* (Version 14.0, updated July 2014) paras 33 and 35 <https://www.hta.gov.uk/sites/default/files/Code_of_practice_1_-_Consent.pdf> accessed 12 May 2016 – archived content available at <https://web.archive.org/web/20170120025305/https://www.hta.gov.uk/sites/default/files/Code_of_practice_1_-_Consent.pdf> last accessed 25 October 2018.

the material risks are.'[67] In order to ensure that informed consent has been obtained, it also suggests that:

> commercial organisations offering services related to the removal, storage and use of human tissue and cells must ensure that materials provided to customers to aid their decision-making, such as marketing and advertising materials, are accurate and abide by the Advertising Standards Agency's guidelines.[68]

Based on the review of companies' terms, which will be set out in Chapter 5, it seems that current practices regarding obtaining consent of many DTC companies may not be sufficient to meet the requirements of the Human Tissue Act. This does leave them open to the possibility of prosecution under the Act for the offence of non-consensual DNA analysis and this could mean that the company could be fined or its employees subject to a term of imprisonment. Given that these are not insignificant penalties, if the industry continues to grow it would be wise for companies to improve their consent mechanisms. What follows is a discussion of the different sub-categories of health-related testing available and their implications for consumers.

(a) Pre-symptomatic Testing

Nature of this Type of Testing
This tests for whether a healthy asymptomatic individual 'has a high probability of developing a condition'.[69] In pre-symptomatic testing, 'a positive result indicates that the patient will develop the condition but does not indicate when this will occur',[70] which means that sometimes receiving such information can be distressing for the individual, especially where there are no treatment options available. Good examples are tests for Huntington's disease or BRCA1 and 2, which are associated with breast cancer.[71] This form

---

[67] HTA, *Code A* (n 55) 11 para 40.

[68] HTA, *Code A* (n 55) 11 para 43.

[69] HGC, *A Common Framework of Principles for direct-to-consumer genetic testing services* (Department of Health, 2010) 2, Table 1<https://ukgtn.nhs.uk/resources/library/article/human-genetics-commission-a-common-framework-of-principles-for-direct-to-consumer-genetic-testing-services-70/> last accessed 22 October 2018.

[70] Elizabeth McPherson, 'Genetic diagnosis and testing in clinical practice' (2006) 4(2) *Clinical Medicine & Research* 123–9, 124 doi: 10.3121/cmr.4.2.123.

[71] HGC, *Common Framework* (n 68) Table 1 (2); EASAC and FEAM, *Direct-To-Consumer Genetic Testing For Health-Related Purposes In The European Union* EASAC Policy Report 18 (July 2012) – archived content available at <https://web.archive.org/web/20121109235113/http://www.easac.eu/fileadmin/Reports/Easac_Genetic_Testing_Web_Complete.pdf> last accessed 25 October 2018; see also EASAC and FEAM, *Direct-to-Consumer Genetic Testing – Summary Document* (EASAC-FEAM Project on

of testing can be useful for monogenic disorders, which have a high level of penetrance. A gene will have high penetrance if the majority of people who possess it will develop the condition. Thus it is not as useful for complex multigenic disorders and as the European Academies of Science Advisory Council (EASAC) and the Federation of European Academies of Medicine (FEAM) have noted, it can be difficult to distinguish between 'high and low penetrance genotypes'.[72] While some of these tests are better validated than many others offered by DTC companies, given the serious impact these test results may have on a person if she is at high risk for a condition such as Huntington's, it may be best to restrict the availability of such tests to a clinical setting.

Companies Operating
As there is some overlap between predisposition and pre-symptomatic testing, companies that perform pre-symptomatic testing generally also offer predisposition testing. Sixty-four companies were identified which offered pre-symptomatic testing. Ten companies provided tests for Parkinson's disease. These included: 23andMe's UK branch; Biotechnology Group Inc; Genetic Centre Company Limited; Map My Gene; and Matrix Genomics. Twenty-nine companies provided tests for Alzheimer's risk. Examples include: 23andMe's UK branch; Map My Gene; Gene Planet; Genetic Healthcare Group; Gonidio; and Graceful Earth.

Implications for Consumers
Pre-symptomatic tests often provide consumers with information about very serious diseases, which can result in psychological harm. Even in clinical settings there is debate over whether all patients should undergo such testing even where they have a family history of a particular disease. The best example is Huntington's disease, as this is a very debilitating illness and at present there are no treatment options. Some patients choose to undergo such testing as they feel the information provided by the test will allow them to make decisions about their lives.[73] However, some people also choose not to undergo such

---

Direct-to-Consumer Genetic Testing, October 2012) 6, 17 <https://www.easac.eu/fileadmin/PDF_s/reports_statements/Easac_12_DTCGT-Lay_Web.pdf> last accessed 22 October 2018; Robin Fears and Volker ter Meulen for the EASAC-FEAM Working Group, 'The perspective from EASAC and FEAM on direct-to-consumer genetic testing for health-related purposes' (2012) 21 *European Journal of Human Genetics* 703–7.

[72] Fears and Volker 704.

[73] Rhona MacLeod et al., 'Experiences of predictive testing in young people at risk of Huntington's disease, familial cardiomyopathy or hereditary breast and ovarian cancer' (2014) 22 *European Journal of Human Genetics* 396–401 <https://www.nature.com/articles/ejhg2013143.pdf> last accessed 25 October 2018.

testing. In the DTC context if such tests are to be offered then as several commentators have suggested, there is a need for genetic counselling, the provision of adequate information and strong informed consent mechanisms. Although it does not appear that companies are currently offering tests for Huntington's disease, they have been offering tests for Parkinson's and Alzheimer's disease and several other serious conditions. While the Huntington's test is well validated, tests for Parkinson's and Alzheimer's disease are not yet standardised.

(b) Susceptibility/Predisposition Testing

Nature of this Type of Testing

This form of testing is 'intended to provide an indication of the absolute lifetime risk and/or relative risk of an individual developing a condition'.[74] Examples are testing for different types of cancer or heart disease.[75] There is some similarity between predisposition and pre-symptomatic testing. However, it 'differs from pre-symptomatic testing in that it informs individuals of an increased or decreased risk of developing the condition in question; however, the degree of certainty is unknown'.[76] Consequently, much predisposition testing is extremely probabilistic and at present will often lack both clinical utility and validity.[77] Thus the usefulness or potential benefit of such tests for individual consumers is questionable.

Companies Operating

Sixty-four companies were identified which offer (or have offered) some type of predisposition testing. Thirty-eight of these offered some form of testing for a person's risk of coronary heart disease, while nine offered tests estimating risk of stroke. Many services will provide people with a risk estimate for different types of cancer, with 39 testing for breast cancer, 23 testing for lung cancer and 20 offering tests for prostate cancer. Fifty-nine tested for diabetes risk; 17 offered tests for Multiple Sclerosis risk. Fifteen companies provided tests for macular degeneration, seven offered tests for migraines and three offered tests for bipolar disorder.[78] Three offered tests for attention-deficit hyperactivity disorder and three tested for schizophrenia.[79]

---

[74] HGC, *Common Framework* (n 68) 2–3, Table 1.

[75] Ibid. 2–3, Table 1.

[76] McPherson (n 69) 124.

[77] Timothy Caulfield, 'Predictive or preposterous? The marketing of DTC Genetic Testing' (2011) 10(3) *Journal of Science Communication* C02 doi: 10.22323/2.10030302; Hogarth et al., 'The current landscape' (n 21).

[78] These were: 23andMe's previous USA website; C2DNA; and Genetic Center Company Limited.

[79] These were: 23andMe's previous USA website; Map My Gene; myDNA.

Examples of companies that have offered predisposition testing are: 23andMe's UK branch; Map My Gene; Genetic Center Company Limited; and Gene By Gene's DNA DTC. 23andMe's UK website offered a health test covering 100 conditions and traits, which includes the following: breast and ovarian cancer; hypertrophic cardiomyopathy; hereditary hemochromatosis; antitrypsin deficiency; early-onset primary dystonia; and factor XI deficiency.[80] Meanwhile, Map My Gene's Disease Susceptibility Test covered 100 diseases, including: ovarian cancer; pancreatic cancer; renal cancer; diabetes; arthritis; and many others.[81]

Implications for Consumers

While such tests may provide some useful information, the majority of tests lack clinical utility and often also clinical validity. As the appropriate interpretation of the effects of gene variants on disease risk are disputed even in the research context,[82] if such tests are to be offered DTC, companies do need to provide sufficient information regarding the limitations of such testing. Also, if such information is to have any benefit for the consumer it is likely that the benefit is really to be realised in the future, when understanding of the role of certain gene variants is better understood. It is also likely that consumers do not understand statistical information sufficiently in order for these test results to offer them real benefit.[83]

At present, the marketing claims made by some DTC companies regarding the benefits of their testing could potentially be construed as misleading,[84] and in line with the various policy guidance previously mentioned, it is

---

[80] 23andMe, 'Health' <23andme.com/en-gb/health/reports/> accessed 19 July 2015.

[81] Map My Gene, 'Disease Susceptibility Test' <mapmygene.com/disease-susceptibility-gene-test.html> accessed 19 July 2015 – archived content available at <https://web.archive.org/web/20150303215031/http://www.mapmygene.com:80/disease-susceptibility-gene-test.html> last accessed 23 October 2018.

[82] Rehm et al. (n 64); Barry, 'Seeking genetic fate . . .' (n 48); CS Bloss, NJ Schork and EJ Topol, 'Effect of direct-to-consumer genomewide profiling to assess disease risk' (2011) 364(6) *New England Journal of Medicine* 524–34 doi: 10.1056/NEJMoa1011893.

[83] CR Lachance, LAH Erby, BM Ford, VC Allen, and KA Kaphingst, 'Informational content, literacy demands, and usability of websites offering health-related genetic tests directly to consumers' (2010) 12(5) *Genetics in Medicine* 304–12 doi 10.1097/GIM.0b013e3181dbd8b2; McGuire et al., 'Social networkers' attitudes . . .' (n 55).

[84] BM Kuehn, 'Inconsistent results, inaccurate claims plague direct-to-consumer gene tests' (2010) 304(12) JAMA 1313–15 doi: 10.1001/jama.2010.1328; Rose Geransar and Edna Einsiedel, 'Evaluating online direct-to-consumer marketing of genetic tests: Informed choices or buyers beware?' (2008) 12(1) *Genetic Testing* 13 <https://doi.org/10.1089/gte.2007.0024> last accessed 18 October 2018.

desirable that DTC companies begin to comply more with existing advertising regulation. There is a need for greater transparency in advertising such tests.[85]

(c) Pharmacogenetic Testing

Nature of this Type of Testing

This form of testing is concerned with assessing an individual's responsiveness to particular drugs or therapies.[86] As very few companies currently perform whole genome sequencing, the majority of tests provided by companies are pharmacogenetic, rather than pharmacogenomics. This is normally depicted as one of the most promising areas of genomic research, largely due to the problems associated with drug responsiveness more generally. For many drugs, a large proportion of the population may be nonresponsive or experience an adverse reaction.[87] The cost of treating patients suffering from adverse drug reactions in the UK alone has been estimated at 'up to £2 billion each year'.[88] Thus if pharmacogenetic testing can assist in identifying individuals likely to respond well to treatment and also identify those likely to have an adverse reaction, this should be beneficial for the general population. Researchers hope that pharmacogenetics will allow us to minimise the occurrence of these adverse events. However, as mentioned in Chapter 1, testing of this type has not yet advanced sufficiently for physicians to be able to make decisions regarding medications solely on the basis of such tests.[89]

---

[85] NP Lewis et al., 'DTC genetic testing companies fail transparency prescriptions' (2011) 30 *New Genetics and Society* 291–307; Geransar and Einsiedel (n 83).

[86] HGC, *Common Framework* (n 68) 2–3.

[87] G Frazzetto, 'The drugs don't work for everyone. Doubts about the efficacy of antidepressants renew debates over the medicalization of common distress' (2008) 9(7) *EMBO Reports* 605–8 doi: 10.1038/embor.2008.116.

[88] Kyla H Thomas, Richard M Martin, John Potokar, Munir Pirmohamed, and David Gunnell, 'Reporting of drug induced depression and fatal and non-fatal suicidal behaviour in the UK from 1998 to 2011' (2014) 15(54) BMC *Pharmacology and Toxicology* 1–11 <https://doi.org/10.1186/2050-6511-15-54> last accessed 25 October 2018.

[89] Angela Chen, '23andMe's genetic test for how you'll react to medication is ahead of its time' *The Verge* (2 November 2018) <https://www.theverge.com/2018/11/2/18055544/23andme-fda-approval-pharmacogenetic-testing-drugs-health-science> last accessed 6 November 2018 – this cites the following study: CA Bousman and BW Dunlop, 'Genotype, phenotype, and medication recommendation agreement among commercial pharmacogenetic-based decision support tools' (2018) 18 *The Pharmacogenomics Journal* 613–22 <https://doi.org/10.1038/s41397-018-0027-3> last accessed 6 November 2018.

Companies Operating

Twenty-four companies were identified which offered this type of testing. Examples of companies offering this type of testing without medical intervention are: Matrix Genomics; Theranostics Lab; GenePlanet; and 23andMe UK.[90] There were others offering their services directly through physicians, and these included: Genelex; Pathway Genomics; and formerly Navigenics.[91] More recent examples of services provided via physicians are CNSDose, Genecept, GeneSight and Neuropharmagen,[92] which are all mentioned in the Bousman and Dunlop study.[93] It should be noted that when 23andMe, ceased offering this testing in the USA, its UK and Canadian websites offered drug response tests for 12 drugs[94] and with its October 2018 FDA approval for pharmacogenetic tests for 33 variants, it is likely to resume offering these tests to consumers in the USA.

Fourteen companies tested for Warfarin response. These companies were: 23andMe UK; Biotechnology Group; C2DNA; Genetic Center Company Limited; Genomic Express; GeneLex; Gene Planet; Gentle; Kimball; Matrix Genomics; myDNA; Pathway Genomics; Theranostics; and the Wellness Gene. There is a difference in terminology in how the test was described. For example, Gentle, C2DNA, myDNA and Theranostics describe their test as one for 'Warfarin sensitivity', while Biotechnology Group Inc and Genetic Center Company Limited use the term 'Warfarin metabolism'.

Eleven companies provided tests for statins.[95] Three test for Clopidrogrel

---

[90] EW Chua and MA Kennedy, 'Current state and future prospects of direct-to-consumer pharmacogenetics' (2012) 3(152) *Frontiers in Pharmacology* 1–8 <https://doi.org/10.3389/fphar.2012.00152> last accessed 25 October 2018; Theranostics Lab, <theranostics.co.nz/wawcs0143590/tn-how-it-works.html> accessed 2 January 2013; 23andMe, 'Drug response' <23andme.com/health/drugs/> accessed 3 January 2013.

[91] Chua and Kennedy (n 89); Navigenics; Pathway Genomics, 'Drug response (medication) insight' <https://www.pathway.com/dna-reports/medication-response> accessed 3 January 2013; GeneLex, 'YouScript' <youscript.com> accessed 3 January 2013; Who'z the Daddy?, <whozthedaddy.com/regions/UK/EN/?gclid=CMm44IbTzLQCFcbLtAodSWgALg> accessed 3 January 2013.

[92] CNSDose, <https://cnsdose.com> last accessed 6 November 2018; GENOMIND, <https://genomind.com/the-genecept-assay/> last accessed 6 November 2018; GeneSight, <https://genesight.com> last accessed 6 November 2018; Neuropharmagen, <http://international.neurofarmagen.com/> last accessed 6 November 2018.

[93] Bousman and BW Dunlop (n 88).

[94] 23andMe (Canada), 'What you can expect' <23andme.com/en-ca/health/reports/> last accessed 24 August 2015; 23andMe (UK), 'What you can expect' <23andme.com/en-gb/health/reports/> last accessed 24 August 2015.

[95] These were: 23andMe; BioLogis; Biotechnology Group; DNA Plus; DNA Testing Centres

and this is normally described as being for Clopidrogrel metabolism, although GenePlanet described this as 'prevention of blood clotting'.[96] Two companies test for responsiveness to particular types of pain medication. Both of these, though, are companies whose services were only available through physicians (Pathway and GeneLex).

Six companies tested for response to anti-depressants generally: 23andMe UK; C2DNA; GeneLex; myDNA; Pathway Genomics; and the Wellness Gene.

Six companies tested for caffeine metabolism: Biotechnology Group Inc;[97] Genomic Express Inc;[98] Theranostics Lab;[99] Pathway Genomics;[100] 23andMe UK;[101] and GenePlanet.[102]

Implications for Consumers
The area of pharmacogenetic genetic testing has been presented as one of the most promising areas of genomic research.[103] However, in the context

---

of Canada; Genetic Center; GeneLex; Gene Planet; myDNA; Theranostics; and the Wellness Gene.

[96] Biotechnology Group Inc, <biotechnologygroup.com/index.html> accessed 22 January 2014. [Checked again 28 January 2014 and still operating]. [Checked again 1 May 2014]; Genetic Center Company Limited, <genetic-center.com> accessed 13 August 2013. [Checked again 28 January 2014 and still operating]. [Checked again 14 April 2014]; GenePlanet, 'Personal Genetic Analysis', <geneplanet.com/personal-genetic-analysis. html/> accessed 3 February 2014. [Checked again 14 April 2014].

[97] Biotechnology Group Inc, <http://www.biotechnologygroup.com/index.html> accessed 22 January 2014. [Checked again 28 January 2014 and still operating]. [Checked again 10 April 2014].

[98] Genomic Express Inc, <https://secure.genomicexpress.com/home.html> accessed 27 January 2014. [Checked again 28 January 2014 and still operating]. [Checked again 14 April 2014].

[99] Theranostics Lab, <http://www.theranostics.co.nz/afawcs0143120/tn-products.html> accessed 5 January 2013. [Checked again 29 January 2014 and still operating]. [Checked again 24 April 2014].

[100] Pathway Genomics, <https://www.pathway.com/about-us/management> accessed 11 February 2013. [Checked again 24 April 2014].

[101] 23andMe (UK), 'Health' <23andme.com/en-gb/health/reports/> accessed 2 July 2015.

[102] GenePlanet, <http://www.geneplanet.com/personal-genetic-analysis.html/> accessed 2 January 2013. [Checked again 28 January 2014 and still operating]. [Checked again 14 April 2014].

[103] NK Gillis and F Innocenti, 'Evidence required to demonstrate clinical utility of pharmacogenetic testing: The debate continues' (2014) 96(6) *Clinical Pharmacology & Therapeutics* 655–7 <https://doi.org/10.1038/clpt.2014.185> last accessed 25 October 2018; Susanne B Haga and Wylie Burke, 'Pharmacogenetic testing: Not as simple as it seems' (2008) 10(6) *Genetics in Medicine* 391–5 <https://www.nature.com/articles/gim200861> last accessed 25 October 2018; ACJW Janssens and PA Deverka, 'Useless until proven effective: The clinical utility of preemptive pharmacogenetic testing' (2014) 96(6) *Clinical*

of tests offered directly to consumers, pharmacogenetics is in fact one of the most challenging types of testing. Pharmacogenetics is the category of health-related DTC that poses the greatest risk of direct harm to consumers. For instance, if a consumer takes a test for drug responsiveness and on the basis of test results increases, decreases or ceases taking their medication without consulting a physician, this could cause severe health consequences including potential death.

Bloss et al.'s study investigated consumer behaviour in the context of pharmacogenetic tests and whether this was associated with increased use of physicians. [104] The study involved:

> [the recruitment of] a sample of adults who purchased a DTC genomic test and had previously received their genomic test results for complex disease risk. All participants additionally underwent PGx testing. At follow-up, to assess the impact of PGx testing on consumer behaviour, healthcare utilisation and psychological status were compared between approximately a third of participants who had received their PGx results and the remaining two-thirds of participants who were still awaiting results. The PGx test included genetic testing for drug effectiveness or risk of side effects for 12 medications.[105]

They concluded that 'risk profiling among a selected sample of persons was associated with statistically significant increases in physician utilisation', and 'testing did not result in any short-term changes in psychological health'.[106] However, they did recommend the need for further evaluation of utility and cost and they highlighted limitations on their study and the need for further research in this area. They observed that their 'sample consisted of a self-selected group of individuals, likely representative of the current population of consumers [. . .] who chose to undergo and pay out of pocket for testing', and that their findings were in contrast with a previous study which has involved a sample of 'young [. . .], healthy, insured population'.[107]

Pharmacology & Therapeutics 652–4 <https://doi.org/10.1038/clpt.2014.186> last accessed 25 October 2018; Matthew B Lanktree et al., 'Positive perception of pharmacogenetic testing for psychotropic medications' (2014) 29(3) *Human Psychopharmacology: Clinical and Experimental* 287–91 <https://doi.org/10.1002/hup.2383> last accessed 25 October 2018.

[104] Cinnamon S Bloss, Nicholas J Schork and Eric J Topol, 'Direct-to-consumer pharmacogenomic testing is associated with increased physician utilisation' (2014) 51(2) *Journal of Medical Genetics* 83–9 <http://dx.doi.org/10.1136/jmedgenet-2013-101909> last accessed 25 October 2018.

[105] Ibid. 83.

[106] Ibid. 89.

[107] Ibid. (n 103) 88.

It seems that physician involvement is something that is particularly desirable in the context of pharmacogenetic testing and the FDA also indicated this in its press release related to the approval of 23andMe's pharmacogenetic tests and alert.[108]

It is clear that companies will use their websites to induce consumers to purchase their products, but there is a need for more transparency regarding the limitations of some DTC services and pharmacogenetic tests should be subject to more oversight than other types of health test provided DTC. This need for transparency and the provision of sufficient information regarding the respective limitations of testing is something that has been stressed in the majority of policy guidance to date. In its recent approval of 23andMe's pharmacogenetic tests, the FDA also stressed that people should not alter their dosage without having follow-up genetic tests in a clinical setting, but it is naive to think that all consumers will do this and it is likely that some people will alter their medication dosage based on a DTC test.

(d) Nutrigenetic Testing

Nature of this Type of Testing

This deals with associations between nutrients and genes and attempts to identify which diet might be best suited to a person based on their genetic makeup. The HGC defined it as 'intended to provide information about an individual's responsiveness to a particular nutrient or diet and how this affects metabolism, health status and risk of disease'.[109] This may be con-

---

[108] FDA, 'FDA authorizes first direct-to-consumer test for detecting genetic variants that may be associated with medication metabolism' (FDA, Press Release, 31 October 2018) <https://www.fda.gov/NewsEvents/Newsroom/PressAnnouncements/ucm624753.htm> last accessed 6 November 2018; 'FDA Tells Patients, Docs to Take Caution When Using Unapproved PGx Tests to Make Treatment Decisions' *GenomeWeb* (1 November 2018) <https://www.genomeweb.com/regulatory-news/fda-tells-patients-docs-take-caution-when-using-unapproved-pgx-tests-make-treatment> last accessed 6 November 2018; FDA, 'The FDA warns against the use of many genetic tests with unapproved claims to predict patient response to specific medications: FDA safety communication' (FDA, Safety Communication, 1 November 2018) <https://www.fda.gov/MedicalDevices/Safety/AlertsandNotices/ucm624725.htm> last accessed 6 November 2018; see also FDA, 'Jeffrey Shuren, M.D., J.D., director of the FDA's Center for Devices and Radiological Health and Janet Woodcock, M.D., director of the FDA's Center for Drug Evaluation and Research on agency's warning to consumers about genetic tests that claim to predict patients' responses to specific medications' (FDA, Statement, 1 Novemer 2018) <https://www.fda.gov/NewsEvents/Newsroom/PressAnnouncements/ucm624794.htm> last accessed 6 November 2018.

[109] HGC, *Common Framework* (n 68) 3, Table 1

sidered as recreational, but where companies also sell supplements or other products, it is likely that it would be considered to be an example of what the Association for Molecular Pathology (AMP) dubbed 'business interest testing'.[110] As with the category of pharmacogenetic testing, most companies offering this type of service are engaged in nutrigenetics, rather than nutrigenomics. There is also some overlap between nutrigenetics and genetic tests for athletic ability. However, at present there is little evidence to support the studies conducted in this area.[111]

Companies Operating

Forty-nine companies were identified that offered this type of testing and the number is likely to increase. As companies providing nutrigenetic testing often provide other services related to diet and fitness and may sell tailored diets and food supplements, they often have more in common with fitness, wellness and nutrition companies than with clinical genetics. Some examples were My Gene Diet (Natures Remedies Ltd),[112] Pathway Genomics,[111] Smart DNA,[112] Inherent Health,[113] Halo Health, and Gene Planet.[114]

Implications for Consumers

The category of nutrigenomics raises issues regarding clinical validity, as many tests currently offered have not been appropriately validated and

---

[110] AMP, *Position Statement: Direct Access Genetic Testing (Direct to Consumer Genetic Testing)* (Association for Molecular Pathology, 2015) <https://www.amp.org/AMP/assets/File/position-statements/2015/AMPpositionstatementDTCtesting-FINAL_002.pdf> last accessed 22 October 2018.

[111] Lewis et al. (n 84) 291–307; Saukko et al., 'Negotiating the boundary between medicine and consumer culture . . .' (n 64); David Castle and Nola M Ries, 'Ethical, legal and social issues in nutrigenomics: The challenges of regulating service delivery and building health professional capacity' (2007) 622(1–2) *Mutation Research – Fundamental and Molecular Mechanisms of Mutagenesis* 138–43 <https://doi.org/10.1016/j.mrfmmm.2007.03.017> last accessed 25 October 2018.

[112] My Gene Diet, <http://www.my-gene-diet.com/products.php> accessed 13 August 2013. [Checked again 29 January 2014 and still operating]. [Checked again 23 April 2014].

[113] Pathway Genomics, 'Pathway fit' <pathway.com/about-us/management> last accessed 3 February 2014.

[114] Smart DNA, <smartdna.net.au/howitworks.html> accessed 13 August 2013. [Checked again 29 January 2014 and still operating]. [Checked again 24 April 2014].

[115] Inherent Health, <inherenthealth.com/our-tests.aspx> accessed 13 August 2013. [Checked again 29 January 2014 and still operating]. [Checked again 15 April 2014],

[116] GenePlanet, 'NutriFit' <http://www.geneplanet.com/nutrifit-en.html> accessed 3 January 2013;

consequently the consumer may be paying for something that is ultimately useless. Some have argued that this type of testing should not be offered by DTC companies unless the tests offered are properly validated.[117] Often companies engaged in testing of this type also market supplements or meal plans. In the AMP's updated *Position Statement*,[118] they included a category dubbed 'business interest', which they did not support, and it seems likely that many nutrigenetic tests would come under this classification. It is possible that some companies in this category are more interested in selling additional products than in providing reliable testing. Again consumer privacy is a significant issue here and companies' policies regarding sale of data, data-sharing and storage need to be carefully monitored.

(e) Carrier Testing

Nature of this Type of Testing
This is aimed at identifying whether a person is a carrier for a particular condition, which might result in having a child affected by that condition. This type of testing has been used quite frequently by the Jewish community in order to identify carriers of Tay-Sachs and Canavan disease, along with other diseases which are common amongst people of Ashkenazi descent.[119] It is also becoming increasingly popular for other population groups, especially in those with a family history of certain autosomal recessive disorders, although carrier screening of the general population is still relatively uncommon.[120] While such testing is generally better validated than many other types of tests currently offered by the DTC industry, it may not be beneficial to offer it without medical intermediaries, especially genetic counsellors, given that undergoing such tests may mean that people make life-changing reproductive decisions.[121]

---

[117] EASAC and FEAM, *Direct-To-Consumer Genetic Testing For Health-Related Purposes In The European Union* (n 70) 10; HGC, *Common Framework* (n 68) 3.

[118] AMP, *Position Statement: Direct Access Genetic Testing (Direct to Consumer Genetic Testing)* (Association for Molecular Pathology, 2015) <https://www.amp.org/AMP/assets/File/position-statements/2015/AMPpositionstatementDTCtesting-FINAL_002.pdf> last accessed 22 October 2018.

[119] Center for Jewish Genetics, 'Jewish Genetic Disorders' <http://www.jewishgenetics.org/?q=content/jewish-genetic-disorders> accessed 3 January 2013 – last accessed 25 October 2018.

[120] P Borry, Lidewij Henneman, Phillis Lakeman, Leo P ten Kate, Martina C Cornel, Heidi C Howard, 'Preconceptional genetic carrier testing and the commercial offer directly-to-consumers' (2011) 26(5) Human Reproduction 972–7 <https://doi.org/10.1093/humrep/der042> last accessed 25 October 2018.

[121] Ibid.

Companies Operating

Seventeen companies were identified which offer (or have offered) carrier testing.[122] For example: 23andMe's UK branch; Biotechnology Group Inc; Counsyl (offers services through a physician); GenePeeks; and Genetic Centre Company Limited.[123]

23andMe UK tested for 43 conditions. Counsyl offered testing for more than 100 conditions. Gentle offered carrier testing for 120 conditions. GenePeeks's Matchright service compared consumers' DNA with that of potential donors to minimise disease risk. Genetic Center Company Limited provided tests for 37 recessive conditions.

Implications for Consumers

As many of the carrier tests offered by DTC companies have been approved and used in clinical settings, there are fewer issues around clinical utility and validity. However, as undergoing carrier testing generally is intended to allow individuals to understand whether they are at heightened risk of having a child affected by a serious illness or disability and may impact upon their reproductive decision making, it is vital that such tests are of the highest quality.[124] In terms of reproductive decision-making, undergoing carrier testing may allow couples to decide whether to use 'prenatal diagnosis followed (or not) by termination of the pregnancy in case of an affected fetus', allow them to understand and 'come to terms with the risk' and also decide whether to use 'pre-implantation genetic diagnosis', 'donor sperm or oocytes'.[125] It may also mean in some communities that couples may choose to adopt or not to have children or may mean that an individual will choose another partner.[126] None of these decisions is trivial and in a clinical setting patients would normally have genetic counselling and receive extensive information regarding the consequences of such testing.

In EASAC and FEAM's report, they highlighted the need for counselling and adequate information in this context. They also stressed that if DTC companies offer this service, they should follow guidelines for

---

[122] These are: 23andMe; All About Truth; Asper Biotech; Biotechnology Group Inc; Boston Paternity; Center for Medical Genetics; Counsyl; DNA Connect; DNA Testing Centres of Canada; DNA Traits; Gentle; GeneLex; GenePeeks; Genetic Center Company Limited; Genex; HomeDNADirect; and Pathway Genomics.

[123] 23andMe, 'Carrier Status' <https://www.23andme.com/health/carrier/> accessed 3 January 2013; Counsyl, <https://www.counsyl.com> accessed 29 May 2014.

[124] Borry et al., 'Preconceptional genetic carrier testing and the commercial offer directly-to-consumers' (n 119)

[125] Ibid. (n 119) 972.

[126] Ibid. (n 119) 972.

quality control, which apply to other medical tests carried out in a clinical context.[127] As learning that a person is a carrier of a serious condition may actually be distressing and might be a factor in reproductive decision-making, it is important that companies do in fact provide sufficient information about the nature of testing so that consumers may make informed decisions.[128]

(f) Companies Offering Services via Physicians

Nature of This Type of Testing
In identifying DTC companies, companies that market their tests online either directly to consumers or directly to physicians but only provide their services through physicians or other intermediaries were also included for the sake of comprehensiveness. (Some companies included are in fact academic laboratories.) This is in part due to the fact that certain companies which began as DTC companies have now shifted to models where testing can only be ordered via a physician and also to capture companies engaged in marketing directly to physicians or consumers. At present, companies that involve physicians offer many types of test, including tests that may not be well validated, such as nutrigenetics and athletic ability tests.

Companies Operating
Forty-one companies were identified that offer genetic testing services that require orders to be made by physicians.[129] Two companies that were quite prominent in the early days of the DTC industry, Navigenics and Pathway Genomics, both shifted to this model. More recently a number of

---

[127] EASAC and FEAM, *Report* (n 70)10; Fears (n 70); Borry et al., 'Preconceptional genetic carrier testing and the commercial offer directly-to-consumers' (n 119).

[128] Borry et al., 'Preconceptional genetic carrier testing and the commercial offer directly-to-consumers' (n 119).

[129] The companies offering testing through physicians are: AccuraScience; American International Biotechnology, LLC (AIBioTech); ARUP Lab; Athleticode; Bio Logis; Bio Wellness Inc; Cancer Genetics Inc; CD Genomics; Center for Medical Genetics; Counsyl; Diagnomics; DNADirect; DNA Traits; Foundation Medicine Inc; GATC Biotech AG; GeneLex; GeneNews Ltd; Genetic Testing Laboratories Inc (GTL); Genewiz; Genomic Express Inc; Genomic Health Inc; Genosense; Gentle; Kimball; Knome; LabCorp; Map My Gene; MEDomics; Molecular Diagnostic Services (PTY) Ltd; Myriad; Navigenics; Pathway Genomics; Pediatrix Medical Group; Perkin Elmer Genetics; Personal Genome Diagnostics Inc; Progenika Inc; Remede; Signal Genetics Inc; Smart DNA; Toldot Genetics; Transnetyx Inc.

companies have entered the market that allow for ordering via physicians: Color Genomics; Veritas Genetics; Helix; and Gene By Gene.

Some of the companies included on my list are more traditional laboratories, which market to physicians. However, several of these have websites that might be construed as advertising directly to consumers or which might be construed as advertising to physicians.

Implications for Consumers

While companies that only allow testing to be ordered through a physician are to some extent engaging in more responsible practices overall, their activities still need to be monitored carefully. While the provision of genetic counselling and supervision of physicians is desirable in DTC more generally, companies which began as DTC without the involvement of medical practitioners and have since shifted to a model involving practitioners have been criticised on the grounds that having a physician on staff or links to company-approved physicians may provide a level of false reassurance.[130] Currently the FDA seems to be taking a stricter approach in relation to DTC companies that allow for ordering directly by consumers, while not requiring the same approvals for tests that can be ordered via a physician.[131] This divergence seems problematic and it is desirable that the FDA alters its stance on this. It needs to be stressed that there are problems generally with the level of general practitioners' understanding of DTC and genetic testing more generally, and the involvement of general practitioners does not necessarily overcome concerns about certain kinds of DTC.[132] Several commentators have also highlighted the need for further education for general practitioners in genetics.[133]

---

[130] Heidi Howard and Pascal Borry, 'Is there a doctor in the house? The presence of physicians in the direct-to-consumer genetic testing context' (2012) 3(2) *Journal of Community Genetics* 105–12, 110–11 doi: 10.1007/s12687-011-0062-0.

[131] Ike Swetlitz, 'Genetic tests ordered by doctors race to market, while "direct-to-consumer" tests hinge on FDA approval' (16 March 2018) *STAT* <https://www.statnews.com/2018/03/16/genetic-tests-fda-regulation/> last accessed 27 October 2018.

[132] Ibid.

[133] Karen P Powell, Carol A Christianson, Whitney A Cogswell, Gaurav Dave, Amit Verma, Sonja Eubanks, and Vincent C Henrich, 'Educational needs of primary care physicians regarding direct-to-consumer genetic testing' (2012) 21(3) *Journal of Genetic Counseling* 469–78; Karen P Powell, Whitney A Cogswell, Carol A Christianson, Gaurav Dave, Amit Verma, Sonja Eubanks, and Vincent C Henrich, 'Primary care physicians' awareness, experience and opinions of direct-to-consumer genetic testing' (2012) 21(1) *Journal of Genetic Counseling* 113–26 <https://www.researchgate.net/profile/Karen_Powell8/publication/51502589_Primary_Care_Physicians%27_Awareness_Experience_and_Opinions_of_Direct-to-Consumer_Genetic_Testing/links/547487340cf2778985abe54c.pdf> last accessed 25 October 2018.

Clinical utility and validity, informed consent and provision of adequate information are still important in this context. Some companies also still have websites that are targeted towards attracting consumers and they also market to physicians, which raises similar issues to those of the direct-to-consumer marketing of pharmaceutical drugs in terms of whether advertising has an impact on physicians' perceptions of testing.[134]

3.4 Ancestry Testing

(a) Nature of this Type of Testing

Generally, this type of testing is 'intended to provide information about an individual's relatedness to a certain ancestor or ancestral group'.[135] It is currently the most popular category of testing.[136] This type of testing is typically classed as recreational, but as certain ethnic groups can be more prone to particular diseases it can also reveal information that is health-related. It may also reveal unknown relatives and false paternity and given recent examples of ancestry testing companies moving into health research, it is important that these tests are monitored. Companies will often offer a variety of tests, focusing on either the paternal line (Y chromosome) or the maternal line (mitochondrial DNA). This will not capture all of a person's ancestry and people with mixed heritage may find test results of limited utility.

---

[134] Catherine A Womack, 'Ethical and epistemic issues in direct-to-consumer drug advertising: Where is patient agency?' (2013) 16(2) *Medicine Health Care and Philosophy* 275–80; Sanjo Adeoye and Kevin J Bozic, 'Direct to consumer advertising in healthcare: History, benefits, and concerns' (2007) 457 *Clinical Orthopaedics and Related Research* 96–104 doi: 10.1097/BLO.0b013e31803427e6.

[135] HGC, *Common Framework* (n 68) 3.

[136] AncestryDNA, 'AncestryDNA breaks holiday sales record for Black Friday to Cyber Monday: More than triple kits sold versus 2016' (AncestryDNA, Press Release, 28 November 2017)
<https://www.ancestry.com/corporate/newsroom/press-releases/ancestrydna-breaks-holiday-sales-record-black-friday-cyber-monday-more> last accessed 25 October 2018; Megan Molteni, 'Ancestry's genetic testing kits are heading for your stocking this year' (1 December 2017) *Wired* <https://www.wired.com/story/ancestrys-genetic-testing-kits-are-heading-for-your-stocking-this-year/> last accessed 25 October 2018; Spencer Wells of National Geographic's Genographic Project speaking at the Consumer Genetics Conference in Boston, MA, USA in September 2013 suggested that the most likely growth area in the immediate future in consumer genetics would be in the field of ancestry testing. See <http://www.globaleventslist.elsevier.com/events/2013/09/consumer-genetics-conference-715f1768/> last accessed 25 October 2018.

(b) Companies Operating

In the initial study, 68 companies were identified offering this type of testing. (As of October 2018, the figure had increased to 81.)[137] Companies will normally have several options and many ancestry testing companies will perform other types of testing for genetic relatedness, including tests for paternity, maternity, grandparents and siblings. Some of the most prominent companies in this category are: AncestryDNA; AncestrybyDNA; FamilyTreeDNA; 23andMe; MyHeritageDNA; easyDNA; National Geographic's Genographic Project; and Nimble Diagnostics.[138]

Thirty-two companies offered testing for both maternal and paternal lineage. Thirteen companies specifically tested for African ancestry and 15 tested for Native American ancestry.[139] It is also common for companies to offer a 'family finder' function, which allows people to connect with others to whom they may be related.

---

[137] These were: 23andMe; Accu-metrics Viaguard; Advanced Healthcare Inc; African Ancestry; African DNA; All About Truth DNA Services; Alpha Biolabs; American Paternity; AncestryDNA; AncestrybyDNA; Any Lab Test Now®; ARCpoint Labs; Atlas Biomed; BritainsDNA; Cambridge DNA Services; Canadian DNA Services; Carigen Caribbean Genetics; DDC, DNA Diagnostics Center; Determigene; DNAme; DNA Ancestry Project; DNA Ancestry & Family Origin; DNA Clinics; DNA Consultants; DNA Dimensions; DNA DTC; DNAForce; DNAme; DNA Heritage; DNA Identifiers; DNA Print Genomics; DNA Services of America; DNA Spectrum; DNA Solutions; DNA Test; DNA Testing Center of America; DNA Testing Centre Inc; DNA Testing Centres of Canada; DNA Tribes; DNA Worldwide; easyDNA; FamilyTreeDNA; Full Genomes Corporation; Genebase; Genetic Testing Laboratories Inc (GTL); Gensys; Genetica DNA Laboratories Inc; GeneTree; Genex Diagnostics Inc; Genomic Express Inc; Gensys; GFI Lab; Health Street; Helix (connected to Illumina); HomeDNAdirect; Home DNA Inc; iGENEA; Indian Biosciences; Insitome; International Bioscience; Legal DNA Testing; Lumigenix; Merrimack Valley Paternity Testing (MVP Testing); MyHeritage; National Geographic's Genographic Project; Nimble Diagnostics; North American DNA Testing; NW DNA; Oxford Ancestors; Paternity Testing Corp; Prophase Genetics; Relative Genetics; Roots for Real; SecureDNA Technologies; ScotlandsDNA; Test Country; Test Diagnostics; YSEQ DNA Origins Project; Who'z the Daddy?

[138] 23andMe, 'Understand the story of your past' <https://www.23andme.com/ancestry/> accessed 3 January 2013; FamilyTreeDNA, <http://www.familytreedna.com> accessed 3 January 2013; Nimble Diagnostics, 'Ancestry DNA Testing' <http://www.nimblediagnostics.com/home/anc.html> accessed 3 January 2013; easyDNA, 'DNA Testing for Ancestry – Find Your Origins Here!' <http://www.easydna.co.uk/dna-ancestry-test.html> accessed 3 January 2013.

[139] These were: Accu-metrics Viaguard; African DNA; Alpha Biolabs; AncestryByDNA; DDC; DNA Consultants; DNA Dimensions; DNA Services of America; DNA Spectrum; Genex; Genomic Express; North American DNA Testing; Genetica; Genebase; and Universal Genetics.

(c) Implications for Consumers

Genetic ancestry testing is the type of DTC service that is experiencing the most growth at present. For example, AncestryDNA in the period between Black Friday and Cyber Monday 2017 sold 1.5 million test kits.[140] The most prominent companies have databases with several million customer samples. 23andMe has collected the samples of more than 5 million customers, while AncestryDNA has more than 10 million.[141] It is also becoming clear that in practice the lines between the activities of DTC companies which perform ancestry testing and those which perform health-related tests are very much blurred. Many companies are not limited to offering merely one type of genetic testing and may offer ancestry together with paternity and health testing. AncestryDNA and Gene By Gene are good examples of this. This also raises the question of whether it is possible to apply different regulatory regimes to ancestry testing and health-related testing. Perhaps it could be argued that while a company is engaged only in ancestry testing it should be subject to less regulatory oversight, but that if it subsequently moves into health research, it should be subject to more oversight. However, this would be very difficult to implement and it is desirable that ancestry companies have more rigorous mechanisms for informed consent and stronger security mechanisms to ensure protection of consumer privacy. In the UK, ancestry testing companies are also likely to come under the remit of the HTA and if that is the case, they would need to provide similar consent mechanisms to companies that provide health tests.

While it is possible for ancestry testing to be conducted as a 'recreational activity', ancestry testing is not necessarily innocuous. The accuracy of ancestry testing in terms of its ability to identify an individual's ancient origins is questionable and while as more research is performed on different ethnic groups ancestry testing will become more accurate, notions of ethnicity and race have historically not generally been used in beneficial ways. So it is possible that an increase in ancestry testing focusing on ethnic origins may serve to fuel further racial divisions, which people have been trying to overcome for some time.[142]

---

[140] AncestryDNA (n 135); and Molteni (n 135).

[141] 23andMe, 'About Us' <https://mediacenter.23andme.com/company/about-us/> last accessed 13 July 2018; AncestryDNA, <https://www.ancestry.co.uk/cs/ireland-dna> last accessed 13 July 2018.

[142] Mark Popovsky, 'Exaggerated benefits and underestimated harms: The direct-to-market consumer genetic test market and how to manage it going forward' (2010) 8 *Dartmouth Law Journal* 65–87; Kim TallBear, 'The emergence, politics, and marketplace of Native

Several DTC companies that perform ancestry testing also offer a family finder service, which connects individuals with others to whom they may be related. This sometimes leads to unexpected discoveries including false paternity and unknown siblings. While this information might be beneficial for some people, it can also cause distress and have a serious impact on families.

Ancestry is also often linked with notions of identity and sometimes when a person learns unexpected information about their origins this may have a significant impact on their conception of their own identity. In terms of accuracy, it will also be of more use to consumers in the future, when more research has been conducted on all population groups, as at present, due to the lack of study of some ethnic groups, the reliability of some ancestry testing may be questionable.[143] The research conducted by the 1000 Genomes Project and the 100,000 Genomes Project is contributing to improvements in this area.[144] However, it is important to understand that everyone has lots of ancestors and ancestry tests may not reveal all of your ancestry. For example, as Kim Tallbear writes:

> Going back only ten generations, each of us has about one thousand ancestors. One could have up to two Native American grandparents and show no sign of Native American ancestry. [. . .] a genetic male could have a maternal grandfather (from whom he did not inherit his Y chromosome) and a paternal grandmother (from whom he did inherit his mtDNA) who were descended from Native American founders, but mtDNA and Y-chromosome analyses would not detect them.[145]

DTC companies also often do not have datasets that are representative of a country's entire population and it is possible to obtain contradictory ethnicity estimates from different companies, as companies also frame their populations differently.[146]

American' in Daniel Lee Kleinman and Kelly Moore (eds), *Routledge Handbook of Science, Technology and Science* (Routledge 2014) 21 doi: 10.4324/9780203101827.ch1.

[143] E Callaway, 'Ancestry testing goes for pinpoint accuracy' (2012) 486 *Nature* 17; Jennifer K Wagner, Jill D Cooper, Rene Sterling, and Charmaine D Royal, 'Tilting at windmills no longer: A data-driven discussion of DTC DNA ancestry tests' (2012) 14(6) *Genetics in Medicine* 586–93 doi: 10.1038/gim.2011.77.

[144] 1000 Genomes Project, <http://www.1000genomes.org/about> accessed 3 January 2013 – this is now IGSR: The International Genome Sample Resource, <http://www.internationalgenome.org/about> last accessed 25 October 2018.

[145] Kim Tallbear, *Native American DNA* (University of Minnesota Press 2013) 43.

[146] Kristin V Brown, 'How DNA testing botched my family's heritage, and probably yours, too' GIZMODO (16 January 2018) <https://gizmodo.com/how-dna-testing-botched-my-familys-heritage-and-probab-1820932637> last accessed 24 October 2018; see also

(d) Indigenous Peoples and DTC Ancestry Services

Another area of concern is the increasing number of companies that specifi-cally offer Native American ancestry testing and it is likely that in the future companies will also market tests for other indigenous peoples. Historically, indigenous peoples in many countries have been marginalised and exploited in many ways, including through their involvement in health research.[147] The example of Havasupai illustrates this point. Here, the Havasupai tribe took legal action against Arizona State University because of research done on their blood samples to which they did not give consent. Havasupai are an American Indian tribe who have a very high incidence of diabetes. They approached researchers and asked for their assistance in researching diabetes. Blood samples from the tribe were taken and subsequently used for other research including research on inbreeding, schizophrenia and migration pat-terns. Havasupai had not given their consent for studies on the last three topics, and they were not informed of the researchers' interests in studying these things. The research on schizophrenia and inbreeding is particularly problematic as Havasupai are a small tribe who still live in an isolated area and such research may cause their clan to be discriminated against.[148] Furthermore, research on migration patterns offends their religious sensibilities as they share a creation story, which tells them that their origins are in America, not Asia. A further issue here is that much research on Native American genetic ancestry has relied on samples appropriated from museums' collections, which at least some Native American groups object to their holding. There have also been disputes over specific samples. See for instance Kennewick Man.[149]

Wendy D Roth and Biorn Ivemark, 'Genetic options: The impact of genetic ancestry testing on consumers' racial and ethnic identities' (2018) 124(1) American Journal of Sociology 150–84 <https://doi.org/10.1086/697487>; Wendy D Roth, 'Genetic ancestry tests don't change your identity, but you might' (5 July 2018) The Conversation <https://the conversation.com/genetic-ancestry-tests-dont-change-your-identity-but-you-might-98 663> last accessed 30 October 2018.

[147] MM Mello and LE Wolf, 'The Havasupai Indian Tribe Case – Lessons for research involving stored biologic samples' (2010) 363 New England Journal of Medicine 204–7 doi: 10.1056/NEJMp1005203.

[148] D Harry, 'Acts of self-determination and self-defence: Indigenous peoples' responses to biocolonialism', in Sheldon Krimsky (ed.) et al., Why We Need a Genetic Bill of Rights: Rights and Liberties in the Biotech Age (Rowman and Littlefield Publishers Inc 2005) 87–9; see also Who Owns Your Body, 'The Havasupai Case' <http://www.whoownsyourbody. org/havasupai.html> last accessed 31 October 2018.

[149] Erick Blakemore, 'Over 9,000 Years Later, Kennewick Man Will Be Given a Native American Burial' Smithsonian.com (28 April 2016) <https://www.smithsonianmag.com/ smart-news/over-9000-years-later-kennewick-man-will-be-given-native-american-bur

Companies providing testing of this type should be subject to more scrutiny. The need for better practices and more oversight of the industry is further demonstrated by two recent examples that have been covered in the American and Canadian press. Firstly, Phil Rogers, an NBC reporter, sent DNA samples from himself and his pet labrador Bailey to three different ancestry testing companies (Orig3n, MyHeritage and Ancestry). Both AncestryDNA and MyHeritage reported that they could not read Bailey's sample, but Orig3n provided a report on the dog, indicating that 'she would be likely to be good at sports requiring quick movement'.[150]

The second example is more concerning. In this case Louis Côté purchased three tests from the Canadian company Accumetrics-Viaguard[151] after becoming concerned regarding their tests during his work for the Confederation of Aboriginal People of Canada (CAPC). This organisation is not officially recognised by the Canadian government or the Assembly of First Nations. The organisation relies heavily on DNA tests, which are all provided by the same company. If an individual receives test results indicating they have more than 1 per cent Native American ancestry, they then can pay 80 CAD to join the organisation. CAPC gives its members a card which looks very similar to the official government-issued Indian status card, which is used by Native Americans to claim tax credits and other benefits. Côté sent samples from himself and his girlfriend's Chihuahua, Snoopy, and received the same ethnicity estimates for both Snoopy and himself. The reports for Côté and Snoopy indicated that they were both 20 per cent Native American with 12 per cent Abanaki and 8 per cent Mohawk. A former member of CAPC, Daniel Brabant, heard about Côté's experience and sent in samples from himself and his poodle. Again, the results indicated that both man and dog had Native American ancestry. CBC News then conducted its own investigation, sending samples from three of its staff, two of whom were born in India and the other in Russia, to both Accumetrics and 23andMe. Accumetrics' results indicated that all three individuals had 20 per cent Native American ancestry 'linking them to specific First Nations communities' and indicating that all three

---

ial-180958947/> accessed 5 April 2019; please also refer to the work of the Indigenous Peoples Council on Biocolonialism if you wish to explore these issues further. Indigenous Peoples Council on Biocolonialism, 'Human Genetics Issues' <http://www.ipcb.org/issues/human_genetics/index.html> accessed 5 April 2019.

[150] 'Bailey the Superdog' *GenomeWeb* (2 May 2018) <https://www.genomeweb.com/scan/bailey-superdog> last accessed 25 October 2018.

[151] Jorge Barrera and Tiffany Foxcroft, 'Heredity or hoax?' *CBC News* (13 June 2018) <https://newsinteractives.cbc.ca/longform/dna-ancestry-test> last accessed 24 October 2018.

had 12 per cent Abanaki and 8 per cent Mohawk ancestry. In contrast, 23andMe's results did not indicate Native American ancestry for any of the employees and instead that 'greater than 99.8 per cent of their DNA was reported as being linked to the regions where they were born'.[152] When contacted, Accumetrics-Viaguard indicated that 'many people find themselves in the range of 20 per cent Indigenous ancestry' and that their results were 'informational'.[153]

CBC News also contacted geneticists Simon Gravel and Steve Carr for their views on the situation. Both were critical of the results, with Gravel saying 'It is not possible to break down someone's ancestry into multiple First Nation groups using only mitochondrial and Y chromosome DNA'. He also said that 'Even the largest companies [. . .] don't report such specific results'.[154] Meanwhile Carr said that 'The results are comical, given that they can't tell the difference between dog and human DNA'.

The above stories highlight that while genetic data can reveal information about our origins, this can also be a double-edged sword, as tests for ethnic ancestry are not standardised and may serve secondary purposes that might not be in an individual's best interests. Ethnic identity itself is complex and for indigenous people's tribal identity a more holistic conception of identity and ancestry is required.[155] DTC companies should be much more cautious and transparent about the limitations of test results.

3.5 Genetic Relatedness Testing

(a) Nature of this Type of Testing

This is done for the purposes of determining genetic relationships. Two of the most significant examples of this are maternity and paternity tests.[156] This testing is generally well validated in the scientific community. It can also be particularly useful in the context of donor-conceived children. However, it can also reveal false paternity and given the mode of delivery of DTC tests it is also open to abuse, as consumers may send in samples belonging to others in order to avoid such things as their maintenance commitments.

---

152 Ibid.
153 Ibid.
154 Barrera and Foxcroft (n 149).
155 CBC News, 'After dog DNA debacle, Indigenous researcher says ancestry testing is "stupid science"' *CBC News Edmonton* (14 June 2018) <http://www.cbc.ca/news/canada/edmonton/dna-testing-indigenous-ancestry-1.4705797> last accessed 1 August 2018; Kim Tallbear, *Native American DNA* (University of Minnesota Press 2013) chapters 2 and 3.
156 HGC, *Common Framework* (n 68) 3.

(b) Companies Operating

In this category the most common type of testing is paternity testing and 83 companies offered this service at the time of review.[157] Ninety-six per cent of the companies that offered paternity testing provided both a 'legal' and a 'peace of mind' option. Sixty per cent of these companies offered both paternity and maternity testing. Thirty-five per cent of the companies identified also offered prenatal paternity testing. Forty-one per cent of the companies offering paternity testing also offered surreptitious (infidelity) testing.

Some examples include: Who'z the Daddy?;[158] Test Country;[159] Gensys;[160] Prophase Genetics;[161] International Biosciences;[162] and Genetic Profiles[163].

---

[157] The companies identified that offer paternity testing are: 23DNA; Accu-metrics Viaguard; Accurate Paternity Testing; Advanced Healthcare Inc; Alpha Biolabs; American Paternity; Any Lab Test Now®; Any Time Lab; ARCpoint Labs; Asper Biotech; AssureDNA; Beta Paternity; Boston Paternity; BRT Labs Inc; Cellmark; Checkmatetest.com; Consumer Genetics; Dadchecksilver; DDC, DNA Diagnostics Centre; Definite DNA; Determigene; DNAForce; DNA Clinics; DNA Connect; DNA Diagnostics Ltd; DNA Dimensions; DNA Findings; DNA Genie; DNA Identifiers; DNA Ireland; DNA Labs; DNA Services of America; DNA Solutions; DNA Test; DNA Test.ie; DNA Testing Center of America; DNA Testing Centre Inc; DNA Testing Centres of Canada; DNA Worldwide; DNAQ owned by Genomics For Life Pty Ltd; easyDNA; Eurofins Medigenomix GmbH; EuroPaternity; Fairfax Identity Labs; Forensics Genetics Center; Genebase; GeneLex; Genetic Profiles; Genetica DNA Laboratories Inc; Gensys; Genetrack Biolabs; Genetic Profiles; Genetic Testing Laboratories Inc (GTL); Genetic Technologies; Genex Diagnostics Inc; GFI Lab; HealthCheckUSA; HomeDNAdirect; Home DNA Inc; Identigene Inc; Independent Forensics; Indian Biosciences; IDNA Systems; International Biosciences; iTest DNA; LabCorp; Medigenomix; Molecular Diagnostic Services (PTY) Ltd; MVP Testing; Nimble Diagnostics; North American DNA Testing; Northgene; Paternity Testing Corp; PaternityUSA; Priority Investigations; Prophase Genetics; Serotech Laboratories Ltd; Silbase Genetics; Sorenson Genomics; SwabTest; Test Country; Test Diagnostics; That DNA Company; Who'z the Daddy?

[158] Who'z the Daddy?, 'Court Approved DNA Tests' <whozthedaddy.com/regions/UK/EN/courtApprovedDNAtests.asp> accessed 5 January 2013. [Checked again 24 April 2014]; Who'z the Daddy?, 'Peace of Mind DNA Tests' <whozthedaddy.com/regions/UK/EN/peaceOfMindDNAtests.asp> accessed 5 January 2013. [Checked again 24 April 2014].

[159] Test Country, 'Paternity DNA Testing' <testcountry.com/categories.html?cat=152&left> accessed 10 August 2013. [Checked again 24 April 2014].

[160] Gensys, 'Do you need a legal or in-home paternity test?' <paternity-answers.com/paternity-test.html> accessed 12 August 2013. [Checked again 14 April 2014].

[161] Prophase Genetics, <prophase-genetics.com/home_legal_paternity2.html> accessed 13 August 2013. [Checked again 24 April 2014].

[162] International Biosciences, 'DNA Testing Services and Prices' <ibdna.com/regions/UK/EN/?page=services#PM_Paternity> accessed 2 February 2013. [Checked again 16 April 2014].

[163] Genetic Profiles, <geneticprofiles.com> accessed 27 January 2014. [Checked again 28

(c) Implications for Consumers

The majority of companies offering paternity testing will sell two versions of the test, which will normally be described as 'legal' or 'court approved' on the one hand and 'peace of mind testing' on the other. The 'legal' option is usually more expensive. The fact that it is common practice to provide these options calls for careful scrutiny of company practices in this context, as sample collection by individual consumers without witnesses does pose a substantial risk of sample contamination or misuse. This type of testing is particularly open to abuse, as some may be motivated to abuse these tests in order to avoid maintenance comitments.

While it did not involve a DTC company, a recent UK case that attracted media attention demonstrates this potential for misuse. John Bullet, wishing to avoid his maintenance[164] commitment, organised for another person to impersonate him and take a paternity test. The mother of the child in question discovered the imposter when she was shown a photo of the man who took the test. Bullett also lied to the Child Support Agency. He was then forced to have a second test, which proved he was the father.[165] While this case did not involve a DTC company it would be easier for a person to send in someone else's sample in the DTC context. Of course anyone who did in fact send in another sample's claiming it was theirs or that they had obtained appropriate consent would be committing the offence of non-consensual DNA analysis set out in the HTA. It is also possible that companies that do not have rigorous systems in place to check consent could also be prosecuted under the Act.

The potential for abuse in this context was also highlighted in the Article 29 Data Protection Working Party's Opinion 03/2012 on developments in biometric technologies in which it stated that 'Insufficient identity checks could allow individuals or entities to submit samples from other individuals' and receive 'sensitive personal data about other people as a result'.[166]

January 2014 and still operating].

[164] Leon Watson, 'Father who didn't want to pay child maintenance sent another man in his place to give DNA for paternity test' *Daily Mail* (5 June 2013) <https://www.dailymail.co.uk/news/article-2336469/Father-didnt-want-pay-child-maintenance-sent-man-place-DNA-paternity-test.html> last accessed 25 October 2018; 'Shamed: Dad who tried to beat DNA paternity test' *Yorkshire Evening Post* (10 May 2013) <https://www.yorkshireeveningpost.co.uk/news/shamed-dad-who-tried-to-beat-dna-paternity-test-1-5660133> last accessed 25 October 2018 – the case was heard in the Leeds Crown Court and the number was S20130486, but the case does not seem to have been reported.

[165] Watson, 'Father who didn't want to pay child maintenance . . .' (n 162); and 'Shamed: Dad who tried to beat DNA paternity test' (n 162).

[166] Article 29 Data Protection Working Party, Opinion 03/2012 on developments in biom-

Companies providing paternity testing will often perform tests on children's DNA samples, which is at odds with most of the policy guidance to date, as generally this guidance has recommended that testing of minors should not be offered DTC. This further supports the need for more monitoring of the industry and specific legal regulation. The wide range of paternity testing services raises issues in criminal law and family law, such as the nature and adequacy of consent, the reliability of testing, and potential harm to individuals, which it is hoped that others will conduct more research on in the future.

If DTC companies continue to offer this kind of testing, it would seem advisable that they improve consent mechanisms and adhere to higher standards, as unreliable parental testing could potentially result in significant harms to families. Companies offering prenatal paternity testing may need to be especially careful.

3.6 Testing for Athletic Ability

(a) Nature of this Type of Testing

This type of testing is carried out in order to identify genetic predisposition to athletic ability. The most common example of this type of testing are services focused on variants of the ACTN3 gene, which have been found to have some association with a person's ability to excel in endurance sports or to be a gifted sprinter.[167] However, the effects of these gene variants have not yet been shown to be the determinative factor in an individual's potential for athletic success. There is some overlap in testing services in this category with the category of nutrigenetics and child talent testing, as companies engaged in this type of testing also commonly provide diet testing and will test children for athletic ability. It is often considered to be an example of lifestyle testing.[168]

(b) Companies Operating

This is a growing area, with 31 companies identified as of 31 October 2018. Some of the most prominent companies in this area were: Athleticode;[169] Atlas

---

etric technologies (27 April 2012) 4.4.5, p 26, <https://ec.europa.eu/justice/article-29/documentation/opinion-recommendation/files/2012/wp193_en.pdf> last accessed 29 January 2019.

[167] Roger Collier, 'Genetic tests for athletic ability: Science or snake oil?' (2012) 184(1) *Canadian Medical Association Journal* E43-5 <https://doi.org/10.1503/cmaj.109-4063> last accessed 25 October 2018.

[168] HGC, *Common Framework* (n 68) 3, Table 1.

[169] Athleticode, <athleticode.com> accessed 10 August 2013. [Checked again 22 January 2014 and still operating]. [Checked again 9 April 2014].

Sport Genomics;[170] Asper Biotech;[171] Genetic Sports Performance; DNA Fit; and Soccer Genomics.

(c) Implications for Consumers

Tests for athletic ability are generally not well validated and even those that have been validated are often of little predictive value.[172] In fact companies selling such tests have been compared with snake oil merchants.[173] While an individual's genetic makeup may play a role in whether she is able to excel in sports it is only one factor and at present it does not seem that this role is determinative, as some successful athletes do not possess the ACTN3 variants. Where companies offer testing for children this raises further issues about the adequacy of consent and the privacy and security of sequenced genetic data, as well as other personal information.

3.7 Testing for Child Talent and Testing of Children

(a) Nature of this Type of Testing

DTC companies offer both testing for child talent and also more general tests related to health. Although child talent testing has not yet proliferated, it is one of the most dubious types of testing currently available. It is also an area of genetic testing which has little credibility in the scientific research community and most tests currently offered lack analytical validity, clinical utility and clinical validity.[174] Talent tests are often categorised

---

[170] Atlas Sports Genetics, <atlasgene.com> accessed 28 August 2013. [Checked again 28 January 2014 and still operating]. [Checked again 9 April 2014].

[171] Asper Biotech, 'Athletic Gene Test' <http://www.asperbio.com/asper-biotech-varia/athletic-gene-test> last accessed 9 April 2014.

[172] AF Patenaude, 'Commentary: Save the children: Direct-to-consumer testing of children is premature, even for research' (2011) 36(10) *Journal of Pediatric Psychology* 1122–7 <https://doi.org/10.1093/jpepsy/jsr068> last accessed 25 October 2018; HC Howard, D Avard, and P Borry, 'Are the kids really all right? Direct-to-consumer genetic testing in children: Are company policies clashing with professional norms?' (2011) 19 *European Journal of Human Genetics* 1122–6; Holly K Tabor and Maureen Kelley, 'Challenges in the use of direct-to-consumer personal genome testing in children' (2009) 9(6–7) *American Journal of Bioethics* 32–4 <https://www.ncbi.nlm.nih.gov/pmc/articles/PMC2792567/pdf/nihms131810.pdf> last accessed 25 October 2018; Amy L Fletcher, 'Field of genes: The politics of science and identity in the Estonian genome project' (2004) 23(1) *New Genetics and Society* 3–14 <https://doi.org/10.1080/1463677042000189589>.

[173] Collier (n 165).

[174] Howard et al. (n 170); Silvia Camporesi, 'Bend it like Beckham! The ethics of genetically testing children for athletic potential' (2013) 7(2) *Sport Ethics and Philosophy* 175–85 <https://doi.org/10.1080/17511321.2013.780183>.

as lifestyle testing.[175] It normally provides information on a wide variety of traits. Companies providing testing for talent encourage consumers that such tests will allow them to identify whether their child is best suited to playing particular sports, has a good memory or high IQ, or has emotional traits. Much policy guidance to date has been opposed to the offering of tests to children more generally and it is desirable that such testing is restricted.

(b) Companies Operating

Only five companies were identified that specifically marketed tests for child talent in a general way.[176] However, companies that provide tests for athletic ability will also often test children (twenty-five such companies were identified).

Map My Gene's DNA Innate Talents service (this is now called Inborn Talent Genetic Test) tested for forty-six talents and traits, which it divided into different categories. This was priced at $1,500 (USD) (as of December 2017). The division of character traits included: optimism; risk-taking; shyness; depression; hyper activeness; and adaptability. The category of IQ included: intelligence; creativity; reading ability; memory; and comprehension. The artistic category included predisposition for: performance; music; drawing; dancing; literature; and linguistics. The EQ category includes: affection; faithfulness; propensity for teenage romance; self-control; self-reflection; and sentimentality. There was also a sports category, which covered: endurance; sprinting; tendency of sport injuries; and sport psychology. The test also covered certain health traits, including obesity and

---

[175] HGC, *Common Framework* (n 68) 3, Table 1.

[176] These are: China Life Science Holding Group Ltd (CLS), <http://www.clsgrouphk.com/en/> accessed 19 December 2017. [Checked again 14 February 2018], last accessed 27 October 2018 and still operating; Genetic Center Company Limited, <http://www.genetic-center.com> accessed 13 August 2013. [Checked again 28 January 2014 and still operating], last accessed 27 October 2018 and may no longer be operating;

The Makings of Me, <http://www.themakingsofme.com> accessed 7 April 2014, last accessed 27 October 2018 and still operating; Map My Gene, <http://www.mapmygene.com/index.htm> accessed 2 January 2013. [Checked again 29 January 2014 and still operating]. [Checked again 16 April 2014]. [Checked again 19 December 2017 and still operating], last accessed 27 October 2018 and still operating;

New Life Genetics, accessed August 2017, checked 19 December 2017 http://newlifegenetics.com accessed 17 October 2016. [Checked again 7 February 2018 and still operating], last accessed 27 October 2018 and still operating; Soccer Genomics, <https://www.soccergenomics.com> accessed January 2018. [Checked again 9 February 2018 and still operating], last accessed 27 October 2018 and still operating.

predisposition to addiction covering alcoholism, smoking and general addiction.[177]

Meanwhile, the Makings of Me provided its My Child's DNA Insights. This is priced at $119 (USD) (as of 27 October 2018). This test covered the following traits: 'Overweight Potential, Height Potential, Memory Performance, Response to Diet, Speed vs. Endurance, Nearsightedness and Morning/Night Person'.[178]

Genetic Center Company Limited previously offered a Child Talent Gene Test, which covered several categories including: intelligence quotient; emotional quotient; focusing potential; and sports potential. The company claims that, the 'Test for Child Talent is carried out to find the Gene that determines the life function and also basic elements to analyze the strengths and weaknesses of a child's capacity in life'.[179]

Finally, the service offered by Soccer Genomics focused specifically on traits associated with playing soccer, including: speed; endurance; strength; risk of injury; nutrition. It offered Player Full Track for $299 (USD) (as of 27 October 2018).

(c) Implications for Consumers

As previously noted, most policy guidance to date has opposed DTC companies offering tests to children, consequently the availability of this testing requires greater oversight and should be restricted. Generally, tests for child talent are also not well validated and are not used widely in clinical settings.[180] The service provided by Soccer Genomics has resulted in renewed concern from the scientific community,[181] with geneticist Stephen Montgomery cre-

---

[177] Map My Gene, 'Inborn Talent Genetic Test' <http://www.mapmygene.com/services/talent-gene-test/> last accessed 27 July 2018.

[178] The Makings of Me, <https://www.themakingsofme.com/dna-test-kit-for-kids.html> last accessed 27 October 2018.

[179] Genetic Center Company Limited, 'Genetic Center Company Limited' <genetic-center.com/index_moduleId-114_pageName-content_pId-30.html> accessed 13 August 2013. [Checked again 28 January 2014 and still operating]. [Checked again 14 April 2014].

[180] Nick Webborn et al., 'Direct-to-consumer genetic testing for predicting sports performance and talent identification: Consensus statement' (2015) 49 BR *Journal of Sports Medicine* 1486–91 doi: 10.1136/bjsports-2015-095343; T Caulfield, P Borry, M Toews, BS Elger, HT Greely, and A McGuire, 'Marginally scientific? Genetic testing of children and adolescents for lifestyle and health promotion' (2015) 2(3) *Journal of Law and the Biosciences* 627–44 doi: 10.1093/jlb/lsv038.

[181] Kristen V Brown, 'Scientist push back against booming genetic pseudoscience market' GIZMODO (14 July 2017) <https://gizmodo.com/scientists-push-back-against-booming-genetic-pseudoscie-1796923059> last accessed 9 August 2018 – this is also mentioned in the chapter Andelka M Phillips, 'Will my genes really help me fit into those

ating a parody website called Yes or No Genomics.[182] Montgomery's website states 'Genetic variants have been connected to human disease! You may be at risk. Would you like to know if you have genetic variants (only $199.95, payable to SPLC)?'[183]

Furthermore, clinical geneticists and physicians often discourage testing of children for late onset conditions.[184] As of October 2018, the American Academy of Pediatrics (AAP) has reaffirmed its policy statement from 2013, which was 'issued in conjunction with the American College of Medical Genetics and Genomics that DTC genetic testing is not appropriate for newborns'.[185] One of the reasons that the AAP discourages the use of DTC tests for newborns is that many tests are focused on 'adult-onset diseases and so treatment is not needed during childhood'.[186] Another concern in this context is that testing of children can also infringe a child's right not to know, and as 'test samples collected by DTC firms are then owned by them and could be sold' this can effectively take away a 'child's right to privacy'.[187]

In this context there is an overall question regarding the adequacy of consent. We should ask who has capacity to consent here and if a parent

---

jeans? Personal genomics and wrap contracts' in Lilian Edwards, Burkhard Schafer, and Edina Harbinja (eds), *Future Law: Emerging Technology, Ethics and Regulation* (forthcoming Edinburgh University Press 2019).

[182] YesOrNoGenomics, <http://montgomerylab.stanford.edu/yesorno.html> last accessed 9 August 2018.

[183] Ibid. (n 180).

[184] Jeffrey R Botkin et al., ASHG Position Statement, 'Points to consider: Ethical, legal, and psychosocial implications of genetic testing in children and adolescents' (2015) 97(1) *American Journal of Human Genetics* 6–21 <https://doi.org/10.1016/j.ajhg.2015.05.022> last accessed 25 October 2018; L Jackson, L Goldsmith, and H Skirton, 'Guidance for patients considering direct-to-consumer genetic testing and health professionals involved in their care: Development of a practical decision tool' (2014) 31(3) *Family Practice* 341–8 <https://doi.org/10.1093/fampra/cmt087> last accessed 25 October 2018.

[185] 'Not for the littlest' *GenomeWeb* (24 October 2018) <https://www.genomeweb.com/scan/not-littlest> last accessed 27 October 2018 – this cites Alyson Sulaski Wyckoff, 'Lack of reliability, privacy plague DTC genetic tests for newborns' *AAP News* (24 October 2018) <http://www.aappublications.org/news/2018/10/24/genetictesting102418> last accessed 27 October 2018; this cites Committee On Bioethics, Committee On Genetics, American College Of Medical Genetics and Genomics Social, Ethical, and Legal Issues Committee, 'Ethical and Policy Issues in Genetic Testing and Screening of Children' (2013) 131(3) from the American Academy of Pediatrics Policy Statement – a statement of reaffirmation for this policy was published at e20181836 <http://pediatrics.aappublications.org/content/131/3/620.short> last accessed 27 October 2018.

[186] 'Not for the Littlest' (n 183).

[187] Ibid.

or guardian is consenting on a child's behalf, is that justifiable for tests of dubious validity?

There is again a need for greater transparency and fair advertising practice in this context, as companies marketing such testing often present genetics in a very deterministic way which does not reflect the respective risks and benefits of testing in an honest way. Given the variety of ways in which genetic data can also be repurposed, the significance of privacy rights in this context should not be underestimated and if companies are permitted to offer such tests, there should be strict time limits on how long an individual's data can be retained.

3.8 Surreptitious ('Infidelity') Testing

(a) Nature of this Type of Testing

This testing is often dubbed 'infidelity' or 'secret' testing on DTC websites. The websites of such companies encourage consumers to submit samples of other individuals without their consent, ostensibly for the purposes of ascertaining whether a person is being unfaithful to their partner.[188] The companies that provide such tests as their primary service may in fact be providing services of very dubious quality, partly due to their acceptance of samples of very poor quality, such as samples collected from bed sheets. It is desirable that such tests are legally prohibited.

(b) Companies Operating

When reviewed, 34 companies offered surreptitious testing services. These tests are often marketed as 'infidelity' tests. Examples of companies specialising in testing of this type include: All About Truth DNA Services; Any Lab Test Now; Infidelity Testing; She Cheated; and Test Infidelity.[189]

However, when examining websites of many seemingly more reputable companies, it becomes apparent that they will sometimes also conduct

---

[188] Albert E Scherr, 'Genetic privacy and the Fourth Amendment: Unregulated surreptitious DNA harvesting' (2012) 47 *Georgia Law Review* 445–526; Eliazbeth E Joh, 'DNA theft: Recognizing the crime of nonconsensual genetic collection and testing' (2011) 91 *Boston University Law Review* 665–700; David Gurwitz and Yael Bregman-Eschet, 'Personal genomics services: Whose genomes?' (2009) 17(7) *European Journal of Human Genetics* 883–9 doi: 10.1038/ejhg.2008.254.

[189] Any Lab Test Now®, <mylabsa.com/index.html> accessed 28 August 2013; Infidelity Testing, <infidelitydnatesting.com> accessed 8 September 2013; All About Truth DNA Services, <allabouttruthdna.com/other-testing-services/infidelity-dna-testing/> accessed 28 April 2014;She Cheated, <shecheated.net> accessed 2 February 2013. [Checked again 24 April 2014]; Test Infidelity, <testinfidelity.com> accessed 20 January 2014. [Checked again 24 April 2014].

tests without consent. Overall, 41 per cent of companies that offer paternity testing also offer 'infidelity testing'.[190] This is also supported by Hazel and Slobogin's study, which found that 'roughly half of companies offering paternity testing also offered some form of surreptitious testing'.[191]

Some companies engaged in health testing or ancestry testing also encourage customers to purchase tests as gifts (for instance, 23andMe allows customers to purchase additional test kits as gifts and when reviewed offer a 20 per cent discount for purchase of multiple kits[192]). Yet others also specifically offer tests for infidelity alongside their other services. For example, Advance Healthcare Inc (which despite its name does not in fact offer health testing, but instead specialises in various tests for genetic relatedness) also offers an infidelity test, for 9,800 rupees.[193]

Furthermore, companies often make claims on their websites in this context, which could be deemed misleading advertising,[194] and they also encourage customers to send in samples of dubious quality.

(c) Implications for Consumers

Surreptitious testing is probably the most concerning type of DTC testing, primarily due to the dubious nature of these services and also companies' marketing practices. Often the content of websites providing testing of this type seems open to challenge on the grounds that it is misleading. Companies often encourage consumers to send in samples of dubious quality belonging to other individuals without their consent and it is possible that some of the services advertised cannot perform in accordance with their claims.[195] Companies offering these services to UK consumers are also

---

[190] These include: Accu-metrics; Advanced Healthcare; All About Truth; Any Lab Test Now; Any Time Lab; Arcpoint; Boston Paternity; Checkmate; DNA Connect; DNA Findings; DNA Identifiers; DNA Q; DNA Services; DNA Test; DNATest.ie; DNA Testing Centre; easyDNA; EuroPaternity; Faifax; Forensics Genetics; GTL; IDNA; International Biosciences; ITest; Labcorp; Medigenomix; MVP; North American; Paternity Testing; PaternityUSA; Serotech; SwabTest; Test Diagnostics; and Universal.

[191] Hazel and Slobogin (n 6) 14.

[192] 23andMe, <23andme.com/store/cart/> last accessed 23 May 2014.

[193] Advanced Healthcare Inc, <advanceddna.in> accessed 28 August 2013, checked again 20 August 2015 – price is current as of 20 August 2015.

[194] Geransar and Einsiedel (n 21).

[195] Scherr, 'Genetic privacy and the Fourth Amendment . . .' (n 186); Eriq Gardner, 'Gene swipe: With more DNA labs, few know whether those chromosomes are yours – or you stole them from someone else' (2011) 97 ABA Journal 50 <http://www.abajournal.com/magazine/article/gene_swipe_few_dna_labs_know_whether_chromosomes_are_yours_or_if_you_stole_/?utm_source=feedburner&utm_medium=feed&utm_campaign=ABA+Journal+Magazine+Stories> last accessed 27 October 2018.

most clearly in breach of the HTA and are likely to be deemed to have committed the offence of non-consensual DNA analysis set out in section 45. Where the content of the website clearly encourages consumers to send in samples belonging to third parties without their consent, the company should be liable to prosecution, but the consumer may also be committing an offence.

Testing of this type is worthy of greater scrutiny and it is desirable that regulators take action against these companies. However, enforcing the legislation in relation to this particular type of testing is likely to be difficult due to its very nature in that companies are encouraging people to send in samples without appropriate consent, clearly in breach of the law.

3.9 Match-making Testing

(a) Nature of this Type of Testing

Fortunately one category of testing which has not yet proliferated is that of DNA-based dating services. This type of testing has been promoted as a means of match making based on two individuals' genetic compatibility.[196] To date, there is little scientific evidence to support this type of service and it is desirable that companies providing such tests are carefully monitored.

(b) Companies Operating

Only four companies offering this type of service have been identified and one of these is no longer operating. These companies are GenePartner, Instant Chemistry, DNA Romance[197] and Scientific Match.[198]

(c) Implications for Consumers

While this type of service has not yet proliferated, it is one of the most dubious services offered by DTC companies. There is very little evidence to support the claims made by companies and the few companies engaged in it often make exaggerated claims about the benefits of testing, which could be potentially misleading. Companies providing these tests to UK consumers are also likely to come within the HTA's remit. Based on the review of

---

[196] Molly C Novy, 'Privacy at a price: Direct-to-consumer genetic testing and the need for regulation' (2010) *Journal of Law, Technology & Policy* 157–80; Timothy Caulfield, 'Predictive or preposterous? The marketing of DTC Genetic Testing' (2011) 10(3) *Journal of Science Communication* C02 doi: 10.22323/2.10030302.

[197] DNA Romance, < https://www.dnaromance.com> last accessed 2 August 2018.

[198] GenePartner, <genepartner.com> accessed 10 February 2013; Instant Chemistry, <instantchemistry.com> accessed 10 April 2014; Dating DNA, <datingdna.com> accessed 10 February 2013; Scientific Match – no longer operating.

companies' contracts and drawing upon related studies,[199] again it seems advisable that companies work to improve their consent mechanisms.

3.10 Conclusion

The DTC industry is engaged in the business of providing genetic tests directly to the public. This technology has come to market very rapidly and without much oversight. Most companies only test for SNPs and not an individual's whole genome, meaning that the utility of test results is limited. Recent advances in genomics have made sequencing of an individual's whole genome possible at a greatly reduced cost and as the science continues to progress, large numbers of people may have their whole genome sequenced and eventually included as part of their medical record. However, the utility of sequencing only a portion of an individual's genome without due consideration of other factors such as family history is questionable. It is important also to stress the ambiguous nature of some genetics research at present. If even in a research context the impact of particular variants upon human health is disputed, some services currently offered to consumers may not be useful to them. Given the ambiguity of the association of particular genetic variants with human health, many tests currently offered by DTC companies cannot perform in the manner described on DTC websites. Therefore, it is unclear what the consumer is really buying.

Given this ambiguity and the nature of testing services, it was necessary to discuss the scientific background to the industry. As such testing can reveal a large amount of personally identifiable and potentially sensitive information about individual consumers and also because genetic information itself has several important features, it is important that companies are transparent about the respective risks and benefits of their tests.

Genetic information by its very nature is different to many other forms of personal information and even if the genetic exceptionalist approach is not accepted, a cautious approach to the treatment of such information seems desirable, because of some of its most significant features. Namely, that genomic data serves as a unique identifier for an individual and can also provide information about those who are related to that individual. This means that testing on an individual is in some ways essentially not an exclusively private act.

While some tests may not be particularly useful at present, DTC companies are continuing to grow, and if legal regulation may not be the only

---

[199] Hazel and Slobogin (n 6); LI Laestadius, Jennifer R Rich, and Paul L Auer, 'All your data (effectively) belong to us: Data practices among direct-to-consumer genetic testing firms' (2016) *Genetics in Medicine* doi:10.1038/gim.2016.136.

solution, involving the industry in developing standards which all DTC companies can adhere to seems a pragmatic strategy. In the UK, the now disbanded Human Genetics Commission did attempt to collaborate with companies in drafting its framework of principles and this could perhaps be a model for future work.

Another shift stems from changes in the location of testing. Thus there is a move from the clinic to the home environment with self-sample collection. Whereas a clinical genetic test would normally be carried out in a hospital or other clinical setting, DTC services normally require the consumer to collect their own sample and send it to the company. This does increase the potential for errors and abuse of the system. Issues of sample contamination or misrepresented identity can arise here.[200]

Recently, there has been a shift in the practice model of some DTC companies. This shift involves more interaction with medical practitioners. Some companies who previously provided their services direct to the consumer without any involvement of a medical practitioner now will only allow people to order their tests through a medical practitioner.[201] Navigenics was a notable example of this, although since its acquisition by Life Technologies it has ceased to offer DTC services. Nevertheless, its previous mode of operations can provide an illustrative example of this shift. Prior to its acquisition, Navigenics moved to a model where it allowed a person to order a test only through 'physicians, clinicians, and wellness programs'.[202] It also provided contact details for physicians who had undergone training with Navigenics and who could assist consumers in ordering a test.[203] At July 2018, Gene By Gene offered whole genome and whole exome sequencing services (at a cost of 2,895 (USD) and 1,095 (USD) respectively) to consumers to order through a physician.[204]

---

[200] Canadian College of Medical Geneticists, 'CCMG Statement on Direct-to-Consumer Genetic Testing' (2012) 81 Clin Genet 1 <https://www.ccmg-ccgm.org/documents/Policies_etc/Pos_Statements/PosStmt_EPP_DTC_FINAL_20Jan2011.pdf> last accessed 25 October 2018.

[201] Heidi Howard and Pascal Borry, 'Is there a doctor in the house? The presence of physicians in the direct-to-consumer genetic testing context' (2012) 3(2) *Journal of Community Genetics* 105–12 doi: 10.1007/s12687-011-0062-0.

[202] Navigenics, <navigenics.com/visitor/what_we_offer/how_it_works/international_orders/> accessed 2 April 2012; Navigenics, 'Our Acquisition by Life Technologies' <navigenics.com> accessed 10 December 2012

[203] Howard and Borry, 'Is there a doctor in the house? The presence of physicians in the direct-to-consumer genetic testing context' (n 199) 109; Navigenics, 'Find a Physician' <navigenics.com/visitor/about_us/find_a_physician/> accessed 5 April 2012

[204] Gene By Gene, 'Whole Exome Sequencing' <https://genebygene.com/pages/research?go

This shift in policy may not be entirely altruistic, as companies may be seeking to limit their liability. Also, as Howard and Borry point out, simply having an ordinary medical physician on the staff may provide a level of false reassurance to consumers, when in fact what is really needed to improve DTC practices in this context is the involvement of qualified clinical geneticists who are best equipped to provide counselling for consumers and explain test results and limitations.[205] An alternative approach would be to require all physicians to have further training in genetics, as many advances in current genomic sequencing technology have been made very recently and were not studied by the majority of physicians practising medicine now.[206]

This chapter has discussed the wide variety of genetic tests currently offered by the DTC industry and the issues that different types of testing raise for consumers. It has demonstrated that the DTC industry is a diverse industry that is growing rapidly with companies taking advantage of new technologies that are not necessarily ready for the market. At present, the industry is continuing to grow and is not subject to specific legal regulation. However, companies offering services to UK consumers should be complying with the provisions of the HTA, the DPA18, and the GDPR. Based on the review of companies' contracts, together with other studies,[207] it seems likely that some companies' consent mechanisms are inadequate and that some companies may be committing an offence under the HTA.

In light of this together with the concerns expressed by policymakers, it is clear that the industry does need to be monitored. At present the adequacy of consent mechanisms and the provision of sufficient information to enable informed decision-making, including sufficient information regarding the respective risks and benefits of testing, the utility and validity of tests, and overall transparency are issues that are raised by all types of DTC test.[208] It

---

to=exome-sequencing> last accessed 27 July 2018; and Gene By Gene, 'Whole Genome Sequencing' <https://genebygene.com/pages/research?goto=exome-sequencing> last accessed 27 July 2018.

[205] Howard and Borry, 'Is there a doctor in the house? The presence of physicians in the direct-to-consumer genetic testing context' (n 199) 110–11.

[206] Sara Pirzadeh-Miller, Cecelia Bellcross, Linda Robinson, and Ellen T Matloff, 'Direct-to-consumer genetic testing: Helpful, harmful, or pure entertainment?' (2011) 8(6) *Community Oncology* 263–8 doi: 10.1016/S1548-5315(12)70021-9.

[207] Lachance (n 82); Lewis et al. (n 84); Laestadius et al. (n 197); Hazel and Slobogin (n 6).

[208] Lewis et al. (n 84) 291–307; Geransar and Einsiedel (n 21); BM Knoppers, 'Consent to "personal" genomics and privacy. Direct-to-consumer genetic tests and population genome research challenge traditional notions of privacy and consent' (2010) 11 *EMBO Reports* 416–9 doi: 10.1038/embor.2010.69.

seems that most companies are not engaging in practices that are in accordance with policy recommendations, especially in the context of the provision of test results. Consumers do need to be provided with sufficient information in order to be able to understand the limitations of test results. This is especially important where companies provide disease risk tests or carrier testing.

For most types of genetic test offered by DTC companies, the results provided to consumers are probabilistic in nature. This means that their level of usefulness to the individual tested is inherently limited.[209] There is also a greater risk that there will be false positives and false negatives. Furthermore, the results and risk information provided to consumers of DTC companies are of a complex nature and it is quite possible that many consumers will have difficulty in understanding the implications of genetic test results. There are also risks associated with being falsely reassured or unnecessarily worried by such results and it is morally questionable whether allowing companies to sell consumers such tests is something that society should condone. Recent work by Edward Esplin et al[210] highlights the need for follow up testing for DTC health tests in order to confirm both positive and negative findings and confirms the conditions imposed by the FDA in its approval of 23andMe's BRCA testing. The work of Eric Giannella is relevant here. Giannella questions the idea of progress which currently dominates Silicon Valley and much of the technology industry. He suggests that '23andMe should have been a long-term research project'[211] rather than a start-up, and this idea has appeal.

[209] Nordgren (n 9); P Saukko, 'State of play in direct-to-consumer genetic testing for lifestyle-related diseases: Market, marketing content, user experiences and regulation' (2013) 72 *The Proceedings of the Nutrition Society* 53 <https://doi.org/10.1017/S0029665112002960> last accessed 18 October 2018; European Society of Human Genetics, 'Direct-to-consumer genetic tests neither accurate in their predictions nor beneficial to individuals, study suggests' *Science News* (31 May 2011) <https://www.sciencedaily.com/releases/2011/05/110530190344.htm> last accessed 25 October 2018.

[210] Julie Karow, '23andMe DTC Breast and Ovarian Cancer Risk Test Misses Almost 90 Percent of BRCA Mutation Carriers' GenomeWeb (5 April 2019) <https://www.genomeweb.com/molecular-diagnostics/23andme-dtc-breast-and-ovarian-cancer-risk-test-misses-almost-90-percent-brca#.XKfbrS1L1PU>.

[211] Eric Giannella, 'Morality and the idea of progress in Silicon Valley' *Berkeley Journal of Sociology* (14 January 2015) <http://berkeleyjournal.org/2015/01/morality-and-the-idea-of-progress-in-silicon-valley/> last accessed 25 October 2018.

In the context of DTC companies which have research divisions and market on the promises of patient-centred and participatory research, it is possible that companies could in the future operate as cooperatives and provide opportunities for profit sharing with their customers. If consumers are required to give up their privacy to some extent and this is done in the name of genetic research being a public good, then there are also possibilities for more truly collaborative research. Companies that offer testing to indigenous groups could also allow customers to decide how a share of their profits is allocated. For instance, a company could provide choices in its contracts that allow consumers to specify that their share of profits is fed back to their tribal group or community.

It is important to note that all DTC companies regardless of the type of testing they offer are united by the fact that they are commercial entities and as such, regardless of the claims made by company representatives regarding their motivations, are all to some extent driven by commercial interests. On the whole, companies strive to be profitable[212] and in the context of DTC, it is the sequenced genetic data that is the primary asset to companies and its main source of profit, as the actual sale of tests does not seem to be especially profitable.[213] As Offit has noted:

> the implicit marketing strategy of these companies is to involve the consumer in a 'voyage of genetic self-discovery,' even if some of the initial paths charted lead nowhere. In the worse-case scenario, the paths may lead to unnecessary medical interventions or false reassurances and missed diagnoses. The incentive for financial profit in such a journey is at fundamental odds with the skeptical nature of scientific inquiry and the conservative nature of clinical translation of new biomedical technologies.[214]

An illustrative example highlighting the commercial nature of DTC company endeavours is that of 23andMe's recent refusal to share data with

---

[212] David Shaywitz, 'Does 23andMe deal mean medical centers are sitting on data worth millions?' *Forbes Pharma & Healthcare* (8 January 2015) <https://www.forbes.com/sites/davidshaywitz/2015/01/08/does-23andme-deal-mean-medical-centers-are-sitting-on-data-worth-millions/> last accessed 25 October 2018; B Williams-Jones, 'Where there's a web, there's a way: Commercial genetic testing and the internet' (2003) 6 *Community Genetics* 46–57 <https://doi.org/10.1159/000069538> last accessed 25 October 2018; Offit (n 71).

[213] Aaron Krol, '23andMe Pursues Health Research in the Shadow of the FDA' *Bio IT World* (24 March 2014) <bio-itworld.com/BioIT_Article.aspx?id=136445> last accessed 25 October 2018.

[214] Offit (n 71) 1354.

Open Humans and also 23andMe has recently been valued at a market cap of $1.5 billion (USD).[215]

The research ventures of DTC companies are also valuable and the databases developed by several of the most prominent companies are being used for profit, as companies partner with pharmaceutical companies and other entities or are sold on to biomedical research companies Examples include: AncestryDNA's recent collaboration with Calico (this partnership has now ended);[216] and 23andMe's partnerships with Pfizer, Genentech and Reset Therapeutics;[217] and the sales of DeCodeMe and Navigenics. It is also possible that physical samples of DNA may also have value for companies, but the focus herein is on the sequenced data, rather than the physical sample itself and the issues raised by companies' treatment of consumers' physical samples will be explored in subsequent research.

Overall, the examination of the content of various DTC websites together with the wide variety of tests available highlights the need for greater transparency by DTC companies. This is supported by the previous studies of Lachance, Laestadius, and Lewis et al. and the more recent study by Hazel and Slobogin.[218]

---

[215] Aaron Krol, 'Open Humans aims to be the social network for science volunteerism' *Bio IT World* (9 April 2015) <http://www.bio-itworld.com/2015/4/9/open-humans-aims-social-network-science-volunteerism.html> last accessed 18 October 2018. Matthew Lynley and Katie Roof, '23andMe hits $1.5B pre-money valuation in latest huge funding round' *TechCrunch* (6 September 2017) <https://techcrunch.com/2017/09/06/23andme-hits-1-5b-pre-money-valuation-in-latest-huge-funding-round/> accessed 29 January 2019.

[216] Erin Brodwin, 'A collaboration between Google's secretive life-extension spinoff and popular genetics company Ancestry has quietly ended' *Business Insider* (1 August 2018) <http://uk.businessinsider.com/google-calico-ancestry-dna-genetics-aging-partnership-ended-2018-7?r=US&IR=T> last accessed 18 October 2018; GenomeWeb Staff Reporter, 'AncestryDNA, Calico to Collaborate on Genetics of Human Longevity' *GenomeWeb* (21 July 2015) <https://www.genomeweb.com/business-news/ancestrydna-calico-collaborate-genetics-human-longevity> last accessed 24 October 2018.

[217] Lagorio-Chafkin (n 13); The Associated Press, 'Pfizer, 23andMe team up to study bowel disease' *Medical Xpress* (12 August 2014) <https://medicalxpress.com/news/2014-08-pfizer-23andme-team-bowel-disease.html> last accessed 24 October 2018; Andrew Ward, 'Google-backed genetic testing company hires veteran scientist' *The Financial Times* (12 March 2015) <https://www.ft.com/content/ead07e84-c8d8-11e4-bc64-00144feab7de> last accessed 24 October 2018; Sullivan (n 13).

[218] Lachance (n 82); Lewis et al. (n 84); Laestadius et al. (n 197); Hazel and Slobogin (n 6).

4

Privacy, Data Protection and Security in the Context of Direct-to-Consumer Genetic Testing Services

4.1 Introduction

The nature of the DTC industry as providers of genetic tests means that privacy and data protection law have relevance to industry governance. As with many other digital service providers, security is also a significant issue here. At present, the European Union is undergoing a time of transition with the implementation of the General Data Protection Regulation (GDPR).[1] Although the UK is also undergoing a broader period of transition with Brexit, the Data Protection Act 2018 (DPA18) transposes the GDPR into the UK's national law. As DTC companies collect genetic data, as well as other types of personal data, which they often use in ongoing research, companies should be complying with the GDPR and applicable data protection law in EU Member States and also other countries that have similar law.

This chapter provides a broad overview of privacy, data protection and security issues raised by DTC services. The aim here is to provide an introduction to a complex area and provide some suggestions for how industry practices and governance could be improved. In the context of privacy policies and notices, it is important to recognise that these documents are often linked with wrap contracts on DTC websites. This is often done through incorporation of terms by reference and for an individual to understand their legal rights in this context, they should really be reading all of these documents. This is problematic, as a number of studies have demonstrated

---

[1] Council Regulation (EU) 2016/679 of 27 April 2016 on the protection of natural persons with regard to the processing of personal data and on the free movement of such data, and repealing Directive 95/46/EC (General Data Protection Regulation) [2016] OJ 2 119/1 <http://eur-lex.europa.eu/legal-content/EN/TXT/?qid=1525272154893&uri=CELEX:32016R0679> last accessed 29 July 2018.

in relation to privacy policies and contracts more generally that consumers are not reading these. One example of this, from 2017, is the work of the Australian consumer advocacy group CHOICE, which examined the privacy policies and contracts of e-readers. They found that Amazon's Kindle contained at least 8 documents in total, which together exceeded 73,000 words,[2] approaching the length of this book. They also hired an actor to read all the documents aloud and this was posted on YouTube in 'nine hour-long instalments'.[3]

We do face a challenge here in that many businesses generally argue that much of what is put in their contracts has to be there. While this is true to a certain degree, it neglects to take into account properly the requirements of consumer protection law and data protection law. Throughout this book, the aim is to highlight the need for doing better in this regard and the need for thinking about compliance in new ways. A further aim is to suggest that governance of DTC and other new technologies should not be looked at in a vacuum. Currently there is not merely one area of law that has relevance to regulating DTC, but several. Companies need to be careful here and think about not only data protection, but also consumer protection, contract and medical devices legislation, as well as human rights.

(a) What is Privacy?

Privacy as an interest differs from confidentiality. There is continuing debate over how to define privacy, but a useful definition is that of Clarke, which suggests that 'Privacy is the interest that individuals have in sustaining a "personal space", free from interference by other people and organisations.'[4] Privacy interests can depend on context and privacy can be viewed as multidimensional. The main dimensions can be described as: 'privacy of the person'; 'privacy of personal behaviour'; 'privacy of personal communications'; and 'privacy of personal data'.[5] With the advances in information technology and the growth in use of the Internet for a variety of purposes,

---

[2] Elle Hunt, 'Amazon Kindle's terms "unreasonable" and would take nine hours to read, Choice says' *The Guardian* (15 March 2017) <https://www.theguardian.com/australia-news/2017/mar/15/amazon-kindles-terms-unreasonable-and-would-take-nine-hours-to-read-choice-says> last accessed 18 October 2018; CHOICE, 'Nine hours of "conditions apply"' <https://www.choice.com.au/about-us/media-releases/2017/march/nine-hours-of-conditions-apply> last accessed 18 October 2018.

[3] Ibid.; The videos are available here: <https://www.youtube.com/watch?v=6QZml7sPbVU&feature=youtu.be> last accessed 24 October 2018.

[4] Roger Clarke, 'Introduction to dataveillance and information privacy, and definitions of terms' <http://rogerclarke.com/DV/Intro.html#Intro> last accessed 18 October 2018.

[5] Ibid.

the final two dimensions are often linked and can be viewed together under the term "informational privacy".[6] The Nuffield Council's description, which resembles Clarke's, is also useful. They note that privacy:

> concerns the interest people have in others' access to themselves, their homes and property, or to information about them. What counts as 'private' can change depending on social norms, the specific context, and the relationship between the person concerned and those who might enjoy access. Informational privacy is maintained by selectively withholding or allowing access or through establishing limits on acceptable behaviour by others (e.g. proscribing voyeurism).[7]

Given the nature of DTC services, the interest that is most relevant here is informational privacy. Informational privacy can be described as 'the interest of individuals in exercising control over access to information about themselves'.[8] Clarke suggests that 'information privacy is the interest an individual has in controlling, or at least significantly influencing, the handling of data about themselves'.[9]

Due to certain aspects of the nature of genetic information, privacy is an important issue in the context of DTC and this has been stressed in the ESHG's Statement and the HGC's Principles. Genetic information can serve as a unique identifier for an individual. It can also be used both in genealogical research and criminal investigations to identify related individuals.[10] As DNA does not change in a way that would make the information non-identifiable over time, stored sequenced data does pose some level of risk to an individual's privacy. Previously, researchers often relied on a variety of techniques of anonymisation, de-identification or pseudonymisation, which generally involve the removal of identifying information or aggregation of individual

---

[6] Ibid.; also see generally G Laurie, *Genetic Privacy: A Challenge to Medico-Legal Norms* (reprint edn, Cambridge University Press 2002).

[7] Nuffield Council on Bioethics, *The Collection, Linking and Use of Data in Biomedical Research and Health Care: Ethical Issues* (Nuffield Council on Bioethics, February 2015) 4 <http://nuffieldbioethics.org/wp-content/uploads/Biodata-a-guide-to-the-report-PDF.pdf> last accessed 24 October 2018.

[8] Jeroen van den Hoven et al., 'Privacy and information technology' in Edward N Zalta (ed.), *The Stanford Encyclopedia of Philosophy* (Winter edn, first published 20 November 2014) <https://plato.stanford.edu/archives/win2014/entries/it-privacy/accessed> 10 June 2015 – last accessed 24 October 2018.

[9] Clarke (n 4).

[10] Tania Simoncelli, 'Dangerous excursions: The case against expanding forensic DNA databases to innocent persons' (2006) 34(2) *Journal of Law, Medicine and Ethics* 390–7 <https://doi.org/10.1111/j.1748-720X.2006.00045.x> last accessed 24 October 2018.

data into larger datasets.[11] However, as will be mentioned in the next section, it has become apparent that it may not be possible to truly anonymise genomic data in a way that prevents re-identification of individuals. This has consequences not only for the individual to whom the genetic data pertains, but also for their family. Given the nature of genetic data, when one family member undergoes genetic testing it will necessarily reveal information about others.[12]

Other types of personal information do not automatically have this implication and thus some scholars such as Woodage have advocated for a change of approach in this context. For Woodage, the nature of genetic information means that it cannot in fact be kept private and so he argues that there is a need to educate people 'about the ways genetic information can be used and misused', to strengthen protections against the misuse of such information and to create legislation which allows individuals 'access to their own genetic records and to know who else has access to the information'.[13] Others have suggested the need for improved cryptographic techniques.[14]

(b) Genetic Privacy

Genetic privacy is an important issue in this context and it is likely that existing data protection law could be used to regulate DTC companies' use, sharing, storage and processing of genetic data. Several policymakers have stressed the importance of adequate privacy protection in this context and, at present, there is a need for companies to improve both their policies and practices regarding protection of the privacy rights of consumers in their genetic data.

As discussed in Chapter 3, providers of DTC genetic tests offer a wide variety of services. Regardless of the type of test though, it is important to recognise that genetic data can both serve as a unique identifier for an individual and be used to identify family members. Furthermore, while in the past it was thought that anonymisation and de-identification techniques might help to minimise privacy risks in this context, there is growing recognition

---

[11] Nuffield Council on Bioethics, *The Collection, Linking and Use of Data in Biomedical Research and Health Care: Ethical Issues* (Nuffield Council on Bioethics, February 2015) 6 <http://nuffieldbioethics.org/wp-content/uploads/Biodata-a-guide-to-the-report-PDF.pdf>.

[12] Ibid. 123.

[13] Trevor Woodage, 'Relative futility: Limits to genetic privacy protection because of the inability to prevent disclosure of genetic information by relatives' (2010) 95 *Minnesota Law Review* 682–713, 684.

[14] M Naveed et al., 'Privacy and security in the genomic era' (2014) arXiv:1405.1891v3 <https://arxiv.org/abs/1405.1891> last accessed 22 October 2018.

that it is not really possible to de-identify genetic data in a way that would make it impossible to re-identify an individual.[15] There have been several recent efforts by researchers which have demonstrated that it is possible to re-identify research participants in large genetic studies. Good examples are the work by Gymrek et al.[16] and Erlich and Narayanan.[17] It has even been demonstrated that identification is possible through reliance on research statistics.[18] This means that the risk of a data leak does not necessarily decrease over time.[19] As Ayday et al. note, due to the shared nature of genetic data, potential data leakage is not a matter that will only affect the individual concerned, but also their family. Genetic data stored in DTC databases if leaked could actually have an impact upon a large family group.

Protection of genetic privacy in the UK largely derives from data protection legislation and a person's interest generally can be seen as a right concerned with informational privacy. In relation to possible issues arising in the context of informational privacy more generally, Taylor notes that the areas of concern can be divided 'into two categories: those associated with unwanted access and those associated with unwanted uses of data'.[20] Given the diverse uses to which genetic information can be put and the trend of DTC companies to in fact make broad use of the information collected from their consumers, it is desirable that data protection law is applied to regulate the industry in a similar way to its use in regulating health research.

At present, the industry lacks harmonised standards as well and it is possible to obtain contradictory results for tests from different health test providers.[21] This is due to a number of factors. Scientific understanding of

---

[15] See for example, Nuffield Council on Bioethics, *The Collection, Linking and Use of Data* (n 7) 69–71.

[16] M Gymrek et al., 'Identifying personal genomes by surname inference' (2013) 339(6117) *Science* 321–4 doi:10.1126/science.1229566.

[17] Yaniv Erlich and Arvind Narayanan, 'Routes for breaching and protecting genetic privacy' (2014) 15 *Nature Reviews Genetics* 409–21.

[18] R Wang, Y Li, XF Wang, H Tang, and X Zhou 'Learning your identity and disease from research papers: Information leaks in genome wide association study' in Proceedings of the 16th ACM Conference on Computer and Communications Security, 534–44 (ACM 2009) <https://www.cs.indiana.edu/pub/techreports/TR680.pdf> last accessed 23 October 2018.

[19] E Ayday, E De Cristofaro, J-P Hubaux, and G Tsudik, 'Whole genome sequencing: Revolutionary medicine or privacy nightmare?' (2015) 48(2) *Computer* 58–66, 62 doi: 10.1109/MC.2015.59.

[20] Mark Taylor, Genetic Data and the Law: A Critical Perspective on Privacy Protection (Cambridge University Press 2012) vol. 16, 2.

[21] US Government Accountability Office, (GAO) Direct-To-Consumer Genetic Tests: Misleading Test Results Are Further Complicated by Deceptive Marketing and Other

how genes function and their association with human health is still developing and tests for many complex diseases have not yet been standardised. Understanding of how epigenetic factors contribute to health is also continuing to develop and there is also growing interest in the impact of the microbiome on human health. Also, some tests offered by DTC companies have not been validated and may have limited use. Most DTC companies are currently not offering services that sequence a whole genome or whole exome and have tended to focus on targeting single nucleotide polymorphisms (SNPs). Furthermore, DTC companies frame their populations in their databases differently.[22] Recent research has also demonstrated that there is a relatively high incidence of false positives in genetic test results provided by DTC companies.[23] It should be noted, though, that it is also possible to obtain different ethnicity estimates from ancestry test providers and also that certain groups, such as indigenous peoples, are underrepresented even in the largest DTC databases.[24] More informational and educational resources are needed to assist consumers in understanding what their individual test results mean for them and to support them to make informed decisions in this context.

Consumers and companies also need to be aware that genetic data collected for one purpose may be used for a wide range of secondary purposes.

Questionable Practice (GAO-10-847T, 2010) Testimony before the Subcommittee on Oversight and Investigations, Committee on Energy and Commerce, House of Representatives 1–8 <http://www.gao.gov/assets/130/125079.pdf> last accessed 24 October 2018; Jessica Cussins, 'Direct-to-consumer genetic tests should come with a health warning' *The Pharmaceutical Journal* (15 January 2015) <https://www.pharmaceutical-journal.com/opinion/comment/direct-to-consumer-genetic-tests-should-come-with-a-health-warning/20067564.article?firstPass=false> last accessed 23 October 2018; Nuffield Council, 'Medical profiling and online medicine: The ethics of 'personalised healthcare' in a consumer age, Nuffield Council on Bioethics (2010) <http://nuffieldbioethics.org/wp-content/uploads/2014/07/Medical-profiling-and-online-medicine-the-ethics-of-personalised-healthcare-in-a-consumer-age-Web-version-reduced.pdf> last accessed 24 October 2018.

22 Andelka M Phillips, 'Only a click away – DTC genetics for ancestry, health, love . . . and more: A view of the business and regulatory landscape' (2016) 8 *Applied & Translational Genomics* 16–22, 17–18 <https://doi.org/10.1016/j.atg.2016.01.001>.

23 Stephany Tandy-Connor, Jenna Guiltinan, Kate Krempely, Patrick Reineke, Stephanie Gutirrez, Philip Gray, and Brigette Tippin Davis, 'False-positive results released by direct-to-consumer genetic tests highlight the importance of clinical confirmation testing for appropriate patient care' (2018) *Genetics in Medicine* doi: doi:10.1038/gim.2018.38 <https://www.nature.com/articles/gim201838> last accessed 24 October 2018.

24 Kristin V Brown, 'How DNA testing botched my family's heritage, and probably yours, too' GIZMODO (16 January 2018) <https://gizmodo.com/how-dna-testing-botched-my-familys-heritage-and-probab-1820932637> last accessed 24 October 2018; Phillips, 'Only a click away' (n 22) 18.

The most prominent DTC companies are engaged in research using consumer data and have also begun to enter into partnerships with other entities. For example, 23andMe has entered into partnerships with at least 14 entities, most notably Pfizer, Genentech, and Reset Therapeutics, while Gene By Gene's FamilyTreeDNA has also acquired DNA Heritage and DNA-Fingerprint, and MyHeritage has partnered with both FamilyTreeDNA and 23andMe.[25] 23andMe has also started a pharmaceutical branch[26] and it also purchased CureTogether in 2012.[27] The activities of another company, Prenetics, highlight the potential links, which genetic testing companies can have with insurance companies. Prenetics aims to offer pharmacogenetic tests to Chinese customers, but it has received significant investment from Ping An, an insurance company based in China with 200 million policy-holders.[28] More recently it has emerged that another American DTC company, the Boston-based Orig3n, has also entered into a partnership with a Chinese insurance company, ZhongAn Online P&C Insurance Co. Ltd. Through this arrangement, ZhongAn will provide a range of genetic testing services to its customer base of 500 million people and the wider Chinese market.[29]

[25] M Sullivan, '23andMe has signed 12 other genetic data partnerships beyond Pfizer and Genentech' *VentureBeat* (14 January 2015) <https://venturebeat.com/2015/01/14/23andme-has-signed-12-other-genetic-data-partnerships-beyond-pfizer-and-genentech/> last accessed 17 August 2018.

[26] Arielle Duhaime-Ross, '23andMe plans to move beyond genetic testing to making drugs' *The Verge* (12 March 2015) <https://www.theverge.com/2015/3/12/8199303/23andme-drug-development-testing> last accessed 24 October 2018; GenomeWeb staff reporter, '23andMe launches therapeutics group with former Genentech exec at helm' *GenomeWeb* (12 March 2015) <https://www.genomeweb.com/drug-discovery-development/23andme-launches-therapeutics-group-former-genentech-exec-helm> last accessed 24 October 2018.

[27] Allison Proffitt, 'Deals center on self-reported patient data services' (2012) 30 *Nature Biotechnology* 1016; 23andMe, '23andMe acquires CureTogether, Inc' (23andMe, Press Release, 10 July 2012), <https://mediacenter.23andme.com/press-releases/23andme-acquires-curetogether-inc/> last accessed 24 October 2018 – archived content available at <https://web.archive.org/web/20130119091334/http://mediacenter.23andme.com/press-releases/> last accessed 24 October 2018.

[28] Alice Woodhouse, 'iGene: Hong Kong biotech start-up Prenetics bringing 48-hour DNA tests to broader Chinese market for safer prescriptions' *South China Morning Post* (4 April 2016) <http://www.scmp.com/tech/science-research/article/1932838/igene-hong-kong-biotech-start-prenetics-bringing-48-hour-dna> last accessed 24 October 2018.

[29] Samantha Hurst, 'Chinese E-Insurer Zhong An has teamed up with biotech company Orig3n For Health Tech Solutions' Crowdfund Insider (2 August 2018) <https://www.crowdfundinsider.com/2018/08/137259-chinese-e-insurer-zhongan-has-teamed-up-with-biotech-company-orig3n-for-health-tech-solutions/> last accessed 24 October 2018.

4.2 General Data Protection Regulation (GDPR)

The GDPR came into force on 25 May 2018. It has direct effect in all EU Member States and so businesses that deal with personal data should be complying with this law. The GDPR seeks to harmonise data protection law across the EU and also to strengthen rights for individuals (data subjects) in their personal data. Specifically, the GDPR provides data subjects with a number of rights, including: right of access; right to have inaccuracies corrected; right to have personal data erased (right to be forgotten); right to object to direct marketing; right to data portability; right to restrict processing of their information; and right to transparency. Although the legislation has direct effect, data protection law in European Member States will continue to be in a period of transition for some time to come, as a number of States are in the process of amending their data protection law. Also, as it is possible to make some derogations, the law in Member States will vary.

As DTC companies offer genetic testing services, depending on the circumstances, DTC companies may qualify as both data processors and data controllers. Article 4(7) defines a 'controller' as:

> the natural or legal person, public authority, agency or other body which, alone or jointly with others, determines the purposes and means of the processing of personal data; where the purposes and means of such processing are determined by Union or Member State law, the controller or the specific criteria for its nomination may be provided for by Union or Member State law.

Article 4(8) defines 'processor' as 'a natural or legal person, public authority, agency or other body which processes personal data on behalf of the controller'.

Genetic information is defined in Article 4(13) of the GDPR, but it is also included within the definition of 'personal data' in Article 4(1). Consequently, as DTC companies collect and process genetic data and often collect other types of personal data as well, they should be complying with the GDPR.

GDPR consent requirements

Given that DTC companies collect and process genetic data and other personal data, where they are offering services to EU and UK consumers they should be complying with the consent requirements set out in Article 4(11). This states that:

'consent' of the data subject means any freely given, specific, informed and unambiguous indication of the data subject's wishes by which he or she, by a statement or by a clear affirmative action, signifies agreement to the processing of personal data relating to him or her.

Genetic data is also included in the prohibition on processing of special categories of personal data set out in Article 9. There are two relevant exceptions set out in Article 9(2). These are: (a) 'explicit consent' of data subject; and (j) the so-called research exemption.

It should be stressed that this is quite a high standard for consent and this may prove challenging for many industries, but given the nature of DTC services, DTC companies should give considerable thought to improving their consent processes. As Article 7 of the GDPR imposes a number of conditions and this includes in Article 7(3) that the 'data subject shall have the right to withdraw his or her consent at any time' provision should be made to accommodate this. This could be done in interface design and companies should also consider having more privacy friendly options. This could include the option to delete genetic data and other personal data as well as to destroy the physical DNA sample after returning tests results to consumers.

As the DTC industry also offers such a diverse range of tests, there will also be issues around the adequacy of consent and who has capacity to consent in the context of particular types of test. For example, a number of policy documents have recommended that DTC services should not be offered to children. In 2018, the AAP reaffirmed its previous 2013 Policy Statement on DTC and advised that DTC tests should not be performed on newborns.[30]

Furthermore, in relation to children the GDPR provides for enhanced protection of children's rights in their personal data. Article 8 sets out conditions in relation to a child's consent in the context of information society

---

[30] 'Not for the littlest' *GenomeWeb* (24 October 2018) <https://www.genomeweb.com/scan/not-littlest> last accessed 27 October 2018 – this cites Alyson Sulaski Wyckoff, 'Lack of reliability, privacy plague DTC genetic tests for newborns' *AAP News* (24 October 2018) <http://www.aappublications.org/news/2018/10/24/genetictesting 102418> last accessed 27 October 2018; this cites Committee On Bioethics, Committee On Genetics, American College Of Medical Genetics and Genomics Social, Ethical, and Legal Issues Committee, 'Ethical and Policy Issues in Genetic Testing and Screening of Children' (2013) 131(3) from the American Academy of Pediatrics Policy Statement – a statement of reaffirmation for this policy was published at e20181836 <http://pediatrics.aappublications.org/content/131/3/620.short> last accessed 27 October 2018.

services. Specifically, in relation to children's consent, it refers to Article 6, which sets out the conditions for lawful processing of data. Article 6(1)(a) allows for lawful processing where the data subject has given their consent. Under Article 8, if Article 6(1)(a):

> applies in relation to the offer of information society services directly to a child, the processing of the personal data of a child shall be lawful where the child is at least 16 years old. Where the child is below the age of 16 years, such processing shall be lawful only if and to the extent that consent is given or authorized by the holder of parental responsibility over the child.
>
> Member States may provide by law for a lower age for those purposes provided that such lower age is not below 13 years.

The UK has lowered the age of consent to 13.[31]

Three recitals are particularly significant here: recitals 38, 40 and 75. Recital 38 provides that:

> Children merit specific protection with regard to their personal data, as they may be less aware of the risks, consequences and safeguards concerned and their rights in relation to the processing of personal data. Such specific protection should, in particular, apply to the use of personal data of children for the purposes of marketing or creating personality or user profiles and the collection of personal data with regard to children when using services offered directly to a child. The consent of the holder of parental responsibility should not be necessary in the context of preventive or counselling services offered directly to a child.

Meanwhile, recital 75 indicates that children should be considered as 'vulnerable natural persons'[32] and recital 40 requires revelant regulatory bodies to create codes of conduct in relation to parental consent.

It has been suggested that it may be possible for DTC companies to take advantage of the research exemption.[33] However, it is submitted that even if this were the case, companies will still need to comply with the consent

---

[31] ICO, Children <https://ico.org.uk/for-organisations/guide-to-the-general-data-protection-regulation-gdpr/applications/children/> last accessed 31 October 2018.

[32] Also see Bird and Bird, 'Guide to GDPR for children' <https://www.twobirds.com/~/media/pdfs/gdpr-pdfs/24--guide-to-the-gdpr--children.pdf?la=en> last accessed 31 October 2018.

[33] Kärt Pormeister, 'Genetic data and the research exemption: Is the GDPR going too far?' (2017) 7(2) International Data Privacy Law 137–146, 145 <https://doi.org/10.1093/idpl/ipx006> last accessed 24 October 2018.

requirements for the initial test and given the commercial nature of DTC companies, it seems likely that they may also need to obtain additional consent for their research activities.

(a) Principles in Relation to the Processing of Personal Data

Article 5 has also has relevance here, as it sets out Principles in relation to the processing of personal data.

Article 5: Principles most relevant for the provision of DTC services

(a) the 'lawfulness, fairness, and transparency' requirement for processing of personal data, which in this context would include both genetic data and other forms of personal data collected in the context of the provision of DTC services

(b) the 'purpose limitation', which requires that personal data be 'collected for specified, explicit and legitimate purposes'

(c) the 'data minimization' principle which requires that personal data collection should be 'adequate, relevant and limited to what is necessary in relation to the purposes for which they are processed'

(e) the 'storage limitation principle', which requires that personal data be 'kept in a form which permits identification of data subjects for no longer than is necessary for the purposes for which the personal data are processed'

(f) the 'integrity and confidentiality' principle, which requires that personal data be 'processed in a manner that ensures appropriate security of the personal data, including protection against unauthorised or unlawful processing and against accidental loss, destruction or damage, using appropriate technical or organisational measures'

In line with these principles, DTC companies and other similar businesses should consider carefully what data is actually necessary for their purposes and where data is to be used in secondary research they should address the need for additional consent. Where possible they should also allow for the possibility of an individual withdrawing their consent to participation in research activities. It may be helpful for businesses to look to models introduced in academic research projects, such as the dynamic consent project.[34]

---

[34] Jane Kaye et al., 'Dynamic consent: A patient interface for twenty-first century research networks' (2015) 23 *European Journal of Human Genetics* 141–46 <https://www.nature.com/articles/ejhg201471> last accessed 22 October 2018.

It may also be useful to consider the use of short summary notices and summary contracts in this context,[35] which could highlight the most significant aspects of data use.

The GDPR also provides for significant penalties for those who infringe its provisions. These are set out in Chapter VIII and Article 83 deals specifically with administrative fines. Significantly, penalties under article 83(5) can result in the organisation involved facing a fine of 20 million euros or up to 4 per cent of the business's 'total worldwide turnover, whichever is higher'. Such a fine can be imposed for a variety of infringements. These are set out in Article 83; the most relevant provisions are listed in 83(5):

(a)   the basic principles for processing, including for consent, pursuant to Articles 5, 6, 7, and 9

(b)   the data subjects' rights pursuant to Articles 12 to 22

(c)   the transfers of personal data to a recipient in a third country or an international organisation pursuant to Articles 44 to 49

(d)   any obligations pursuant to Member State law adopted under Chapter IX

Data controllers and processors can also face fines of up to 10 million euros or '2% of total worldwide turnover, whichever is higher' under Article 83(4) if they fail to meet their obligations under Articles 8, 11, 25, 39, 42 and 43.

DTC companies have a lot in common with companies that produce wearable devices, such as fitness bands and smart watches. Unfortunately, as with a number of other IoT devices, products are often coming to market with security vulnerabilities and the studies by the NCC, HPE Fortify, Citizen Lab and Open Effect[36] have highlighted a number of security flaws

---

[35] Andelka M Phillips, 'Reading the fine print when buying your genetic self online: Direct-to-consumer genetic testing terms and conditions' (2017) *New Genetics and Society* 36(3) 273–95, 285–6 <http://dx.doi.org/10.1080/14636778.2017.1352468>; NS Good, J Grossklags, DK Mulligan, and JA Konstan, 'Noticing Notice: A Large-scale Experiment on the Timing of Software License Agreements' in Proceedings of the SIGCHI Conference on Human Factors in Computing Systems ACM (San Jose, California 2007) 607–16 <http://people.ischool.berkeley.edu/~jensg/research/paper/Grossklags07-CHI-noticing_notice.pdf> last accessed 24 October 2018.

[36] Andrew Hilts, Christopher Parsons, and Jeffrey Knockel, *Every Step You Fake: A Comparative Analysis of Fitness Tracker Privacy and Security* (Open Effect Report 2016) <https://citizenlab.org/2016/02/fitness-tracker-privacy-and-security/> last accessed 24 October 2018; HPE Fortify, *Internet of Things Security Study: Smartwatches* (2015) <https://www.ftc.gov/system/files/documents/public_comments/2015/10/00050-98093.pdf>

in these devices. This highlights the importance of thinking about security infrastructure early on for any company offering new services that are data driven, bearing in mind the penalties set by the GDPR.

4.3 The UK's Data Protection Legislation

Although the UK is undergoing a period of uncertainty in relation to Brexit, it has enacted new data protection legislation in the form of the Data Protection Act 2018 (DPA18), which came into force on the same day as the GDPR (25 May 2018). The DPA18 replaces the previous Data Protection Act 1998. The new Act governs the use and processing of personal data and sensitive personal data and the Information Commissioner's Office (ICO) remains the regulatory body responsible for enforcing the Act. Regardless of what happens with Brexit, as the GDPR has already been passed and has direct effect across all the Member States, companies marketing to UK consumers still need to comply with the GDPR. The GDPR does allow for Member States to 'make provisions for how it applies in their country'[37] and it is the DPA18 which does this. The DPA18 also transposes the GDPR into the UK's domestic law. Consequently, businesses need to comply with both the provisions of the GDPR and the DPA18. For present purposes, it should be noted that genetic data is treated under the DPA18 in a similar way to the GDPR and specifically, that processing of sensitive data includes the processing of genetic data under section 86(7)(b). This is also in accordance with the previous UK legislation and in its Framework of Principles, the HGC also classed genetic information as sensitive personal information.

---

last accessed 24 October 2018; HP, 'HP Study Reveals Smartwatches Vulnerable to Attack' *HP News Advisory* (22 July 2015) <http://www8.hp.com/us/en/hp-news/press-release.html?id=2037386#.W3ahQS2ZPUo> last accessed 24 October 2018; HP, 'HP Study Reveals 70 Percent of Internet of Things Devices Vulnerable to Attack' (29 July 2014) <http://www8.hp.com/us/en/hp-news/press-release.html?id=1744676#.W3ag 5i2ZPUo> last accessed 24 October 2018; Norwegian Consumer Council, *Consumer protection in Fitness wearables* (NCC, November 2016) <http://www.sverigeskonsumenter.se/Documents/Rapporter/Consumer%20protection%20in%20fitness%20wearables.pdf> last accessed 24 October 2018; Norwegian Consumer Council, *#WatchOut Analysis of smartwatches for children* (NCC, October 2017) <https://fil.forbrukerradet.no/wp-content/uploads/2017/10/watchout-rapport-october-2017.pdf> last accessed 24 October 2018.

[37] ICO, 'Data Protection Act 2018' <https://ico.org.uk/for-organisations/data-protection-act-2018/> last accessed 1 August 2018; the ICO has also released an 'Introduction to the Data Protection Bill' <https://ico.org.uk/media/for-organisations/documents/2258303/ico-introduction-to-the-data-protection-bill.pdf> and guidance on the GDPR, see ICO, 'Guide to the General Data Protection Regulation (GDPR)' <https://ico.org.uk/for-organisations/guide-to-the-general-data-protection-regulation-gdpr/> last accessed 24 October 2018.

In its Opinion 03/2012 on developments in biometric technologies, the Article 29 Data Protection Working Party (Working Party) raised a number of concerns in the context of the use of DNA. Regarding linkability, it stated:

> Given the amount and variety of information that can be derived from DNA sequencing, DNA provides high potential for misuse as the extracted data can be easily linked with other databases allowing profiling of the individual. A familial search also allows creating links with relatives.[38]

It also highlighted the need for appropriate consent and transparency, the potential for repurposing data, and suggested that DNA counted as sensitive data.[39] The Opinion recommends undertaking Privacy Impact Assessments for a variety of biometric technologies, including DNA tests, and its guidance could be drawn upon for Privacy Impact Assessments involving DTC companies.[40] The HGC and the ESHG have also stressed the importance of protecting privacy in the DTC context.

A comparison can also be made between DTC companies and cloud computing service providers, as the DTC industry's use of wrap contracts raises similar issues to those of cloud computing.[41] The European Data Protection Supervisor and the Working Party have both released opinions on cloud computing.[42] The Working Party's report highlighted the lack of transparency and chain of accountability in cloud computing contracts.[43] In 2015, the Working Party released a further opinion on 'the Data Protection Code

---

[38] Article 29 Data Protection Working Party, Opinion 03/2012 on developments in biometric technologies (27 April 2012) para. 4.4.5, 26–7 <https://ec.europa.eu/justice/article-29/documentation/opinion-recommendation/files/2012/wp193_en.pdf> last accessed 18 October 2018.

[39] Ibid. 26–7, para. 4.4.5. DNA.

[40] Ibid. (n 38) para. 5.3.

[41] K McGillivray, 'Conflicts in the cloud: Contracts and compliance with data protection law in the EU' (2014) 17 *Tulane Journal of Technology and Intellectual Property* 217.

[42] Ibid. – citing Article 29 Data Protection Working Party, Opinion 05/2012 on Cloud Computing, European Commission 27 (1 July 2012) <http://ec.europa.eu/justice/data-protection/article-29/documentation/opinion-recommendation/files/2012/wp196_en.pdf> last accessed 12 May 2016 – archived content is now accessible at <https://ec.europa.eu/justice/article-29/documentation/index_en.htm> last accessed 24 October 2018; and Peter Hustinx, Opinion of the European Data Protection Supervisor on the Commission's Communication on 'Unleashing the Potential of Cloud Computing in Europe' European Data Protection Supervisor 4 (16 November 2012) <https://secure.edps.europa.eu/EDPSWEB/webdav/shared/Documents/Consultation/Opinions/2012/12-11-16_Cloud_Computing_EN.pdf> last accessed 24 October 2018.

[43] Ibid. – citing Article 29 Data Protection Working Party, Opinion 05/2012 on Cloud Computing, European Commission 27 (1 July 2012) 6, 8.

of Conduct for Cloud Service Providers [. . .] drafted by the Cloud Select Industry Group (C-SIG), a working group composed of representatives of the industry'.[44] Significantly for present purposes, the 2015 Opinion sought to assess whether the Code addressed the following matters:

1. liability: the Code must prevent the adoption of terms of service that unduly limit obligations and responsibilities. The Code must specify (in an Annex) when the CSP is a co-controller, a controller or a processor, and allocate liabilities

2. transparency on the location(s) of the data processing

3. processing of special categories and sensitive data (such as financial or health data);

4. applicability of the European definition of personal data requirements for international transfers and law enforcement access requests

5. security measures and the level of detail on those measures[45]

It is suggested that one way forward for improved industry governance is the creation of a code of conduct and such a code should take into account these matters.

(a) Data Security and Personal Data Breaches

The GDPR defines a personal data breach in article 4(12) as: 'a breach of security leading to the accidental or unlawful destruction, loss, alteration, unauthorised disclosure of, or access to, personal data transmitted, stored or otherwise processed'. Article 33 of the GDPR makes it mandatory to report personal data breaches to the relevant supervisory bodies, 'unless the personal data breach is unlikely to result in a risk to the rights and freedoms of natural persons'. Section 67 of the UK's DPA18 is substantively the same in effect.

Article 34 requires the reporting of data breaches to the data subjects affected. Section 68 of the UK's DPA18 is also substantively the same in effect. It requires notification of data subjects of a personal data breach, where the 'breach is likely to result in a high risk to the rights and freedoms of individuals'.

---

[44] Article 29 Data Protection Working Party, Opinion 02/2015 on C-SIG Code of Conduct on Cloud Computing (22 September 2015) <http://ec.europa.eu/justice/data-protect ion/article-29/documentation/opinion-recommendation/files/2015/wp232_en.pdf> last accessed 29 May 2016 – archived content now available at <https://ec.europa.eu/ justice/article-29/documentation/opinion-recommendation/files/2015/wp232_en.pdf> last accessed 24 October 2018.

[45] Ibid. (n 44) Opinion 02/2015 on C-SIG Code of Conduct on Cloud Computing, 'Summary' 2.

Under the GDPR, organisations can face significant penalties for a number of matters, including data breaches. In 2018, there have been revelations of two data breaches at DTC companies,[46] namely MyHeritage and AncestryDNA.[47] Given the nature of their services and the requirements of the GDPR in relation to data breaches, the DTC industry does need to consider its security infrastructure. Businesses of all types are vulnerable to security breaches and many products, particularly developments in the IoT, have been shown to have security vulnerabilities.[48] Given the recent occurrence of mega breaches, such as that of Equifax and Yahoo,[49] this is likely to be a very significant issue for businesses in future. It has now also been demonstrated that it is possible to infect DNA with malware, which may pose other challenges for companies dealing with genetic data in the future.[50] It is important to remember here that an individual's stored genetic data cannot be changed in the way we might reset a bank password and so taking a proactive stance on ensuring high security standards is vital for DTC companies if they wish to retain consumer trust.

[46] Deven Coldewey, 'MyHeritage breach exposes 92M emails and hashed passwords' *TechCrunch* (5 June 2018) <https://techcrunch.com/2018/06/05/myheritage-breach-exposes-92m-emails-and-hashed-passwords/?guccounter=1> last accessed 24 October 2018; Ancestry, 'RootsWeb Security Update' (23 December 2017) <https://blogs.ancestry.com/ancestry/2017/12/23/rootsweb-security-update/> last accessed 24 October 2018; Francis Navarro, 'Ancestry.com suffers big data leak – 300,000 user credentials exposed' Komando (28 December 2017) <https://www.komando.com/happening-now/435921/ancestry-com-suffers-big-data-leak-300000-user-credentials-exposed> last accessed 24 October 2018; Angela Chen, 'Why a DNA data breach is much worse than a credit card leak' *The Verge* (6 June 2018) <https://www.theverge.com/2018/6/6/17435166/myheritage-dna-breach-genetic-privacy-bioethics> last accessed 24 October 2018.

[47] Ibid. Coldewey; and Navarro.

[48] See for example, Andrew Hilts et al., *Every Step You Fake: A Comparative Analysis of Fitness Tracker Privacy and Security* (n 36); and NCC, *Consumer Protection in Fitness wearables* (n 36); and NCC, *#WatchOut Analysis of Smartwatches for Children* (n 36).

[49] Nick Clements, 'Equifax's enormous data breach just got even bigger' *Forbes* (5 March 2018) <https://www.forbes.com/sites/nickclements/2018/03/05/equifaxs-enormous-data-breach-just-got-even-bigger/#5ded590d53bc> last accessed 24 October 2018; Nicole Perlroth, 'Yahoo breach found to affect all 3 billion' *The New York Times* (New York, 3 October 2017) <https://www.nytimes.com/2017/10/03/technology/yahoo-hack-3-billion-users.html> last accessed 24 October 2018.

[50] Amy Nordrum, 'Researchers embed malware into DNA to hack DNA sequencing software' *IEEE Spectrum* (10 August 2017) <https://spectrum.ieee.org/the-human-os/computing/software/researchers-embed-malicious-code-into-dna-to-hack-dna-sequencing-software> last accessed 3 May 2018.

(b) GDPR Requirements for Privacy Policies and Notices.

The GDPR sets a number of requirements in relation to these documents. Article 13 sets out the types of information that should be provided to data subjects in relation to processing of information. There is also a transparency requirement in relation to privacy notices in Article 12(1). Article 12(7) also requires that information that is provided to a data subject be provided in a meaningful way, including that the information presented is 'easily visible, intelligible and clearly legible'.

Article 12(1): Transparency requirement in relation to privacy notices

information [. . .] and any communication [. . .] relating to processing to the data subject in a concise, transparent, intelligible and easily accessible form, using clear and plain language, in particular for any information addressed specifically to a child. The information shall be provided in writing, or by other means, including, where appropriate, by electronic means. When requested by the data subject, the information may be provided orally, provided that the identity of the data subject is proven by other means.

Compliance with the GDPR may prove challenging for some businesses and it may be that more reform is needed to assist with governance of new technologies. However, creating privacy policies that are user-friendly and assist data subjects in understanding how their data is used can also be seen as an opportunity. Particularly for services that deal with sensitive information, such as genetic data, developing consumer trust could allow for a competitive advantage. If data protection authorities and consumer regulators could provide model privacy policies and contracts for specific industries and also work with all stakeholders to produce industry codes of conduct, this could also allow for better protection of the rights of individuals, but also allow them to make more informed choices about whether to engage with such services. Some businesses have already begun to be more innovative in relation to their privacy policies. An interesting example of this is the work of Booking.com, which now has a video explaining its privacy policy.[51]

---

[51] Booking.com, 'Privacy Statement' (3 May 2018) <https://www.booking.com/content/privacy.html?label=gen173nr-1FCAEoggJCAlhYS DNYBGhpiAEBmAExuAEHyAEN2AEB6AEB-AECkgIBeagCAw;sid=8594fab5943c0dc 80412889630bdbff3> last accessed 24 October 2018.

4.4 Privacy Policies, Privacy Notices and Website Design

As with many other digital services, DTC companies often include privacy policies, privacy statements or privacy notices[52] on their websites. While the research on which this book is based has primarily focused on contracts rather than privacy policies, it is useful and important to discuss privacy policies in the DTC context. At a basic level, privacy policies and notices should set out a business's practices in relation to processing personal data. There are now a number of interesting and promising projects focusing on making these documents more effective and better understood by consumers, but currently many policies may not be drafted in a manner that is consumer friendly and may be difficult for the average consumer to understand. Some good examples of projects trying to assist people with understanding privacy policies are the Usable Privacy Policy Project[53] and Hamza Harkous et al.'s Polisis[54] and PriBot.[55] PriBot allows you to ask it questions about the privacy policies of different websites.

The work of McDonald and Cranor provides an illustrative example of the challenges for businesses and consumers in e-commerce. In their 2008 study, they found that it would take approximately 201 hours a year for the average American consumer to read all the privacy policies they encountered.[56] Given how things have changed in the last decade with the widespread adoption of smartphones and the use of applications on smartphones and other devices, the number of privacy policies and the time it takes to read them has also increased.

The recent study of privacy policies by Hazel and Slobogin focusing

---

[52] New Zealand Privacy Commissioner, 'Privacy Statements' <https://www.privacy.org. nz/privacy-for-agencies/privacy-statements/> last accessed 24 October 2018; Irish Data Protection Commission, 'Guidelines for the contents and use of privacy statements on websites' <https://www.dataprotection.ie/docs/PrivStatements/m/290.htm> last accessed 2 May 2018 – checked 24 October 2018 and the link is not working.

[53] The Usable Privacy Policy Project, <https://usableprivacy.org> last accessed 2 May 2018.

[54] Polisis, 'Welcome to Polisis!' <https://pribot.org/polisis> last accessed 24 October 2018 – this is an artificial-intelligence-based project that generates summaries of privacy policies.

[55] PriBot <https://pribot.org/bot> last accessed 24 October 2018 – this allows you to chat with a PriBot and ask questions about different websites' privacy policies.

[56] Aleecia M McDonald and Lorrie Faith Cranor, 'The cost of reading privacy policies' (2008) 4 *Journal of Law and Policy for the Information Society* 543–68 <https://kb.osu. edu/bitstream/handle/1811/72839/1/ISJLP_V4N3_543.pdf> last accessed 24 October 2018; also see Cranor Lorrie Faith, and Hoke Candice, Pedro Leon, and Au Alyssa, 'Are They Worth Reading? An In-Depth Analysis of Online Advertising Companies' Privacy Policies' (31 March 2014) 2014 TPRC Conference Paper <http://dx.doi.org/10.2139/ ssrn.2418590>

on US-based DTC companies,[57] as well as the study by Laestidius et al. on data practices of DTC companies, are enlightening and support the need for reform.[58] Hazel and Slobogin's study was conducted in 2017 and they collected their data on privacy policies in February and October 2017. They 'developed an analysis instrument designed to assess the information these policies provided regarding the collection, use and sharing of genetic data'.[59] The analysis instrument was applied on a pilot basis to a small subset of policies and then 'applied to all policy documents by two independent legal research assistants' with disputes being resolved by a third party.[60] Significantly, they found that all companies with a privacy policy publicly available reserved the right to make changes and 'very few provided for individualised consumer notification'. 'The majority [. . .] stated that any changes to the policy would be reflected on the website and the consumer was encouraged to routinely re-read the policy documents'.[61]

In preliminary analysis of company privacy policies, conducted as part of the preparation for this book, it was found that 25 per cent of companies do state that they will share genetic information with law enforcement agencies.[62] Hazel and Slobogin's more recent study found that:

> over two-thirds of companies (69%; 38 of 55) addressed the sharing of information with law enforcement or other governmental authorities, but policies varied significantly in the amount of information provided to the consumer about the process. [. . .] Only 11% of companies with policies governing law enforcement disclosure (4 of 38) stated that they would attempt to notify the consumer if they were the subject of such a request, if such notification was permitted by law.[63]

---

[57] James Hazel and Christopher Slobogin, 'Who knows what, and when? A survey of the privacy policies proffered by U.S. direct-to-consumer genetic testing companies' (19 April 2018, last revised 18 October 2018) *Cornell Journal of Law and Public Policy* and Vanderbilt Law Research Paper No 18–18 <https://ssrn.com/abstract=3165765> last accessed 24 October 2018.

[58] LI Laestadius, Jennifer R Rich, and Paul L Auer, 'All your data (effectively) belong to us: Data practices among direct-to-consumer genetic testing firms" (2016) 19 *Genetics in Medicine* 513–20 doi:10.1038/gim.2016.136.

[59] Hazel and Slobogin (n 57).

[60] Ibid. 12–13.

[61] Ibid. 15.

[62] Andelka M Phillips, 'Genomic privacy and direct-to-consumer genetics – Big consumer genetic data – What's in that contract?' (presented at GenoPri'15 [The 2nd Workshop on Genome Privacy and Security] and published as part of IEEE Conference Proceedings 2015) <https://www.computer.org/csdl/proceedings/spw/2015/9933/00/9933a060.pdf> last accessed 23 October 2018.

[63] Hazel and Slobogin (n 57) 23.

This supports my preliminary findings and lends further support to the need to improve privacy policies and contracts.

The Norwegian Consumer Council's (NCC) work is also extremely helpful here. They are 'an interest group for consumers funded by the Norwegian government'.[64] Part of their work is 'to promote consumer rights such as privacy, security and balanced contracts in digital products and services'.[65] In their 2018 report into privacy settings they found that 'design, symbols and wording' often 'nudge users away from privacy friendly choices'.[66]

Meanwhile, the NCC's earlier *APPFAIL* report examined the terms of use and privacy policies of 20 common smartphone applications to assess their compliance with EU data protection and consumer protection law. In relation to the issue of informed consent they noted that: 'If terms are very difficult to read as they are very long, ambiguous or written in overly technical, complex or vague language, a strong case can be made that informed consent is not possible for most consumers'.[67] In the context of DTC services, given the complex nature of genetic test results, companies really do need to make sure that their policies are easier to read.

Obar and Oeldorf-Hirsch's research is also useful in thinking about how people interact with contracts and privacy policies.[68] Their studies used a fictitious social networking platform called NameDrop to explore four research questions:[69]

1. 'To what extent will participants ignore privacy and terms of service policies for fictitious social networking service NameDrop?'
2. 'To what extent will participants fail to notice "gotcha" clauses in NameDrop policies?'

[64] NCC, *Deceived by Design* (June 2018) 4 <https://www.forbrukerradet.no/undersokelse/no-undersokelsekategori/deceived-by-design/> last accessed 25 October 2018.

[65] Ibid. 4.

[66] Ibid. 3.

[67] NCC, *APPFAIL Threats to Consumers in Mobile Apps* (March 2016) 24 <https://www.forbrukerradet.no/undersokelse/2015/appfail-threats-to-consumers-in-mobile-apps/> last accessed 18 October 2018.

[68] Jonathan A Obar and Anne Oeldorf-Hirsch, 'The biggest lie on the Internet: Ignoring the privacy policies and terms of service policies of social networking services' (2018) *Information, Communication & Society* 1–20 <https://doi.org/10.1080/1369118X.2018.1486870> last accessed 22 October 2018; and JA Obar and A Oeldorf-Hirsch, 'Clickwrap impact: Quick-join options and ignoring privacy and terms of service policies of social networking services' (2017) in Proceedings of the 8th International Conference on Social Media and Society ACM 8 <https://ssrn.com/abstract=3017277> last accessed 29 October 2018.

[69] Obar and Oeldorf-Hirsch, 'The biggest lie on the Internet' 5.

3. 'To what extent will participants read privacy and terms of service policies for real social networking services?'
4. 'What attitudes about privacy and terms of service policies predict the extent to which participants ignore them?'

This work involved a survey of 543 undergraduate university students.[70] All participants had the option to read terms of service and privacy policies, but at the beginning they were given the option of skipping the terms of service with a 'quick-join option'. Seventy-four per cent of the participants chose the 'quick-join option' and 78 per cent indicated that they use quick-join options often.[71] The policies included two gotcha clauses: a child assignment clause; and a clause allowing for data-sharing with the NSA.[72] These gotcha clauses can also be viewed as what Kim calls 'crook' provisions.

In relation to the reading time and gotcha clauses the results are particularly significant. The privacy policy (PP) should have taken an average of 29 to 32 minutes to read, while the terms of service (TOS) should have taken 15 to 17 minutes to read. In the study, the actual median reading time for both respectively was 13.60 seconds and 14.04 seconds, with 81 per cent spending less than one minute reading the privacy policy and 86 per cent spending less than one minute reading the terms of service.[73] Overall, '96% spent less than 5 minutes on the PP and 98% spent less than 5 minutes on the TOS'.[74]

Only 1.7 per cent (9 out of 543) of those surveyed 'mentioned the child assignment clause', '11 (2%) mentioned concerns with data sharing', and only one person actually mentioned the NSA clause.[75] These results highlight just how few people are likely to notice problematic terms when they engage with wrap contracts and privacy policies.

Three attitude factors were identified in the study. These were: information overload; the attitude that policies were difficult to understand; and the attitude that participants had nothing to hide. However, it was the attitude of information overload which was a 'negative predictor of reading terms of service when signing up' and this was also a negative predictor for reading privacy policies when they change.[76]

---

[70] Ibid. 5.
[71] Ibid. 8.
[72] Ibid. 10–11.
[73] Ibid. 10.
[74] Ibid. 10.
[75] Ibid. 11.
[76] Ibid. 11–12.

In their related paper, Obar and Oeldorf-Hirsch provide an 'exploratory analysis' drawing data from their previous 'qualitative survey addressing participant perceptions of the role of clickwrap agreements, specifically quick-join options, in facilitating consent to the policies of social networking services'.[77] In their results from the qualitative data, three themes emerged:

1. the quick-join option fails to notify users about the consent process
2. the quick-join option suggests that the consent process is unimportant
3. the quick-join option discourages engagement with the consent process[78]

Thinking about these findings in the DTC context, it seems advisable that companies move away from using quick-join features. Also, given the nature of DTC services, the industry could treat improving industry practices as an opportunity to rethink ways of doing things. While the rise of e-commerce and many new digital technologies have changed our lives in significant ways, business practices are remarkably uniform in e-commerce, regardless of the product or service being sold. Businesses in general for too long have simply relied on wrap contracts and privacy policies, without really trying to distinguish themselves by providing better terms or enhancing consumers' choices. The DTC industry should look beyond merely rewording contracts and policies to thinking about how they can actually make their relationships with consumers more balanced. This may actually necessitate redesigning user interfaces, so that consumers are provided with informational tools and also given time to digest material, rather than being steered towards purchase, as they are in most e-commerce.

PriBot

In October 2018, I used PriBot to explore some current versions of DTC privacy policies and put questions to PriBot. I plan to conduct further research on this in the future.

As this exchange further confirmed that DTC companies still have work to do to improve their policies, it is set out below. In relation to 23andMe's privacy policy:

---

[77] Obar and Oeldorf-Hirsch, 'Clickwrap impact' (n 68).
[78] Ibid. 11–12.

Me: 'How long is my data retained?'

PriBot: 'I searched well, Looks like the policy doesn't have an answer to your question'. *And:* 'It can either be that the company retains data indefinitely or because it does not retain any data in the first place'.

Me: 'What types of personal information do you collect?'

Pribot: 'I couldn't find statements confirming data collection'. *And:* 'I searched well, Looks like the policy doesn't have an answer to your question.'[79]

4.5 US Privacy Law

Given that the majority of DTC companies as well as all the most prominent companies are bases in America, American privacy law also has relevance here. Much of American privacy law is sectoral, so protection does vary in different contexts.

(a) Health Insurance Portability and Accountability Act

This Act ordinarily applies to genetic tests carried out in a clinical setting and affords the protection of confidentiality to test results. The American Society of Human Genetics in its Statement on DTC has recommended that DTC companies should comply with Health Insurance Portability and Accountability Act (HIPAA) requirements.[80] If HIPAA were to apply to DTC companies that provide tests for health purposes it should improve protection for consumers' privacy in this context by requiring companies to keep test results confidential, although given the way that DTC companies have began to partner with other entities, compliance with HIPAA may prove challenging.

(b) Genetic Information Nondiscrimination Act 2008

Meanwhile, in the USA the Genetic Information Nondiscrimination Act (GINA) was enacted in 2008. It is aimed chiefly at preventing discrimination in health insurance and employment[81] and it prohibits genetic

---

[79] PriBot, <https://pribot.org/bot?company=https:%2F%2Fwww.23andme.com%2Fen-int%2Fabout%2Fprivacy%2F> last accessed 31 October 2018.

[80] K Hudson, G Javitt, W Burke, P Byers, and ASHG Social Issues Committee, 'ASHG Statement on direct-to-consumer genetic testing in the United States' (2007) 81(3) *American Journal of Human Genetics* 635–7 <https://www.ncbi.nlm.nih.gov/pmc/articles/PMC1950839/> last accessed 24 October 2018.

[81] Woodage (n 13) 690.

discrimination in the context of employment and insurance, but the Act leaves many gaps. For instance, it does not apply to life insurance, long-term care, disability insurance or the military.[82] Michelle Irick has suggested it might be possible and desirable to amend GINA so that its remit is extended to cover the DTC industry.[83] This idea has appeal, especially given the possibility that DTC companies might share data with insurance companies. As previously noted, several prominent companies have already entered partnerships with the pharmaceutical industry, so this possibility may be quite likely.

(c) Preserving Employee Wellness Programs Act Bill

The Preserving Employee Wellness Programs Act bill (HR 1313) was originally proposed in March 2017.[84] It has not yet been enacted, but if it does pass it will reduce the protections provided for genetic privacy in the workplace. Specifically, it will permit employers to require employees to undergo genetic testing and share results as part of workplace wellness programmes. The American Society of Human Genetics (ASHG) has stated its opposition to the bill[85] and has also submitted two letters to the US House Committee on Education and the Workforce;[86] the second letter is a joint letter with a number of other organisations.[87]

(d) American State Law

It is also useful to recognise that some US states have stronger protection for an individual's rights in their genetic data. These are not always privacy

---

[82] A Foster, 'Critical dilemmas in genetic testing: Why regulations to protect the confidentiality of genetic information should be expended' (2010) 62(2) *Baylor Law Review* 537–72; Naveed et al. (n 14) 10.

[83] Michelle D Irick, 'Age of an information revolution: The direct-to-consumer genetic testing industry and the need for a holistic regulatory approach' (2012) 49 *San Diego Law Review* 279, 328–9.

[84] Bill HR 1313 <https://www.congress.gov/bill/115th-congress/house-bill/1313/text> last accessed 24 October 2018.

[85] American Society of Human Genetics, 'ASHG opposes H.R.1313, the Preserving Employee Wellness Programs Act Bill would undermine genetic privacy protections' (American Society of Human Genetics, Press Release, 8 March 2017) <http://www.ashg.org/press/201703-HR1313.html> last accessed 24 October 2018.

[86] ASHG, Letter to House Committee on Education and the Workforce (7 March 2017) <http://www.ashg.org/policy/pdf/HR1313_letter_030717.pdf> last accessed 24 October 2018.

[87] ASHG, Multi-organization Letter to House Committee on Education and the Workforce (7 March 2017) <http://www.ashg.org/policy/pdf/HR1313_groupletter_030717.pdf> last accessed 24 October 2018.

rights, but property rights with several states having enacted legislation declaring genetic information to be personal property. Notable examples are Alaska, Georgia, Florida and Oregon.[88] The provisions classifying genetic information as property are mainly found in insurance legislation and are primarily aimed at preventing discrimination based on genetic information, particularly where a person has a pre-existing condition. Alaskan law provides stronger protection for individuals than GINA, as its 'statute provides a private cause of action against individuals who analyze, collect, or retain DNA samples without consent, or individuals that release the results of DNA testing'.[89] Lousiana also has a statute prohibiting discrimination on the grounds of genetic information.[90]

The study by Miller and Tucker is also relevant here. Their research addressed the impact state genetic privacy laws have on the uptake of personalised medicine, focusing on the example 'of genetic testing for predispositions for certain types of cancer'.[91] They examined the effects of 'different types of state privacy laws on genetic testing rates'.[92]

> [approaches that allow individuals greater] control over redisclosure encourage the spread of genetic testing, whereas an approach of notification and informed consent deters individuals from obtaining genetic tests. We also find that there is little effect, either positive or negative, from regulation that prevents discriminatory use of this data.[93]

---

[88] Seth Axelrad, *State Statutes Declaring Genetic Information to be Personal Property* <http://www.aslme.org/dna_04/reports/axelrad4.pdf> last accessed 31 October 2018.

[89] Chelsea Weiermiller, 'The future of direct-to-consumer genetic testing: Regulation and innovation' (2015) 16(5) *North Carolina Journal of Law & Technology* – online issue 137–71, 153 <http://scholarship.law.unc.edu/ncjolt/vol16/iss5/5> last accessed 31 October 2018; see also Alaska Stat. § 18.13.010(a)(2).

[90] See 2011 Louisiana Laws Revised Statutes Title 22 – Insurance – LA Rev Stat § 22:1023 <https://law.justia.com/codes/louisiana/2011/rs/title22/rs22-1023/> last accessed 31 October 2018.

[91] AR Miller and C Tucker, 'Privacy protection, personalized medicine, and genetic testing' (25 May 2017) 1–52, 44 (May 25, 2017). Available at SSRN: <https://ssrn.com/abstract=2411230> or <http://dx.doi.org/10.2139/ssrn.2411230> last accessed 6 November 2018. The earlier version AR Miller and C Tucker, 'Privacy protection, personalized medicine, and genetic testing' (9 July 2015) is available at: <https://www.ftc.gov/es/system/files/documents/public_comments/2015/09/00010-97509.pdf> last accessed 6 November 2018; and it is also published as AR Miller and C Tucker, 'Privacy protection, personalized medicine, and genetic testing' (2017) 64(10) *Management Science* 4471–965 <https://doi.org/10.1287/mnsc.2017.2858>

[92] Miller and Tucker (n 91) SSRN Version 1–55, 44.

[93] Ibid.

Their findings generally lend support for 'privacy regimes that focus on establishing rules of data ownership rather than merely informing the consumer how their data will be used and focusing on notification and obtaining upfront consent'.[94] They do note in discussion of their study's limitations that it was limited to thinking about such approaches in the context of genetic testing and may not be applicable to other types of data. However, as herein the focus is also on genetic tests their findings are useful in thinking about improving regulation of DTC.

4.6 Canadian Genetic Privacy Law

It is useful to consider Canada's approach to genetic privacy, which has recently undergone significant reform and considerably strengthened the right to genetic privacy and Canadians' rights more generally in their genetic information. As mentioned in Chapter 1, this new act, the Genetic Non-Discrimination Act 2017 (GNA),[95] creates a number of offences in relation to genetic tests.

Significantly, section 3 of GNA prohibits requiring an individual to undergo a genetic test, while section 4 prohibits requiring an individual to disclose genetic test results. The Act does allow for individual to consent to disclosure of results, but this consent must be explicit and in writing.[96] Those who do not comply with the Act could be committing an offence and the Act sets substantial penalties for offences, including under section 7(a) 'a fine not exceeding $1,000,000 or to imprisonment for a term not exceeding five years, or to both'.

The GNA is a useful example, which should be considered by other countries interested in improving regulation of the DTC industry, and enhances privacy rights for individuals. It can also been seen as being in line with the provisions of the EU's GDPR.

It is also useful to note here the work of the Health Law Institute at the University of Alberta, which conducted a study on the privacy policies and practices of DTC companies.[97] Its report analysed the pri-

94 Ibid. 45.
95 Genetic Non-Discrimination Act 2017 (CA) <https://laws-lois.justice.gc.ca/eng/acts/G-2.5/page-1.html#h-3>
96 OPC, 'Direct-to-consumer genetic testing and privacy' (OPC, updated December 2017) <https://www.priv.gc.ca/en/privacy-topics/health-genetic-and-other-body-information/02_05_d_69_gen/> last accessed 27 October 2018.
97 Health Law Institute, Analysis of Privacy Policies and Practices of Direct-to-Consumer Genetic Testing Companies: Private Sector Databanks and Privacy Protection Norms (Health Law Institute, report funded by the Office of the Privacy Commissioner of Canada, 2010) 11 <https://www.priv.gc.ca/en/opc-actions-and-decisions/research/funding-

vacy policies of 32 companies 'against the fair information principles developed by the Canadian Standards Association in the Model Code for the Protection of Personal Information and incorporated into the federal Personal Information Protection and Electronic Documents Act' (PIPEDA).[98] The report concluded that there was much variation in these policies and that regarding privacy protection practices many companies made claims on their websites which were 'no more than advertising claims'. It also found that many policies were internally inconsistent and it ended with a list of questions it 'recommended consumers should consider before purchasing genetic tests'.[99] Some of the questions are very much aligned with the requirements of the GDPR. These include asking: whether the company has provided sufficient information regarading the purpose for which personal data is collected; whether the company has provided sufficient information to enable the consumer 'to make an informed choice about whether to buy genetic testing services'; whether the company limits the amount of data it collects; whether the company will share 'personal information or biological sample with third parties without your consent'.[100]

4.7 Secondary Use of Genetic Databases: The Golden State Killer and Beyond

There are many ways that genetic data may be used beyond the original purpose of its collection. Companies are often using such data in research projects, but they have also begun to enter partnerships with third parties. Under Article 9(2) of the GDPR, in relation to special categories of data, which includes genetic data, a person's consent needs to be both explicit and specific. Consequently, where such data is to be used for additional purposes not contemplated at the time of collection, additional consent is likely to be required. This means that DTC companies will need to work on their consent mechanisms in order to meet these obligations for consumers based in the EU and UK.

---

for-privacy-research-and-knowledge-translation/completed-contributions-program-pr ojects/2009-2010/p_200910_07/> last accessed 23 October 2018; see also Personal Information Protection and Electronic Documents Act 2000 <https://laws-lois.justice.gc.ca/ eng/acts/P-8.6/ Documents Act> last accessed 29 October 2018.

[98] Ibid. 3.

[99] Ibid. 33–4.

[100] Ibid. 35.

(a) Secondary Use by Law Enforcement

It is also possible that data may be used by third parties, such as law enforcement. The recent Golden State Killer[101] case is an illuminating example of how law enforcement may use genetic databases in criminal investigations. In this case, DNA evidence that had been collected from crime scenes in the 1970s and 1980s was used by investigators in the process of familial DNA matching.[102] Details of the case are still emerging, but it seems the samples were used to create a profile on a public genetic genealogical website GEDmatch[103] and compared against possible relatives on that site. GEDmatch is not a DTC company, but allows people to upload their genetic data to its database. It allows for this type of sharing under its Site Policy.[104] More recently it has been revealed that Gene By Gene, which owns the DTC ancestry company FamilyTreeDNA, 'received a federal subpoena from the Eastern District of California in March 2017 asking for "limited information" about a single customer account'.[105]

A suspect, James DeAngelo, was subsequently identified through this process and charged. Familial DNA matching is controversial, as it often involves searching the genetic profiles of innocent people in order to find a potential relative, who may have been involved in the commission of a crime.

---

[101] Megan Thielking, 'Lawmakers press genetic testing companies for details on their privacy policies' STAT (21 June 2018) <https://www.statnews.com/2018/06/21/congress-genetic-testing-companies-privacy-policies/> last accessed 24 October 2018; Tamar Lapin, '"Golden State Killer" cleared of 1978 double-murder cold case' New York Post (14 June 2018) <https://nypost.com/2018/06/14/golden-state-killer-cleared-of-1978-double-murder-cold-case/> last accessed 24 October 2018; Rachel Becker, 'Golden State Killer suspect was tracked down through genealogy website GEDmatch' The Verge (26 April 2018) <https://www.theverge.com/2018/4/26/17288532/golden-state-killer-east-area-rapistgenealogy-websites-dna-genetic-investigation> last accessed 24 October 2018; and Tina Hesman Saey, 'Why using genetic genealogy to solve crimes could pose problems' ScienceNews (7 June 2018) <https://www.sciencenews.org/article/why-police-using-genetic-geneaology-solve-crimes-poses-problems?mode=pick&context=2782&tgt=nr> last accessed 24 October 2018.

[102] Also see Andelka M Phillips, 'Genetics goes online – privacy in the world of personal genomics' Privacy Laws and Business International Report (October 2018) 19–21.

[103] Saey, 'Why using genetic genealogy to solve crimes could pose problems' (n 101) and Lapin, '"Golden State Killer" cleared of 1978 double-murder cold case' (n 101).

[104] Megan Molteni, 'The key to cracking cold cases might be genealogy sites' Wired (1 June 2018) <https://www.wired.com/story/police-will-crack-a-lot-more-cold-cases-with-dna/>; GEDmatch, <https://www.gedmatch.com/tos.htm> last accessed 2 August 2018.

[105] Phillips, 'Genetics goes online – privacy in the world of personal genomics' (n 102) 19–20 citing Peter Aldhous, 'Cops forced a company to share a customer's identity for the Golden State Killer investigation' BuzzFeed News (1 May 2018) <https://www.buzzfeednews.com/article/peteraldhous/family-tree-dna-subpoena-golden-state-killer#.klPB3w6vpm>

It also should be noted that the suspect has now been cleared in at least one of the murder cases, which highlights just how challenging using this technique is.[106] Furthermore, since this case came to light, Parabon NanoLabs has now uploaded data from approximately 100 crime scenes on to GEDmatch's database in the hopes of finding further matches.[107]

In the past, concern was expressed regarding the retention of DNA profiles of innocent persons in criminal databases, most notably the UK's National DNA Database (NDNAD) and the USA's Combined DNA Index System (CODIS).[108] Given that the age of criminal responsibility can actually be very low (for example, the age of criminal responsibility is 10 in England, Wales and Northern Ireland; and at the time of writing, 8 in Scotland), it does seem advisable to restrict such retention of DNA profiles of minors or at least to place time limits on such retention. Furthermore, it should be noted that as mentioned above in discussion of the GDPR's requirement for the age of consent for children in the context of data processing (in the UK this is 13),[109] the age of criminal responsibility throughout the UK is lower than the age of consent for data processing. In the DTC context, where companies perform tests on minors, the retention of genetic information needs to be monitored. It is advisable that time limits should be implemented generally as well, so that companies do not retain genetic information indefinitely.

(b) Secondary Use by Immigration Services

Rather surprisingly, given Canada's Genetic Non-Discrimination Act, it has emerged that the Canadian Border Services Agency (CBSA) has been making use of DTC ancestry services in deportation cases. In an ongoing deportation case, Global News has obtained court documents which show

---

[106] Lapin, '"Golden State Killer" cleared of 1978 double-murder cold case' (n 101).

[107] Peter Aldhous, 'DNA data From 100 crime scenes has been uploaded to a genealogy website – just like the Golden State Killer' *BuzzFeed News* (17 May 2018) <https://www.buzzfeednews.com/article/peteraldhous/parabon-genetic-genealogy-cold-cases> last accessed 24 October 2018.

[108] Frederick R Bieber, Charles H Brenner and David Lazer, 'Finding criminals through DNA of their relatives' (2006) 5778 *Science* 1315–16 doi: 10.1126/science.1122655; Helen Wallace, 'The UK national DNA database' (2006) 7 *EMBO Reports* – Special Issue S26–30 <https://onlinelibrary.wiley.com/doi/pdf/10.1038/sj.embor.7400727> last accessed 24 October 2018; Lila Kazemian, Ken Pease, and David P Farrington, 'DNA retention policies: The potential contribution of criminal career research' (2011) 8(1) *European Journal of Criminology* 48–64 doi: 10.1177/1477370810373731.

[109] ICO, *Guide to the GDPR*, see 'What is valid consent?' <https://ico.org.uk/for-organisations/guide-to-data-protection/guide-to-the-general-data-protection-regulation-gdpr/consent/what-is-valid-consent> accessed 29 January 2019.

'a CBSA representative admitting to using familytreedna.com to contact the long-lost cousins of Franklin Godwin, who was accepted as a refugee from Liberia'.[110] Godwin's lawyer, David Cote, told Global News that they were using FamilyTreeDNA in order to try to trace family members and through this process link Godwin to another country. Godwin's DNA sample was taken while he was being detained by immigration. CBSA is now claiming that 'Godwin is a Nigerian national and have focused their efforts in deporting him there. However, Cote says Godwin was left in the dark and was not told how his DNA sample would be used'.[111] The CBSA declined to be interviewed by Global News regarding the case, but interestingly FamilyTreeDNA have indicated that they were not 'aware that their website was being used by the CBSA, the company said they have never worked with the Canadian government, and that using data in that way would violate their terms of service'.[112] This case is ongoing and the final outcome will have significance for how such data is used by immigration services.

(c) Secondary Use and Insurance

Predictive genetic tests can reveal information about an individual's risk level for developing a particular condition or disease. This type of information can be used by the insurance industry and could influence decisions on the insurance coverage available to an individual. Given that DTC companies have already begun to partner with the pharmaceutical industry,[113] and we are

---

[110] Emanuela Campanella, 'Government using ancestry websites to deport immigrants: Lawyer, court documents' *Global News* (1 November 2018) <https://globalnews.ca/news/4616715/ancestry-dna-test-deportation-cbsa/> last accessed 6 November 2018.

[111] Ibid.

[112] Ibid.

[113] See the recent example of 23andMe and GlaxoSmithKline and its earlier partnerships with Pfizer and others: Laura Geggel, '23andMe is sharing its 5 million clients' genetic data with drug giant GlaxoSmithKline' *Livescience* (26 July 2018) <https://www.livescience.com/63173-23andme-partnership-glaxosmithkline.html> last accessed 22 October 2018; GlaxoSmithKline, 'GSK and 23andMe sign agreement to leverage genetic insights for the development of novel medicines' (25 July 2018) <https://www.gsk.com/en-gb/media/press-releases/gsk-and-23andme-sign-agreement-to-leverage-genetic-insights-for-the-develop ment-of-novel-medicines/> last accessed 2 August 2018; M Sullivan, '23andMe has signed 12 other genetic data partnerships beyond Pfizer and Genentech' *VentureBeat* (14 January 2015) <https://venturebeat.com/2015/01/14/23andme-has-signed-12-other-genetic-data-partnerships-beyond-pfizer-and-genentech/> last accessed 17 August 2018; Christine Lagorio-Chafkin, '23andMe exec: You ain't seen nothing yet' *Inc* (7 January 2015) <http://www.inc.com/christine-lagorio/23andMe-new-partnerships.html> last accessed 17 August 2018; The Associated Press, 'Pfizer, 23andMe team up to study bowel disease' *Medical Xpress* (12 August 2014) <https://medicalxpress.com/news/2014-08-pfizer-23andme-

starting to see partnerships with the insurance industry, there is the potential for DTC companies to share a person's genetic data with insurers. For example, the Hong Kong-based start-up Prenetics, which offers a variety of genetic testing services, has received investment from Ping An Ventures, an insurance company with 200 million policy holders in China.[114]

In the UK there has been a Concordat and Moratorium by the Association of British Insurers, which was extended several times and has now been replaced by a code of practice released in October 2018. (Please see the Appendix for the commitments made in this Code.) The new Code addresses the: 'use insurers can make of genetic test results of individuals who are applying for insurance and refers to two different kinds of genetic tests:

- **Diagnostic genetic tests** confirm or rule out a diagnosis based on existing symptoms, signs or abnormal non-genetic test results which indicate that the condition in question may be present.
- **Predictive genetic tests** predict a future risk of disease in individuals without symptoms of a genetic disorder.[115]

The Code addresses how 'genetic information is treated by insurers who provide life, critical illness and income protection insurance'.[116]

This can be compared with the work of the Canadian Life and Health Insurance Association (CLHIA), which has followed a similar line with its Position Statement on Genetic Tests.[117] In its Statement it provides that:

---

team-bowel-disease.html> last accessed 24 October 2018; Andrew Ward, 'Google-backed genetic testing company hires veteran scientist' *The Financial Times* (12 March 2015) <https://www.ft.com/content/ead07e84-c8d8-11e4-bc64-00144feab7de> last accessed 24 October 2018.

[114] Woodhouse, 'iGene: Hong Kong biotech' (28)

[115] ABI and HM Government, Code on Genetic Testing and Insurance (October 2018) 4 <https://www.abi.org.uk/globalassets/files/publications/public/genetics/code-on-genetic-testing-and-insurance_embargoed.pdf> accessed 5 April 2019.

[116] ABI and HM Government, Code on Genetic Testing and Insurance (October 2018) at 5.

[117] See Office of Canadian Privacy Commissioner, 'Canadian Life and Health Insurance Association, Position Statement on Genetic Testing' OPC News (9 July 2014) <https://www.priv.gc.ca/en/opc-news/news-and-announcements/2014/s-d_140709/> citing Canadian Life and Health Insurance Association, 'Position Statement on Genetic Testing' (CLHIA 2010) at footnote 3. CLHIA, 'Position Statement on Genetic Testing' (CLHIA 2010) – the statement is archived and available at <https://web.archive.org/web/20130523005959/http://www.clhia.ca/domino/html/clhia/clhia_lp4w_lnd_webstation.nsf/resources/Guidelines/$file/Genetic_Testing_CLHIA_Industry_Position_2010.pdf> last accessed 24 October 2018.

insurers would not require an applicant for insurance to undergo genetic testing. However, if genetic testing has been done and the information is available to the applicant for insurance and/or the applicant's physician, the insurer would request access to that information just as it would for other aspects of the applicant's health history.

This policy is based on the general principle that the insurance contract is a 'good faith' agreement and that both parties have an obligation to disclose any information that may be relevant to the contract so that the contract can be entered into on an 'equal information' footing. [118]

The Office of the Canadian Privacy Commissioner has recommended extending this moratorium and, as previously noted, Canada now has stronger genetic privacy law with the passing of the Genetic Non-Discrimination Act 2017. GNA prohibits insurers and employers from requiring that an individual undergo a genetic test or requiring them to reveal genetic test results.

In contrast, the situation in Australia may be likely to become less favourable for consumers:

> Lobbyists for Australian life insurers have proposed an AUD$500,000 (USD$360,000) cap on policies for individuals who disclose adverse genetic testing results [. . .] life insurers in Australia cannot require customers to take genetic tests, but can ask about testing and base coverage or rate decisions on disclosed adverse results. This, it says, has led to concerns that some people would forgo testing because it could affect their insurance coverage and to Parliament to call on the Financial Services Council to make changes. [119]

In relation to DTC company policies in relation to use of test results in the context of insurance, Kristen Brown's 2017 Gizmodo article is noteworthy. Brown, with assistance from legal scholars, read and compared the contracts and policies of AncestryDNA, 23andMe and Illumina's Helix. [120] In relation to insurance they highlight that having a DTC test and sharing those results could impact upon your ability to get insurance. They refer to a clause in 23andMe's Terms of Service which is still included in their

---

[118] CLHIA, 'Position Statement on Genetic Testing' (n 97)

[119] 'Cap Proposed' *GenomeWeb* (5 November 2018) <https://www.genomeweb.com/scan/cap-proposed> last accessed 6 November 2018.

[120] Kristen V Brown, 'What DNA Testing Companies' Terrifying Privacy Policies Actually Mean' *GIZMODO* (18 October 2017) <https://gizmodo.com/what-dna-testing-companies-terrifying-privacy-policies-1819158337> last accessed 24 October 2018.

most recent Terms of Service. The clause is included under the heading 'Important Issues Regarding 23andMe Services', clause (p):

> You should be aware that, if you are asked by an insurance company whether you have learned Genetic Information about health conditions and you do not disclose this to them, this may be considered to be fraud or a breach of the policy that you subsequently purchase.[121]

(d) Social Networking Functions of DTC Websites

It is common for companies that offer ancestry tests to have social networking features on their websites that allow consumers to connect with unknown relatives. These functions also allow for sharing of a wide variety of data, including information about a person's health and potentially their genetic data if they wish to share it. While this can have positive outcomes, it can also result in serious impacts on families when unexpected information emerges. An article by George Doe highlights some of the challenges in this area,[122] stemming from the author's experience of purchasing tests as gifts for their parents. In this case, the DTC company in question connected the author's father with an unknown child, which led the author's parents to end their marriage. This type of scenario is also likely to become more common as more people engage with these services and businesses should consider this in their consumer contracts and their privacy policies.

Given how significant family relationships can be to an individual's wellbeing and identity, and in light of the research relating to peoples' interaction with contracts, privacy policies and privacy settings, DTC businesses should look beyond merely reformatting these contracts and policies. They should also think about how this could be addressed in a way that truly enhances consumer understanding and puts them in control of their data. It should be borne in mind that whenever an interface enables sharing, it also raises the possibility that data and content that is shared may be saved and stored by others on the site. This in turn can create difficulties when it comes to account deletion, as it may not be possible for a DTC company to completely ensure that all content is deleted. This is a challenge that has arisen in the

---

[121] 23andMe, 'Terms of Service Europe', <https://www.23andme.com/en-eu/about/tos/> this version was downloaded on 1 August 2018.

[122] George Doe, 'With genetic testing, I gave my parents the gift of divorce' *Vox* (9 September 2014) <https://www.vox.com/2014/9/9/5975653/with-genetic-testing-i-gave-my-parents-the-gift-of-divorce-23andme> last accessed 2 May 2018.

context of online harassment, particularly in relation to the posting of videos and images.[123]

4.8 Indigenous Peoples and Data Sovereignty

As mentioned in Chapter 3, a number of DTC companies are marketing tests specifically for Native American ancestry. Such tests are quite controversial and the recent examples of some DTC companies not distinguishing between human and canine DNA samples[124] and providing ancestry test results for dogs highlight the potential for abuse and misuse of DNA tests. While the GDPR aims to strengthen data protection rights for citizens in the EU and to some extent some of the GDPR's purpose is to put people back in control of their data, the idea of data sovereignty for indigenous peoples can be viewed as referring 'to the proper locus of authority over the management of data about indigenous peoples, their territories and ways of life'.[125] 'Early expressions of indigenous data sovereignty can be seen in indigenous oral traditions, which included a complex set of rights and responsibilities concerning the use of community-held information'.[126] Movements promoting indigenous data sovereignty are growing. A good example is the work of Te Mana Raraunga (Maori Data Sovereignty Network).[127] Included in Te Mana Raraunga's Charter is the idea that data has special value for Maori people and that 'Maori data should be subject to Maori governance'.[128] While this is one example from one nation, it exemplifies conceptions of indigenous data sovereignty in that data is seen as something that should be under the control of the indigenous people to whom it relates. In reflecting on this, DTC companies should review their practices in relation to tests for indigenous ancestry. There is a need for

---

[123] See for example the Canadian case of *Jane Doe 464533* v *N.D* [2017] OJ No 60 (QL) <https://www.canlii.org/en/on/onsc/doc/2017/2017onsc127/2017onsc127.html> last accessed 24 October 2018.

[124] CBC News, 'After dog DNA debacle, Indigenous researcher says ancestry testing is "stupid science"' *CBC News Edmonton* (14 June 2018) <http://www.cbc.ca/news/canada/edmonton/dna-testing-indigenous-ancestry-1.4705797> last accessed 24 October 2018; Jorge Barrera and Tiffany Foxcroft, 'Heredity or hoax?' *CBC News* (13 June 2018) <https://newsinteractives.cbc.ca/longform/dna-ancestry-test> last accessed 24 October 2018.

[125] Tahu Kukutai And John Taylor (eds), *Indigenous Data Sovereignty Toward An Agenda* (Australian National University Press 2016) 14 <http://dx.doi.org/10.22459/CAEPR38.11.2016> last accessed 24 October 2018.

[126] Ibid. 14–15.

[127] Te Mana Raraunga Māori Data Sovereignty Network <https://www.temanararaunga.maori.nz> last accessed 24 October 2018.

[128] Te Mana Raraunga, 'Māori Data Sovereignty Network Charter' <http://planetmaori.com/Files/Content/2016/Te_Mana_Raraunga_Charter.pdf> last accessed 24 October 2018.

increased transparency and also a much more cautious approach in relation to tests for ancestry that purport to provide estimates of indigenous ancestry.

4.9 Privacy Best Practices for Consumer Genetics Testing Services

At the end of July 2018,[129] a number of prominent DTC companies made voluntary commitments to improving protection of consumer privacy. A set of guidelines was developed in collaboration with the Future of Privacy Forum.[130] The companies that have expressed support for these Practices to date are: Ancestry, 23andMe, Helix, MyHeritage, Habit, . . . African Ancestry and Living DNA (and previously FamilyTreeDNA).[131]

Main commitments of the Future of Privacy Forum guidelines,
Privacy Best Practices for Consumer Genetic Testing Services[132]

1. 'Transparency: Provide clear and complete information regarding the Company's policies and procedures for the management of personal data (personally identifiable information, Genetic Data, and protected health information) and de-identified information'[133]
2. 'Consent: Obtain express consent for collection, analysis, sharing, or reporting of Genetic Data';[134] [. . .] 'informed consent for research'[135]
3. 'Use and Onward Transfer: [. . .] collecting, using, and sharing Genetic Data in ways that are compatible with reasonable Consumer expectations for the context in which the data was collected'[136]

---

[129] Tony Romm and Drew Harwell, 'Ancestry, 23andMe and others say they will follow these rules when giving DNA data to businesses or police' *The Washington Post* (31 July 2018) <https://www.washingtonpost.com/technology/2018/07/31/ancestry-and-me-others-say-they-will-follow-these-rules-when-giving-dna-data-businesses-or-police/?noredirect=on&utm_term=.0f9962a4c6e8> last accessed 24 October 2018.

[130] Ibid.; Carson Martinez, 'Privacy Best Practices for Consumer Genetic Testing Services' Future of Privacy Forum (31 July 2018) <https://fpf.org/2018/07/31/privacy-best-practices-for-consumer-genetic-testing-services/> last accessed 24 October 2018.

[131] Carson Martinez, 'Privacy Best Practices for Consumer Genetic Testing Services' Future of Privacy Forum (31 July 2018, updated January 2019) <https://fpf.org/2018/07/31/privacy-best-practices-for-consumer-genetic-testing-services/> accessed 6 April 2019.

[132] Future of Privacy Forum, *Privacy Best Practices for Consumer Genetic Testing Services* (31 July 2018) <https://fpf.org/wp-content/uploads/2018/07/Privacy-Best-Practices-for-Consumer-Genetic-Testing-Services-FINAL.pdf> last accessed 24 October 2018. Full Commitments set out in the Addendum.

[133] Ibid. 3.

[134] Ibid. 4.

[135] Ibid. 5.

[136] Ibid. 7.

4. 'Provide the Consumer with access to their Genetic Data and inform the Consumer of what rights they have to correct or amend the record, how to report security concerns, and how long their Genetic Data and the original Biological Sample will be maintained'[137]
5. 'Accountability: Designate a responsible office or official who is accountable for the organization's compliance with the Privacy Principles'[138]
6. 'Security: Maintain a comprehensive security program that is reasonably designed to protect the security, privacy, confidentiality, and integrity of Genetic Data against risks – such as unauthorized access or use, or unintended or inappropriate disclosure or breach – through the use of administrative, technological, and physical safeguards appropriate to the sensitivity of the information'[139]
7. 'Consumer education: Make available to Consumers resources that advise about the implications and consequences of genetic testing, research, and data sharing'.[140]

While this is a positive step and all of these commitments are laudable, it needs to be stressed these are voluntary guidelines and not law. In relation to a number of the commitments, based on the review discussed in Chapter 5 together with the studies by Hazel and Slobogin[141] and Laestadius et al.,[142] in order to comply with these commitments DTC companies that agree to follow these Best Practices still have work to do in order to meet these commitments and will need to reform their privacy policies and wrap contracts in order to meet these obligations. For example, in Hazel and Slobogin's study of privacy policies they found that:[143]

95% of companies (52 of 55) provided no information regarding how the company would deal with a security breach or whether an affected consumer would be notified. Of the 5% of companies (3 of 55) that provided for consumer notification in the event of a security breach, only two states that consumers would be notified.

---

[137] Ibid. 7.
[138] Ibid. 9.
[139] Ibid. 9.
[140] Ibid. 10.
[141] Hazel and Slobogin (n 57)
[142] Laestadius et al. (n 13)
[143] Hazel and Slobogin (n 57) 19.

Furthermore, regardless of any voluntary commitments, DTC companies that offer services to consumers based in the EU will still be caught by the provisions of the GDPR and should be complying with it.

4.10 Conclusion

This chapter has given a brief introduction to a very complex area. It should be stressed that regardless of whether or not one chooses to take a genetic exceptionalist approach, the nature of genetic data does mean that it is different to some other forms of personal data. Remember that stored genetic data is immutable, can serve as both a unique identifier for an individual and can also be used to identify family members. Stored genetic data can also be used for a wide variety of secondary research purposes and it can also be shared with other entities, such as law enforcement and insurers.

DTC companies as for-profit entities are seeking to profit from their services and from the use of consumers' data. As will be seen in the following chapter, which provides a review of DTC wrap contract terms, DTC companies do seek to acquire very broad intellectual property rights in any products developed from consumer data in their contracts while granting the consumer very limited rights in their data. This is not in accordance with the GDPR and it may be that new ventures will emerge in future that empower the consumer more and put them in control.

In the last two years, a number of entities have begun to explore the use of blockchain for the storage of genomic data. At a basic level, 'blockchain is literally just a chain of blocks, but not in the traditional sense of those words. When we say the words "block" and "chain" in this context, we are actually talking about digital information (the "block") stored in a public database (the "chain").'[144] For example Zenome, which has as its slogan 'Your DNA is an asset'[145], Luna DNA, which describes itself as 'a community owned database that rewards individuals Luna Coins for contributing their DNA and other medical information',[146] and Nebula Genomics, which claims that it 'will leverage blockchain technology to eliminate middlemen and empower people to own their personal genomic data. This will effectively lower sequencing costs and enhance data privacy, resulting in growth of genomic data'.[147] These

---

[144] Luke Fortney, 'Blockchain, explained' *Investopedia* (updated 19 December 2018) <https://www.investopedia.com/terms/b/blockchain.asp> accessed 29 January 2019.

[145] Zenome <https://zenome.io> accessed 27 February 2018 – last accessed 24 October 2018.

[146] Luna DNA <https://www.lunadna.com> accessed 27 February 2018 – last accessed 24 October 2018.

[147] Nebula Genomics <https://www.nebulagenomics.io> accessed 27 February 2018 – last accessed 24 October 2018.

ventures do need to be monitored, as several mention the idea of consumers profiting from their DNA in marketing and the possibility of property rights in genomic data, which at present may not be supported in law, particularly in the US. Furthermore, as genomic data is shared amongst families, but also can be used to identify individuals, the use of blockchain for genomic data storage also poses privacy and security risks, as well as issues related to quality and informed consent.[148] Other ventures, such as Tim Berners-Lee's Decentralised Web project,[149] may hold more promise in heading towards a future where the individual can truly be in control of their data.

---

[148] Bristena Oprisanu, '"Wow such genetics. So data. Very forever?" An overview of the blockchain genomics trend' Bentham's Gaze (19 March 2018) <https://www.benthamsgaze.org/2018/03/19/wow-such-genetics-so-data-very-forever-an-overview-of-the-blockchain-genomics-trend>; see also Angela Chen, 'Why a DNA data breach is much worse than a credit card leak' *The Verge* (6 June 2018).

[149] MIT Internet Policy Research Initiative, Decentralized Web <https://internetpolicy.mit.edu/research/decentralized-information-group/> last accessed 24 October 2018.

5

Clicking Away Rights in DNA:
A Review of DTC Contracts

5.1 Introduction

This chapter sets out the findings of a review of the wrap contracts used by DTC companies that provide testing for health purposes.[1] This takes the form of a descriptive comparative document analysis of these contracts. It provides an outline of the typical terms likely to be included in a DTC contract and a discussion of terms which are likely to be deemed unfair and unenforceable under UK law. In this chapter it will be argued that several terms commonly included in DTC contracts are likely to be deemed to be unfair terms under UK law and consequently unenforceable. Given the frequency of use of these terms it is suggested that the best means of enhancing protection for consumers in this context in the short-term is for the Competition & Markets Authority (CMA) to begin to take pre-emptive action and work with the industry to discontinue the use of such terms. Specifically, the following terms are likely to be deemed to be unfair or fail to meet transparency requirements:

1. clauses allowing for unilateral variation of the contract
2. clauses disclaiming liability for fitness for purpose or for personal injury caused by the company's negligence

---

[1] Please see the related papers: Andelka M Phillips, 'Reading the fine print when buying your genetic self online: Direct-to-consumer genetic testing terms and conditions' (2017) *New Genetics and Society* 36(3) 273–95, 285–6 <http://dx.doi.org/10.1080/14636778.201 7.1352468>; Andelka M Phillips, 'Only a click away – DTC genetics for ancestry, health, love . . . and more: A view of the business and regulatory landscape' (2016) 8 *Applied and Translational Genomics* 16–22 <https://doi.org/10.1016/j.atg.2016.01.001>; and Andelka M Phillips, 'Genomic privacy and direct-to-consumer genetics – Big consumer genetic data – What's in that contract?' (presented at GenoPri'15 [The 2nd Workshop on Genome Privacy and Security] and published as part of IEEE Conference Proceedings 2015) <https://www.computer.org/csdl/proceedings/spw/2015/9933/00/9933a060.pdf> last accessed 23 October 2018.

3. clauses limiting scope of purpose
4. clauses purporting to bind the consumer to resolve any disputes in another jurisdiction
5. consent clauses

This chapter will also provide a brief overview of contract and consumer protection law, as it relates to DTC contracts. In so doing it will make reference to the applicable UK legislation, namely the Consumer Rights Act 2015 (CRA) and the work of the CMA. As it will always be difficult for an individual consumer to pursue litigation against a large company, if certain terms currently included in these contracts seem likely to be deemed as unfair, it is desirable that the CMA works with the industry to prevent the use of such terms.

This chapter provides a case study of the contracts of DTC companies that provide health testing. The choice was made to focus on health testing companies as it was not possible to analyse the contracts of the entire industry herein and companies that are engaged in offering health testing can be viewed as a good example that is representative of the broader issues raised by the DTC industry. Namely, DTC companies that perform health testing offer a diverse range of tests, often may provide testing for other purposes and are often entering into the medical research space with their research ventures and partnerships and mergers with other companies. Thus, the health testing industry highlights the potential for data sharing in this context. It also is the most reflective of the shift from patient to consumer, as these companies are often offering tests, which were only previously offered in a clinical setting. These are normally to be found on websites as Terms of Use, Terms of Service, Terms and Conditions, Privacy Policy or Privacy Statement. All documents were downloaded between 2011 and 2014. It should be noted that where examples of actual wording have been used this was to accurately describe the drafting as at the time when the documents were downloaded. The extractions were for the purposes of research.

Most versions were accessed between January 2013 and November 2014. Some companies may have altered their terms and their policies since November 2014 and these changes cannot be considered herein. However, the study by Hazel and Slobogin[2] which examined privacy policies and con-

---

[2] James Hazel and Christopher Slobogin, 'Who knows what, and when? A survey of the privacy policies proffered by U.S. direct-to-consumer genetic testing companies' (19 April 2018, last revised 18 October 2018) Cornell Journal of Law and Public Policy and Vanderbilt Law Research Paper No 18–18 <https://ssrn.com/abstract=3165765> last accessed 24 October 2018.

tracts collected from DTC websites in 2017 demonstrated that a number of the terms identified herein as problematic persist in more recent versions of the contracts and privacy policies.[3] As noted in the earlier chapters, it is also likely that DTC companies' consent mechanisms will not be sufficient to meet the requirements of the Human Tissue Act or of data protection law and the DTC industry does have some work to do in order to ensure compliance specifically in relation to the requirements of the GDPR.

In analysing these documents it appears that many contracts and privacy policies have not been specifically drafted to address the issues raised by the DTC industry. Although it is not possible to explore this issue in depth here it is concerning given the nature of DTC services and more research is needed. Furthermore, while some privacy policies of DTC companies have also been analysed as part of this research project, this work is primarily concerned with the contracts used by DTC companies. Consequently, the focus will be on contractual terms and how these might be challenged under contract law, rather than with discussion of whether the terms included in DTC privacy policies comply with data protection law. However, as discussed in Chapter 4, the Hazel and Slobogin and Laestadius et al.'s studies[4] demonstrate that there are problems with current privacy policies and data practices and the ICO and other data protection authorities should also have a role in regulating the DTC industry.

It should be noted though that sometimes privacy policies and terms and conditions are combined in one document and consequently some terms that are included in documents entitled 'Privacy Statement'(s) will be considered herein. Furthermore, given the tendency to combine privacy policies with contracts, the impact of unilateral variation clauses is increased, as clauses of this type may permit a company to alter their policies on use, storage, sharing and sale of stored genetic information in significant ways that may have serious consequences for consumers. As will be seen later in this chapter, that very few companies that allow for unilateral variation in their contracts will also notify their customers of changes means that clauses of this type need to be monitored and it would be beneficial for consumers if the CMA could work to discontinue the inclusion of these terms. Hazel and Slobogin also found that companies reserved the right to alter privacy policies and 'very few companies provided for individualised consumer notification of any potential changes'.[5]

---

[3] Ibid. (n 2) 11 and 15.
[4] Ibid.; LI Laestadius, Jennifer R Rich, and Paul L Auer, 'All your data (effectively) belong to us: Data practices among direct-to-consumer genetic testing firms' (2016) 19 *Genetics in Medicine* 513–20 doi:10.1038/gim.2016.136.
[5] Hazel and Slobogin (n 2)15.

It is important to again note the importance of the shift from providing genetic tests in a clinical setting to providing them directly to consumers in their homes. The significance of this shift is compounded by the other features of the DTC industry chiefly related to the fact that it is an Internet-based industry. Many web-based services can be viewed as fostering a sense of impulsivity, and this environment 'may be less conducive to informed contracting than the offline one' as users may not assign the 'same significance to a mouse click as a signature on a paper form', may 'expect speed and instant gratification', and may be 'overeager, even "click-happy"[. . .]'[6]

The work of Obar and Oeldorf-Hirsch[7] and Frischmann and Selinger[8] also highlights that the designed environment of clickwrap is fostering a culture of ignoring contracts and privacy policies. Studies have also indicated that the illusion of being in control may lead to poor decision-making by consumers. For example, the NCC suggests that through using dark patterns 'the idea of giving consumers better control over their personal data is circumvented [. . .] and at odds with the notion of consent being freely given'.[9] They suggest that user interfaces can nudge consumers away from making informed decisions and away from privacy-friendly options. Their 2018 *Deceived by Design* report[10] focused on how design can be used to manipulate consumers to share personal information about themselves and illustrates this with examples. They indicate that:

> that users who perceive that they are given more control, are also susceptible to take more risks when disclosing sensitive information. This is called the control paradox [. . .] This makes it particularly important that the controls are actually effective, and that they do what users expect. If users are only

---

[6] Nancy S Kim, *Wrap Contracts: Foundations and Ramifications* (Oxford University Press 2014) 59–61 and Robert A Hillman, 'On-line consumer standard-form contracting practices: A survey and discussion of legal omplications' (2005) Cornell Law Faculty Publications Paper 29 <http://dx.doi.org/10.2139/ssrn.686817>

[7] Jonathan A Obar and Anne Oeldorf-Hirsch, 'The biggest lie on the Internet: Ignoring the privacy policies and terms of service policies of social networking services' (2018) *Information, Communication & Society* doi: 10.1080/1369118X.2018.1486870.

[8] BM Frischmann and E Selinger, 'Engineering humans with contracts' (September 2016) Cardozo Legal Studies Research Paper N. 493. <https://papers.ssrn.com/sol3/papers.cfm?abstract_id=2834011>; BM Frischmann and E Selinger, *Re-Engineering Humanity* (Cambridge University Press 2018) chapter 5.

[9] NCC, *Deceived by Design* (June 2018) 4 <https://www.forbrukerradet.no/undersokelse/no-undersokelsekategori/deceived-by-design/> last accessed 25 October 2018.

[10] NCC, *Deceived by Design* (n 9) 4.

given an illusion of control, this can be considered a dark pattern used to manipulate users.[11]

The NCC also highlights the use of 'dark patterns' (a term coined by Harry Brignull[12]), which they characterise as exploitative design choices, which can 'push consumers toward choices that benefit the service provider'.[13] Dark patterns are also 'ethically problematic, because they mislead users into making choices that are not in their interest, and deprive them of their Agency'.[14] They also highlight that the use of dark patterns 'is particularly problematic given the power imbalances and information asymmetries that already exist between many service providers and their users'.[15]

In light of this, it is possible that the very nature of the online environment may actually be detrimental to consumers in the context of providing DTC services. Given the complex nature of test results and the uses to which genetic data may be put, the digital environment may not be conducive to enabling consumers to make informed decisions regarding the purchase of these tests. While more studies are needed, there is also evidence to suggest that many consumers may misunderstand the effect of online contracts and privacy policies. Studies by Haynes,[16] Kacen et al.[17] and Thompson[18] highlight the difficulties in this area, as it seems many consumers think that the mere existence of a privacy policy on a website means that the company will not share or sell personal data, when in fact the opposite is often true, with many policies serving as notice that companies will share or sell data.

---

[11] Ibid. 31.

[12] Ibid. 7; see Dark Patterns, 'What are dark patterns?' <https://darkpatterns.org/> last accessed 23 October 2018.

[13] Ibid. 4.

[14] Ibid. 7.

[15] Ibid. 7.

[16] Allyson Haynes Stuart, 'Online privacy policies: Contracting away control over personal information' (2006) 111(3) *Penn State Law Review* 587–624 <https://ssrn.com/abstract=2316378> last accessed 24 October 2018.

[17] Jacqueline J Kacen, James D Hess and Wei-Yu Kevin Chiang, 'Bricks or clicks? Consumer attitudes toward traditional stores and online stores' (2013) 18(1) *Global Economics and Management Review* 12–21 <https://doi.org/10.1016/S2340-1540(13)70003-3> last accessed 25 October 2018.

[18] David Thompson, 'I agreed to what? A call for enforcement of clarity in the presentation of privacy policies' (2012) 35(1) *Hastings Communications and Entertainment Law Journal* 203–26 <h ps://repository.uchastings.edu/hastings_comm_ent_law_journal/vol35/iss1/4> last accessed 25 October 2018.

(a) Summary of Review

Of 102 companies identified that provide health-related genetic testing, 31 companies did not have terms and conditions publicly available. Of the 31 that did not have terms available, some of the websites did have sections on their websites entitled Terms and Conditions, but when the link was clicked upon no terms or text were available. Consequently, this chapter's focus is on the 71 companies which did have terms and conditions available. It is likely that companies which did not have terms and conditions available do in fact have contracts and policies, which are only made available once a person registers on the site and makes a purchase.[19] Therefore it should not be assumed that they do not have terms and conditions, or that companies which have their terms and conditions available are necessarily engaged in more responsible business practice than those which do not.

(b) The Work of the Competition & Markets Authority (CMA)

The CMA was formed in 2014 and it has taken over some of the functions of the OFT and the Competition Commission. Under the Consumer Rights Act the CMA has authority to take enforcement actions against companies which are using unfair terms or notices. It can apply to a court for an injunction against specific companies. However, it cannot take on individual cases on behalf of individual consumers, which means that in practice if consumers seek redress their options may be limited. It can be very difficult for individuals to sue such large companies.[20] It is hoped that the CMA will monitor DTC companies' practices where they offer services to UK-based consumers.

CMA has recently released its findings report *Consumer Law Compliance Review: Cloud Storage*.[21] This review was concerned with assessing whether cloud storage providers' terms and business practices complied with consumer protection law. It should be noted that the report has already had some degree of success with improving terms, as several cloud service providers have made commitments to improve their terms.[22] The report is very relevant to the present discussion, as it indicates the types of terms and business practice which the CMA is likely to view as problematic and potentially unfair.

---

[19] Hazel and Slobogin (n 2) 14–15.

[20] Kim, *Wrap Contracts* (n 6)

[21] CMA, *Consumer Law Compliance Review: Cloud Storage Findings Report* (2016) <https:// assets.digital.cabinet-office.gov.uk/media/57472953e5274a037500000d/cloud-storage-findings-report.pdf> last accessed 25 October 2018.

[22] CMA, 'Cloud storage: Consumer compliance review' homepage <https://www.gov.uk/ cma-cases/cloud-storage-consumer-compliance-review> last accessed 25 October 2018.

For each of the terms that the CMA finds problematic, it also makes recommendations on how terms and business practice might be improved. Some of these suggestions could usefully be adapted to the DTC context.

(c) The Nature of Contract

Contracts at their most basic level can be defined as legally enforceable or legally binding promises. Central to the traditional conception of a contract are the concepts of offer and acceptance and consideration.[23] Here one person will make an offer, which is in turn accepted by another, normally in exchange for something else, 'consideration'. Contract law is the law of bargaining and there is a strong emphasis on freedom of will and an important purpose of contract law generally is 'to promote individual autonomy'.[24] There is much academic literature regarding the theoretical justifications for contract law and the legal enforcement of contracts.[25] For Radin, there are essentially 'two main branches: welfare theories and autonomy theories'.[26] Autonomy theories are centred on 'an exchange of promises, or on agreement'.[27] In such theories, 'in order for any entitlement to be transferred [. . .] voluntariness of transfer is an indispensable premise of justice'.[28]

Much of the enforcement of contracts can also be justified on pragmatic grounds as it allows businesses to conduct their affairs with more certainty. It is this justification that has been largely relied upon by courts in enforcing standard form contracts and standard form contracts have developed as a consequence of industrialisation and the development of the mass market.[29]

Unfortunately, while the model of parties agreeing on a bargain that is to their mutual advantage is still important today, especially in the online environment, it does not always reflect reality. In wrap contracts specifically the element of voluntariness may be lacking. Generally, parties will be held to be bound by the agreements they have made and there are strong arguments concerned with autonomy, which are used to justify a cautious approach to questioning the validity of a bargain once made.[30]

---

[23] AS Burrows, *A Casebook on Contract* (4th edn, Hart Publishing 2013) 3–4.

[24] Kim, *Wrap Contracts* (n 6) 207.

[25] See generally Gregory Klass, George Letsas and Prince Saprai (eds), *Philosophical Foundations of Contract Law* (Oxford University Press 2014); and MJ Radin, *Boilerplate* (Princeton Press 2013) chapter 4.

[26] Radin 57.

[27] Ibid. 57.

[28] Ibid. 59.

[29] Kim, *Wrap Contracts* (n 6) 20–6.

[30] Ibid. 9–13.

In contract law, the emphasis is normally on whether a person has given appropriate assent to the terms of the agreement. It should be noted that assent can be passive and sometimes may be implied from a course of dealing or on the basis of constructive or actual knowledge.[31] In the context especially of standard form contracts, courts have upheld the validity of contracts where one party has not in fact read the terms. Wrap contracts are a form of adhesion contract and Kim also views the way assent has been constructed in contracts of adhesion more generally as problematic. She writes that 'assent in the context of adhesive contracts thus became construed to mean acquiescence rather than active agreement [. . .] assent is often stripped of any requirement of volition or desire to enter into a contract'.[32]

However, in a clinical setting, the emphasis in genetic testing has been on individuals giving appropriate consent, which should be voluntary and informed.[33] More generally, in relation to medical treatment, valid consent of the patient is required and it is possible that operating on a patient without appropriate consent could breach their rights under Article 3 of the European Convention on Human Rights, which affords protection against 'torture or inhuman or degrading treatment'.[34] Valid consent in a medical setting arguably requires a much higher standard than contractual assent. Doctors are required to provide patients with information regarding the treatment they are considering before obtaining consent and when doctors provide information to patients regarding procedures, 'it is not enough to ensure this advice is provided – attempts must be made to make sure it is understood'.[35] This can be demonstrated by reference to the General Medical Council's guidance on consent, which suggests that in obtaining consent, doctors 'should check whether the patient needs any additional support to understand information, to communicate their wishes, or to make a decision'.[36] It is also far less

---

[31] Ewan McKendrick, *Contract law: Text, cases, and materials* (5th edn, Oxford University Press 2012) 80–115, 313–37.

[32] Kim, *Wrap Contracts* (n 6) 27.

[33] J Herring, *Medical Law and Ethics* (4th edn, Oxford University Press 2012)155–62; and NHS Choices, 'Consent to treatment' (NHS Choices) <https://www.nhs.uk/conditions/consent-to-treatment/> accessed 31 July 2015 – last accessed 25 October 2018. This provides that 'Consent is required from a patient regardless of the intervention – from a physical examination to organ donation'.

[34] Herring, *Medical Law and Ethics* (n 33) 149, citing *R (N)* v *Dr M, A Health Authority Trust and Dr O* [2002] EWHC 1911.

[35] Ibid. 173.

[36] General Medical Council, *Consent: patients and doctors making decisions together* (General Medical Council, 2008) para 21 <https://www.gmc-uk.org/static/documents/content/Consent_-_English_0617.pdf> last accessed 25 October 2018.

likely that consent will be implied in the context of medical treatment, as the rights of patients to refuse treatment are afforded strong legal protection. The position in UK law is that a person may 'refuse treatment even if without the treatment she or he will die'.[37] The importance of obtaining valid consent to treatment was reaffirmed in the recent case of *Montgomery (Appellant)* v *Lanarkshire Health Board (Respondent) (Scotland)*, which has overruled the previous House of Lords decision of *Sidaway* v *Board of Governors of the Bethlem Royal Hospital*[38]

Yet DTC contracts and many other Internet companies tend to treat the concepts of consent and assent interchangeably and sometimes in the context of a terms of service agreement companies will mention consent to the contract rather than assent or acceptance. This practice may potentially be more common also due to the broader trend of Internet industries borrowing or copying the terms of their competitors.[39] This conflation is problematic and is another feature highlighting the paradigm shift from patient to consumer apparent in the DTC context and the potential inadequacy of current consent mechanisms if these are compared to the requirements for consent in a medical setting.

On the matter of the validity of DTC contracts, it is also possible that an argument could be made against the validity of wrap contracts in this context on the basis that many DTC companies are providing insufficient notice of their terms.[40] Such an argument would rely on the position established in *Parker* v *South Eastern Railway Co*,[41] and affirmed in the case law since, which is that:

> a term will only become incorporated in the contract if notice of the term has been given and that notice is reasonably sufficient in all the circumstances. This is a question of fact, 'in answering which the tribunal must look at all the circumstances and the situation of the parties'.[42]

---

[37] Herring, *Medical Law and Ethics* (n 33) 552 citing *Re T (Adult: Refusal of Treatment)* [1992] 4 ALL ER 649, [652]–[653]; *Airedale NHS Trust* v *Bland* [1993] 1 All ER 821, [860] (Lord Keith), [866] (Lord Goff), [881 (Lord Browne-Wilkinson), and [889 (Lord Mustill); *Re AK* [2001] 1 FLR 129.

[38] [2015] 2 All ER 1031, [2015] UKSC 11; [1985] 1 All ER 643, [1985] UKHL 1, [1985] AC 871. Philip S Rathbone, 'New rules of consent: The patient decides' (2015) 350 *British Medical Journal*: h1534 doi: https://doi.org/10.1136/bmj.h1534 <https://www.bmj.com/content/350/bmj.h1534/rr-3> accessed 29 January 2019.

[39] Kim, *Wrap Contracts* (n 6) 60–1.

[40] Richard Lawson, *Exclusion Clauses and Unfair Contract Terms* (11th edn, Thomson Reuters [Professional] UK Limited 2014) 9–12.

[41] (1877) LR 2 CPD 416.

[42] Lawson (n 40) 9–10.

(d) Brief Discussion of Clickwrap and Browsewrap in the DTC Context

All the DTC contracts and privacy policies examined herein are wrap contracts, either clickwrap (click-through) or browsewrap. These are a new type of adhesion contract known as the wrap contract, which have arisen in the digital environment. Clickwrap contracts 'do not permit a user to progress until and unless the user clicks on a box containing the words "I agree" or some similar expression of agreement'[43]. Meanwhile, browsewrap contracts normally have their terms only accessible by means of a hyperlink to another page or another website. These are also mass consumer standard form contracts (sometimes referred to as 'boilerplate') also referred to as contracts of adhesion. Adhesion contracts have terms that are offered on a 'take it or leave it' basis.[44] However, while wrap contracts might be treated as adhesion contracts, they are not necessarily the same as older forms of adhesion contracts and may represent a separate class of contract.[45]

Both clickwrap and browsewrap have developed from shrink-wrap agreements (also referred to as shrink-wrap licences), which were originally conceived in order to protect the rights of software developers. Shrink-wrap contracts are included on the packaging of software products and a person normally signals their assent to be bound by these contracts by ripping the packaging open.[46] There are now also 'tapwraps', which are the contracts encountered on mobile devices which allow a person to agree to terms with a tap of the finger.[47] Companies also often engage in the practice of 'multiwrapping', which Kim uses to refer to 'the use of more than one type of Wrap contract'.[48]

These contractual forms are common to all forms of online commerce. DTC companies and other Internet companies use wrap agreements because it allows them to set the terms of the bargain and to minimise their risk.[49] This can in fact be seen as a form of private legislation skewed in favour of the industry. As it is frequently the case that people do not read these contracts and they cost little for the company to create, there is a growing

---

[43] Kim, *Wrap Contracts* (n 6) 35; Nancy S Kim, 'Exploitation by wrap contracts – click "Agree"' (2014) 39(2) California Bar IP Journal *New Matter* 10–17 <https://ssrn.com/abstract=2461272> last accessed 25 October 2018.

[44] Kim, *Wrap Contracts* (n 6) 4–5; Kayleen Manwaring, 'Enforceability of clickwrap and browsewrap terms in Australia: Lessons from the US and the UK' (2011) 5(1) *Studies in Ethics, Law, and Technology* 1–17 doi: 0.2202/1941-6008.1102.

[45] See generally Kim, *Wrap Contracts* (n 6).

[46] Ibid. Kim (n 6).

[47] Ibid. 3.

[48] Ibid. 93.

[49] Kim, *Wrap Contracts* (n 6) 73.

trend for companies to make their contracts longer and more one-sided. In e-commerce more generally, it is common practice for companies to borrow and copy from the contracts of their competition[50] and the examples in this chapter will be illustrative of this practice as sometimes the terms used by different companies use wording that is identical or extremely similar. Function may dictate the form used in the sense that lawyers tend to prefer to follow the use of a form of drafting already used as a precedent, which has been thought to address a particular legal risk in order to ascertain a greater measure of certainty. The drafting may be outdated, taken from other contexts or yet be untested in the provision of DTC services. As such, this copying may be inappropriate and lead to an opposite, less certain or unexpected outcome.

Caution should be exercised in copying from models used in other digital services as they may employ drafting which does not adequately address the risk or is otherwise inappropriate for the particular context and therefore potentially exploitative, risky or deficient.

Such deficiencies are pertinently illustrated in recent studies. For example, the NCC's *Deceived by Design* report did not focus on the DTC context, but instead upon leading digital service providers by sampling their settings and showing:[51]

> how default settings and dark patterns, techniques and features of interface design meant to manipulate users, are used to nudge users towards privacy intrusive options. The findings include privacy intrusive default settings, misleading wording, giving users an illusion of control, hiding away privacy-friendly choices, take-it-or-leave-it choices, and choice architectures where choosing the privacy friendly option requires more effort for the users.

The NCC has undertaken studies which variously assist consumers and also advocate best practices for digital businesses which may seek to both enable consumers to comprehend what they are agreeing to and at the same time enable the business to interact in a compliant and, therefore, more certain way.[52]

The digital environment has been criticised as potentially problematic for consumers at a design level. In contrast to the privacy by design model, digital services may also feature exploitative design choices, characterised as 'dark

---

[50] Ibid. 61.

[51] NCC, *Deceived by Design* (June 2018) 4 <https://www.forbrukerradet.no/undersokelse/no-undersokelsekategori/deceived-by-design/> last accessed 25 October 2018.

[52] NCC, *APPFAIL Threats to Consumers in Mobile Apps* (March 2016) <https://www.forbrukerradet.no/undersokelse/2015/appfail-threats-to-consumers-in-mobile-apps/> last accessed 18 October 2018.

patterns' by the Norwegian Consumer Council. Websites and their terms and conditions might in some ways also be viewed under such an analysis as undermining 'consent', such as by employing legalese language which requires interpretation by a lawyer in order to be deciphered, and using other structures, which use dark patterns to drive consumers towards choices that benefit the service provider.

The relevance of this to providing DTC services is that DTC services have tended to use models designed to work in the general digital service provider context. Those models may be inadequate and inappropriate even for such digital services. Copying such models may alter the position of consumers of DTC service providers such that cumulatively the deficiencies make the bargain one sided, or potentially less than fair.

Brief Note on the Spreadex *v* Cochrane Case

Spreadex is the only UK case to date specifically dealing with a wrap contract. Briefly, the case concerned an online betting account. Cochrane had joined Spreadex's online betting platform, but while he was away from home, his girlfriend's five-year-old son used his account to place bets and accrued a £50,000 debt which the company wanted Cochrane to repay. The main clause that was in dispute was clause 10(3), which was included in Spreadex's 49-page Customer Agreement. The clause purported to make the customer responsible for all transactions made with their account. The clause read: '[. . .] You will be deemed to have authorised all trading under your account number'.[53]

Donaldson J questioned whether there was in fact valid consideration provided in the circumstances, due to the fact that Spreadex was merely providing a platform and although Cochrane had created an account the service was not activated in essence until he had in fact placed a bet. According to the Court:

> The provision of an on-line interactive platform is in effect simply a more modern equivalent of the expressed readiness of a potential contracting party (also covered in the Consumer Agreement) to enter into contracts by receiving and responding orally to telephone calls.[54]

The Court then went on to hold that clause 10(3) did result in 'not only a significant imbalance in the parties' rights and obligations but one which viewed overall is unfair within the meaning of the UTCCR'.[55] The judge went on to state that:

[53] *Spreadex* [8].
[54] *Spreadex Ltd* v *Cochrane* [15].
[55] Ibid. [20].

It would have come close to a miracle if he had read the second sentence of Clause 10(3), let alone appreciated its purport or implications, and it would have been quite irrational for the claimant to assume that he had.[56]

As *Spreadex* is only a High Court case it is not strong authority, but if courts were to take a similar approach to other wrap contracts this could be beneficial for consumers and might mean that several terms commonly included in DTC contracts could be deemed unfair by the courts. Although the facts of this case do not resemble the situation where a dispute might potentially arise between a DTC company and consumer, the Court's approach here is relevant to this discussion. Significantly, the length of the contract in *Spreadex* was treated as weighing against the company and in line with the CMA's guidance it is likely that particularly lengthy contracts may be treated as failing transparency requirements. If companies bury unexpected terms in very long contracts, it seems more likely that they might be viewed as unfair and unenforceable.

(e) The Typical DTC Contract

A DTC contract will often include the following terms: a clause allowing the company to unilaterally alter its terms; clauses indicating that services are provided for informational purposes and do not constitute medical advice; a clause governing consent; a clause governing acceptance of the contract; exclusion clauses disclaiming liability; clauses requiring consumers to indemnify the company; clauses disclaiming warranties; clauses governing intellectual property; clauses governing disclosure of data; clauses making arbitration compulsory, which may include waivers of class actions and class arbitrations; clauses prescribing the choice of law or jurisdiction for setting disputes; and clauses limiting remedies and damages. As will be seen from the examples given, the majority of these terms are open to challenge on the grounds of their unfairness.

DTC contracts generally resemble contracts used by Internet service providers. Loos and Luzak's study comparing the terms included in the contracts of Google, Twitter, Facebook and Dropbox[57] suggested that many of these terms would be likely to be deemed unfair under EU law. In this study they primarily relied upon the provisions of the Unfair Terms Directive and the case law of the Court of Justice of the European Union (CJEU) in investigating potential unfairness. They examined the following types of term: terms

---

[56] Ibid. [21].

[57] Marco Loos and Joasia Luzak, 'Wanted: A bigger stick. On unfair terms in consumer contracts with online service providers' (2015) 39 *Journal of Consumer Policy* 63–90 <https://doi.org/10.1007/s10603-015-9303-7> last accessed 18 October 2018.

providing for unilateral alteration of terms or unilateral changes to the nature of the service offered; 'exclusions or limitations of liability'; 'international jurisdiction clauses'; and 'choice-of-law clauses'.[58] They concluded their analysis 'by illustrating the overarching problem of many online contractual terms, namely, their lack of transparency',[59] which is at odds with the requirement of Article 5 of the Unfair Terms Directive, which requires that 'terms must always be drafted in plain, intelligible language'.[60] In line with their work, as will be demonstrated by the examples provided in this chapter, as many terms commonly included in DTC contracts resemble those included in those of Internet service provider contracts using similar language, it seems likely that they would also be construed as unfair under EU law and that they may also fail to meet transparency requirements.

To date most clickwrap and browsewrap disputes have centred on forum selection and arbitration clauses.[61] 23andMe has faced a number of class actions in the last few years, which do fit into this pattern, as the cases have focused on the arbitration clause in 23andMe's Terms of Service.

However, overall arbitration clauses are not as common in the contracts of DTC companies providing health services as they are in online contracts more generally and while they are significant this chapter will also consider several other clauses, which should be seen as important in relation to their impact on consumers' rights in the DTC context and which are frequently included in DTC contracts.

DTC contracts include many terms and are normally thousands of words in length. For example, 23andMe's Terms of Service is 9,081 words, while its Privacy Statement is 32 pages and 15,807 words long; Gene By Gene's DNA DTC Terms and Conditions runs to 3,645 words and its consent document is 4,718 words; and DNA Spectrum's Terms of Service is 5,165 words long.[62] It is common for online contracts generally to be at least 6,000 words in length. Examples from other industries are the iTunes agreement, which is 19,972 words long, and Amazon's Terms and Conditions at 36,275 words long.[63] The UK consumer organisation Which? has also studied the lengths of the contracts

---

[58] Ibid. 66–8.

[59] Ibid. (n 57) 3, and 24–5.

[60] Ibid. (n 57) 24, citing Directive 93/13/EEC of 5 April 1993 On Unfair Terms On Consumer Contracts.

[61] Manwaring (n 44) 1–17, 13.

[62] Copies of all contracts and privacy policies are on file with the author.

[63] Wigley + Company Solicitors, 'To read or not to read . . . Online Ts and Cs. Or Hamlet' (Wigley + Company Solicitors 2015) <http://www.wigleylaw.com/assets/Uploads/To-read-or-not-to-read.pdf > last accessed 18 October 2018.

for many popular services and found that Google's All-Inclusive terms and conditions were 10,640 in length and Windows Live's terms were 14,714.[64]

While all the terms included in DTC contracts are interesting, what follows is a discussion of the terms that are considered most important for consumers. The examples provided are from companies categorised as providers of health-related testing, regardless of their location and including those offering their services through physicians. Central to this discussion is whether some of these terms qualify as unfair terms in accordance with the definition provided in section 62 of the Consumer Rights Act, that is, whether they cause a 'significant imbalance in the parties' rights and obligations under the contract to the detriment of the consumer'.[65]

Brief Note on ACCC *v* Valve

The case of *ACCC* v *Valve*[66] is relevant as it is one of the very few cases that has been brought by a regulatory body regarding a wrap contract internationally. It is an Australian case, initiated by the Australian Competition and Consumer Commission (ACCC) in August 2014.[67] It centred on three versions of Valve's Steam User Subscriber Agreement and whether this breached the Australian Consumer Law (ACL) by making false and misleading representations to Australian consumers.

In 2016 the Federal Court ruled against Valve, finding that it 'had engaged in misleading or deceptive conduct and made false or misleading representations'.[68] The Federal Court decided in ACCC's favour, fining Valve

---

[64] Maartje Elshout, Millie Elsen, Jorna Leenheer, Marco Loos, and Joasia Luzak, *Study on Consumers' Attitudes Towards Terms Conditions (T&Cs) Final Report* (Report for the European Commission, Consumers, Health, Agriculture and Food Executive Agency [CHAFEA] on behalf of Directorate-General for Justice and Consumers, 22 September 2016) <https://ssrn.com/abstract=2847546> 14 citing Which? study – Rich Parris, 'Online T&Cs longer than Shakespeare plays – who reads them?' *The Conversation* (23 March 2012) <https://conversation.which.co.uk/technology/length-of-website-terms-and-conditions/> last accessed 25 October 2018.

[65] Consumer Rights Act 2015 s 62.

[66] *Australian Competition and Consumer Commission* v *Valve Corporation* (No 3) [2016] FCA 196; *Australian Competition and Consumer Commission* v *Valve Corporation* (No 7) [2016] FCA 1553; *Australian Competition and Consumer Commission* v *Valve Corporation* (No 8) [2016] FCA 1584.

[67] Australian Competition and Consumer Commission, 'Federal Court finds Valve made misleading representations about consumer guarantees' (ACCC, Press Release, 29 March 2016) <https://www.accc.gov.au/media-release/federal-court-finds-valve-made-misleading-representations-about-consumer-guarantees> last accessed 25 October 2018.

[68] ACCC, 'High Court dismisses Valve's special leave to appeal application' (20 April 2018) <https://www.accc.gov.au/media-release/high-court-dismisses-valve's-special-leave-to-appeal-application> last accessed 25 October 2018.

$3 million (AUD). The Court's decision was confirmed in 2017 by the Full Federal Court.[69] There were a number of further appeals to the Australian High Court, but the latest appeal was dismissed by the High Court (the highest Australian court) in April 2018,[70] which can be seen as a victory for consumers and Australia's consumer protection law.

> ### *ACCC* v *Valve*: Court Findings in relation to breaches of law
>
> The Federal Court found that Valve breached the law in relation to its user agreement and refund policy by leading consumers to believe that:
>
> 1. consumers were not entitled to a refund for digitally downloaded games purchased from Valve via the Steam website or Steam Client (in any circumstances)
> 2. Valve had excluded statutory guarantees and/or warranties that goods would be of acceptable quality
> 3. Valve had restricted or modified statutory guarantees and/or warranties of acceptable quality[71]

The ruling is significant because Valve is an American company based in Washington State (it operates an online game distribution network known as Steam).[72] The earlier decisions and the most recent High Court dismissal of Valve's request supports the ACCC's view that companies providing products and services to Australian consumers should be complying with Australian law.

---

[69] ACCC, 'Full Federal Court confirms that Valve misled gamers' (Press Release, 22 December 2017) <https://www.accc.gov.au/media-release/full-federal-court-confirms-that-valve-misled-gamers> last accessed 25 October 2018; *Valve Corporation* v *Australian Competition and Consumer Commission* [2017] FCAFC 224.

[70] S Fogel, 'Valve loses appeal over $2.3 million fine in Australia' *Variety* (20 April 2018) <https://variety.com/2018/gaming/news/valve-australia-fine-1202772984/> last accessed 1 August 2018; ACCC, 'High Court dismisses Valve's special leave to appeal application' (20 April 2018) <https://www.accc.gov.au/media-release/high-court-dismisses-valve's-special-leave-to-appeal-application> last accessed 25 October 2018.

[71] ACCC, 'Federal Court finds Valve made misleading representations about consumer guarantees' (Press Release, 29 March 2016) <https://www.accc.gov.au/media-release/federal-court-finds-valve-made-misleading-representations-about-consumer-guarantees> last accessed 25 October 2018.

[72] Davies Collinson Cave, 'Valve ordered to pay $3 million for misleading Australian gamers on Steam' *Lexology* (19 January 2018) <https://www.lexology.com/library/detail.aspx?g=952517e9-bda4-4ce1-88fe-c6c1835a9d62> last accessed 25 October 2018.

(f) Brief Note on 23andMe Class Actions

Several class actions have been filed against 23andMe. The class actions allege a variety of claims related to 'false advertising, unfair competition, and consumer protection'.[73] Nine cases have been filed and eight of these were consolidated for pre-trial purposes (there are also three pending arbitrations). On 28 April 2014, 23andMe filed an omnibus motion to compel arbitration.

In May 2014, lead counsel were appointed by the Court and the Casey Gerry Ankcorn group led the case.[74] This was followed on 28 of May 2014 by the plaintiffs filing a motion in opposition, with 23andMe filing a reply on 4 June.

Then in June 2014, Koh J ruled to compel arbitration granting the motion, thus upholding the arbitration clause in the 23andMe agreement. The plaintiffs' claims were dismissed without prejudice, but the plaintiffs filed a Notice of Appeal on 23 July 2014 and the appeal was scheduled for a hearing before the Court of Appeal of the Ninth Circuit on 31 October 2014. The case number is 14-16405.[75] It seems the actions have now been divided into two groups and 23andMe has argued that its Terms of Service bar class arbitration. According to an article by Kendall, a hearing held in San Francisco in June 2015 was decided in favour of 23andMe.[76]

The reasoning in the *Tompkins* order has been criticised and the criticism may be justified. Central to understanding the criticism is an understanding of the process which a consumer follows in purchasing a DTC test from 23andMe. When a consumer purchases a test, they are essentially ordering a service, and this does involve several steps. The consumer will purchase the test online and this involves paying the purchase price and only then will they receive a test kit in the post. The consumer will then use the kit to collect a sample of their DNA and send it back to the company for sequencing. After the company receives the sample they will sequence it and communicate the results to

---

[73] *Tompkins* v *23andMe, INC* (District Court, ND California 2014).

[74] Marisa Kendall, 'Koh appoints lead lounsel in scrum over 23andMe suits' *The Recorder* (15 May 2014) <https://www.law.com/therecorder/almID/1202655508972/?slret urn=20180925003615> last accessed 25 October 2018; Benjamin Cohn and Dalga Surofchy, 'Fighting for the right to know: OBR-Bay debates FDA regulation of DTC genetic testing' (Oxbridge Biotech Roundtable, 2014) <http://www.oxbridgebiotech.com/review/featured/23andme-debate/> last accessed 27 May 2014.

[75] Ankcorn Law Firm, '23andMe: Going up on appeal' <http://www.markankcorn.com/blog/2014/8/3/23andme-going-up-on-appeal> last accessed 23 September 2014.

[76] Marisa Kendall, 'SF judge sides with 23andMe on class claims' *The Recorder* (10 June 2015) <therecorder.com/id=1202729012905?keywords=Marisa+Kendall> last accessed 15 May 2014.

the consumer. For many companies, once the consumer receives the kit the consumer is required to register the kit online and create an online account, which is sometimes used for communication of results, other communication and social networking functions if these are offered by the company. In the 23andMe case, terms were allegedly only viewable when consumers registered their kits and not when they made their initial orders. Koh J interpreted this registration process as constituting a new contract. This interpretation has been criticised and it seems that the better view is that this should be viewed as an amendment to the original contract, because a consumer may be using the test kit to access a service, but the object of their contract with the company is the provision of genetic sequencing, not the provision of a test kit. Specifically the judgement has been criticised on the grounds that:

> it treats the registration process as a completely new contract, when I see it as an amendment of the existing contract formed when the buyer made the purchase. If it's an amendment, then the delivery of services can't provide new consideration because that's why the buyer bought the services in the first place. As a result, the resolution ignores the buyer's economic realities.[77]

Furthermore, if the test was purchased as a gift, the purchaser would have had no opportunity to read the arbitration clause and thus to agree to it, as they are not obliged to create an account, which is problematic and means that the purchaser of a gift has not given assent to the terms of the contract and consequently enforcement of contractual terms against purchasers of gifts is open to challenge.

In September 2017, 23andMe settled these class actions.[78] Under the settlement, individuals who purchased tests between 16 October 2007 and 22 November 2013 are entitled to either a $40 (USD) certificate of the cost of the 23andMe genetic testing kit or the sum of $12.50 (USD) in cash compensation.[79]

---

[77] E Goldman, '23andMe's browsewrap fails, but its post-purchase clickthrough works anyway – Tompkins v. 23andMe' *Technolgy & Marketing Law Blog* (2 July 2014) <https://blog.ericgoldman.org/archives/2014/07/23andmes-browsewrap-fails-but-its-post-purchase-clickthrough-works-anyway-tompkins-v-23andme.htm> last accessed 25 October 2018.

[78] KCC, 'Davis-Hudson, et al. v. 23andMe, Inc. Settlement' <http://www.23andmesettlement.com> last accessed 1 August 2018; Paul Tassin, '23andMe DNA testing kit class action settlement' *Top Class Actions* (19 September 2017) <https://topclassactions.com/lawsuit-settlements/closed-settlements/820889-23andme-dna-testing-kit-class-action-settlement/> last accessed 25 October 2018.

[79] KCC, Davis-Hudson, et al. v. 23andMe, Inc. Settlement Frequently Asked Questions <http://www.23andmesettlement.com/faqs.aspx#a1> last accessed 25 October 2018.

5.2 Challenging Unfair Terms in DTC Contracts

Below is a discussion of some of the terms commonly included in DTC contracts with a focus on those that are likely to be open to challenge on the grounds of unfairness.

(a) The Consumer Rights Act 2015

The Consumer Rights Act 2015 (CRA) came into force on 1 October 2015. The Act is of great significance in the context of discussing potentially unfair terms as it consolidates previous UK legislation governing unfair terms in business to consumer contracts and implements EU directives. It essentially replaces the Unfair Contract Terms Act 1977 and the Unfair Terms in Consumer Contracts Regulations 1999 (UTCCR) and implements aspects of the Consumer Rights Directive and the Unfair Contract Terms Directive. The Act applies to both contract terms and notices. As this is the most current law, this chapter takes the provisions of this Act as its central focus, but it will touch upon the previous Unfair Contract Terms Act and the Unfair Terms Regulations. Because it is intended to consolidate previous legislation and continue to implement the Unfair Terms Directive, the new Act does resemble the UTCCR and the Directive.

Key Provisions of the Consumer Rights Act

For present purposes there are a number of provisions that have significance in examining the terms of DTC companies. The term 'consumer' is defined in section 2(3) in a similar way to in the EU Directives and so should cover consumers in the context of DTC services.

Section 62 of the Act requires terms and notices to be fair and sets out the test for determining fairness. According to section 62(4), 'A term is unfair if, contrary to the requirement of good faith, it causes a significant imbalance in the parties' rights and obligations under the contract to the detriment of the consumer'.

In its *Unfair Contract Terms Guidance,* the CMA states that:[80]

> **Significant imbalance** is concerned with the parties' rights and obligations under the contract. The requirement is met if a term is so weighted in favour of a business that it tilts the rights and obligations under the

---

[80] Competition & Markets Authority, *Unfair Contract Terms Guidance – Guidance on the Unfair Terms Provisions in the Consumer Rights Act 2015* (CMA, CMA37, 31 July 2015) para 2.16 <https://assets.publishing.service.gov.uk/government/uploads/system/uploads/attachment_data/file/450440/Unfair_Terms_Main_Guidance.pdf> last accessed 25 October 2018.

contract significantly in its favour, for instance by granting the trader undue discretion or imposing a disadvantageous burden on the consumer.

As assessing fairness requires consideration of the surrounding circumstances and the other terms agreed upon and the subject matter of the contract, it seems that in the context of assessing the fairness of particular terms in a DTC contract, a court should consider the environment in which such contracts are made. Namely, that these are wrap contracts often entered into by the consumer in their home and they are for a service which has normally only been offered to people in a clinical setting. While much e-commerce is concerned with the sale of ordinary consumer products, DTC services are novel and represent disruptive innovation. Where companies provide tests for health purposes, the information they provide is of a complex nature and it may be that using wrap contracts to govern DTC services may not be providing sufficient protection for consumers.

Section 68 of the Act requires contractual terms and notices to be transparent. In order to be transparent, terms and notices must be drafted in 'plain and intelligible language'. This is similar to the requirements for notices under the GDPR.

Part 1 of the Act also blacklists certain types of term and section 65 has the effect of voiding those terms. Schedule 2 also provides a non-exhaustive and indicative list of terms that are likely to be deemed unfair. This list closely resembles the list provided in the Consumer Rights Directive.[81] As this list is indicative only it is possible that some terms of a type specified in the schedule will not in fact be deemed to be unfair and likewise, terms of a type not specified in the schedule may be deemed to be unfair.

(b) Unilateral Variation Clauses

Summary of Review of Unilateral Variation Clauses
Clauses allowing DTC companies to alter their terms are particularly common, with 72 per cent of the 71 companies with terms available including such a clause.[82] Of these companies, 39 per cent include a term which

---

[81] Council Directive 93/13/EEC of 5 April 1993 on unfair terms in consumer contracts <https://eur-lex.europa.eu/legal-content/EN/TXT/?uri=CELEX%3A31993L0013> last accessed 18 October 2018; and Directive 2011/83/EU of the European Parliament and of the Council of 25 October 2011 on consumer rights, amending Council Directive 93/13/EEC and Directive 1999/44/EC of the European Parliament and of the Council and repealing Council Directive 85/577/EEC and Directive 97/7/EC of the European Parliament and of the Council <http://eur-lex.europa.eu/legal content/EN/TXT/?qid=152 5272546102&uri=CELEX:32011L0083> last accessed 18 October 2018.

[82] Andelka M Phillips, 'Genomic privacy and direct-to-consumer genetics – Big consumer genetic data – What's in that contract?' (presented at GenoPri'15 [The 2nd Workshop

allows them to alter their terms 'at any time', while 32 per cent allow for alteration of terms 'from time to time'. Only a very small minority of companies with variation clauses, 6 per cent, will notify consumers of changes by email. Furthermore, 30 per cent of companies will deem acceptance to altered terms through continued use of the website. Twenty-eight per cent recommend that the customer checks their website periodically to ascertain whether changes have been made to their terms or privacy policy.

Hazel and Slobogin's more recent study of privacy policies and terms and conditions of DTC websites found that:

> two-thirds of companies (37 of 55) provided information regarding the effect of changes to privacy policies [. . .] all of which reserved the right to modify their privacy documents [. . .] the majority of companies stated that any changes to the policy would be reflected on their website, and the consumer was encouraged to routinely re-read the policy documents [. . .] Companies either stated that consumers would be bound by the new terms immediately, or after a specified time period (usually 30 days).[83]

Clauses of this type are very likely to be construed as being unfair according to the CMA's *Draft Guidance*[84] and its *Unfair Contract Terms Guidance* (final guidance).[85] These are also covered in the CRA's grey list in sections 10 and 11 of Schedule 2, but the CMA in its *Unfair Terms Explained* also suggests that these may be blacklisted under Part 1 of the CRA.[86]

In its *Cloud Computing Compliance Review*[87] report, the CMA indicated that several examples of clauses of this type may cause consumer detriment[88] and that they view such clauses as unfair under the CRA.[89]

---

[83] on Genome Privacy and Security] and published as part of IEEE Conference Proceedings 2015) <https://www.computer.org/csdl/proceedings/spw/2015/9933/00/9933a060.pdf> last accessed 23 October 2018.

[83] Hazel and Slobogin (n 2) 15.

[84] Competition & Markets Authority (CMA), *Draft Guidance on Unfair Contract Terms – Consultation Document* (CMA, CMA37con, 2015) <https://assets.publishing.service. gov.uk/government/uploads/system/uploads/attachment_data/file/398202/CMA37con_ Unfair_contract_terms_guidance_consultation.pdf> last accessed 25 October 2018.

[85] Competition & Markets Authority, *Unfair Contract Terms Guidance – Guidance on the Unfair Terms Provisions in the Consumer Rights Act 2015* (n 80).

[86] Competition & Markets Authority, *Unfair Contract Terms Explained* (CMA, CMA37(a), 31 July 2015) 13–4, paras 65–8 <https://assets.publishing.service.gov.uk/government/ uploads/system/uploads/attachment_data/file/450410/Unfair_Terms_Explained.pdf> last accessed 26 October 2018.

[87] CMA, *Consumer Law Compliance Review* (n 22).

[88] CMA, *Consumer Law Compliance Review* para 5.24.

[89] Ibid. para 5.25.

Relevant here is that this includes terms that 'allow the provider to change the terms or the service in any way for any reason and at any time' or those that 'do not require providers to give consumers notice of changes' are of concern.[90]

While such clauses may be understandable from a company's perspective, if these are to be included then companies should be making efforts to provide sufficient notice of such clauses to consumers in order to meet the requirements of transparency. Loos and Luzak[91] have argued that such terms are likely to be deemed unfair in accordance with the Unfair Terms Directive, which from 2015 has been implemented in the UK through the CRA. Such clauses are listed in paragraph 1(j) of Annex I of the Directive as of a type that might be deemed to be unfair. As Lord Denning in *J Spurling* v *Bradshaw*[92] suggested in obiter dicta:

> the more unreasonable a clause is the greater the notice which must be given of it. Some clauses would need to be printed in red ink on the face of the document with a red hand pointing to it before the notice could be held to be sufficient.[93]

The English case law following on from *Spurling* has taken this to mean that the more onerous the term is, the greater the level of notice required. As Hedley writes, 'some US cases have refused to apply terms which are considered unconscionably biased against consumers' interests' and although UK 'notions of "unconscionability" do not stretch so far, nonetheless consumer protection legislation will in many cases lead to the same result'.[94] American courts have often held that 'an opportunity to read is enough', but it is possible that UK courts will require more, as they have previously 'held that rather minimal notice may mean that the consumer agrees to the terms only in so far as they are usual and reasonable'.[95] Thus, very broad variation clauses are likely also to be unfair where there is insufficient notice and in the context of many DTC companies' contracts it seems that there would be insufficient notice.

---

90   CMA, *Consumer Law Compliance Review* (n 22) para 5.24.
91   Loos and Luzak (n 57) 6–10.
92   [1956] 2 All ER 121.
93   Lawson (n 40) 18, citing *J Spurling* v *Bradshaw* [1956] 2 All ER 121, [125].
94   Steve Hedley, *The Law of Electronic Commerce and the Internet in the UK and Ireland* (2nd edn, Cavendish Publishing Limited 2006) 248.
95   Ibid. 248, citing *Interfoto Picture Library Ltd* v *Stiletto Visual Programmes Ltd* [1989] QB 433.

Examples of Unilateral Change of Terms Clauses Specifying that a Company can Change Terms from Time to Time

The following examples highlight the similarity in language used by different companies. Also, significant here is that 23andMe and Gene By Gene, which owns DNA DTC, are probably the two largest and most prominent companies, so it is interesting that their clauses often use identical or nearly identical language.

23andMe includes as clause 26 of the contract analysed, in their Terms of Service (termed TOS), a provision that seems to reserve any making of changes to 23andMe:

> 23andMe may make changes to the TOS from time to time.

However, when these changes are made:

> 23andMe will make a new copy of the TOS available on its website and any new additional terms will be made available to you from within, or through, the affected Services.

How this will work by being made available 'from within, or through, the affected Services' is unclear.

The clause goes on to state that the user acknowledges and agrees that if the user makes use of the services after the date on which these TOS are changed then 23andMe will treat 'that use as acceptance of the updated TOS'.[96]

Meanwhile, Gene By Gene's DNA DTC includes clause 20 in its Terms of Service. This is a very similarly worded clause to the same effect.

Similar to the examples above, Asper Biotech and DNA Traits use identical wording in their variation clauses, which allow them to change their terms at any time, with such modifications to be posted on the website and continued use of the website and services to be an acceptance of such changes.

Asper Biotech and DNA Traits variation clauses

Asper Biotech includes the following clause in its Terms and Conditions:

> Asper Biotech may revise these Terms and Conditions at any time and for any reason. Modifications may be posted on the website. By

---

[96] 23andMe, TOS <www.23andme.com/about/tos/> – archived content available at: <http://web.archive.org/web/20130807140525/www.23andme.com/about/tos/> last accessed 31 October 2018.

continuing use of the website and Asper Biotech services after such changes are made you will be accepting such changes.[97]

DNA Traits includes the following clause in its Terms and Conditions:

DNATraits may revise these Terms and Conditions at any time and for any reason. Modifications may be posted on the website. By continuing use of the website and DNATraits services after such changes are made you will be accepting such changes.[98]

Meanwhile, Cancer Genetic Inc's clause is included under the subtitle 'Updates'. It is concerned not merely with updating website content, but also with their making changes to the terms at any time without notice:

Cancer Genetics, Inc. periodically makes updates and/or revisions to the content contained on the CancerGenetics.com website. All content contained on this website is subject to change at any time without notice. Cancer Genetics, Inc. may revise or modify these Terms of Use at any time without notice.[99]

DNA Spectrum's clause is concerned with stating what the agreement is, namely both the Terms and the Privacy Policy. It may amend or modify the agreement by posting the new terms on its website but no other amendment to the agreement may be made 'except in a written document signed by (the user) and DNA Spectrum'.

DNA Spectrum's variation clause

Whole Agreement and Amendment

This Agreement and the Privacy Policy constitutes the entire agreement between you and DNA Spectrum with respect to the subject matter hereof and supersedes and replaces all prior or contemporaneous understandings or agreements, written or oral, regarding such subject matter. DNA Spectrum may amend or modify this Agreement at any time by posting the new terms on its website. This Agreement may not be otherwise amended except in a written document signed by you and DNA Spectrum.[100]

---

[97] Asper Biotech, T&C.
[98] DNA Traits, T&C.
[99] Cancer Genetics Inc, TOU.
[100] DNA Spectrum, TOS.

Gentle's clause 14 allows the company to alter terms 'at any time' after publication of the modification to their terms on the website. In contrast, GenePlanet allows itself to alter both its Terms and Conditions and Privacy Statement 'at any time' by notice on their website but provides for confirmation of acceptance by the user by clicking on an acceptance icon. How effective such notice may be will depend upon how this is done. GenePlanet's clause in its Terms and Conditions is as follows:

> 1. (2) We may revise these Terms and Conditions at any time and for any reason. Any such revised terms shall be posted on the Website and where such revisions are material they shall be notified to you by means of a notice on the Website indicating the date of revision and you shall be asked to confirm your acceptance to such revised Terms and Conditions by clicking on an acceptance icon.[101]

(c) *Choice of Law and International Jurisdiction*

The question of the jurisdiction that is to govern disputes arising between companies and consumers is an important matter, especially in relation to affording adequate protection to both parties. It is common practice for companies to specify their governing jurisdiction of choice in their contracts. Such clauses stipulate that the law of a particular jurisdiction should govern any disputes which might arise between the company and consumer. In the context of DTC, the jurisdiction that will govern disputes arising between companies and consumers varies widely.

However, for disputes involving UK-based consumers, if provisions of the Consumer Rights Act were to apply and clauses were deemed to be unfair, English law would probably apply to any dispute that arose between the company and consumer. Specifically, this is addressed in section 32 of the Act and also in section 20 of Schedule 2. In accordance with these provisions it is likely that a clause purporting to bind a UK-based consumer to have to resolve any potential disputes in another jurisdiction would not be enforceable.

The only UK case on wrap contracts did involve an American company but was still litigated in the UK.[102]

Furthermore, it is also likely that many terms purporting to choose a jurisdiction outside the EU to govern disputes will be unenforceable in accordance with Articles 17 to 19 of the Brussels I-Regulation.[103] This argument was made

---

[101] GenePlanet, T&C

[102] *Spreadex Ltd* v *Cochrane* [2012] EWHC 1290.

[103] Regulation (EU) No 1215/2012 of 12 December 2012 on jurisdiction and the recognition and enforcement of judgments in civil and commercial matters (recast) OJ 2012,

by Loos and Luzak in their study of the terms of Internet service providers.[104] These articles 'create specific jurisdiction for consumer contracts'[105] and it seems that DTC services should fall within the scope of Article 17.

Loos and Luzak then cited the joint declaration of the Council and Commission on Article 15 of the equivalent provision of the previous Brussels I-Regulation, which stated:

> *inter alia*, that for the specific rules of the Brussels I-Regulation pertaining to consumer contracts to apply, the contract concluded must fall within the framework of the targeted activities, and that the mere fact that an Internet site is accessible from the consumer's place of residence is not sufficient for their applicability [. . .] This joint declaration identifies as relevant factors in determining whether the requirements of (then) Article 15 of the Brussels I-Regulation are met the fact that the Internet site solicits the conclusion of contracts by consumers at a distance and that the contract is in fact concluded at a distance.[106]

It seems likely that many DTC companies would fall within the Regulation's remit, as many DTC websites do solicit sales from UK consumers and from consumers in other EU countries.

In the context of choice of law clauses, Loos and Luzak also refer to the Rome I Regulation,[107] which under Article 3, paragraph 1, allows for 'parties to a contract' to choose the law they wish to govern their contract, so long as 'the choice is made expressly or clearly demonstrated by the terms of the contract of the circumstances of the case'. They argue that this:

> could suggest that a choice-of-law clause included in standard contract terms would not suffice to prescribe a valid choice for the applicable law, unless the trader has specifically drawn the consumer's attention to the term, e.g., by indicating that a choice-of-law clause is included in the standard contract terms. According to Articles 3, paragraph 5, and 10 Rome I-Regulation the existence and the validity of the consumer's consent to a choice-of-law clause is to be decided on the basis of the chosen law. This implies that the consent may be void or voided under the chosen applicable

---

L 251/1 <https://eur-lex.europa.eu/legal-content/EN/ALL/?uri=celex%3A32012R1215> last accessed 26 October 2018.

[104] Loos and Luzak (n 57) 19.

[105] Ibid. (n 57) 19.

[106] Ibid. (n 57) 19.

[107] Council Regulation (EC) No 593/2008 of 17 June 2008 on the law applicable to contractual obligations (Rome I) <https://eur-lex.europa.eu/legal-content/EN/ALL/?uri=CELEX%3A32008R0593> last accessed 26 October 2018.

law in cases of, for instance, duress, fraud or other vices of consent, but also by virtue of the rules on the incorporation of standard terms or those on unfair contract terms.[108]

Such clauses even where validly incorporated are also potentially unfair in accordance with Article 3 of the Unfair Terms Directive, as they may give:[109]

> the false impression to the consumer that her national law is irrelevant for the dispute she has with the online service provider, for instance by falsely claiming that the law of the country where the service provider is located is applicable with the exclusion of any other law.

In the context of DTC contracts, which are all standard form contracts, it seems likely that many companies are not providing sufficient notice of their choice of law clauses for them to be effective.

Summary of Review of Jurisdictional Clauses

Overall there is much commonality in the language used in these clauses regardless of which jurisdiction is specified. Of the 102 companies offering health-related testing, 55 have offices based in the USA. Usually the company chose its home jurisdiction as the forum for settlement of all disputes. American companies normally specify their home state's law. Of the 71 companies with terms available, 51 per cent do have a choice of law clause. Of the companies which specify their forum of choice, the jurisdiction most commonly chosen is that of the state of California with 13 per cent of companies choosing this. This is consistent with the fact that California is also the state in the USA which has more DTC companies based in it than any other state, with 24 per cent (17) companies in total. The companies that chose to be governed by Californian law in their contracts were 23andMe[110], Counsyl,[111] DNA Direct, DNA Plus, Genomic Health Inc,[112] myDNA, Navigenics, Pathway

---

[108] Loos and Luzak (n 57) 22.

[109] Ibid. 23.

[110] 23andMe, <https://www.23andme.com/health/> last accessed 5 January 2013. [Checked again 22 January 2014 and still operating]. [Checked again 24 April 2014]. [Checked again 28 September 2014].

[111] Counsyl, <https://www.counsyl.com> last accessed 28 January 2014. [Checked again 10 April 2014].

[112] Genomic Health Inc, <http://www.genomichealth.com/en-US.aspx#.UuuKSv07S44> last accessed 15 January 2014. [Checked again 31 January 2014 and still operating]. [Checked again 14 April 2014]. [Checked again 28 September 2014]. [Checked again 28 September 2014].

Genomics,[113] and Test Country.[114] Those companies based in California which do not specify California as their jurisdiction of choice were Athleticode,[115] Diagnomic,[116] easyDNA[117] (its administration office is in California and its registered office is in the British Virgin Islands), Genomic Express Inc,[118] MEDomics,[119] PHENOM Biosciences Inc,[120] vuGene,[121] and DeCODEme.[122]

Two companies specified their choice of law as that of the state of Massachusetts and two specify Texas as their choice of law. However, six companies were located in Massachusetts and the only two specifying Massachusetts law were Perkin Elmer and Inherent Health. The other companies located in Massachusetts were Interleukin Genetics Inc,[123] Knome,[124] PerioPredict™, Genetic Risk Test[125], and Progenika Inc.[126] The three companies located in Texas were Gene By Gene, DNA DTC, and DNA Traits. It should be noted that Gene By Gene in fact owns both these latter companies and that DNA DTC now is just known as Gene By Gene.

---

113 Pathway Genomics, <https://www.pathway.com/about-us/management> last accessed 11 February 2013. [Checked again 24 April 2014].

114 Test Country, <http://www.testcountry.com> last accessed 10 August 2013. [Checked again 24 April 2014].

115 Athleticode, <http://athleticode.com> last accessed 10 August 2013. [Checked again 22 January 2014 and still operating]. [Checked again 9 April 2014]. [Checked again 28 September 2014].

116 Diagnomics, <http://www.diagnomics.com> last accessed 27 January 2014. [Checked again 28 September 2014].

117 easyDNA, <http://www.easy-dna.com> last accessed 5 August 2014. [Checked again 28 September 2014]. [Checked again 28 September 2014].

118 Genomic Express Inc, <https://secure.genomicexpress.com/home.html> last accessed 27 January 2014. [Checked again 28 January 2014 and still operating]. [Checked again 28 September 2014].

119 MEDomics, <http://www.medomics.com> [Checked again 29 January 2014 and still operating]. [Checked again 22 April 2014]. [Checked again 28 September 2014].

120 PHENOM Biosciences, <http://www.phenombio.com/about-us> last accessed 30 April 2014.

121 vuGene, <http://www.mygenesdirect.com> last accessed 2 January 2013. [Checked again 29 January 2014 and website not displaying]. [Checked again 24 April 2014].

122 DeCODEme, <http://www.decodeme.com> last accessed 22 August 2013. [Checked again 28 January 2014 and still operating].

123 Interleukin Genetics, <http://ilgenetics.com/content/products-services> last accessed 15 April 2014.

124 Knome, <http://www.knome.com/knome-blog/direct-to-consumer-genomics-reinvents-itself/> last accessed 10 August 2013. [Checked again 16 April 2014].

125 PerioPredict™, 'What is PerioPredict™?' <http://periopredict.com/patient/about.php> last accessed 15 April 2014.

126 Progenika Inc, <http://www.progenika.com/us/index.php> [Checked again 29 January 2014 and still operating]. [Checked again 24 April 2014].

Five companies specify that English or UK law should govern, although 11 companies were located in the UK. The companies that chose for their disputes to be governed by English law were BioClinics, DNAFit, DNA Genie, International Biosciences and Test Diagnostics. The companies which are located in the UK but which do not specify their jurisdiction of choice in their contracts are BioClinics (Genetic Health Management), easyDNA, Genetic Health, ION (Institute for Optimal Nutrition), Matt Roberts, My Gene Diet (Natures Remedies Ltd), and Nimble Diagnostics.

Two companies were located in Germany (Bio Logis and Genosense) and both specifed German law as their jurisdiction of choice. Of the two companies located in Slovenia, GenePlanet and LifeGenetics, LifeGenetics specified that Slovenian law should govern disputes, whereas GenePlanet relied on Irish law.

There were nine companies located in Australia. However, all nine companies either had no terms available or no choice of law, so no available contract specifies Australian law as its jurisdiction of choice. The companies based in Australia were Darwin Dieticians,[127] DNA Bioservices,[128] DNAFit,[129] FitGenes,[130] Lumigenix,[131] Molecular Diagnostic Services (PTY) Ltd,[132] MyGene,[133] Remede,[134] and Smart DNA[135].

Similarly, none of the companies based in Canada specified that Canadian law should govern their disputes. This is despite the fact that there were four

[127] Darwin Dietitians, <http://www.darwindietitians.com.au> last accessed 22 August 2013. [Checked again 28 January 2014 and still operating]. [Checked again 10 April 2014]. [Checked again 28 September 2014].

[128] DNA Bioservices, <http://www.dnabioservices.com.au/> last accessed 13 May 2014. [Checked again 28 September 2014].

[129] DNAFit, <http://www.dnafit.com/uk/> last accessed 15 August 2013. [Checked again 28 January 2014 and still operating]. [Checked again 11 April 2014]. [Checked again 28 September 2014].

[130] FitGenes, <http://www.fitgenes.com> last accessed 27 January 2014. [Checked again 28 January 2014 and still operating]. [Checked again 14 April 2014]. [Checked again 28 September 2014].

[131] This company no longer appears to be operating.

[132] Molecular Diagnostic Services (PTY) Ltd, <http://www.mdsafrica.net/site/default.asp> last accessed 27 January 2014. [Checked again 28 September 2014].

[133] My Gene, <http://www.mygene.com.au> last accessed 13 August 2013. [Checked again 29 January 2014 and website suspended]. [Checked again 22 April 2014]. [Checked again 28 September 2014].

[134] Remede, <http://remede.com.au/dna-profiles-nutrigenomics/> last accessed 7 April 2014. [Checked again 24 April 2014]. [Checked again 28 September 2014].

[135] Smart DNA, <http://www.smartdna.net.au/howitworks.html> last accessed 13 August 2013. [Checked again 28 September 2014].

companies located in Canada: Accu-metrics Viaguard, C2DNA (Canadian Centre for DNA Diagnostics),[136] DNA Testing Centres of Canada,[137] and YOUology.[138]

Examples of Jurisdiction Clauses
23andMe specifies its forum of choice in section 28(b) of its Terms of Service, which also provides for arbitration.

> **Applicable law and arbitration**
>
> Except for any disputes relating to intellectual property rights, obligations, or any infringement claims, any disputes with 23andMe arising out of or relating to the Agreement ('Disputes') shall be governed by California law regardless of your country of origin or where you access 23andMe . . .[139]

Although Gene By Gene's DNA DTC specifies a different jurisdiction as its forum of choice and arbitration, which has remarkably similar wording, it does allow for injunctive relief to enforce the arbitrator's award.

> **Gene By Gene's DNA DTC's clause in its Terms and Conditions Applicable law and arbitration**
>
> Except for any disputes relating to intellectual property rights, obligations, or any infringement claims, any disputes with DNA DTC arising out of or relating to the Agreement ("Disputes") shall be governed by Texas law regardless of your country of origin or where you access DNA DTC . . . Either party may obtain injunctive relief (preliminary or permanent) and orders to compel arbitration or enforce arbitral awards in any court of competent jurisdiction.[140]

---

[136] C2DNA, <http://www.c2dna.com/index.html> last accessed 28 August 2013. [Checked again 28 January 2014 and still operating]. [Checked again 10 April 2014]. [Checked again 28 September 2014].

[137] DNA Testing Centres of Canada, <http://dnatestingcanada.com/about-us/> last accessed 7 April 2014. [Checked again 12 April 2014]. [Checked again 28 September 2014].

[138] YOUology, <http://www.youology.com/about-youology.html> last accessed 7 April 2014. [Checked again 24 April 2014]. [Checked again 28 September 2014].

[139] 23andMe, TOS.

[140] DNA DTC, T&C.

(d) Indemnity Clauses

Summary of Review of Indemnity Clauses

Broad indemnity clauses are also very common in DTC contracts with 44 per cent of companies requiring the consumer to indemnify the company. Overall 37 per cent of companies go so far as to require the consumer to indemnify the company against third-party actions, which might arise through the consumer sharing test results with a healthcare practitioner.

In accordance with the CMA's *Draft Guidance*[141] and its final guidance[142] it is likely that such indemnity clauses would be deemed unfair, as they either allow a company to protect itself from the consequences of its negligence 'or [. . .] transfer a risk to the consumer when the business can insure against it and the consumer cannot'.[143] These terms are also dealt with in the grey list of the CRA in sections 10 and 11 of Schedule 2.

Examples of Indemnity Clauses

Again, the clauses of the most prominent DTC companies are remarkably similar and particularly broad in scope.

It should be noted that were 23andMe's clause to be effective it would require the consumer to indemnify its affiliates, which would now include its pharmaceutical partners together with the other platforms it has purchased such as Cure Together.

23andMe's indemnity clause

23andMe's section 14 of its TOS specifies indemnifying 23andMe, in broad terms which refers also to '[. . .]affiliates, officers, agents, contractors, partners, employees, successors, and assigns' regarding 'any claim, or demand [. . .] made by any third party due to or arising out of User Content' submitted, posted, or transmitted 'through the Service; use of the Service; connection to the Service; violation of the TOS; [. . .]your violation of any rights of another'.[144]

This goes on to cover liability arising out of 'the use or disclosure of any information obtained from genotyping the saliva sample and/or analysing

---

[141] CMA, *Draft Guidance on Unfair Contract Terms* (n 84).
[142] CMA, *Unfair Contract Terms Guidance – Guidance on the Unfair Terms Provisions in the Consumer Rights Act 2015* (n 85) para 5.14.3.
[143] CMA, *Unfair Contract Terms Explained* (n 86) para 84.
[144] DNADTC, T&C.

the Genetic Information' and refers to a user providing 'their Genetic and/ or Self-Reported Information to third parties – whether intentionally or inadvertently, or to third parties for diagnostic or other purposes and to all liability arising from such disclosure or use'.

Gene By Gene's DNA DTC's clause contained in their Terms and Conditions closely resembles that of 23andMe. Similarly, section 13 of myDNA's Terms and Conditions provides for indemnities including for such diagnostic disclosure or use.

DNA DTC's clause in its Terms and Conditions

7. Indemnity

You agree to defend and hold DNA DTC, and its subsidiaries, affiliates, officers, agents, contractors, partners, employees, successors, and assigns harmless from any claim, or demand, including reasonable attorneys' fees, made by any third party due to or arising out of any information you submit, misuse of the results delivered to you, violation of the Terms and Conditions, or your violation of any rights of another party. If you have submitted a saliva sample or otherwise provided your own personal information, you will defend and hold harmless DNA DTC, its employees, contractors, successors, and assigns from any liability arising out of the use or disclosure of any information obtained from genotyping your saliva sample and/or analyzing your results, which is disclosed to you consistent with our Privacy Statement or results from any third-party add-ons to tools we provide. In addition, if you choose to provide your results and personal information to third parties – whether individuals to whom you facilitate access, intentionally or inadvertently, or to third parties for diagnostic or other purposes – you agree to defend and hold harmless DNA DTC, its employees, contractors, successors, and assigns from any and all liability arising from such disclosure or use of your results and personal information.[145]

Likewise, C2DNA has a clause in its Terms of Use which specifies that use of the site is at the user's sole risk and then goes on to provide for broad indemnities 'against any and all losses, claims, demands, expenses (including lawyer's fees) or liabilities of whatever nature or kind asserted by, suffered or

---

[145] DNADTC, T&C.

incurred by third parties arising out of [. . .] (the User's) use of the content on this Site'.[146]

(e) Exclusion Clauses

Summary of Review of Exclusion Clauses

Overall, exclusion clauses broadly disclaiming liability are very common with 80 per cent of companies including such a clause. Fourteen per cent of DTC company contracts examined herein disclaim liability for personal injury or death caused by their negligence.[147] This is a term of a type that is blacklisted in section 65 of the Consumer Rights Act and is consequently automatically void and unenforceable. Meanwhile, 38 per cent of companies disclaim liability for fitness for purpose and 44 per cent specify that their services are provided on an 'as is' basis and 30 per cent also specify that they provide 'no warranty' for their services.[148] It is quite likely that many of the terms of this type would be deemed to be unfair in accordance with the Act. The Act implies certain terms into consumer contracts. This includes a requirement that providers of goods, services and digital content must ensure that their products and services are all 'of satisfactory quality'. For the supply of goods and digital content, this entails a requirement that the product or service be fit for purpose. Section 10 requires that goods must be fit for a particular purpose, while section 34, which deals with the supply of digital content, specifies that in relation to the supply of digital content, 'fitness for all the purposes for which digital content of that kind is usually supplied'. Meanwhile, section 49 provides that in relation to the supply of services, there is a requirement that services are to be 'performed with reasonable care and skill'. Section 31(1)(b) specifies that consumer contracts cannot exclude liability for fitness for purpose for the sale of goods. In relation to the supply of digital content, under section 47 suppliers cannot exclude liability for either the requirement that content be of 'satisfactory quality' or the requirement that it be 'fit for a particular purpose'. Finally, under section 57 suppliers of services also cannot exclude liability from the requirement to perform services with reasonable care and skill. As the nature of the provision of DTC genetic tests involves the sale and provision of goods, services and digital content, DTC companies providing tests to UK customers

---

[146] C2DNA, TOU.

[147] These are: Asper Biotech; BioClinics; DDC Diagnostics Centre; DeCODEme; DNA Traits (owned by Gene By Gene); Test Diagnostics; and The Makings of Me.

[148] Andelka M Phillips, 'Think before you click: Ordering a genetic test online' (2015) 11 *SciTech Lawyer* 8 <https://www.americanbar.org/publications/scitech_lawyer/2015/winter/think_before_you_click_ordering_genetic_test_online/> last accessed 22 October 2018.

are likely to be caught by the requirements of the Act in relation to all three categories. Consequently, it seems likely that contractual clauses attempting to disclaim liability for 'fitness for purpose' are likely to be unenforceable.

Examples of Disclaimer and Exclusion of Liability Clauses

23andMe's disclaimer clauses are to be found in section 7 and section 23 of its Terms of Service. Section 7 addresses confidentiality and security obligations of the user with requirements to notify 23andMe 'of any unauthorized use of your password or account or any other breach of security, and (b) ensure that you exit from your account at the end of each session'. It also provides that: '23andMe cannot and will not be liable for any loss or damage arising from your failure to comply with this Section'.[149]

23andMe disclaimer clauses

Section 23 of 23andMe's Terms of Service is unhelpfully expressed in capital letters, which obstruct ease of understanding. The broad disclaimers of warranties and exclusions of liability, at the time reviewed, are stated in detail but in lower case, to illustrate their scope:[150]

(1) your use of the services are at your sole risk. The services are provided on an 'as is' and 'as available' basis. 23andme expressly disclaims all warranties of any kind, whether express or implied, including, but not limited to, the implied warranties of merchantability, fitness for a particular purpose, and noninfringement.

(2) 23andme makes no warranty that (a) the services will meet your requirements; (b) the services will be uninterrupted, timely, unfailingly secure, or errorfree; (c) the results that may be obtained from the use of the services will be accurate or reliable; (d) the quality of any products, services, information, or other material purchased or obtained by you through the services will meet your expectations and (e) any errors in the software will be corrected.

(3) any material downloaded or otherwise obtained through the use of the services is done at your own discretion and risk and that you will be solely responsible for any damage to your computer system or loss of data that results from the download of any such material.

---

[149] 23andMe, TOS.
[150] 23andMe, TOS.

(4) no advice or information, whether oral or written, obtained by you from 23andme or through or from the services shall create any warranty not expressly stated in the TOS.

(5) you should always use caution when giving out any personally iden- tifying information about yourself or those for whom you have legal authority. 23andme does not control or endorse any actions resulting from your participation in the services and, therefore, 23andme specifi- cally disclaims any liability with regard to any actions resulting from your participation in the services.

In the same clause there is a broad limitation of liability stated to be within the limits allowed by applicable laws:

that 23andme shall not be liable for any direct, indirect, incidental, special, consequential, or exemplary damages, including but not limited to, damages for loss of profits, goodwill, use, data or other intangible losses (even if 23andme has been advised of the possibility of such dam- ages), resulting from:

(a) the use or the inability to use the services;

(b) any action you take based on the information you receive in through or from the services,

(v) your failure to keep your password or account details secure and confidential,

(d) the cost of procurement of substitute goods and services resulting from any goods, data, information, or services purchased or obtained or messages received or transactions entered into through or from the services;

(e) unauthorized access to or alteration of your transmissions or data;

(f) the improper authorization for the services by someone claiming such authority; or (g) statements or conduct of any third party on the services.[151]

Counsyl's clause is included in section 11 of their Terms of Service, and similarly is expressed in capitals and features broad exclusions. However, it does concede that some of the limitations may not apply where: 'some juris- dictions do not allow the exclusion of certain warranties or the limitation or exclusion of liability for incidental or consequential damages'.[152]

---

[151] 23andMe, TOS.
[152] Counsyl, TOS.

In its *Cloud Computing Compliance Review*, in the context of cloud computing, the CMA indicated concern over terms which:

> [1] attempt to exclude or restrict a consumer's statutory rights and remedies under the CRA, for example, excluding liability where the provider has failed to use reasonable skill and care when providing the service despite the potential for consumers to have large amounts of data saved or stored, place an unreasonably low cap on liability (outside of a consumer's statutory remedies)

> [2] contain confusing or contradictory information, so that it is not possible for consumers to know what liability is or is not excluded in any particular situation

> [3] include significant amounts of unnecessary 'legal jargon' (for example, 'mutatis mutandis', 'workmanlike effort' and 'implied warranties of merchantability'). Businesses should, of course, generally avoid using jargon at all in their terms. We had particular concerns about the amount and complexity of legal jargon in providers' liability terms.[153]

They indicated that they viewed these as likely to be unfair under the CRA and that many exclusion clauses are also likely to be blacklisted under the Act and that 'Blacklisted terms are automatically unenforceable by a trader against a consumer'. In the context of DTC, it would seem likely that several of the exclusion clauses mentioned in Chapter 5 are likely to be deemed unfair. Those purporting to exclude liability for fitness for purpose or limiting the scope of purpose for health tests to non-medical purposes seem particularly likely to be deemed unfair.

(f) Arbitration Clauses

Summary of Review of Arbitration Clauses

Arbitration clauses are often included in wrap contracts and these are normally included in order to place limitations on how disputes between consumers and companies are to be resolved. Often these clauses will specify that any disputes must be resolved through arbitration proceedings and they will also specify the jurisdiction where claims should be brought. While most clickwrap and browsewrap contract disputes have centred on such clauses,[154] only 13 per cent (9) out of 71 companies reviewed actually include such a clause. This can be compared with 15 per cent (10) out of 68

---

[153] Ibid. para 5.59.
[154] Manwaring (n 44) 1–17, 13.

for ancestry testing companies. However, although they may not be particularly common, 23andMe does include such a clause and this clause has been central to the class action litigation against 23andMe previously mentioned in Chapter 4.

The nine companies which include arbitration clauses are: 23andMe; Any Lab Test Now; Counsyl; DNA DTC (owned by Gene By Gene); DNA Spectrum; Foundation Medicine Inc; Genetic Testing Laboratories Inc; myDNA; and Pathway Genomics. Overall, the clauses are very similar in their wording, despite differences in the jurisdiction specified for where claims are to be brought. Of these nine, four specify that the proceedings are to be brought in the state of California, with 23andMe and myDNA allowing for claims to be brought in San Francisco. Pathway specifies San Diego and Counsyl specifies Santa Clara County. Of the other five, four specify another American state as their venue of choice. Only one, Foundation Medicine, does not limit the jurisdiction, allowing for dispute resolution to be 'facilitated by the International Centre for Dispute Resolution/ American Arbitration Association'.[155]

Examples of Arbitration Clauses
What follows concerns the text of the arbitration clauses of 23andMe, Any Lab Test Now (which relies on PayPal's User Agreement), Counsyl, DNA DTC and Pathway Genomics.

23andMe's arbitration clause is contained in section 28(b) of its Terms of Service.

23andMe's arbitration clause (Terms of Service section 28[b])

With the exception of 'disputes relating to intellectual property rights, obligations, or any infringement claims', any disputes arising out of or relating to the Agreement are to be 'governed by California law' 'regardless of country of origin' or where their services are accessed.

notwithstanding of any conflicts of law principles and the United Nations Convention for the International Sale of Goods.

The final and binding arbitration is to be:

under the rules and auspices of the American Arbitration Association, to be held in San Francisco, California, in English, with a written decision

---

[155] Foundation Medicine, TOU.

stating legal reasoning issued by the arbitrator(s) at either party's request, and with arbitration costs and reasonable documented attorneys' costs of both parties to be borne by the party that ultimately loses

To compel arbitration to enforce the arbitrator's decision:

Either party may obtain injunctive relief (preliminary or permanent) and orders to compel arbitration or enforce arbitral awards in any court of competent jurisdiction.[156]

Any Lab Test Now relies on the PayPal User Agreement and the relevant sections are 14(3)(a)–(c) which explain arbitration procedures, the cost of arbitration and contain a narrow opt-out provision for new PayPal users only. This is by a specific form of notice, which must be postmarked no later than 30 days after the date the user accepts the User Agreement for the first time.

Gene By Gene's DNA DTC's clause in its Terms and Conditions specifies that:

any disputes with DNA DTC arising out of or relating to the Agreement ('Disputes') shall be governed by Texas law regardless of your country of origin or where you access DNA DTC, and notwithstanding of any conflicts of law principles and the United Nations Convention for the International Sale of Goods.

Any Disputes shall be resolved by final and binding arbitration under the rules and auspices of the American Arbitration Association, to be held in Houston, Texas, in English, with a written decision stating legal reasoning issued by the arbitrator(s) at either party's request, and with arbitration costs and reasonable documented attorneys' costs of both parties to be borne by the party that ultimately loses. Either party may obtain injunctive relief (preliminary or permanent) and orders to compel arbitration or enforce arbitral awards in any court of competent jurisdiction.[157]

Pathway Genomics' more succinctly provides that:

All disputes between Pathway and you arising under these Terms and Conditions shall be decided by arbitration in accordance with the rules of the American Arbitration Association by a single arbitrator in San Diego, California, U.S. The award rendered by the arbitrator shall be final. In the

---

[156] 23andMe, TOS.
[157] DNA DTC, T&C.

event of any legal action or proceeding related to this website, such action or proceeding shall be brought exclusively in a federal or state court of competent jurisdiction sitting in California.[158]

(g) Waiver of Class Arbitrations and Class Actions

Counsyl's Terms of Service specifies that the laws of California shall apply but without regard to its conflicts of law principles. It provides that:

> any dispute, claim, or controversy in connection with or arising under the use of our Service or this agreement, its construction, existence, interpretation, validity, or any breach hereof which cannot be amicably settled between the parties, shall be finally and exclusively resolved by binding arbitration under the Rules of Arbitration of the American Arbitration Association then prevailing.[159]

It goes on to include a waiver of class arbitrations and class actions.

(h) Brief Note on AT & T Mobility LLC v Concepcion

A waiver of class arbitrations and class actions clause was considered by the Supreme Court of the United States in *AT &T Mobility LLC v Concepcion Et Ux.*[160] Here, the Supreme Court decided by a 5–4 majority that the Federal law relating to arbitration applied, which meant that consumers could be required contractually to bring claims in arbitration individually rather than by class action.

It had been alleged by Concepcion, in a consolidated class action that AT & T had engaged in false advertising and fraud by charging sales tax on 'free' phones. The District Court had denied AT & T's motion to compel arbitration under the Concepcion's contract. Relying on a California Supreme Court's Discover Bank decision, it found the arbitration provision unconscionable because it disallowed classwide proceedings. Notwithstanding that both the District Court and the Ninth Circuit agreed that the provision was unconscionable under California law, the Supreme Court majority favoured the view that section 2's saving clause in the Federal Arbitration Act (FAA) should not apply. That section, which makes arbitration agreements 'valid, irrevocable, and enforceable, save upon such grounds as exist at law or in equity for the revocation of any contract preserves

---

[158] Pathway Genomics, T&C.
[159] Counsyl, TOS.
[160] 563 US 333 (2011) 9 USC §2 (2018) <https://supreme.justia.com/cases/federal/us/563/333/> last accessed 26 October 2018.

generally applicable contract defences',[161] was said not to suggest an intent to preserve state-law rules that stand as an obstacle to the accomplishment of the FAA's objectives. The Supreme Court majority decision detailed what those objectives were and how they would be defeated if interpreted in this way. Whilst these are oversimplifications, the degree to which the FAA limitation should apply to a particular DTC contract's terms may depend to some extent upon how genuinely consensual they are. Congress might eventually clarify this.

Other means to resolve this are possible. One approach is that the DTC industry might, through striving for a consumer-focused best practice, improve the way in which DTC contracts are worded. Alternatively, regulators might address this on behalf of consumers.

(i) Consent, Assent and Acceptance of Terms

Summary of Review of Consent, Assent and Acceptance Clauses

It should also be noted that consent, assent and acceptance of contractual terms are quite separate things. These concepts are covered in greater depth in the next chapter. Consent and assent and/or acceptance are often conflated in the contracts and privacy policies of DTC companies. This conflation is another factor highlighting the consequences of the paradigm shift from patient to consumer in the DTC context. In a clinical or research setting the emphasis is normally on obtaining valid consent and a patient will be asked to provide appropriate consent before undergoing any form of medical treatment. Likewise, a research participant is also required to give adequate consent to participate in research. As previously mentioned, the Human Tissue Act also sets requirements for consent and creates an offence for non-consensual DNA analysis. This means that DTC companies that are not meeting appropriate standards may face prosecution; and the recent ruling in *Montgomery* v *Lanarkshire Health Board*[162] may mean that DTC companies providing tests for health purposes or engaging in health research may need to have better consent mechanisms and provide more comprehensive information to their consumers. Prior to the advent of DTC, patients were also expected to provide appropriate consent before undergoing genetic testing and also undergo pre- and post-test genetic counselling. This continues to be a requirement of genetic testing carried out in a clinical setting.

---

[161] Ibid, citing Federal Arbitration Act 1925 9 U S C §2 <https://www.law.cornell.edu/uscode/text/9/2> last accessed 30 October 2018.
[162] (Scotland) [2015] UKSC 11; Mark Campbell, 'Montgomery v Lanarkshire Health Board' (2015) 44(3) Common Law World Review 222–8.

In contrast, in a normal commercial setting where terms are agreed upon in a contract, the emphasis in contract law has been on demonstrating assent or acceptance of the terms of the contract and what constitutes that assent or acceptance. Of the 71 companies with terms available, 31 per cent do not have specific clauses addressing consent. The remaining 69 per cent (49 companies) do have some clause addressing consent or acceptance of terms.[163] However, consent and assent are often treated as synonymous in DTC contracts and the way in which both are treated in the contracts is problematic. For instance, of the 49 companies, 53 per cent deem either acceptance, agreement or consent to their terms merely through use or viewing of the website (this is representative of 35 per cent of the total 71 companies examined). Twenty-two per cent have clauses deeming acceptance or agreement and 13 per cent have clauses deeming consent.

The companies that included clauses that deemed acceptance of their terms or agreement with their terms through use or viewing of their website or services included 23andMe, 23DNA, DNA Direct, easyDNA, GenePlanet, Genomic Health, GTL, GenoVive, Inherent Health, International Biosciences, Indian Biosciences, Map My Genome, My Gene Diet, myDNA, Personal Genome Diagnostics, Phenom, and VuGene.

The nine companies that included clauses that deemed consent through use or viewing of the website were ARUP, Cancer Genetics Inc, DNADTC, DNA Spectrum, Genomic Health, Halo Health, Inherent Health, Life Genetics, and The Makings of Me.

Only 10 companies mentioned 'informed consent' anywhere in their contracts and privacy policies. These companies were Counsyl, DeCODEme, DNA Spectrum, DNA Traits, easyDNA, GenePeeks, Gentle, Inherent Health, Map My Gene, and Navigenics.[164] Only a small minority of companies that had consent clauses also had separate consent documents. The best examples were 23andMe, Gene By Gene's DNA DTC, Counsyl, Navigenics (which is no longer DTC), and myDNA.

In the context of DTC where test results may have relevance for a person's health, it seems unacceptable for companies to deem consent merely through use or visiting of the website, as visiting a website does not necessitate viewing of terms. It does seem desirable that more information and resources to assist with understanding contractual terms be provided and doing this on the web is not difficult or particularly costly.

There are several issues which need to be considered in examining

[163] Phillips, 'Think before you click' (n 146).
[164] Please note that Navigenics is no longer offering DTC services.

acceptance and consent mechanisms in the DTC context. These include the level of consumers' understanding of terms in DTC contracts; whether they have in fact given consent to the contract; and the limits of their consent (for instance, whether they have provided adequate consent for their data to be used in research and shared by the company with third parties; and whether the consumer has capacity to consent). For instance as genetic information is shared between family members, whether all relevant family members ought to give their consent before one individual is tested; and also whether they have in fact given valid assent or acceptance of terms. It is submitted that the current practice of deeming either acceptance or consent through viewing or visiting a website provides insufficient protection for consumers and unnecessarily favours companies. While in more conventional e-commerce this may be permissible to some extent, DTC companies are collecting large amounts of potentially sensitive information from their consumers, including information that would more usually be recorded in a patient's medical records.

Furthermore, in accordance with the provisions of the Consumer Rights Act it is likely that deemed consent or assent clauses might be deemed to be unfair terms in accordance with the grey list in Schedule 2, as such terms seem to be within the remit of section 10 which deals with terms that have 'the object or effect of irrevocably binding the consumer to terms with which the consumer has had no real opportunity of becoming acquainted before the conclusion of the contract'.

Examples of Consent Clauses

23andMe's Terms of Service included in section 6 'User Representations' provides a list of things that by accessing their services the user is agreeing to, acknowledging and representing what the user is said to understand. To illustrate this accurately, some excerpts are included below.

> (a) [. . .] that information you learn from 23andMe is not designed to diagnose, prevent, or treat any condition or disease or to ascertain the state of your health and that you understand that the 23andMe services are intended for research, informational, and educational purposes only.[165]

This goes on to state that the user acknowledges that: '23andMe urges you to seek the advice of your physician or other health care provider if you have questions or concerns arising from your Genetic Information' and is taking 'responsibility for all possible consequences' resulting from their

---

[165] 23andMe, TOS.

sharing with others access to both their 'Genetic Information' and 'Self-Reported Information'.[166]

Furthermore, 23andMe's Consent Document also covers how consent is to be manifested by 'Giving consent by checking the appropriate box below' and describes what is being consented to, namely that the consumer agrees to let 23andMe investigators use their 'Genetic & Self-Reported Information for 23andWe research, as described above'.

> 'Genetic & Self-Reported Information' refers to:
>
> Your genetic data
> Information you enter into surveys and forms
> Information you enter via features labeled with the 23andWe research logo
> Data you authorize us to import for research
> Your age and ethnicity
>
> Self-Reported Information includes any information you submitted prior to giving consent. If you have elected to have your saliva sample stored, we may also use the results of further analysis of your sample in 23andWe research. To protect your privacy, your Genetic & Self-Reported Information does not include identifying Registration Information you provided when you purchased the Personal Genome Service® or created an account (such as name, address, email address, user ID, password, or credit card information).[167]

DNA DTC's Consent Document contains a clause about how it promotes the advances said to have been made by 'citizen science' and mentions that it believes that:

> [. . .] through RUO tests, individual consumers can play a significant role in advancing the discovery of genetic factors behind diseases and traits.

This leads on to the acknowledgement:

> In view of that, by checking the box below, and by ordering an RUO DNA test for your own use, you agree to participate in the research and development initiatives as stated in the Company's and Terms and Conditions and Privacy Document below.[168]

DNA DTC used the abbreviation RUO, which stands for Research Use Only tests and in describing the nature of its services in its Consent

---

[166] 23andMe, TOS.
[167] 23andMe, Consent.
[168] DNA DTC, Consent Document.

Document it further states that 'DTC RUO tests are for research, informational and educational use only' and it further explains that as many of its tests have not been widely used in clinics, its customers are encouraged to participate in research that will contribute to advancing understanding of genetics, but that they use these services at their 'own risk'.

Examples of Acceptance Clauses
Gene By Gene's DNA DTC in its Terms and Conditions covers its requirements for acceptance of terms and regarding use and storage by describing what it does and using a form of ultimatum that before using their services or website the user must '[. . .] review and accept this and the general Agreement containing your rights and responsibilities as a user of the website and services operated and offered by DNADTC.com'. But if the user does not agree, then the user 'must not use the website and services offered by DNADTC.com'.

DNA DTC may establish limits concerning the maximum number of days that the results will be retained and also regarding the maximum disk space that will be allotted for these. The user is said to:

> acknowledge and agree that DNA DTC has no responsibility or liability for the deletion of or failure to store any of your results or for the loss of those results due to malfunction or destruction of data servers or other catastrophic events.[169]

Interleukin's Inherent Health includes a clause in its Privacy Policy, titled 'NOTICE TO VISITORS OUTSIDE OF THE UNITED STATES'. It then warns that:

> You should be aware that the United States and other countries have not harmonized their privacy regulations. Because Interleukin and its servers is [sic] located in the United States, we have written our Privacy Policy to satisfy United States regulations [. . .][170]

It then specifies that by registering as a customer the individual 'expressly agrees':

> to the transfer into and out of the United States and the use of your personally identifiable information as necessary to provide the services that you request. You also agree to the level of privacy protection set out in this Privacy Policy.[171]

---

[169] DNA DTC, T&C.
[170] Inherent Health, Privacy.
[171] Inherent Health, Privacy.

Meanwhile DNA Direct in section 15 of its Terms of Use includes the following clause:

> [. . .] You and DNA Direct expressly agree to submit to the exclusive jurisdiction and venue of the courts in California in all disputes arising out of or relating to the use of this Service.[172]

Examples of deemed consent clauses

An extract from ARUP's Online Privacy Policy states 'Your Consent: By visiting and using ARUP's website and the contents therein, you consent to the collection, use, and disclosure of information as described in this policy.'[173]

23DNA's Privacy Policy mentions that their 'computer systems are currently based in the United States, so your personal data will be processed by us in the United States'. Then it deems agreement to the privacy policy and 'consent to the transfer of all such information to the United States and to the processing of that information as described in this privacy policy'.[174]

Examples of Deemed Acceptance Clauses

The Makings of Me includes two clauses deeming consent. These are contained in section 6 of its Terms of Use and a section of its Privacy Policy. Section 6 reads:

> By using this Site and/or any of its Services, you agree to these Terms, including any modifications we make, and further waive any rights or claims you may have against us.[175]

Its Privacy Policy includes the following section:

> What if you do not agree with our Privacy Policy?
> By visiting our website and voluntarily providing personal information to the website, you agree to the terms of the online Terms of Use Agreement and this Privacy Policy. [. . .][176]

Perkin Elmer includes the following clause:

> By using this site or downloading materials from this site, you agree to these terms and conditions. If you do not agree to be bound by these terms

---

[172] DNA Direct, TOU.
[173] Arup, Privacy.
[174] 23DNA, Privacy.
[175] The Makings of Me, TOU.
[176] The Makings of Me, Privacy.

and conditions, please do not use this site or download materials from this site.[177]

Genomic Health in its section on Governing Law includes the following:

By choosing to visit our Websites or otherwise provide information to Genomic Health, you agree [. . .][178]

(j) Scope of Purpose

Summary of Review of Scope of Purpose Clauses
While in the context of DTC conducted for purposes that are not health related it may appear reasonable that a company is not providing medical advice or medical information, the situation is less clear where tests are carried out for health purposes. This is accentuated when DTC companies are also engaged in medical research, which as previously noted is true of all the most prominent DTC companies.

Of the 71 companies examined, 51 per cent have clauses of this type. Of these, 12 companies specifically state that their services are provided for 'informational purposes'. Forty-five per cent of companies overall include a statement indicating that they do not provide or intend to provide medical advice with 15 per cent also stating that their services are not intended to be a substitute for medical advice and 27 per cent indicate in some way that their services are not intended as medical advice. Three companies specifically use the phrase 'we do not provide medical advice' (23andMe, DNA DTC and The Makings of Me). Twenty per cent mention that their services are not intended as diagnoses.

It is likely that such terms may be deemed to be unfair under the CRA, as the Act implies obligations into contracts for services and the supply of digital content. Specifically, digital content, which in this case would include genetic test results, should be fit for purpose (section 35), should match description (section 36) and should be of satisfactory quality (section 34). In relation to scope of purpose clauses, the provision requiring services, section 36, which requires digital content to match description is key. In the context of DTC companies providing health tests, where website content encourages consumers to believe they are buying tests that have a medical purpose or will be relevant for medical treatment decisions, a scope of purpose clause suggesting that services are not for medical purposes may be deemed to be unfair.

---

[177] Perkin Elmer, T&C.
[178] Genomic Health Inc, Legal.

Examples of Scope of Purpose Clauses
Clauses have been referred to explicitly to illustrate the scope of the purposes ascribed.

23andMe's clause, when reviewed, read:

> 5. 23andMe Services are for research, informational, and educational use only. We do not provide medical advice.
>
> The Genetic Information provided by 23andMe is for research, informational, and educational use only. This means two things. First, many of the genetic discoveries that we report have not been clinically validated, and the technology we use, which is the same technology used by the research community, to date has not been widely used for clinical testing. Second, in order to expand and accelerate the understanding and practical application of genetic knowledge in health care, we invite all genotyped users to participate in 23andWe Research. Participation in such research is voluntary and based upon an IRB-approved consent document. As a result of the current state of genetic knowledge and understanding, our Services are for research, informational, and educational purposes only. The Services are not intended to be used by the customer for any diagnostic purpose and are not a substitute for professional medical advice. You should always seek the advice of your physician or other health care provider with any questions you may have regarding diagnosis, cure, treatment, mitigation, or prevention of any disease or other medical condition or impairment or the status of your health. 23andMe does not recommend or endorse any specific course of action, resources, tests, physician or other health care providers, drugs, biologics, medical devices or other products, procedures, opinions, or other information that may be mentioned on our website.[179]

DNA DTC's clause is remarkably similar:

> 1. [. . .] DNA DTC RUO tests are for research, informational and educational use only. We do not provide medical advice. In other words, some of the genetic information that is reported may have not been clinically validated, and the technology we use, which is the same technology used by the research community, to date has not been widely used for clinical testing. For this reason, our customers are encouraged to participate in DNA DTC's research initiatives that may

---

[179] 23andMe, TOS.

contribute to a better understanding of the results of genetic testing. The use of DNA DTC services or website information is solely at your own risk.

2. Client Representations and Warranties.

By accessing DNA DTC Services, you agree to, acknowledge, and represent as follows:

You understand that information you learn from DNA DTC is not designed to diagnose, prevent, or treat any condition or disease or to ascertain the state of your health and that the DNA DTC services are intended for research, informational, and educational purposes only. You acknowledge that DNA DTC urges you to seek the advice of your physician or other health care provider if you have questions or concerns arising from your Genetic Information.[180]

Meanwhile, the wording of Genetic Performance and Gonidio are also very similar. Genetic Performance's clause reads:

It is not the intention of genetic performance to provide specific medical advice but rather to provide you with information to better understand your genetic predispositions. Specific medical advice will not be provided, and genetic performance urges you to consult with a qualified physician for diagnosis and for answers to your personal questions. [. . .]

Individuals with specific concerns about their health status or genetic testing should consult with a doctor or a genetic counselor.[181]

Gonidio's clause reads:

It is not the intention of Gonidio to provide specific medical advice but rather to provide you with information to better understand the health risks and benefits associated with your genotype. Specific medical advice will not be provided, and Gonidio urges you to consult with a qualified physician for diagnosis and for answers to your personal questions. [. . .]

Individuals with specific concerns about their health status or genetic testing should consult with a doctor or a genetic counselor. [182]

[180] DNA DTC, T&C.
[181] Genetic Performance, T&C.
[182] Gonidio, TOS.

(k) Property and Intellectual Property

Summary of Review of Intellectual Property and Property Clauses

It is also common for companies to include broad clauses on intellectual property and property more generally, such as a clause waiving the consumers' property rights in their genetic information. While a person does not normally retain property rights in their excised tissue or DNA, important privacy[183] and security issues are raised by DTC companies' use, storage and potential sharing or sale of consumers' data. These clauses as currently framed are often unnecessarily broad in scope and are likely to fail the requirements of transparency under the CRA and the Unfair Terms Directive terms. They are also likely to be in breach of data protection law and not be consistent with the Human Tissue Act.

As DTC companies are commercial entities and their main assets consist of the sequenced information collected from consumers together with their research ventures, it seems that companies do need to be more transparent about the property rights they are allocating to themselves. At present, these clauses are very similar to the clauses used by social networking websites meaning that companies also often acquire licences to use user-generated content, which in this context may actually include a person's health information and information which would normally be included in a medical record and which would ordinarily be subject to confidentiality protection. It is possible that at present many consumers are not necessarily aware of the implications which such clauses may have upon their rights in their sequenced genetic information and other types of personal information.

Examples of Property Waiver Clauses

23andMe's Terms of Service includes the following clause:

> 6. (k) Waiver of Property Rights: You understand that by providing any sample, having your Genetic Information processed, accessing your Genetic Information, or providing Self-Reported Information, you acquire no rights in any research or commercial products that may be developed by 23andMe or its collaborating partners. You specifically understand that you will not

---

[183] Hsiao-Ying Huang, and Masooda Bashir, 'Direct-to-consumer genetic testing: Contextual privacy predicament' Proceedings of the 78th ASIS&T Annual Meeting: Information Science with Impact: Research in and for the Community (2015) American Society for Information Science 50.

receive compensation for any research or commercial products that include or result from your Genetic Information or Self-Reported Information.[184]

Meanwhile, Gene By Gene's DNA DTC's Terms and Conditions includes the following clauses:

2. Client Representations and Warranties

[. . .]Waiver of Property Rights: You understand that by providing any sample, having your sample processed, accessing your results, or providing personal information, you acquire no rights in any research or commercial products that may be developed by DNA DTC or its collaborating partners. You specifically understand that you will not receive compensation for any research or commercial products that include or result from your sample, results or personal record. You agree that you have the authority, under the laws of the state or jurisdiction in which you reside, to provide these representations. In case of breach of any one of these representations you will defend and indemnify the Company against any liability, costs, or damages arising out of the breach of the representation.

6. Your Proprietary Rights

Your sample, once submitted to and analyzed by us, cannot be returned to you. Any test results derived from your sample remains your information, subject to rights as established under the Terms and Conditions and Privacy Statement. You understand that you should not expect any financial benefit from DNA DTC as a result of having your results processed; made available to you; or, as provided in our Privacy Statement and Terms of Service, shared with research partners, including commercial partners.

Waiver of Property Rights. As stated above, you understand that by providing any sample, having your sample processed, accessing your results, or providing personal information, you acquire no rights in any research or commercial products that may be developed by DNA DTC or its collaborating partners. You specifically understand that you will not receive compensation for any research or commercial products that include or result from your sample, results or personal record.[185]

Examples of Intellectual Property Clauses

23andMe's clause 22 in their TOS protects their proprietary rights in their services, software, domain names and all kinds of intellectual property therein and trademarks. All information presented to the consumer through

[184] 23andMe, TOS.
[185] DNA DTC, T&C.

their services is also protected by the proprietary rights clause. This refers also to the end-user licence agreement, if any, for the software used in the services.

The services and software are also said to contain both proprietary and confidential information. These are worded thoroughly to protect their property rights.

However, a narrow licence is granted in clause 22 to use the software and services on a single computer for the sole purpose of enabling the consumer to 'use and enjoy the benefit of the Services as provided by 23andMe, in the manner permitted by the TOS'. [186]

And this narrow licence may not be assigned. Seemingly, the content of the services may include the information returned to the consumer and as such no rights in that material are granted.

The bargain reflected overall would seem to be that whilst the consumer waives all rights and the services are provided, the content of the services and any material provided back to the consumer is owned by and confidential to 23andMe. In particular the consumer agrees:

> not to– and not to permit anyone else to – modify, rent, lease, loan, sell, distribute, or create derivative works of, reverse engineer, decompile, or otherwise attempt to extract the source code of the Services or Software or any part thereof, in whole or in part

It is set out in full to show the detail of their proprietary rights wording. It is expressed in legalistic language which would require interpretation by a lawyer.[187]

Examples of Licence Clauses
Clauses have been referred to explicitly to illustrate their complexity and language.

23andMe includes provisions relating to both the User Content and the Services Content. The user is responsible for the former and the interests of 23andMe in the latter are protected in clauses which grant to the user a narrow (in the sampled version clause 9) and limited licence to copy some services content for non-commercial purposes only (in the sampled version clause 13).

> The User content is the User's responsibility, but the User grants to 23andMe:

---

[186] 23andMe, TOS.
[187] 23andMe, TOS.

a perpetual, irrevocable, worldwide, royalty-free, and non-exclusive license to reproduce, adapt, modify, translate, publish, publicly perform, publicly display, distribute, reproduce, edit, reformat, and create derivative works from any User Content that you submit, post, or display on or through the Services. You acknowledge and agree that this license includes a right for 23andMe to make such User Content available to other companies, organizations, or individuals with whom 23andMe has relationships, and to use such User Content in connection with the provision of those services. [188]

As the contrast is interesting the clauses are set out below for comparison. Please note they may have been replaced by subsequent drafting so comparison with their current terms is advisable.

9. Limited License

You acknowledge that all User Content, whether publicly posted or privately transmitted, is the sole responsibility of the person from which such User Content originated. This means that you, and not 23andMe, are entirely responsible for all User Content that you upload, post, email, or otherwise transmit via the Service.

You acknowledge that the Services content presented to you as part of the Services, whether original 23andMe Services content or sponsored content within the Services, is protected by copyright and/or other intellectual property rights that are owned by 23andMe and/or the sponsors who provide that content to 23andMe (or by other persons or companies on their behalf). 23andMe grants you a Limited License to copy and distribute free of charge, for noncommercial purposes only, any of the Services content with the exception of content from 'MD's Perspectives' in the 'For the Experts' section of the website and any other content marked as not subject to this Limited License on the website, provided you: (i) provide the Services content as it appears on the 23andMe website with no changes including but not limited to presenting selections which might tend to misrepresent the substance of the Services content; (ii) include the following attribution on the first page of any materials you distribute: © 23andMe, Inc. 2007–2012. All rights reserved; distributed pursuant to a Limited License from 23andMe; (iii) agree you have no right to offer anyone else any further right with respect to this Services content. Aside from the Limited License provided in this paragraph, you may not modify, rent, lease, loan, sell, distribute, or create derivative works based on this

---

[188] 23andMe, TOS.

Services content (either in whole or in part) unless you have been specifically told that you may do so by 23andMe or by the owners of that content, in a separate agreement.

13. Material Provided to 23andMe – Your Proprietary Rights

User Content. 23andMe does not claim ownership of the User Content you provide to 23andMe (including feedback and suggestions) or post, upload, input, or submit to the Service. Unless otherwise specified, you retain copyright and any other rights you already hold over User Content that you create and submit, post, or display on or through the Services. However, by submitting, posting, or displaying User Content, you give 23andMe, its affiliated companies, sublicensees (including but not limited to sublicensees who avail themselves of the Limited License granted in Section 9 above) and successors and assigns a perpetual, irrevocable, worldwide, royalty-free, and non-exclusive license to reproduce, adapt, modify, translate, publish, publicly perform, publicly display, distribute, reproduce, edit, reformat, and create derivative works from any User Content that you submit, post, or display on or through the Services. You acknowledge and agree that this license includes a right for 23andMe to make such User Content available to other companies, organizations, or individuals with whom 23andMe has relationships, and to use such User Content in connection with the provision of those services.

You understand that 23andMe, in performing the required technical steps to provide the Services to our users, may (a) transmit or distribute your User Content over various public networks and in various media; and (b) make such changes to your content as are necessary to conform and adapt that content to the technical requirements of connecting networks, devices, services, or media. You acknowledge and agree that this license shall permit 23andMe to take these actions. You represent and warrant to 23andMe that you have all the rights, power, and authority necessary to grant the above license.[189]

The Makings of Me includes the following clause which also grants a non-exclusive, worldwide royalty free and perpetual licence: [190]

Waiver of Rights: You agree to grant to Mapme a non-exclusive, worldwide, royalty-free, perpetual license, with the right to sublicense, to reproduce, distribute, transmit, create derivative works of, publicly display and

---

[189] 23andMe, TOS.
[190] The Makings of Me, TOU.

publicly perform any materials and other information (including, without limitation, ideas contained therein for new or improved products or services) you submit to public areas of Mapme (such as BBSs, forums and chat rooms) by all means and in any media now known or hereafter developed. You hereby waive all rights, legal, moral or otherwise, in any such materials and information, and you hereby warrant that any such materials and information originate with you, or that you have the right to submit such materials and information. You agree that you shall have no recourse against Mapme for any alleged or actual infringement or misappropriation of any proprietary right in your public communication.

DNA Spectrum's provision in the Intellectual Property clause of its TOS also has a similar broad licence which is worldwide, extensive and irrevocable. The wording is set out below to enable comparison: [191]

While you retain any and all rights accruing to you with respect to your User-generated Content, you grant us, our agents and affiliates a worldwide, irrevocable, perpetual, non-exclusive, fully sub-licensable, transferable, royalty-free license to copy, reproduce, edit, adapt, modify, (publicly) display, publish, translate, distribute and otherwise use such content for any purpose in any existing or future form(s) or media.

These licences are all expressed in complex legalistic language, which a consumer may not readily understand.

5.3 Conclusion

This chapter has presented a review of 71 contracts used by DTC companies engaged in the provision of health-related services. As has been shown through the examples of actual clauses, there is overall a lack of transparency in the sense that DTC contractual terms may be construed not to be written in plain and intelligible language and may be overly lengthy. There is also much commonality in the types of clause used and also the language used by different companies, which might also indicate that companies are copying terms from their competitors. Companies may also be copying terms from other web-based industries, as many of the terms used resemble the contracts of companies engaged in other types of e-commerce. The similarities between different companies' contracts results in limitations on consumers' choices as it means that even where consumers are interested in purchasing genetic tests on terms that are more favourable, they may in fact find it difficult to find companies with better terms. Given this tendency it is hoped that the CMA

---

[191] DNA Spectrum, TOS.

will work with the industry to improve the terms or take enforcement action against it.

Certain types of terms commonly included in DTC contracts include: clauses allowing for unilateral variation of the contract; clauses disclaiming liability for fitness for purpose or for personal injury caused by the company's negligence; clauses limiting scope of purpose; clauses purporting to bind the consumer to resolve any disputes in another jurisdiction; and consent clauses. These are likely to be deemed unfair and regulators should take an interest in policing these terms. The frequency of these terms highlights the need for greater oversight of the industry and indicates that self-regulation may not be providing sufficient protection to consumers. It is also likely that consent mechanisms in particular may not be in compliance with either the Human Tissue Act or the DPA and that where companies provide health tests they may in fact need to adhere to higher standards in line with the decision in *Montgomery*.[192]

It is argued that many terms currently used do cause an imbalance in the rights of parties to the contract to the detriment of the consumer. It is also suggested that overall it is likely that many DTC contracts fail to meet the CRA's requirement for transparency and as transparency has also been frequently stressed in policy guidance, it is clear that there is a need for better practice.

It seems that in the context of the DTC industry, the use of wrap contracts does need to be considered more carefully. As consumers are becoming habituated to agreeing to unseen terms online and also routinely ignore such terms,[193] they are also likely to be underestimating any risks of potential harm from entering into such contracts.[194] While it might be argued that purchasing shoes on Amazon is not an activity likely to result in harm for that consumer, the DTC context is different and involves more potential risk. While an individual might provide quite significant amounts of personal information to a company when making an ordinary purchase online, when a person orders a DTC she provides both a physical sample of herself and access to her genetic information. Genetic information can be used as a unique identifier of the individual tested, but it can also be used to identify her relatives. Where DTC companies are also engaged in health research they are also acquiring large amounts of health information about the consumer, which might be potentially sensitive and would normally only have been provided by the individual as part of medical treatment or participation in medical research.

---

[192] (Scotland) [2015] UKSC 11.
[193] Obar and Oeldorf-Hirsch, 'The biggest lie on the Internet' (n 32).
[194] Kim, *Wrap Contracts* (n 6) 59.

Given the length of DTC contracts and the language used it is possible that consumers will not necessarily understand the legal information contained in these documents and they may also not be sufficiently cognizant of the implications of entering into a contract online.

DTC companies may also wish to consider what consumer best-practice engagement and contracting might look like. Seemingly there could be a competitive advantage, from a consumer perspective, in attracting consumers who perceive that a particular company has more consumer-friendly terms. Whether or not the DTC industry will strive to improve contracts so that they are more consumer friendly remains to be seen. If businesses do wish to maintain consumer trust and conduct ethical and responsible health research, they could treat improving their contracts, privacy policies, and web interfaces as opportunities, which could in turn lead to the development of industry standards and delivering on some of the rhetoric and claims commonly made in the marketing of DTC services.

6

Future Directions for DTC Governance

Today's world is one of constant tracking, where personal data fuels many new products and services. Numerous emerging and new technologies offer novel opportunities for us to learn about ourselves and allow companies to learn about us as well. The Internet of Things is rapidly expanding the range of entities that can profile us and analyse us. Smartphones and travel cards track our movements across cities and across countries. Wearable fitness monitors track our exercise and can also reveal our location. New consumer services such as DTC promise to give us insights into our identities, our essence – but at what cost?

This book has sought to provide an introduction to the DTC industry and the challenges it poses for regulation. This chapter will discuss possible future directions for improved industry governance. Several suggestions are made, as given the nature of DTC services and the variety of areas of law which might be drawn upon to regulate the industry, there are both short-term fixes and longer-term solutions to be considered. While the law often struggles to keep up with technology, with the wide range of new technologies coming to market which have the potential to change the way we live and affect our lives in significant ways, regulators, legislators, lawyers, researchers, technology companies and the public need to come together and engage in open discussion so that laws can be created that can respond to the specific issues raised by particular technologies and regulate them appropriately.

The public also needs to have access to balanced information about new technologies in general so that individuals can make informed choices about whether to engage with particular services and products.[1] There are numerous historical examples of why it might not be beneficial for consumers or companies to leave sole responsibility for regulating to the industry itself. It is

---

[1] Andelka M Phillips and IS Mian, 'Governance and of future spaces: A discussion of some issues raised by the possibilities of human–machine mergers' discussion paper presented at the Data For Policy Government by Algorithm? Conference (London, 6–7 September 2017) <https://zenodo.org/record/896110#.WcDnv8iGPIU>

hoped that the suggestions made herein will assist both regulators and industry in thinking of new ways to improve governance and also to help consumers.

6.1 Note for Readers Interested in Purchasing DTC Tests

If you are reading this book in part because you are considering engaging with a DTC service, there are a number of issues you should consider. Firstly, do compare a few different companies' services and actually read all their policies. Consider what the benefit is that you are seeking from undergoing testing. If you have serious medical concerns, consider the option of discussing genetic testing with your physician or going to a specialist clinic. Also, think about insurance coverage. If you have a family history of a particular medical condition or disease, which may have a genetic link, think carefully about where would be best to undergo testing. If you would be obliged to reveal test results to an insurer and you have concerns about this, then you may want to wait until the industry matures more.

If you do not have an interest in your genetic makeup for medical reasons, but are interested in exploring your family origins, remember that your genetic information is shared with your family. Remember too that stored genetic data can be used for a wide variety of secondary purposes and may be shared with third parties. It may be wise to discuss the possibility of having a test with family members. If you or your family have concerns about future use, you may want to take some time to think about testing and delay a decision for a few weeks. If you do not have a pressing need to undertake testing you could wait until the industry matures more and there are more businesses offering more privacy-centric services.

6.2 Suggestions for Reform

DTC services challenge existing governance mechanisms and while consumer protection and data protection law should have direct applicability to the industry, to improve industry governance there is a need for thinking beyond existing legislation. One possibility is to create new legislation focused on regulating the use of genetic data used by commercial entities at a domestic level. Countries could then appoint new regulatory bodies to deal specifically with industry. Although it might seem that different types of DTC test should be regulated differently, as it is common for companies to merge and partner with others and offer a variety of different types of tests, both health and recreational, there is a need for higher standards across the industry.

Codes of conduct could also serve as good short-term strategies to improve industry governance and they seem particularly desirable in relation to DTC companies that provide tests for health purposes, as they could serve to improve standards across the industry and afford greater protection to consumers. However, as with *Best Practices for Consumer Genetic Testing Services*,[2] we will have to see how the commitments made in such voluntary measures live up to their promise.

Chapter 5 explored the wrap contracts of DTC companies and previous chapters have drawn upon other studies of DTC privacy policies, as well as studies of contracts and privacy policies for other digital services. Overall it is argued that there is a need for reform of contracts and privacy policies, so that companies comply with consumer protection and data protection law. Transparency is vital here, but contracts need also to be fair and balanced. Improving contracts should not simply be about expressing existing terms that protect business in a more easily understood way. In order for contracts to actually improve from a consumer standpoint, they need to be more balanced. As contracts and privacy policies link to each other and incorporate terms by reference, if there are problems with one document, then there are likely to be difficulties with the other. Allowing a broad power to alter terms without notice is particularly problematic, as this could also allow for a business to change their privacy policy. Such broad alteration clauses can also have the effect that the overall contract may lack certainty, as where terms can change at any time without notice, it is not really possible to know what the terms of that contract are.

The review of the contracts of DTC companies considered how specific terms might be challenged under existing contract and consumer protection law. In light of the lack of specific legal regulation of the industry, we can view the use of wrap contracts as the main means of governance of the relationships between companies and consumers at present. This situation means that contract law and consumer protection law are the current mechanism that consumers are most likely to draw upon in seeking redress, but it may not be the best suited to protection of their interests in this context. (The class actions against 23andMe in the USA have centred on its contract.)

(a) The Canadian Example

In thinking about the way forward for regulation of the DTC industry and protecting the rights of individuals in this context, it is helpful to look at the recent Canadian reforms. As mentioned previously, in Chapters 1 and

---

[2] Carson Martinez, 'Privacy Best Practices for Consumer Genetic Testing Services' Future of Privacy Forum (31 July 2018) <https://fpf.org/2018/07/31/privacy-best-practices-for-consumer-genetic-testing-services/> last accessed 18 October 2018; Future of Privacy Forum, *Privacy Best Practices for Consumer Genetic Testing Services* (31 July 2018) <https://fpf.org/wp-content/uploads/2018/07/Privacy-Best-Practices-for-Consumer-Genetic-Testing-Services-FINAL.pdf> last accessed 24 October 2018.

4, Canada's Genetic Non-Discrimination Act has strengthened Canadians' genetic privacy rights considerably. The Act:

> prohibits any person from requiring an individual to undergo a genetic test as a condition of providing goods or services or entering into a contract. It also prohibits any person from requiring the disclosure of existing genetic test results as a condition of engaging in those activities.[3]

Under the Act, Canadians who choose to have a genetic test are not required to either share test results with an employer or insurer or to consent to further disclosure.[4]

The Canadian Office of the Privacy Commissioner has produced guidance regarding DTC genetic tests,[5] issued after the enactment of GNA. This guidance is particularly helpful for anyone interested in undergoing a DTC test, as it lists a number of questions which you should consider before purchasing a DTC test.[6]

Questions you might ask a company before purchasing a DTC test

The following questions are taken from guidance from the Canadian Officer of the Privacy Commissioner:

1. What are the purposes of the genetic test (health-related, ancestry, paternity or maternity testing) and are they consistent with your expectations?
2. What personal information will the company collect in addition to your biological sample and are you satisfied with its explanations regarding how it will process and protect the data?
3. With whom does the company propose to share your test results (e.g. researchers, pharmaceutical companies, marketers, patient groups, related or affiliated companies, etc.) and have you been given the opportunity to consent to this voluntarily and in writing? *You are within your rights to refuse such disclosures.*

---

[3] OPC, *Policy Statement on the Collection, Use and Disclosure of Genetic Test Results* (OPC, updated December 2017) <https://www.priv.gc.ca/en/privacy-topics/health-genetic-and-other-body-information/s-d_140710/> last accessed 27 October 2018.

[4] OPC, 'Direct-to-consumer genetic testing and privacy' (OPC, updated December 2017) <https://www.priv.gc.ca/en/privacy-topics/health-genetic-and-other-body-information/02_05_d_69_gen/> last accessed 27 October 2018.

[5] OPC, *Policy Statement* (n 3).

[6] OPC, 'Direct-to-consumer genetic testing and privacy' (n 4).

4. What kind of lab performs the testing and is it certified by an accredited body?
5. Will your information be processed outside Canada?
6. How long will your personal information, biological sample and test results be retained and why? Once the service is completed and the related retention period is expired, will your sample be destroyed and your related personal information be deleted?
7. How can you access the personal information about you that is on file, including a record of how your data has been used and whether and with whom it has been shared (in accordance with your prior consent)?
8. If the policy does not clearly answer your questions and explain what will happen to your personal information, including your biological samples and test results, contact the company directly for more information. They should provide contact information for somebody who can answer privacy-related questions or concerns. If you are still not satisfied with the responses provided, know that you can contact one of our Offices and consider filing a privacy complaint.

Personal questions you might ask yourself before purchasing a DTC test

The following questions are taken from guidance from the Canadian Officer of the Privacy Commissioner:

1. Would talking to my doctor or genetic counsellor help me make a more informed decision about whether a direct-to-consumer genetic test would meet my needs?
2. Am I comfortable finding out things about myself or my family members that I did not expect or that I may not want to know?
3. How will receiving this information affect me and the kinds of life choices I will make?
4. Have I spoken to my family members about the potential implications this may have for them?

(b) Potential for Secondary Use of Data

The use of genetic data from a commercial database in the Golden State Killer case illustrates just how easily genetic data can be repurposed beyond what consumers might expect their data to be used for. In the past, concern has been also been expressed regarding governments retaining identifiable DNA profiles, primarily in the context of criminal databases, such as the UK's National DNA Database (NDNAD) and the USA's Combined DNA Index System (CODIS).[7] Given the significance of individuals' rights in this context, where private companies are collecting and retaining DNA there should be greater scrutiny of their activities.

While some tests currently offered by DTC companies may have little predictive value, stored sequenced data may allow individuals to be identified and may also enable people to learn much about the individuals, which they may not want shared. With continuing advances in biometrics, it is possible that hackers may target DNA databases. There is potential here for data protection authorities in the EU and privacy regulators elsewhere to also take on a role in regulating DTC as well given the privacy concerns raised by the nature of DTC services. It is desirable that entities such as the UK's ICO and Ireland's Data Protection Commissioner contribute to improving regulation of this industry. Canada's GNA and the Canadian OPC's guidance on DTC could also provide useful models for other countries.

In an age where a range of technology companies are acquiring vast amounts of personal data, the activities of companies providing DNA tests and combining them with other sources of personal data do need to be monitored. The public needs sufficient information about the industry to be able to make an informed choice about whether or not to engage with it. At present there is a real need for companies not only to improve their contracts and privacy policies, but also to be more transparent about the nature of the services they provide and the uses to which consumer data may be put.

(c) A Role for Consumer Protection and Data Protection Regulators

In the short term, one possible strategy for enhancing consumer protection in this context is for the CMA and consumer regulators in other countries, such as the ACCC in Australia, to undertake compliance reviews of the DTC industry, similar to the CMA's review of cloud storage providers. Especially

---

[7] See National DNA Database Strategy Board, <https://www.gov.uk/government/groups/national-dna-database-strategy-board> last accessed 26 October 2018; National Institute of Justice, 'What is CODIS?' <https://www.nij.gov/journals/266/Pages/backlogs-codis.aspx> last accessed 26 October 2018; Frederick R Bieber, Charles H Brenner and David Lazer, 'Finding criminals through DNA of their relatives' (2006) 5778 *Science* 1315–6 doi: 10.1126/science.1122655; Helen Wallace, 'The UK national DNA database' (2006) 7 *EMBO Reports* – Special Issue S26–30 <https://onlinelibrary.wiley.com/doi/pdf/10.1038/sj.embor.7400727> last accessed 24 October 2018; Lila Kazemian, Ken Pease, and David P Farrington, 'DNA retention policies: The potential contribution of criminal career research' (2011) 8(1) European Journal of Criminology 48–64 doi: 10.1177/1477370810373731.

in the area of genetic tests for health purposes, I do suggest that the Human Tissue Authority, the MHRA and ICO in the UK have a greater role to play in regulating the industry. However, due to ongoing reform of data protection and medical devices law, it is important to consider current industry practice and how matters might be improved for consumers and companies based on current business practice. Given the legislation on unfair terms and the previous work of the Office of Fair Trading, a useful strategy in the short term is for the new CMA to take on an active stance as regulator for this industry in the UK and to work with the industry to discontinue the use of certain terms and increase transparency.

Currently the industry is using wrap contracts to govern several matters, including the sale of tests, participation in research activities, the use, sharing and storage of genetic and other types of personal information, and use of their websites. As the industry is at present largely unregulated, the use of these contracts allows the industry to effectively engage in private legislation, which has the consequence of causing an imbalance in the respective rights of the parties – consumer and company– which is heavily skewed in favour of companies and is likely to be detrimental to the rights of consumers.

In analysing DTC contracts, much commonality was found in the terms included and the language used. At present, the majority are skewed heavily in the company's favour. A variety of terms commonly included in these contracts seem likely to be deemed unfair and consequently unenforceable under UK law. (It is likely that these are also unenforceable under EU consumer protection law). These include terms allowing for unilateral variation, exclusion clauses, indemnity clauses, choice of law clauses, and consent and assent clauses. It is therefore desirable that companies do reform their contracts and omit some of these terms. Overall, contracts also do not represent a fair balance between the respective parties' interests and due to the nature of genetic information it is desirable that companies engage in better practice. They could look to governance mechanisms developed in the medical research context.

The pattern observed amongst DTC contracts fits in with broader trends in online contracting more generally, where consent or assent to a website's terms are often deemed through use of the website. It might be argued that a consumer purchasing a shirt on Amazon accepts certain potential risks and accepts the possibility that there may be certain additional contractual clauses that they might not necessarily want. They accept all this in exchange for ease of purchase and lower prices. It seems though that even in this situation the paradigm is one that needs to change: while companies are entitled to minimise their own level of risk, online contracts ought to be written in clear, concise and comprehensible language, displayed in readable formats with any unexpected clauses highlighted, so that a consumer can enter into the bargain knowingly. Currently many consumers do not expect that anything surprising would be included in the contract, but often this is not the case.

Companies could work with the CMA and other consumer regulators to improve their contracts. As many companies do want to conduct medical research based upon data they have collected from consumers, it is a two-way street and sharing of information will benefit all parties in the long term. Regulatory reform is also needed, but improving contracts and privacy policies would be a cost-effective and useful strategy in the short term. Contracts could be developed so that they were shorter and more interactive with attention being drawn to key clauses, by using bold font or other visual aids.

Companies could also develop something akin to Nancy Kim's suggested model of specific assent or HeLEX's dynamic consent.[8] Contracts could allow more opportunities for customers to opt out of particular services, and provide more information about use, storage and disclosure of data. Making sure that documents are available in printer-friendly, easily readable formats is very important. Currently, some companies make additional consent and contractual documents available only after purchase or after creating an account. A better practice would be to make all documents publicly available on DTC websites without requiring registration, as this would allow people the opportunity to save the documents and consider them before purchase.

Given the implementation of the GDPR and the UK's DPA18, the ICO and other data protection and privacy regulators should also engage in more oversight of the industry. They could assist with educational initiatives to help consumers/data subjects understand the respective risks, benefits and limitations of DTC services and the privacy implications of undergoing testing.

(d) DTC as One Example of Personalised Medicine

DTC services for health purposes are representative of a broader paradigm shift from patient to consumer in the field of personalised medicine. These services, as they are offered via the Internet internationally, do challenge existing governance mechanisms, especially those based nationally. They raise similar issues to those of wearable health-monitoring devices, such as Fitbit, Jawbone and Garmin, or innovations in the field of biometrics. In an increasingly globalised world where legal regulation is no longer restricted to national laws, DTC highlights some of the problems associated more generally with regulation of Internet-based industries.

---

[8] Jane Kaye et al., 'Dynamic consent: A patient interface for twenty-first-century research networks' (2015) 23 *European Journal of Human Genetics* 141–6 <https://www.nature.com/articles/ejhg201471> last accessed 22 October 2018.

For health-related testing, relying on medical device regulation does seem one of the most attractive options although this still leaves many other types of DTC largely unregulated. Although in the EU the IVD Regulation has been enacted, many of its provisions do not come into force until 2022, which does limit the amount of protection it affords to consumers in the short term.

Meanwhile, in the USA, as mentioned in Chapter 1, the FDA has created a pathway for approval for DTC tests for health purposes.[9] However, DTC offerings, which only allow for ordering via a physician, are not yet subject to the same approvals process[10] and it is desirable that this does change in the future. It would also be beneficial if the FDA could work with the FTC to produce more guidance for consumers on this industry.

(e) The Need for Quality Checks

Companies are also often selling products that may not in fact be fit for purpose and may also not live up to the marketing claims made on DTC websites. Lack of regulation here also makes it difficult to regulate advertising of such tests, as it 'makes it difficult to determine what is false advertising as opposed to innovative new use'.[11] While it was not possible to address this matter in this book, it is hoped that future research will be able to explore in detail the manner in which DTC tests are advertised. In this context, it is possible that the ordinary consumer, even were she to be reasonably observant and circumspect assuming she is neither a geneticist nor legally trained, would have difficulty in understanding her test results and the implications that they have, and also she will likely have difficulty with understanding the terms of the wrap contract. It is also very likely that she has not provided valid consent to undergo a genetic test. It is also likely that in accordance with Kim's work, she has also not provided valid assent to the contract. While contract law does protect autonomy, there should be some degree of mutuality and a person should be aware that she has entered into a contract. DTC contracts as they are currently framed attempt to bind the consumer in

[9] US Food and Drug Administration, 'FDA allows marketing of first direct-to-consumer tests that provide genetic risk information for certain conditions' (FDA, Press Release, 6 April 2017) <https://www.fda.gov/newsevents/newsroom/pressannouncements/ucm551185. htm> last accessed 30 July 2018.

[10] Ike Swetlitz, 'Genetic tests ordered by doctors race to market, while "direct-to-consumer" tests hinge on FDA approval' STAT (16 March 2018) <https://www.statnews. com/2018/03/16/genetic-tests-fda-regulation/> last accessed 27 October 2018.

[11] MF Myers, 'Health care providers and direct-to-consumer access and advertising of genetic testing in the United States' (2011) 3(81) Genome Medicine 1–13, 4 <https://doi. org/10.1186/gm297> last accessed 20 October 2018.

a manner that is not transparent and it is possible that many terms included in these contracts are open to challenge on the grounds of unfairness.

In line with the views of Hudson and Javitt, and with the Association for Molecular Pathology's Revised Position Statement, ensuring that DTC tests are of high quality is vital.[12] It is also desirable that there is greater protection provided for consumers in this context, especially in relation to the protection of consumers' privacy in their genomic sequence data and also in other types of personal data which DTC companies may collect. As previously noted, there is a need to both strengthen and harmonise the standards used by different DTC companies and at a minimum it is desirable that the tests offered by DTC companies providing tests for health purposes are 'fit for purpose'.

Where consumers participate in research focused on serious psychiatric diseases, addiction susceptibility, or late-onset diseases, which may be untreatable, different standards may need to be developed and adhered to.[13] While web-based interfaces can be beneficial for consumers, they need to be used carefully. It might be advisable for DTC companies to look to web-based models used in the research context such as HeLEX's dynamic consent model.[14] It would be helpful if online genetic counselling services were made available to consumers.

It is important to recognise that DTC as an Internet-based industry does pose challenges for regulation if the focus of regulation is solely on national regulatory systems. The majority of DTC companies that provide health-related testing are based in the USA. UK-based consumers who purchase tests from companies such as 23andMe will have their biological samples sent overseas and their genetic information and other types of personal information will in fact be processed, stored and shared in other countries. This data flow is borderless and it may be naïve to focus too much on regulating at a national level, even though specific regulation at a national level is desirable. It does

---

[12] Gail H Javitt and Kathy Hudson, 'Federal neglect: Regulation of genetic testing – Government needs to ensure that genetic tests provide useful medical information and that the test results are reliable' (2006) 22(3) *Issues in Science and Technology* 59–66 <https://www.jstor.org/stable/43314223> last accessed 22 October 2018.

[13] R Mathews, W Hall, and A Carter, 'Direct-to-consumer genetic testing for addiction susceptibility: A premature commercialisation of doubtful validity and value (2012) 107(12) *Addiction* 2069–74 <https://doi.org/10.1111/j.1360-0443.2012.03836.x> last accessed 24 October 2018; S Pirzadeh-Miller et al., 'Direct-to-consumer genetic testing: Helpful, harmful, or pure entertainment?' (2011) 8(6) *Community Oncology* 263–8 doi: 10.1016/S1548-5315(12)70021-9; CA Bellcross, PZ Page, and D Meaney-Delman, 'Direct-to-consumer personal genome testing and cancer risk prediction' (July 2012) 18(4) *Cancer Journal* 293–302 doi: 10.1097/PPO.0b013e3182610e38.

[14] Kaye et al., 'Dynamic consent' (n 8)

seem that the ideal regulatory response is to be found in international law. For instance, part of the Data Protection Directive's success has been due to its extra-jurisdictional reach.[15] Here the IVD Regulation might be useful as it would significantly restrict DTC for health purposes in the EU, prohibiting direct-to-consumer advertising and requiring a prescription in order to purchase a genetic test for health purposes. Although, as previously noted, this approach still does have flaws, partly because it allows manufacturers to limit the ostensible purposes of their testing.[16] It is also questionable what counts as advertising; for instance, does website content constitute advertising or the mere provision of information regarding tests? Also, restricting advertising may increase advertising to physicians, which may result in impartiality.[17] It should be noted as well that the IVD Regulation will not catch recreational DTC.

Some types of DTC service may not in fact offer any real benefit to consumers. This is primarily due to the fact that some tests currently offered lack clinical utility and may also lack clinical validity and consumers are often not well equipped to understand the genetic test results they receive from DTC companies. The ideal 'average consumer' contemplated in English and EU case law may be 'well informed, reasonably observant and circumspect', but as has been noted this ideal often does not reflect reality.[18] Moreover, in the context of the provision of services that are complex in nature, it may be even less likely that an ordinary consumer would really meet these standards. Ongoing work by a colleague, Jan Charbonneau, highlights the problems ordinary consumers may encounter when presented with genetic risk information.[19]

Ideally, new industry-specific regulatory authorities are needed. An analogy can be made here with the financial services sector, which has its own specific industry regulator in several countries including the UK. Here there

---

[15] McKay Cunningham, 'Next generation privacy: The Internet of Things, data exhaust, and reforming regulation by risk of harm' (2015) 2(2) *Groningen Journal of International Law* 115–44, 122 <https://ssrn.com/abstract=2549849> last accessed 24 October 2018.

[16] Louiza Kalokairinou, Heidi Carmen Howard, and Pascal Borry, 'Changes on the horizon for consumer genomics in the EU' (2014) 346(6207) *Science* 296–8 doi: 10.1126/science.1256396.

[17] Ibid. 298.

[18] I Benöhr, *EU Consumer Law and Human Rights* (Oxford University Press 2013) 17; L Waddington, 'Reflections on the protection of "vulnerable" consumers under EU law' (2013) 2 Maastricht Faculty of Law Working Paper 5–6 <http://dx.doi.org/10.2139/ssrn.2532904> last accessed 24 October 2018.

[19] Jan Charbonneau, 'Straight from the lab to the market: General public engagement with direct-to-consumer genetic testing (conference slides)' (DTC genetics – consumers, contracts and complexities, King's College London, 19 June 2015); see also University of Tasmania, *The Age of Personalised Medicine: Regulatory Challenges for Australia* <http://www.utas.edu.au/law-and-genetics/research-and-projects/personalised-medicine>

has been recognition that the nature of financial services[20] means that consumers may require specific additional protection and such regulation is not necessarily viewed as overly paternalistic. The UK's FCA also has powers to challenge unfair terms and it works together with the CMA.[21] The FCA's guidance for consumers on unfair terms highlights a number of terms which it deems to be likely to be unfair. This includes clauses that allow businesses to change terms without notice, those that purport to bind the consumer to unknown terms, and those that try to limit a person's legal rights.[22]

(f) Rethinking the User Interface

The DTC industry should also look beyond merely rewording contracts and privacy policies – to the design of their user interfaces. Given the nature of their services, consumers should not be rushed into a decision. Instead the user interface could create stopping points that slow down consumers. For instance, once a consumer has registered on a site, companies could allow for a time period for consideration of purchase and a time period after the DNA sample has been received that allows a person to change their mind. We live in an age when we want everything instantly, but when it comes to serious decisions about new services that handle sensitive data, slowing down the process of decision making could lead to benefits for both consumers and industry.

Projects such as POLISIS, Pribot and the Useable Privacy Policies Project can provide useful insight into how we might go about making things better. However, there is also growing concern more generally about interface and specifically application design. Many products are being designed to grab a user's attention[23] and nudge them towards making a quick decision,[24] and

[20] Financial Conduct Authority, *Consumer Vulnerability* (FCA, Occasional Paper No 8, 2015) 22, citing Office of Fair Trading, *Vulnerable Consumer Groups: Quantification and Analysis* (Office of Fair Trading, Research Paper 15 1998, 1998) <https://www.fca.org.uk/pub lications/occasional-papers/occasional-paper-no-8-consumer-vulnerability> last accessed 23 October 2018.

[21] FCA, 'Unfair contract terms' (FCA, last updated 17 May 2018) <https://www.fca.org.uk/ firms/unfair-contract-terms> last accessed 29 October 2018.

[22] FCA, 'Unfair contracts: Consumers' <https://www.fca.org.uk/consumers/unfair-contracts-consumers> last accessed 29 October 2018.

[23] See generally, Adam Atler, *Irresistable: Rise of Addictive Technology and the Business of Keeping us Hooked* (Penguin 2017).

[24] BM Frischmann and E Selinger, 'Engineering humans with contracts' (September 2016) Cardozo Legal Studies Research Paper No 493 <https://papers.ssrn.com/sol3/papers. cfm?abstract_id=2834011>; BM Frischmann and E Selinger, *Re-Engineering Humanity* (Cambridge University Press 2018) chapters 1, 2, 5; Norwegian Consumer Council, *Deceived by Design* (June 2018) <https://www.forbrukerradet.no/undersokelse/no-under sokelsekategori/deceived-by-design/> last accessed 26 July 2018.

often these are also designed in a way that can cause addiction.[25] In light of these aspects of design, the idea of creating a privacy-friendly interface that also allows for stopping points is something that DTC companies should seriously consider. This is something that other companies engaging in consumer-focused health services, such as the wearable technology sector, should also think about. In the DTC context, when thinking about how to improve interface design in order to enhance protection of consumers' privacy, companies should consider turning family finder settings off by default and providing consumers with more information about the possible consequences of being connected with unknown relatives.[26]

6.3 Final Thoughts

This book has sought to provide an introduction to the world of DTC genetic tests and the regulation of the industry. It is hoped that it will stimulate further discussion of improved governance of the industry. In closing, I wish to remind all readers that in the context of new and emerging technologies and particularly new services that are offered via the Internet, the rules on how businesses do things are not set in stone. Much current business practice in the digital space has evolved with little direct oversight, but that does not mean this needs to remain the case. There are opportunities here for us to think about how things should be done and the type of world we want to live in. While genetic research holds great promise, such research does need to be conductly ethically and with respect to those involved. If genetic tests are to be offered as a consumer service, then everyone needs to be able to understand the nature of the thing being sold to them. People need to be able to make an informed choice whether to purchase DTC genetic tests and companies need to be obtaining informed consent from their customers. This informed consent cannot be achieved through deeming acceptance to contracts or privacy policies through simply visiting a website or using a service.

---

[25] Tristan Harris, 'How technology is hijacking your mind – from a magician and Google's design ethicist' *Thrive Global* (19 May 2016) <https://www.thriveglobal.com/stories/8466-how-technology-is-hijacking-your-mind-from-a-magician-and-google-design-ethicist> – also see Harris's website for other papers <http://www.tristanharris.com/essays/>; also see Center for Humane Technology <http://humanetech.com>

[26] Guido Pennings, 'Genetic databases and the future of donor anonymity' (2019) 34(5) *Human Reproduction* 786–90 doi:10.1093/humrep/dez029.

Addendum

Since submitting the manuscript for this book, there have been a number of developments, which I should like to mention in closing. I do hope to release a second edition of this volume in the future, which can provide further updates. My own thoughts on regulation of this industry have also progressed. I do strongly believe that together with drawing upon existing law, such as the GDPR and the Consumer Rights Directive, much more needs to be done in terms of specific oversight of the industry. Existing regulators should have a role to play in this, but we also need new legislation at the national level directed at regulating the industry and creating a new regulatory body to govern businesses dealing with genetic information is advisable. In some countries this may come under the supervision of existing privacy and data protection regulators or human tissue regulators, such as the UK's Human Tissue Authority. In thinking about improving regulation of DTC at the national level, the Canadian Genetic Non-Discrimination Act could provide a useful model for improving privacy protection in this context.

I wish to begin by noting developments in the Golden State Killer case with several prosecutors in the case seeking the death penalty.[1] In light of this, I should like to stress that regardless of whether or not James DeAngelo is convicted of the crimes with which he has been charged, the manner in which this investigation was conducted should cause concern. When we think about the use of genetic databases for the purposes of assisting with finding suspects, we should consider not only the rights of innocent relatives, but also the privacy rights of suspects, who may in fact also be innocent. These suspects

---

[1] Darrell Smith and Sam Stanton, 'Prosecutors to seek death penalty in Golden State Killer case' *The Mercury News* (10 April 2019) <https://www.mercurynews.com/2019/04/10/prosecutors-to-seek-death-penalty-in-golden-state-killer-case/> accessed 15 April 2019; Katie Dowd, 'Golden State Killer suspect appears in court nearly one year after arrest' *San Francisco Chronicle* (10 April 2019) <https://www.sfgate.com/bayarea/article/joseph-deangelo-hearing-sacramento-trial-13757418.php> accessed 15 April 2019.

are not notified by law enforcement when their genetic data is uploaded to a public genetic database, such as GEDmatch.[2] We also need to remember the presumption that you are innocent until proven guilty and the right to a fair trial. We should also recognise that if the popularity of DTC tests continues to rise more people could have their data used in criminal investigations without their knowledge. A recent *MIT Technology Review* article suggests that by early '2019, more than 26 million consumers had added their DNA to four leading commercial ancestry and health databases.'[3] According to Regalado's article, this estimate was made by relying on a combination of sources including the 'public statements of the four largest ancestry companies, our own reports, and data maintained by the International Society of Genetic Genealogy and tracked by genealogy blogger Leah Larkin.'[4] While this is an estimate, it is one that is likely to be fairly accurate and it should help us in understanding the number of people who could be impacted by secondary use of these databases.

Since DeAngelo's arrest, 'more than 20 people' have also been arrested using similar methods.[5] These arrests highlight that sharing with law enforcement and other entities has moved beyond being a hypothetical possibility, it has begun to happen, and there needs to be much more public debate and oversight of this type of sharing. Together with this, DNA transfer is an issue that is often overlooked when using DNA evidence in criminal investigations and legal proceedings. In the past year there has been renewed concern about DNA transfer and how this can implicate innocent people. DNA transfer, or 'touch-transfer' happens all the time – we shed our DNA constantly and can leave traces of our DNA everywhere we go whenever we touch a thing, another person or an animal.[6] This can take the form of skin particles, saliva

---

[2] Nila Bala, 'Criminal Suspects Deserve Genetic Privacy, Too' *Slate* (18 March 2019) <https://slate.com/technology/2019/03/genetic-genealogy-law-enforcement-suspects-dna-privacy-gedmatch.html> accessed 16 April 2019 – this cites.

[3] Antonio Regalado, 'More than 26 million people have taken an at-home ancestry test' MIT Technology Review (11 February 2019) <https://www.technologyreview.com/s/612880/more-than-26-million-people-have-taken-an-at-home-ancestry-test/> accessed 16 April 2019.

[4] Ibid.

[5] Bala (n 2), this cites Megan Molteni, 'The Future Of Crime-Fighting Is Family Tree Forensics' *Wired* (26 December 2018) <https://www.wired.com/story/the-future-of-crime-fighting-is-family-tree-forensics/> accessed 16 April 2019.

[6] Marina Medvin, 'Framed By Your Own Cells: How DNA Evidence Imprisons The Innocent' *Forbes* (20 September 2018) <https://www.forbes.com/sites/marinamedvin/2018/09/20/framed-by-your-own-cells-how-dna-evidence-imprisons-the-innocent/#6f6d24a44b86> accessed 16 April 2019 – this cites Leslie A Pray, 'Legislative Landmarks of Forensics: California v. Greenwood and Shed DNA' (2008) 1(1) Nature Education 75 <https://

or fingerprints. We can leave saliva traces on other people and on things such as walls when we talk. We can do this both unintentionally and without any knowledge that we have done it. The case of Lukis Anderson illustrates how severe the consequences can be for innocent people, when DNA evidence is given significant weight, without other supporting evidence.[7] In Anderson's case he was implicated in a murder and burglary and spent several months in prison[8] before it was proven that 'he was drunk and unconscious at a hospital when the victim was killed in his mansion miles away.'[9] The mere fact that a person's DNA is found at a crime scene cannot then be taken to mean conclusively that she was even present at that crime scene and this needs more attention. Investigators, juries, and courts need to make sure they look at the whole picture and are not overly reliant on DNA evidence where there is no other supporting evidence, as although DNA evidence is very useful, it could just mean that a suspect left traces of themselves that have no relation to a crime. Criminals who are aware of the possibility of leaving DNA traces will often take steps to avoid this, such as wearing gloves. As was noted in a recent *Wired* article 'Eleven leading DNA transfer scientists contacted for this story were in consensus that the criminal justice system must be willing to question DNA evidence.'[10] Forensic scientists have a role to play in this, but there needs to be more information provided to the public about this as well, as often people's perceptions of DNA evidence may be influenced by the way such evidence is presented in police television shows and films, and people need to understand that the mere presence of DNA does not equate with guilt in the absence of other facts connecting an individual to a crime.

In early 2019, it also emerged that FamilyTreeDNA has been collaborating with the American Federal Bureau of Investigation (FBI) to

---

www.nature.com/scitable/topicpage/legislative-landmarks-of-forensics-california-v-green wood-776> accessed 16 April 2019.

[7] Katie Worth, 'Framed For Murder By His Own DNA' *Wired* (19 April 2018) <https:// www.wired.com/story/dna-transfer-framed-murder/> accessed 12 April 2019; see also Roland AH Van Oorschot and Maxwell K Jones, 'DNA fingerprints from fingerprints' (1997) 387(6635) Nature 767 doi: 10.1038/42838; and Peter A Smith, 'When DNA Implicates the Innocent' (2016) 314(16) Scientific American 11-12 <https://www.scienti ficamerican.com/article/when-dna-implicates-the-innocent/> accessed 14 April 2019.

[8] Seth Augenstein, 'Secondary Transfer a New Phenomenon in Touch DNA' *Forensic Magazine* (9 November 2015) <https://www.forensicmag.com/article/2015/11/secondary-transfer-new-phenomenon-touch-dna> accessed 16 April 2019 – citing Henry K Lee, 'How innocent man's DNA was found at killing scene' (26 June 2013) <https://www.sfgate. com/crime/article/How-innocent-man-s-DNA-was-found-at-killing-scene-4624971.php> accessed 16 April 2019.

[9] Lee, 'How innocent man's DNA was found at killing scene' (n 8).

[10] Worth, 'Framed For Murder By His Own DNA' (n 7).

investigate violent crime.[11] After FamilyTreeDNA's agreement with the FBI was revealed, the company was removed from the supporters of the Future of Privacy Forum's Privacy Best Practices.[12] Initially, in order for a consumer to opt out of sharing with the FBI, they had to opt out of all DNA matching, but FamilyTreeDNA has since introduced the option of allowing consumers to opt out of DNA matching by law enforcement.[13]

Another point to note is that DTC services do vary significantly and less prominent companies offering dubious types of tests, particularly child talent and surreptitious testing need much more scrutiny. While there continues to be a lack of oversight for the industry as a whole, this also allows unscrupulous players to operate. For instance, residents in some of Louisville, Kentucky's most vulnerable communities have recently been targeted by unmarked vans and individuals were offered $20(USD) for mouth swabs and also asked for health insurance information.[14] Some of those requesting the mouth swabs claimed to be connected with 'Passport Health Plan, which manages Kentucky's Medicaid program, though Passport says they are not related.'[15] In response to this, together with another scam where people received 'calls offering medical devices through Medicare'[16] on the 9th of April 2019 Kentucky's Attorney General has issued a scam alert. According to the alert in both schemes 'scammers try to steal the victim's insurance and personal information in order to receive reimbursement for services or

[11] Matthew Haag, 'FamilyTreeDNA Admits to Sharing Genetic Data With F.B.I.' *The New York Times* (4 February 2019) <https://www.nytimes.com/2019/02/04/business/family-tree-dna-fbi.html> last accessed 6 April 2019.

[12] Carson Martinez, 'Privacy Best Practices for Consumer Genetic Testing Services' Future of Privacy Forum (31 July 2018, updated January 2019) <https://fpf.org/2018/07/31/privacy-best-practices-for-consumer-genetic-testing-services/> accessed 6 April 2019.

[13] Adam Vaughan, 'Home DNA-testing firm will let users block FBI access to their data' New Scientist (13 March 2019) <https://www.newscientist.com/article/2196433-home-dna-testing-firm-will-let-users-block-fbi-access-to-their-data/> accessed 6 April 2019.

[14] P Ashley, 'Residents concerned about DNA-for-cash transactions in Louisville' Wave 3 News (1 April 2019) <http://www.wave3.com/2019/04/01/residents-concerned-about-dna-for-cash-transactions-louisville/> accessed 3 April 2019.

[15] 'Kentucky AG on DNA-for-Cash Scheme' GenomeWeb (12 April 2019) <https://www.genomeweb.com/scan/kentucky-ag-dna-cash-scheme#.XLUk5i9L10s> accessed 16 April 2019; Matthew Glowicki, 'Beshear urges those who received money for DNA samples to call fraud hotline' Louiscille Courier Journal (8 April 2019, updated 8 April 2019) <https://www.courier-journal.com/story/news/crime/2019/04/08/kentucky-ag-asks-dna-cash-customers-call-fraud-hotline/3405027002/> accessed 16 April 2019.

[16] Office of the Attorney General of Kentucky, 'Beshear: Fraudulent Medical Billing Scams Targeting Kentuckians' (Scam Alert 9 April 2019) <https://ag.ky.gov/scams/Pages/Current-Scam-Alert.aspx> accessed 16 April 2019.

medical devices that were not provided or medically necessary.'[17] Anyone 'who may have provided their Medicaid information to a suspicious person or company are encouraged to call the Office of the Attorney General's Medicaid Fraud Hotline.'[18]

Another development worthy of note is that the Association of British Insurers (ABI) together with the UK Government has released its Code of Practice on Genetic Testing and Insurance.[19] This document unlike the previous versions of the Concordat and Moratorium is open ended and may, it is hoped, serve to improve protection for UK consumers in the long-term, although further reform is still needed, given that this is voluntary and does not apply to all insurers operating in the UK.

In March 2019, the UK House of Commons' Science and Technology Committee has launched an inquiry into personal genomics, which it refers to as commercial genomics.[20] It is seeking submissions and as this book is being finalised prior to the closing of this consultation, so it is not possible to comment on its conclusion, but it is hoped that this inquiry will lead to regulatory reform within the UK at least, and perhaps provide a model for other countries considering how to improve industry governance.

Another very recent development is the US Food and Drug Administration's (FDA) warning letter to Inova regarding the marketing of Inova's MediMap tests in the US.[21] Inova is not strictly a DTC company, as its services are only available for order by physicians, but it does provide test results

[17] Ibid.

[18] Ibid.

[19] ABI, 'ABI and Government publish updated Code on Genetic Testing & Insurance' (23 October 2018) <https://www.abi.org.uk/news/news-articles/2018/10/abi-and-government-publish-updated-code-on-genetic-testing--insurance/> accessed 5 April 2019.

[20] Science and Technology Committee (Commons), Commercial genomics inquiry – final deadline for submissions 26 April 2019 <https://www.parliament.uk/business/committees/committees-a-z/commons-select/science-and-technology-committee/inquiries/parliament-2017/commercial-genomics-17-19/> accessed 6 April 2019. I have made a written submission to the Inquiry and have also met with the Committee's chair, Rt Hon Norman Lamb MP in May 2019.

[21] GenomeWeb Staff Reporter, 'FDA Warns Inova to Stop Performing MediMap Tests Without Proper Regulatory Approvals' GenomeWeb (4 April 2019) <https://www.genomeweb.com/business-news/fda-warns-inova-stop-performing-medimap-tests-without-proper-regulatory-approvals#.XKfaTy1L0_U> accessed 5 April 2019; Warning Letter from US Food and Drug Administration to Inova Genomics Laboratory (4 April 2019) <https://www.fda.gov/ICECI/EnforcementActions/WarningLetters/ucm634988.htm?utm_campaign=040419_PR_FDA%20issues%20warning%20letter%20to%20Inova%20Genomics%20Laboratory&utm_medium=email&utm_source=Eloqua> accessed 6 April 2019.

directly to patients. In its letter the FDA expressed concern regarding the clinical utility of the MediMap tests. It also expressed concern regarding the direct return of results to patients, stating that: 'This could lead to patients inappropriately increasing, decreasing, or stopping their medication without their physician's involvement, which poses significant risks to patient safety'.[22] This recent action may signal that the FDA will be taking a more active stance in regulating genetic testing services in the future. Since receiving the FDA's warning letter Inova has announced that it will be ceasing to offer its pharmacogenetic tests.[23]

A further recent development is the release of a study, which found that 23andMe's BRCA test 'misses almost 90 percent of BRCA mutation carriers, both in those with and those without a personal or family history of cancer.'[24] This study focussed on clinical utility of BRCA testing provided by 23andMe, and according to Edward Esplin, (one of the study's authors):

> the data confirms the caveats contained in the FDA's authorization of 23andMe's BRCA test and suggests that confirmatory testing is needed for those with a positive result as well as those with a negative result from limited DTC testing. 'Both of these types of individuals should receive clinical genetic testing,' he said. This, Esplin and his colleagues wrote in their conference abstract, 'begs the question of what role, if any, does DTC testing for these three mutations really play in the healthcare of individuals who either have an indication for testing or are seeking to know their risks.'[25]

This recent work highlights the current limitations for individuals of these types of tests and as previously mentioned those with an interest in taking health tests through DTC companies should think carefully about whether this is the best place to get the information they want. If you have a serious

[22] Ibid Warning Letter from US Food and Drug Administration to Inova Genomics Laboratory (4 April 2019)

[23] Staff Reporter, 'Inova Decides to End PGx Test Offerings in Response to FDA Warning Letter' GenomeWeb (15 April 2019) <https://www.genomeweb.com/regulatory-news/inova-decides-end-pgx-test-offerings-response-fda-warning-letter#.XLZMmS9L1PU> accessed 17 April 2019.

[24] Julie Karow, '23andMe DTC Breast and Ovarian Cancer Risk Test Misses Almost 90 Percent of BRCA Mutation Carriers' GenomeWeb (5 April 2019) < https://www.genomeweb.com/molecular-diagnostics/23andme-dtc-breast-and-ovarian-cancer-risk-test-misses-almost-90-percent-brca#.XKfbrS1L1PU>.

[25] Ibid. See also Marco Leung, 'Be wary of direct-to-consumer genetic testing' Medium (25 April 2019) <https://medium.com/@marcoleung/be-wary-of-direct-to-consumer-genetic-testing-d21a039b617a> accessed 27 June 2019.

medical concern, it is recommended that you discuss this with a physician and if you do need genetic testing, this should be done in a medical clinic.

In closing, the GDPR affords people certain rights in their personal data and as well as the requirement for explicit consent to undergo genetic testing, businesses should be adhering to the principles set out in relation to their processing. They should also make provision for consumers to withdraw their consent in accordance with the right to erasure, even though this may be technically difficult. Given the variety of uses to which our genetic data can be put, protecting people's privacy in this context is of vital importance and the industry needs much more specific regulatory oversight in order to both improve standards and protect people's rights.

Finally, while reviewing final proofs for this book there have been three developments I also wish to mention. Firstly, in considering how to improve interfaces, so that consumers can make more informed choices online, there is a Bill being considered in the USA called the Deceptive Experiences to Online Users Reduction (DETOUR) Act.[26] This legislation if passed would ban a number of practices that have 'the purpose or substantial effect of obscuring, subverting, or impairing user autonomy, decision-making, or choice to obtain consent or user data'.[27] The Bill in its current framing only applies to entities that have more than 100,000,000 users, which is quite a substantial figure and it is desirable that this figure is reduced, so that other operators with significant numbers of users would come within its remit. If this legislation is enacted it may lead to improvements in the way a number of industries operate. Secondly, in May 2019, GEDmatch changed its site policy, which means that its users are now opted out of law enforcement matching by default and must specifically opt in if they wish to participate in this. At the time of writing, only around 50,000 out of over 1 million users have specifically opted into law enforcement matching.[28] This is a positive change and does demonstrate that people may not be comfortable with this type of secondary use and the issue of such secondary use by law enforcement and other entities requires much more public debate. Lastly, in June 2019 three companies, Helix, 23andMe, and Ancestry have 'formed the Coalition

[26] S. 1084: Deceptive Experiences to Online Users Reduction Act <https://www.govtrack.us/congress/bills/116/s1084/text> accessed 21 June 2019.

[27] Ibid section 3(a)(1)(A).

[28] Adam Vaughan, 'DNA database opts a million people out from police searches' *New Scientist* (20 May 2019) <https://www.newscientist.com/article/2203857-dna-database-opts-a-million-people-out-from-police-searches/> accessed 21 June 2019

for Genetic Data Protection'[29] and this group is going to lobby the American Congress in relation to the issue of genetic privacy.[30] What impact this group will have on improving regulation of the industry in the US remains to be seen, but it is vital that all stakeholders including the public have a say in improving regulation internationally as well, given the nature of DTC services, which are sold internationally. Other countries will need to consider how to improve governance of DTC at the national level. Given the issues at stake, voluntary self-regulation is not the optimal strategy for improving standards and affording better protection to consumers' rights. A wider public debate is needed, together with new tailored legislation that can be actively enforced. In the long term it is desirable that new regulatory bodies are created that oversee not just DTC, but other consumer facing services that handle sensitive data.

[29] 'New Privacy Coalition' *GenomeWeb* (25 June 2019) <https://www.genomeweb.com/scan/new-privacy-coalition#.XRRRky1L10s> accessed 27 June 2019.

[30] Ibid citing Alex Gangitano, 'DNA testing companies launch new privacy coalition' *The Hill* (25 June 2019) <https://thehill.com/regulation/lobbying/450124-dna-testing-companies-launch-new-privacy-coalition> accessed 27 June 2019.

The Commitments

Made by the Association of British Insurers on behalf of its members

1. Insurers will always treat applicants fairly. They will not require or pressure any applicant to undertake a predictive or diagnostic genetic test in order to obtain insurance. Insurers will not treat any applicant differently if they have had a predictive genetic test, except as detailed below.

2. Insurers will only ask applicants to disclose the result of a predictive genetic test and take the result of this test into account, for conditions that have been approved as being relevant under this Code, and for policies above the following financial limits:

   a. Life insurance – £500,000 (per person)

   b. Critical illness insurance - £300,000 (per person)

   c. Income protection - £30,000 (per annum)

   The list of approved relevant predictive genetic tests is given in Appendix I. The current list only includes a predictive genetic test for Huntington's disease, in applications for life insurance cover which totals over the financial limit of £500,000.

3. Insurers will <u>not</u> ask an applicant to disclose the results of a predictive genetic test:

   a. taken after insurance cover has started, for the duration of that cover;

   b. of another person, such as a blood relative; or

   c. obtained exclusively in the context of scientific research

4. Where insurers ask an applicant to disclose the result of a predictive genetic test in the limited circumstances described in Commitment 2, they will not impose disproportionate terms, conditions or exclusions related to that result.

5. Insurers will provide all applicants with clear information before an application for insurance cover is completed explaining:

   a. What they will and will not have to disclose regarding genetic test results, in accordance with this Code.

   b. How their insurance decision may be affected if an applicant decides voluntarily to disclose any favourable predictive genetic test result.

6. If a predictive genetic test result is given to an insurer by the applicant, either accidentally or voluntarily, an insurer may take it into account if it is to the applicant's benefit. For instance, if a predictive genetic test result was disclosed which ruled out a risk which was otherwise suggested by family history, the insurer may take this into account to offer more favourable terms. If the result is unfavourable to the applicant, the insurer will ignore the result unless Commitment 2 applies.

7. Insurers who transact life, critical illness or income protection insurance will:

   a. Report annually to the ABI their continued compliance with the Code

   b. Maintain a complaints procedure relating to their compliance with this Code according to the detail set out in the following Q&A's

   c. Report annually to the ABI all complaints received relating to the operation of the Code

8. Insurers who transact life, critical illness or income protection insurance will nominate at least one appropriately trained genetics underwriter (NGU), who is responsible for all matters relating to genetic information and the operation of this Code. The full duties and responsibilities of the NGU are given in Appendix II. The number of NGUs should be proportionate to the scale of the business.

Privacy Best Practices for
Consumer Genetic Testing Services

I. TRANSPARENCY: *Provide clear and complete information regarding the Company's policies and procedures for the management of personal data (personally identifiable information, Genetic Data, and protected health information) and de-identified information.*[4]

   a. **Privacy Notices:** Privacy policies should be prominent, publicly accessible, and easy to read. They should specify the Company's data collection, consent, use, onward transfer, access, security, and retention/deletion practices.
      i. A high-level overview of the key principles should be provided preceding the full privacy policy. This overview should be a short document or statement that provides basic, essential information about the Company's collection, use, and sharing of Genetic Data.
      ii. Policies that vary for different categories of data should clearly spell out when each applies. For example, if the policy for Genetic Data is different than that of other data (e.g. registration data, browsing (cookies or website) tracking, and/or personal information), these policies should be described clearly and separately.

   b. **Deidentification and Genetic Data**: Deidentified information is not subject to the restrictions in this policy, provided that the deidentification measures taken establish strong assurance that the data is not identifiable.
      i. We note that currently, Genetic Data held *at the individual-level* that has been de-identified[5] cannot be represented as strongly protecting individuals from re-identification, based upon existing deidentification tools and standards.[6] Such data may be protected in other ways and used for research with appropriate consent and security controls (See Principle VI: Security, below).
      ii. Aggregation of individual reports may provide strong assurance that personal data is not identifiable, if appropriate safeguards are in place.[7]

---

[4] *See infra* Annex A (defining "deidentified information").

[5]*See, e.g.,* U.S. Dep't Health & Hum. Services, Office for Civil Rights, *Guidance Regarding Methods for De-identification of Protected Health Information in Accordance with the Health Insurance Portability and Accountability Act (HIPAA) Privacy Rule* (Nov. 26, 2012), https://www.hhs.gov/hipaa/for-professionals/privacy/special-topics/de-identification/index.html (presenting guidance for the HIPAA Safe Harbor Method).

[6] Commercial, technical protections and capabilities are currently being developed, but to date, protections for genetic data include strong security protocols, including removal of quasi-identifiers (demographic and other personal health information); retention separate from or without matching datasets; encryption; access controls; and contractual restrictions on sharing and use. Without a corollary dataset for matching, the risks remain minimal.

[7] The Federal Trade Commission (FTC) has identified its standards for reasonable de-identification for the protection of Consumer data, encompassing three steps: 1) reasonably deidentify the data using available practices to an extent appropriate to the sensitivity of the data, 2) commit to not attempting to re-identifying data, 3) when sharing deidentified data, contractually prohibit additional parties from attempting to reidentify (and monitor compliance). *See* Fed. Trade Comm'n, *Protecting Consumer Privacy in an Era of*

c. **Policy Change**: Policies should indicate that material changes will not be made without first providing prominent notice and obtaining Consumer consent before data is used in any manner inconsistent with terms initially provided.

d. **Transfer of Ownership**: Policies should indicate that in the case of merger or acquisition by another entity, the successor entity is subject to these same commitments for the Genetic Data and biological sample already collected.[8]

e. **Transparency Reporting:** Companies should provide a public report describing requests from law enforcement for Genetic Data. Such reports should be made on at least an annual basis.[9]

II. CONSENT: *Obtain express consent for collection, analysis, sharing, or reporting of Genetic Data.*

a. *Initial Express Consent*: Initial express consent must describe data collection and uses of the commercial genetic product or services purchased by the Consumer, including the inherent contextual uses. Inherent contextual uses—such as providing the specific genetic analysis product or service, data use for product and service review and improvement, or new product development—should be clearly defined. Companies should clearly specify the uses of the Genetic Data, who will have access to test results, and how that data will be shared.

b. **Separate Express Consent:**[10] Separate express consent will be required for:
   i. Onward transfer of individual-level information (i.e., Genetic Data and/or personal information about a single individual) to third-parties for any reason, excluding vendors and service providers;[11]

Rapid Change (Mar. 2012), https://www.ftc.gov/sites/default/files/documents/reports/federal-trade-commission-report-protecting-consumer-privacy-era-rapid-change-recommendations/120326privacyreport.pdf.
Under the HIPAA Privacy Rule, there are no restrictions on the use or release of deidentified data. Data is deidentified if it neither identifies nor provides a reasonable basis to identify an individual. This can be accomplished either by an expert determination using generally accepted statistical and scientific principles and methods for rendering information not individually identifiable (or a HIPAA-specific Safe Harbor option based on removing enumerated fields). *See* U.S. Dep't Health & Hum. Services (HHS), *Summary of the HIPAA Privacy Rule* (2003), https://www.hhs.gov/sites/default/files/privacysummary.pdf.

[8] The FTC has addressed both "material change" and "merger or acquisition" data use issues in its enforcement actions, and has made clear that it could be an unfair practice under Section 5 for a company to alter its privacy policies in a way that's inconsistent with the promises made when the information was collected, without notice and new consent. *See* Jamie Hine, Fed. Trade Comm'n, *Mergers and Privacy Promises* (Mar. 25, 2015), https://www.ftc.gov/news-events/blogs/business-blog/2015/03/mergers-privacy-promises.

[9] Peter Micek, *Transparency Reporting Index*, Access Now (2016), https://www.accessnow.org/transparency-reporting-index/.

[10] Express consent means a Consumer's statement or clear affirmative action in response to a clear, meaningful, and prominent notice regarding the collection, use, and sharing of data for a specific purpose.

[11] Vendors and service providers are companies that act under the direct authority of the data controller or processor and are authorized to process personal data in support of providing the data controller's commercial product or service. For the purposes of this document, a company's vendors and service providers are not third parties, provided that appropriate contractual controls bind such vendors and service providers.

      ii. Incompatible secondary uses[12] of Genetic Data; and

      iii. Consumers or organizations that submit biological samples or Genetic Data on behalf of other individuals (others, elderly relatives, etc.).

          a) Policies should require that the individual submitting the Biological Sample or the Genetic Data is the owner or include reasonable steps to ensure that consent has been obtained from the owner of the Biological Sample or Genetic Data.[13]

c. **Informed Consent for Research:**[14] Informed consents should include basic elements,[15] such as an acknowledgment of the voluntary nature of the research, a statement concerning the confidentiality of data, and a description of risks, benefits, and purpose of the research. Informed consent will be required when:

      i. Genetic Data is transferred to third parties for research purposes; and

      ii. Research is done under the control of the Company (i.e. internal research) for the purpose of publication or generalizable knowledge (this excludes product development, quality control, or data processing to support inherent contextual uses), unless otherwise approved by an institutional review board (IRB)[16] or internal ethical

---

[12] Incompatible secondary uses include those uses outside of the primary purpose of the purchased service and the inherent contextual uses. Incompatible secondary uses do not include activities intended to develop or improve new or current products.

[13] With regard to minors or those incapacitated, appropriate permissions to submit a Biological Sample or Genetic Data on behalf of another may vary from consent, power of attorney, guardianship, etc., depending on the nature of the relationship between the Data/Sample owner and the Data/Sample submitter.

[14] Informed consent is the process of providing an individual with adequate information about the research to allow for an informed decision about the individual's voluntary participation in a research study.

[15] According to the HHS Office of Research Protections, the 8 basic elements of an informed consent include:

A. "a statement that the study involves research, an explanation of the purposes of the research and the expected duration of the subject's participation, a description of the procedures to be followed, and identification of any procedures which are experimental;

B. a description of any reasonably foreseeable risks or discomforts to the subject;

C. a description of any benefits to the subject or to others which may reasonably be expected from the research;

D. a disclosure of appropriate alternative procedures or courses of treatment, if any, that might be advantageous to the subject;

E. a statement describing the extent, if any, to which confidentiality of records identifying the subject will be maintained;

F. for research involving more than minimal risk, an explanation as to whether any compensation and an explanation as to whether any medical treatments are available if injury occurs and, if so, what they consist of, or where further information may be obtained;

G. an explanation of whom to contact for answers to pertinent questions about the research and research subjects' rights, and whom to contact in the event of a research-related injury to the subject; and

H. a statement that participation is voluntary, refusal to participate will involve no penalty or loss of benefits to which the subject is otherwise entitled, and the subject may discontinue participation at any time without penalty or loss of benefits to which the subject is otherwise entitled."

Additional elements of informed consent may apply. Additional elements of informed consent may apply. See 45 C.F.R. § 46.116 (2009), https://www.hhs.gov/ohrp/regulations-and-policy/regulations/45-cfr-46/index.html#46.116.

[16] An IRB is a group designated to review research protocols and related materials (including informed consents) and assure that appropriate steps have been taken to protect the rights and welfare of human research subjects. IRBs have the authority to approve, modify, or disapprove research. See 45 C.F.R. § 46.107–115 (2009), https://www.hhs.gov/ohrp/regulations-and-policy/regulations/45-cfr-46/index.html.

review process.[17]

d. **Marketing:**[18] Companies should provide Consumers with the ability to opt-out of communications from the Company, excluding communications that provide information about the maintenance of accounts or related to an ongoing product or service provided

    i. Marketing to a Consumer based on Genetic Data is not permitted, unless the Consumer has provided separate express consent for such marketing or otherwise is clearly described in the initial express consent as a primary function of the product or service.

    ii. Marketing to a Consumer because they have ordered or purchased a genetic product or service is not permitted, unless the Consumer has been provided the ability to opt-out of such marketing.

    iii. Marketing to any individual is not permitted when based on (a) the Genetic Data of a Consumer who is a relative or (b) the order or purchase of a genetic product or service by a Consumer who is a relative.[19]

    iv. Marketing does not include the provision of customized content or offers by the Company on its own websites and services.

e. **Minors' (Under 18) Genetic Data:** Consumer-facing services should not be marketed to, or offered directly to anyone under the age of 18.

    i. Processing and analysis of samples and account activation for those under 18 may be provided with the consent of a parent or guardian.

    ii. Companies should provide a method for minors to be provided access to their Genetic Data and to become the primary holder of their account after they reach the age of 18.

---

[17] An ethical review process (also referred to as a corporate IRB, Consumer subject review board, or corporate ethics boards) has been proposed for the ethical review for data that is not typically covered by the Common Rule. The purpose of these reviews is to identify both the risks and the benefits of the research and to balance the prospective risks to the Consumer, prospective benefits to Consumers or to the public, the rights and interests of the Consumer, and the legitimate interests of the company. See Dennis D. Hirsch, et al., *Roundtable: Beyond IRBs: Designing Ethical Review Processes for Big Data*, 72 Wash. & Lee L. Rev. Online 406–498 (2016), https://scholarlycommons.law.wlu.edu/wlulr-online/vol72/iss3/; Ryan Calo, *Consumer Subject Review Boards: A Thought Experiment*, 66 Stan. L. Rev. Online 97 (Sept. 2013), http://www.stanfordlawreview.org/online/privacy-and-big-data/consumer-subject-review-boards.

[18] Under the HIPAA Privacy Rule, marketing is defined as "a communication about a product or service that encourages recipients of the communication to purchase or use the product or service." Covered entities must obtain written authorization for any use or disclosure of PHI for marketing communications, except those in-person or which involve a promotional gift of nominal value. HIPAA exempts certain types of communications from the definition of marketing, such as communications made (1) for treatment of the individual; (2) for case management or care coordination, or to direct or recommend alternative treatments, therapies, providers, or settings; and (3) to describe health-related products or services provided by the covered entity or included in a plan of benefits. For example, "a hospital's Wellness Department could start a weight-loss program and send a flyer to all patients seen in the hospital over the past year who meet the definition of obese, even if those individuals were not specifically seen for obesity when they were in the hospital," because the wellness program is about the covered entity's own health-related service. *See* U.S. Dep't Health & Hum. Services, Office for Civil Rights, *Marketing [45 CFR 164.501, 164.508(a)(3)]* (Apr. 3, 2003), https://www.hhs.gov/sites/default/files/ocr/privacy/hipaa/understanding/coveredentities/marketing.pdf.

[19] "Refer a friend" communications or communications that facilitate a Consumer's sharing of results and recommending the purchase of products or services to others are not covered by this section.

III. USE AND ONWARD TRANSFER: *Commit to collecting, using, and sharing Genetic Data in ways that are compatible with reasonable Consumer expectations for the context in which the data was collected.*

a. **Prohibited Sharing:** Genetic Data, by definition linked to an identifiable person, should not be disclosed or made accessible to third parties, in particular, employers, insurance companies, educational institutions, or government agencies, except as required by law or with the separate express consent of the person concerned. (See Principle IV(d): Law Enforcement Access, below)

b. **Vendors/Service Providers:** Companies are responsible to ensure that any vendors and service providers are bound to the same level as the Company's privacy commitments under these Principles, and the associated policies, and such partners have no independent rights to use Genetic Data or other personal information outside the scope of their role in providing the primary product or service. In the case of a Company ending or selling its business, it should either dispose of Consumers' Genetic Data and Biological Samples securely, or ensure recipient third party commitments consistent with the original notices provided to the Consumer.[20]

c. **Research:** As discussed under "Principle II: Consent," sharing of individual-level Genetic Data with third parties for additional research should only be allowed with specific separate express consent or informed consent from the Consumer.[21]

IV. ACCESS, INTEGRITY, RETENTION, AND DELETION: *Provide the Consumer with access to their Genetic Data and inform the Consumer of what rights they have to correct or amend the record, how to report security concerns, and how long their Genetic Data and the original Biological Sample will be maintained.[22]*

a. **Access:** Companies should provide a method for Consumers to access their Genetic Data through the services, as well as:
    i. Provide a process for Consumers to indicate the handling of their account, such as granting access, deletion, and/or transferring account control, in case of death or if a Consumer becomes incapacitated; and/or

---

[20] Per FTC guidance, effective vendor oversight includes: reasonable due diligence in selecting vendors; limiting shared data to those required by business needs; contractual requirement for vendors to ensure collection, use, and retention policies to protect PII; and most significantly, adequate monitoring of vendor privacy and security practices. The GDPR likewise clearly delineates responsibilities between "controllers" and "processors" for handling personal information, with responsibility and liability for Controllers as ultimate owners of the data. Controllers should: Only use processors that provide sufficient guarantees of their abilities to implement the technical and organizational measures necessary; Carry out data protection impact assessment prior to contract; Contractually ensure vendor compliance responsibilities and practices.

[21] Companies should take note of the range of guidance provided by organizations on data sharing practices (See Annex C: Genetic Data Sharing Policies, below).

[22] Retention and deletion/destruction policies should clearly identify practices regarding both the physical sample(s) provided, and the data derived or obtained from analysis of those samples.

       ii. Implement a process for a successor to request the transfer of an account after the death or if a Consumer becomes incapacitated.

b. **Integrity:** Genetic Data should be maintained at an industry standard of accuracy.[23]

c. **Retention:** Companies should set reasonable practices for Genetic Data retention and data minimization, taking into account the existence of active Consumer accounts, inherent contextual uses, and regulatory retention requirements.[24]

       i. Retention practices should address both the Biological Sample provided and Genetic Data.

d. **Deletion:** Unless otherwise required by law,[25] Companies should provide Consumers clear and prominent methods to delete their account and Genetic Data and destroy their Biological Sample, and describe any relevant limitations.

       i. For Consumers who have agreed to an informed consent for research, companies may not be able to delete or remove their Genetic Data from active or completed research, or from published results and findings. If deletion is requested, Genetic Data should not be used for any future or new research.

       ii. Companies should remove or restrict access to Genetic Data when deletion is not possible due to legal or technological requirements or other limitations.

e. **Law Enforcement Access:** Genetic Data may be disclosed to law enforcement entities without Consumer consent when required by valid legal process.[26] When possible, companies will attempt to notify Consumers on the occurrence of personal information releases to law enforcement requests.[27] Companies

---

[23] Nat'l Human Genome Research Inst., *Regulation of Genetic Tests* (Jan. 17, 2018), https://www.genome.gov/10002335/regulation-of-genetic-tests

[24] For example, retention may be limited due to regulatory or accreditation requirements. The Clinical Laboratory Improvement Amendments (CLIA) require that a data be stored according to retention requirements for CLIA certified laboratories. *See infra* Appendix B, Section IV for more information about CLIA. The College of American Pathologists (CAP) Laboratory Accreditation Program was granted authority by the Centers for Medicare and Medicaid Services (CMS) to inspect laboratories performing testing on human or animal specimens in lieu of a CMS inspection. CAP accredited laboratories are required to retain certain documents and specimens for quality testing and assurance. Coll. of Am. Pathologists, *Laboratory General Checklist: CAP Accreditation Program* 19 (July 28, 2015), http://www.cap.org/ShowProperty?nodePath=/UCMCon/Contribution%20Folders/DctmContent/education/OnlineCourseContent/2016/LAP-TLTM/resources/AC-laboratory-general.pdf#page=19.

[25] *See infra* Appendix B, Section IV for more information about CLIA.

[26] If a Consumer has agreed to provide their data for research, Genetic Data may be subject to confidentiality protections. For federally funded research, the 21st Century Cures Act guards against inappropriate use of the Freedom of Information Act (FOIA) to gain access to participants' genetic information by allowing the Secretary of the Department of Health and Human Services (HHS) to disqualify such research data from FOIA requests if: "(A) an individual is identified; or "(B) there is at least a very small risk, as determined by current scientific practices or statistical methods, that some combination of the information, the request, and other available data sources could be used to deduce the identity of an individual." *See* 21st Century Cures Act, Pub. L. No. 114-255, § 2013, 130 Stat. 1033 (2016), https://www.congress.gov/114/plaws/publ255/PLAW-114publ255.pdf.

[27] HIPAA limits the type of information that covered entities may disclose to law enforcement, absent a warrant or other prior process, when law enforcement is seeking to identify or locate a suspect. It

should consider the feasibility of applying for certificates of confidentiality for relevant research.[28]

V. ACCOUNTABILITY: *Designate a responsible office or official who is accountable for the organization's compliance with the Privacy Principles.*

    a. **Enforcement:** Implement reasonable policies, procedures, and practices to ensure that these Principles guide the collection, use, sharing, and storage of Genetic Data by the Company. Provide public/consumer facing commitments that are enforceable by the FTC, State Attorneys General, or other authorities.

    b. **Training:** Implement training programs for personnel who handle Genetic Data. Consider creating internal privacy review boards to evaluate and approve new technologies and services involving Genetic Data.

VI. SECURITY: *Maintain a comprehensive security program that is reasonably designed to protect the security, privacy, confidentiality, and integrity of Genetic Data against risks – such as unauthorized access or use, or unintended or inappropriate disclosure or breach – through the use of administrative, technological, and physical safeguards appropriate to the sensitivity of the information.*

    a. **Protection:** Genetic Data requires high levels of security and confidentiality. Genetic Data should be protected through a combination of mechanisms including, at a minimum: secure storage of human biological materials and data, encryption of digital records, data-use agreements, and contractual obligations, and accountability measures (e.g. training, access controls and logs, and independent audits).

VII. PRIVACY BY DESIGN: *Implement technological controls that support or enforce compliance with these Principles in addition to policy, legal, and administrative measures.*

    a. **Assessment:** Companies should undertake a comprehensive evaluation of the Genetic Data required at each step to ensure only appropriate data is collected and that reasonable Genetic Data retention practices are in place

---

specifically prohibits disclosure of DNA information for this purpose, absent some other legal requirements such as a warrant. *See* U.S. Dep't Health & Hum. Services, Office for Civil Rights, *Will this HIPAA Privacy Rule Make It Easier for Police and Law Enforcement Agencies to Get My Medical Information?* (Dec. 20, 2002), https://www.hhs.gov/hipaa/for-individuals/faq/349/will-hipaa-make-it-easier-for-law-enforcement-to-get-my-medical-information/index.html.

[28] For non-federally funded research, investigators may apply for a certificate of confidentiality (CoC) through the NIH, as laid out in Section 2012 of the 21st Century Cures Act. CoCs protect the privacy of research participants by protecting identifiable health information from compelled disclosure. While CoCs are typically reserved for federally funded research, the NIH also considers requests for COCs for non-federally funded research in which identifiable, sensitive information is collected or used, including individual level human genomic data. *See* Nat'l Inst. of Health, Certificates of Confidentiality Kiosk, *Certificates of Confidentiality: Background Information* (2017), https://humansubjects.nih.gov/coc/background.

(see Principle IV(c): Retention, above).[29]

VIII. CONSUMER EDUCATION: *Make available to Consumers resources that advise about the implications and consequences of genetic testing, research, and data sharing.*

    a. **Education:** Companies should inform Consumers about the basics of genetics and genetic testing; the risks, benefits, and limitations of genetic testing; and the appropriate interpretation and use of results.[30] Companies should do so by providing such materials themselves or pointing to appropriate third-party resources.

---

[29] *See, e.g.*, Fed. Trade Comm'n, *Internet of Things: Privacy and Security in a Connected World* (Jan. 2015), https://www.ftc.gov/system/files/documents/reports/federal-trade-commission-staff-report-november-2013-workshop-entitled-internet-things-privacy/150127iotrpt.pdf; Commision Regulation (EU) 2016/679, of the European Parliament and of the Council of 27 April 2016 on the Protection of Natural Persons with regard to the Processing of Personal Data and on the Free Movement of such Data, and Repealing Directive 95/46/EC (General Data Protection Regulation), 2016 O.J. (L 119) 1, https://eur-lex.europa.eu/legal-content/EN/TXT/?uri=uriserv:OJ.L_.2016.119.01.0001.01.ENG; Hugo Teufel III, U.S. Dept. of Homeland Security, Privacy Policy Guidance Memorandum (Memorandum No. 2008-01, Dec. 29, 2008), https://www.dhs.gov/xlibrary/assets/privacy/privacy_policyguide_2008-01.pdf.

[30] For FDA approved devices, other special controls may apply, such as requirements to include limiting statements about what genetic risk information the test does and does not provide and how other factors such as environmental and lifestyle risk factors may affect the risk of developing disease, among others. *See* 21 C.F.R. § 866.5950 (2018), https://www.ecfr.gov/cgi-bin/text-idx?SID=26b6a62c2603684a93b9bffa0095289a&mc=true&node=pt21.8.866&rgn=div5#se21.8.866_1595 0.

Bibliography

Adams SD, Evans JP and Aylsworth AS, 'Direct-to-consumer genomic testing offers little clinical utility but appears to cause minimal harm' (2013) 74 *North Carolina Medical Journal* 494–9.

Adeoye S and Bozic KJ, Direct to consumer advertising in healthcare: History, benefits, and concerns' (2007) 457 *Clinical Orthopaedics and Related Research* 96–104 doi: 10.1097/BLO.0b013e31803427e6.

Adeyemo A and Rotimi C, 'Genetic variants associated with complex human diseases show wide variation across multiple populations' (2010) 13 *Public Health Genomics* 72–9 <https://doi.org/10.1159/000218711> last accessed 25 October 2018.

Adjin-Tettey E, 'Potential for genetic discrimination in access to insurance: Is there a dark side to increased availability of genetic information?' (2013) 50 *Alberta Law Review* 577–614.

Allyse M, '23 and Me, We, and You: Direct-to-consumer genetics, intellectual property, and informed consent' (2013) 31(2) *Trends in Biotechnology* 68–9.

AMP, *Association for Molecular Pathology Position Statement: Direct Access Genetic Testing (Direct to Consumer Genetic Testing)* (Association for Molecular Pathology, 2015).

Ancker JS et al., 'Consumer experience with and attitudes toward health information technology: A nationwide survey' (2013) 20(1) *Journal of the American Medical Informatics Association* 152–6 <https://doi.org/10.1136/amiajnl-2012-001062> last accessed 23 October 2018.

Angrist M, *Here Is a Human Being* (Harper Perennial 2011).

Annes JP, Giovanni MA and Murray MF, 'Risks of presymptomatic direct-to-consumer genetic testing' (2010) 363 *New England Journal of Medicine* 1100–1 doi: 10.1056/NEJMp1006029.

Article 29 Data Protection Working Party, Opinion 02/2015 on C-SIG Code of Conduct on Cloud Computing (22 September 2015) <http://ec.euro pa.eu/justice/data-protection/article-29/documentation/opinion-recommenda tion/files/2015/wp232_en.pdf> last accessed 29 May 2016 – archived content now available at <https://ec.europa.eu/justice/article-29/documentation/ opinion-recommendation/files/2015/wp232_en.pdf> last accessed 24 October 2018.

Article 29 Data Protection Working Party, Opinion 03/2012 on developments in biometric technologies (27 April 2012) 4.4.5, 26, <https://ec.europa. eu/justice/article-29/documentation/opinion-recommendation/files/2012/

wp193_en.pdf> last accessed 18 October 2018.<recommendation/files/2012/
wp193_en.pdf> last accessed 29 May 2016.

Asper Biotech, 'Athletic gene test' <http://www.asperbio.com/asper-biotech-varia/
athletic-gene-test> last accessed 9 April 2014.

Association for Molecular Pathology, *Association for Molecular Pathology Position
Statement:On Direct Access Genetic Testing (Direct to Consumer Genetic Testing)*
(Association for Molecular Pathology, 2007) <https://www.amp.org/AMP/
assets/File/position-statements/2007/AMPDTCPositionStatement_Final.pdf>
last accessed 22 October 2018.

Association for Molecular Pathology, *Position Statement: Direct Access Genetic Testing
(Direct to Consumer Genetic Testing)* (Association for Molecular Pathology,
2015) <https://www.amp.org/AMP/assets/File/position-statements/2015/AMP
positionstatementDTCtesting-FINAL_002.pdf> last accessed 22 October 2018.

Association of British Insurers, Concordat and Moratorium on Genetics and
Insurance (Department of Health, 2011) <https://assets.publishing.service.
gov.uk/government/uploads/system/uploads/attachment_data/file/2168
21/Concordat-and-Moratorium-on-Genetics-and-Insurance-20111.pdf> last
accessed 24 October 2018 – note that archived content is also available at <http://
webarchive.nationalarchives.gov.uk/20130123204306tf_/http://www.dh.gov.
uk/en/Publicationsandstatistics/Publications/PublicationsPolicyAndGuidance/
DH_4105905> last accessed 24 October 2018.

Ayday E et al., 'Whole genome sequencing: Revolutionary medicine or privacy
nightmare?' (2015) 48(2) *Computer* 58–66, 62 doi: 10.1109/MC.2015.59.

Ayres I and Schwartz A, 'The no-reading problem in consumer contract law' (2014)
66 *Stanford Law Review* 545.

Bamshad MJ et al., 'Exome sequencing as a tool for Mendelian disease gene discovery' (2011) 12 *Nature Reviews Genetics* 745–55.

Barnhizer DD, 'Escaping toxic contracts: How we have lost the war on assent in wrap
contracts' (2014) 44 *Southwestern Law Review* 215–29.

Barry P, 'Seeking genetic fate: Personal genomics companies offer forecasts of disease
risk, but the science behind the packaging is still evolving' (2009) 176(1) *Science
News* 16 <https://onlinelibrary.wiley.com/doi/abs/10.1002/scin.5591760123>

Behesti B, 'Cross-jurisdictional variation in Internet contract regulation' (2013) 8(1)
Journal of International Commercial Law and Technology.

Benöhr I, *EU Consumer Law and Human Rights* (Oxford University Press 2013).

Bieber FR, Brenner CH and Lazer D, 'Finding criminals through DNA of their relatives' (2006) 5778 *Science* 1315.

Bloss C, Schork NJ and Topol E, 'Direct-to-consumer pharmacogenomic testing is
associated with increased physician utilisation' (2014) 51(2) *Journal of Medical
Genetics* 83–9 <http://dx.doi.org/10.1136/jmedgenet-2013-101909> last
accessed 25 October 2018.

Borry P and Henneman L, 'Debating the clinical utility of direct-to-consumer
genetic testing for addiction susceptibility' (2012) 107(13) *Addiction* 2076–7
<https://doi.org/10.1111/j.1360-0443.2012.03939.x>

Borry P et al., 'Legislation on direct-to-consumer genetic testing in seven European
countries' (2012) 20 *European Journal of Human Genetics* 715.

Botkin JR et al., ASHG Position Statement, 'Points to consider: Ethical, legal, and
psychosocial implications of genetic testing in children and adolescents' (2015)

97(1) *American Journal of Human Genetics* 6–21 <https://doi.org/10.1016/j.ajhg.2015.05.022> last accessed 25 October 2018.

Brandie H, Emily E and Charis E, 'Prospective comparison of family medical history with personal genome screening for risk assessment of common cancers (2012) 20 *European Journal of Human Genetics*.

Brett GR et al., 'An exploration of genetic health professionals' experience with direct-to-consumer genetic testing in their clinical practice' (2012) 20 *European Journal of Human Genetics* 825.

Bright S, 'Unfairness and the consumer ccontract regulations' in Burrows A and Peel E (eds), *Contract Terms* (Hart 2007).

Bunnik EM, Janssens A and Schermer MH, 'Informed consent in direct-to-consumer personal genome testing: The outline of a model between specific and generic consent' (2014) 28 *Bioethics* 343.

Burrows A, *A Casebook on Contract* (4th edn, Hart Publishing 2013).

Callaway E, 'Ancestry Testing Goes For Pinpoint Accuracy' (2012) 486 *Nature* 17.

Cameron E, 'Major cases: The scrutiny of computer contracts: At last' (1996) 10 *International Review of Law, Computers & Technology* [serial online] 331.

Cammack R et al. (eds), *Oxford Dictionary of Biochemistry and Molecular Biology* (2nd edn, Oxford University Press 2006).

Camporesi S, 'Bend it like Beckham! The ethics of genetically testing children for athletic potential' (2013) 7(2) *Sport Ethics and Philosophy* 175–85.

Caplan A and Matloff E, 'Direct to confusion: Lessons learned from marketing BRCA testing' (2008) 8(6) *American Journal of Bioethics* 5.

Castle D and Ries NM, 'Ethical, legal and social issues in nutrigenomics: The challenges of regulating service delivery and building health professional capacity' (2007) 622 *Mutation Research/Fundamental and Molecular Mechanisms of Mutagenesis* 138.

Caulfield T, 'Direct-to-consumer testing: If consumers are not anxious, why are policymakers?' (2011) 130 *Human Genetics* 23.

Caulfield T, 'DTC genetic testing: Pendulum swings and policy paradoxes' (2012) 81 *Clinical Genetics* 4.

Caulfield T, 'Predictive or Preposterous? The marketing of DTC genetic testing' (2011) 10 *Journal of Science Communication* 3.

Caulfield T and McGuire A, 'Direct-to-consumer genetic testing: Perceptions, problems, and policy responses' (2012) 63 *Annual Review of Medicine* 23.

Charbonneau J, 'Straight from the lab to the market: General public engagement with direct-to-consumer genetic testing (conference slides)' (DTC Genetics – Consumers, Contracts and Complexities, King's College London, 19 June 2015).

Christofides E and O'Doherty K, 'Company disclosure and consumer perceptions of the privacy implications of direct-to-consumer genetic testing' (2016) 35(2) *New Genetics and Society* 101–23 doi: 10.1080/14636778.2016.1162092.

Cohn B and Surofchy D, 'Fighting for the right to know: OBR-Bay debates FDA regulation of DTC genetic testing' (Oxbridge Biotech Roundtable, 2014) <http://www.oxbridgebiotech.com/review/featured/23andme-debate/> last accessed 27 May 2014.

Collier R, 'Genetic tests for athletic ability: Science or snake oil?' (2012) 184(1) *Canadian Medical Association Journal* E43–5 <https://doi.org/10.1503/cmaj.109-4063> last accessed 25 October 2018.

Competition & Markets Authority, *Consumer Protection: Guidance on the CMA's Approach to Use of its Consumer Powers* (Competition & Markets Authority, CMA7, March 2014).

Competition & Markets Authority, *Draft Guidance on Unfair Contract Terms Consultation Document* (Competition & Markets Authority, CMA37con, 26 January 2015).

Competition & Markets Authority, *Unfair Contract Terms Explained* (Competition & Markets Authority, CMA37(a), 31 July 2015).

Competition & Markets Authority, *Unfair Contract Terms Guidance - Guidance on the Unfair Terms Provisions in the Consumer Rights Act 2015* (Competition & Markets Authority, CMA37, 31 July 2015).

Competition & Markets Authority, *Update on Cloud Storage Consumer Compliance Review* (CMA, 1 April 2016) <https://assets.digital.cabinet-office.gov.uk/media/56fe3227ed915d117d000037/Investigation_update-1_April_2016.pdf> last accessed 29 May 2016.

Competition & Markets Authority, *Consumer Law Compliance Review: Cloud Storage* (CMA, Findings Report, 2016) <https://assets.digital.cabinet-office.gov.uk/media/57472953e5274a037500000d/cloud-storage-findings-report.pdf> last accessed 29 May 2016.

Conklin K and Hyde R, 'If small print "terms and conditions" require a PhD to read, should they be legally binding?' *The Conversation* (10 May 2018) <https://theconversation.com/if-small-print-terms-and-conditions-require-a-phd-to-read-should-they-be-legally-binding-75101> last accessed 18 October 2018.

Conklin K, Hyde R and Parente F, 'Assessing plain and intelligible language in the Consumer Rights Act: A role for reading scores?' (2018) *Legal Studies* ISSN 1748-121X (in press) <http://eprints.nottingham.ac.uk/51073/> last accessed 18 October 2018.

Cornel MC, van El CG and Borry P, 'The challenge of implementing genetic tests with clinical utility while avoiding unsound applications' (2014) 5 *Journal of Community Genetics* 7.

Cranor LF, Hoke C, Leon P and Au A, 'Are they worth reading? An In-depth analysis of online advertising companies' privacy policies (31 March 2014) 2014 TPRC Conference Paper <http://dx.doi.org/10.2139/ssrn.2418590>

Cranor LF, Leon P and Ur B, 'A large-scale evaluation of US financial institutions' standardized privacy notices' *ACM Transactions on the Web (TWEB)* 10, no. 3 (2016) 17 <http://delivery.acm.org/10.1145/2920000/2911988/a17-cranor.pdf?ip=115.188.134.190&id=2911988&acc=OA&key=4D4702B0C3E38B35%2E4D4702B0C3E38B35%2E4D4702B0C3E38B35%2E1BEBFB956F94DAC2&__acm__=1552165885_805eda794d1ee2d3e22f298fe8563271> last accessed 5 April 2019.

Cunningham M, 'Next generation privacy: The Internet of Things, data exhaust, and reforming regulation by risk of harm' (2015) 2(2) *Groningen Journal of International Law* 115–44.

Curnutte M and Testa G, 'Consuming genomes: Scientific and social innovation in direct-to-consumer genetic testing' (2012) 31 *New Genetics and Society* 159.

Curren L and Kaye J, 'Revoking consent: A "blind spot" in data protection law?' (2010) 26 *Computer Law & Security Review* 273.

Daley L et al., 'Personal DNA testing in college classrooms: Perspectives of students and professors' (2013) 17 *Genetic Testing and Molecular Biomarkers* 446.

David G and Yael B-E, 'Personal genomics services: Whose genomes?' (2009) 17 *European Journal of Human Genetics* 883.

Dickenson D, *Body Shopping: The Economy Fueled by Flesh and Blood* (Oneworld 2008).

Dickenson D, *Me Medicine vs. We Medicine: Reclaiming Biotechnology for the Common Good* (Columbia University Press 2013).

Dickenson D, *Property in the Body* (2nd edn, Cambridge University Press 2017).

Dohany L et al., 'Psychological distress with direct-to-consumer genetic testing: A case report of an unexpected BRCA positive test result' (2012) 21 *Journal of Genetic Counseling* 399.

Downes L and Nunes P, 'Regulating 23andMe won't stop the new age of genetic testing' *Wired* (1 January 2014) <wired.com/2014/01/the-fda-may-win-the-battle-this-holiday-season-but-23andme-will-win-the-war/> last accessed 25 August 2015.

Dreyfuss J, 'How accurate can genetic predictions be?' (2012) 13 *BMC Genomics* 340.

Dvoskin R and Kaufman D, 'Tables of direct-to-consumer genetic testing companies and conditions tested – August 2011' (2011) <dnapolicy.org/images/reportpdfs/NewMethodsForDTCTable_updated_Jan2012.pdf>

EASAC and FEAM, *Direct-To-Consumer Genetic Testing For Health-Related Purposes In The European Union* EASAC Policy Report 18 <http://www.easac.eu/home/reports-and-statements/detail-view/article/direct-to-co.html> last accessed 10 December 2012.

Edwards K et al., 'Genetics researchers' and IRB professionals' attitudes toward genetic research review: A comparative analysis' (2012) 14 *Genetic Medicine* 236.

Elshout M, Elsen M, Leenheer J, Loos M, and Luzak J, *Study on Consumers' Attitudes Towards Terms Conditions (T&Cs) Final Report* (Report for the European Commission, Consumers, Health, Agriculture and Food Executive Agency [CHAFEA] on behalf of Directorate-General for Justice and Consumers, September 22, 2016) <https://ssrn.com/abstract=2847546>

Emerging Science and Bioethics Advisory Committee, 'Emerging Science and Bioethics Advisory Committee (closed)' <gov.uk/government/groups/emerging-science-and-bioethics-advisory-committee> last accessed 5 August 2015.

Erlich Y and Narayanan A, 'Routes for breaching and protecting genetic privacy' (2014) 15 *Nature Reviews Genetics* 409.

European Academies Science Advisory Council (EASAC) and the Federation of European Academies of Medicine (FEAM), *Direct-to-Consumer Genetic Testing Summary Document* (EASAC-FEAM Project on Direct-to-Consumer Genetic Testing, October 2012).

European Commission, *Consumer Vulnerability Across Key Markets in the European Union* (2016) <https://ec.europa.eu/info/publications/understanding-consumer-vulnerability-eus-key-markets_en>

European Society of Human Genetics, 'Statement of the ESHG on direct-to-consumer genetic testing for health-related purposes' (2010) 18 *European Journal of Human Genetics* 1271.

European Society of Human Genetics, 'Direct-to-consumer genetic tests neither accurate in their predictions nor beneficial to individuals, study suggests' (2011) <http://www.sciencedaily.com/releases/2011/05/110530190344.htm> last accessed 3 November 2011.

Evans HM, 'Do patients have duties?' (2007) 33 *Journal of Medical Ethics* 689.

Evans JP and Burke W, 'Genetic exceptionalism. Too much of a good thing?' (2008) 10 *Genetics in Medicine* 500.

Evans JP, Burke W and Khoury M, 'The rules remain the same for genomic medicine: The case against "reverse genetic exceptionalism"' (2010) 12 *Genetics in Medicine* 342.

Evans JP and Green RC, 'Direct to consumer genetic testing: Avoiding a culture war' (2009) 11 *Genetics in Medicine* 568.

Fabian B, Ermakova T and Lentz T, 'Large-scale readability analysis of privacy policies' *Proceedings of the International Conference on Web Intelligence* (August 2017) *ACM* <https://www.researchgate.net/profile/Benjamin_Fabian/publi cation/317400012_Large-Scale_Readability_Analysis_of_Privacy_Policies/ links/59b17226aca2728472d12f9b/Large-Scale-Readability-Analysis-of-Privacy-Policies.pdf> last accessed 5 April 2019.

FCA, *Consumer Vulnerability* (FCA, Occasional Paper No 8, 2015).

FDA, *Cybersecurity Vulnerabilities of Hospira Symbiq Infusion System* (FDA Safety Communication, 31 July 2015).

Feero W and Guttmacher A, 'Genomic Medicine – An Updated Primer' (2010) 362 *New England Journal of Medicine* 2001.

Field Dawn and Davies Neil, *Biocode: The New Age of Genomics* (Oxford University Press 2015).

Finlay T, *UK Users' and Genetics Clinicians' Experiences of Direct-to-Consumer Genetic Testing* (PhD thesis, Cardiff University 2015).

Fletcher AL, 'Field of genes: The politics of science and identity in the Estonian genome project' (2004) 23 *New Genetics and Society* 3.

Food and Administration Administration, 'Anticipated details of the draft guidance for industry' (2014) Food and Drug Administration staff and clinical laboratories: framework for regulatory oversight of laboratory developed tests (LDTs).

Foster A, 'Critical dilemmas in genetic testing: Why regulations to protect the confidentiality of genetic information should be expanded' (2010) *Baylor Law Review* 537.

Frazzetto G, 'The drugs don't work for everyone. Doubts about the efficacy of antidepressants renew debates over the medicalization of common distress' (2008) 9 *EMBO Reports* 605.

Frebourg T, 'Direct-to-consumer genetic testing services: What are the medical benefits?' (2012) 20 *European Journal of Human Genetics* 483.

Frischmann BM and Selinger E, 'Engineering humans with contracts' (September 2016) Cardozo Legal Studies Research Paper No. 493 <https://papers.ssrn.com/ sol3/papers.cfm?abstract_id=2834011>.

Frischmann BM and Selinger E *Re-Engineering Humanity* (Cambridge University Press 2018).

Frueh FW et al., 'The future of direct-to-consumer clinical genetic tests' (2011) 12 *Nature Reviews Genetics* 511.

Frumkin A et al., '"The most important test you'll ever take"?: Attitudes toward confidential carrier matching and open individual testing among modern-religious Jews in Israel' (2011) 73 *Social Science & Medicine* 1741.

Gabel J, 'Redeeming the genetic Groupon: Efficacy, ethics, and exploitation in marketing DNA to the masses' (2012) 81 *Mississippi Law Journal.*

Gardner E, 'Gene swipe: With more DNA labs few know whether those chromosones are yours – or you stole them from someone else' (2011) 97 *ABA Journal* 50.

Genetics and Public Policy Center, 'Survey of direct-to-consumer testing statutes and regulations' (2007) <dnapolicy.org/news.release.php?action=detail&pressrelease_id=81> accessed 10 October 2012 – checked again 15 June 2014.

Genetics and Public Policy Center, *Table of Direct-to-Consumer Genetic Testing Companies Listed Alphabetically* (Gentics and Public Policy Center, 2011).

GenomeWeb staff reporter, 'Study finds clinical worries over DTC tests in Europe' *GenomeWeb Daily News* (31 May 2011) <genomeweb.com/dxpgx/study-finds-clinical-worries-over-dtc-tests-europe> last accessed 10 December 2012.

GenomeWeb Staff Reporter, 'FDA warns Inova to stop performing medimap tests without proper regulatory approvals' *GenomeWeb* (4 April 2019) <https://www.genomeweb.com/business-news/fda-warns-inova-stop-performing-medimap-tests-without-proper-regulatory-approvals#.XKfaTy1L0_U> last accessed 5 April 2019.

Giannella E, 'Morality and the idea of progress in Silicon Valley' *Berkeley Journal of Sociology* <http://berkeleyjournal.org/2015/01/morality-and-the-idea-of-progress-in-silicon-valley/> last accessed 12 April 2015.

Gibbs S, 'DNA-screening test 23andMe launches in UK after US ban' *The Guardian* (2 December 2014) <theguardian.com/technology/2014/dec/02/google-genetic-testing-23andme-uk-launch> last accessed 4 December 2014.

Gillis N and Innocenti F, 'Evidence required to demonstrate clinical utility of pharmacogenetic testing: The debate continues' (2014) 96 *Clinical Pharmacology & Therapeutics* 655.

Ginsburg D, 'Genetics and genomics to the clinic: A long road ahead' (2011) 147 *Cell* 17.

Ginsburg GS and Willard HF, 'Genomic and personalized medicine: Foundations and applications' (2009) 154 *Translational Research* 277.

Goddard K et al, 'Health-related direct-to-consumer genetic tests: A public health assessment and analysis of practices related to internet-based tests for risk of thrombosis' (2009) 12 *Public Health Genomics.*

Goh AM et al., 'Perception, experience, and response to genetic discrimination in Huntington's disease: The Australian results of The International RESPOND-HD study' (2013) 17 *Genetic Testing And Molecular Biomarkers* 115.

Goldman E, '23andMe's browsewrap fails, but its post-purchase clickthrough works anyway – Tompkins v. 23andMe' (2014) <http://blog.ericgoldman.org/archives/2014/07/23andmes-browsewrap-fails-but-its-post-purchase-clickthrough-works-anyway-tompkins-v-23andme> last accessed 3 July 2014.

Goldsmith L et al., 'Direct-to-consumer genomic testing: Systematic review of the literature on user perspectives' (2012) 20 *European Journal of Human Genetics* 811.

Good NS et al., *Noticing Notice: A Large-Scale Experiment on the Timing of Software License Agreements* (ACM 2007).

Goold I, Greasley K, Herring J, and Skene L (eds), *Persons, Parts and Property: How Should We Regulate Human Tissue in the 21st Century?* (Bloomsbury 2016).

Gray S et al., 'The impact of risk information exposure on women's beliefs about direct-to-consumer genetic testing for BRCA mutations' (2012) 81 *Clinical Genetics* 29.

Greenbaum D and Gerstein M, 'The role of cloud computing in managing the deluge of potentially private genetic data' (2011) 11 *American Journal of Bioethics* 39.

Griffiths A et al., *Introduction to Genetic Analysis* (10th edn, GH Freeman and Company 2012).

Gustafson D, 'Expanding on the role of patient as consumer' (1991) 17 *Quality Review Bulletin* 324.

Gymrek M et al., 'Identifying personal genomes by surname inference' (2013) 339 *Science* 321.

Haga SB et al., 'Public knowledge of and attitudes toward genetics and genetic testing' (2013) 17 *Genetic Testing And Molecular Biomarkers* 327.

Haga SB and Burke W, 'Pharmacogenetic testing: Not as simple as it seems' (2008) 10 *Genetics in Medicine* 391.

Hall TO et al., 'Risk prediction for complex diseases: Application to Parkinson Disease' (2012) 15 *Genetics in Medicine* 361.

Hamburg MA and Collins FS, 'The path to personalized medicine' (2010) 363 *New England Journal of Medicine* 301.

Harris A, Wyatt S and Kelly SE, 'The gift of spit (and the obligation to return it): How consumers of online genetic testing services participate in research' (2013) 16 *Information, Communication & Society* 236.

Harvard PGP, 'Sharing personal genomes' <personalgenomes.org/harvard> last accessed 3 August 2015.

Hastings R et al., 'The changing landscape of genetic testing and its impact on clinical and laboratory services and research in Europe' (2012) 20 *European Journal of Human Genetics* 911.

Hayden EC, 'The $1,000 genome' (2014) 507 *Nature* 294.

Hayden EC, 'Technology: The $1,000 genome' (2014) 507 *Nature*.

Haynes AW, 'Online privacy policies: Contracting away control over personal information' (2006) 111 *Penn State Law Review* 587.

Hazel J and Slobogin C, 'Who knows what, and when?: A survey of the privacy policies proffered by U.S. direct-to-consumer genetic testing companies' (19 April 2018, last revised 18 October 2018) *Cornell Journal of Law and Public Policy* and Vanderbilt Law Research Paper No 18–18 <https://ssrn.com/abstract=3165765> last accessed 24 October 2018.

Health Law Institute, *Analysis of Privacy Policies and Practices of Direct-to-Consumer Genetic Testing Companies: Private Sector Databanks and Privacy Protection Norms* (Report funded by the Office of the Privacy Commissioner of Canada, 2010).

Hedley S, *The Law of Electronic Commerce and the Internet in the UK and Ireland* (2nd edn, Cavendish Publishing Limited 2006).

Herring J, *Medical Law and Ethics* (4th edn, Oxford University Press 2012).

Herring J, *Medical Law and Ethics* (8th edn, Oxford University Press 2018).

Hillman RA, 'On-line consumer standard-form contracting practices: A survey and discussion of legal implications' (2005) Cornell Law Faculty Publications Paper 29 <http://dx.doi.org/10.2139/ssrn.686817>

Hilts A, Parsons C, and Knockel J, *Every Step You Fake: A Comparative Analysis of Fitness Tracker Privacy and Security* (Open Effect Report, 2016) <https://citizenlab.org/2016/02/fitness-tracker-privacy-and-security/> last accessed 24 October 2018.

Hofmann B, Solbakk JH and Holm S, 'Consent to biobank research: One size fits all?' in Solbakk JH, Holm S and Hoffman B (eds), *The Ethics Of Research Biobanking* (Springer 2009).

Hoffman DA, 'From promise to form: How contracting online changes consumers' (2016) 91 *New York University Law Review* 1595 (2016); Temple University Legal Studies Research Paper No 2016–10; University of Pennsylvania, Institute for Law and Economics Research Paper No 17–7<https://ssrn.com/abstract=2724661> or http://dx.doi.org/10.2139/ssrn.2724661.

Hogarth S, Melzer D and Zimmern R, 'The regulation of commercial genetic testing services in the UK' (2005) A briefing for the Human Genetics Commission Cambridge.

Holtzman NA and Watson MS, 'Promoting safe and effective genetic testing in the United States: Final report of the Task Force on Genetic Testing' (1997).

Howard H, Avard D and Borry P, 'Are the kids really all right? Direct-to-consumer genetic testing in children: Are company policies clashing with professional norms?' (2011) 19 *European Journal of Human Genetics* 1122.

Howard H and Borry P, 'Survey of European clinical geneticists on awareness, experiences and attitudes towards direct-to-consumer genetic testing' (2013) 5 *Genome Medicine* 45.

Howard H, Knoppers B and Borry P, 'Blurring lines. The research activities of direct-to-consumer genetic testing companies raise questions about consumers as research subjects' (2010) 11 *EMBO Reports* 579.

Howard HC and Borry P, 'Direct-to-consumer genetic testing: More questions than benefits?' (2008) 5 *Personalised Medicine* 317.

Huang, H-Y and Bashir M, 'Direct-to-consumer genetic testing: Contextual privacy predicament' Proceedings of the 78th ASIS&T Annual Meeting: Information Science with Impact: Research in and for the Community (2015) American Society for Information Science 50.

Hughes JT, 'Consent and forgetting: What privacy pros can learn from one family's unexpected experience' (2014) <https://privacyassociation.org/news/a/consent-and-forgetting-what-privacy-pros-can-learn-from-one-familys-unexpected-experience/> last accessed 14 September 2014.

Human Genetics Commission, *Genes Direct: Ensuring the Effective Oversight of Genetic Tests Supplied Directly to the Public* (Department of Health, 2003).

Human Genetics Commission, *More Genes Direct* (Department of Health, 2007)

Human Genetics Commission, *Human Genetics Commission Final Report* (Department of Health, 2012).

Hunt E, 'Amazon Kindle's terms "unreasonable" and would take nine hours to read, Choice says' *The Guardian* (15 March 2017) <https://www.theguardian.com/australia-news/2017/mar/15/amazon-kindles-terms-unreasonable-and-would-take-nine-hours-to-read-choice-says> last accessed 18 October 2018.

Hustinx P, Opinion of the European Data Protection Supervisor on the Commission's Communication on 'Unleashing the Potential of Cloud Computing in Europe',

European Data Protection Supervisor (16 November 2012) <https://secure.edps.europa.eu/EDPSWEB/webdav/site/mySite/shared/Documents/Consultation/Opinions/2012/12-11-16_Cloud_Computing_EN.pdf> last accessed 12 May 2016.

Irick M, 'Age of an information revolution: The direct-to-consumer genetic testing industry and the need for a holistic regulatory approach' (2012) 49 *San Diego Law Review* 279.

Jackson L, Goldsmith L and Skirton H, 'Guidance for patients considering direct-to-consumer genetic testing and health professionals involved in their care: Development of a practical decision tool' (2014) *Family Practice.*

Janssens A and Deverka P, 'Useless until proven effective: The clinical utility of preemptive pharmacogenetic testing' (2014) 96 *Clinical Pharmacology & Therapeutics* 652.

Joh EE, 'DNA theft: Recognizing the crime of nonconsensual genetic collection and testing' (2011) 91 *Boston University Law Review* 665.

Joly Y, Ngueng Feze I and Simard J, 'Genetic discrimination and life insurance: A systematic review of the evidence' (2013) 11 *BMC Medicine* 25.

Jostins L and Barrett JC, 'Genetic risk prediction in complex disease' (2011) 20 *Human Molecular Genetics* R182.

Kacen JJ, Hess JD and Kevin Chiang W-Y, 'Bricks or clicks? Consumer attitudes toward traditional stores and online stores' (2013) 18 *Global Economics and Management Review* 12.

Kalf R et al., 'Variations in predicted risks in personal genome testing for common complex diseases' (2014) 16 *Genetic Medicine* 85.

Kalokairinou Louiza, Howard Heidi Carmen and Borry Pascal, 'Changes on the horizon for consumer genomics in the EU' (2014) 346 (6207) *Science* 296–8 doi: 10.1126/science.1256396.

Kalokairinou L, Howard HC, Slokenberga S et al., 'Legislation of direct-to-consumer genetic testing in Europe: A fragmented regulatory landscape' (2018) 9(2) *Journal Of Community Genetics* 117–32, 118 <https://link.springer.com/article/10.1007/s12687-017-0344-2>

Katz J, 'Informed consent – a fairy tale-law's vision' (1977) 39 *University of Pittsburg Law Review* 137.

Kaufman DJ et al., 'Risky business: Risk perception and the use of medical services among customers of DTC personal genetic testing' (2012) 21 *Journal of Genetic Counseling* 413.

Kaye J, 'The regulation of direct-to-consumer genetic tests' (2008) 17 *Human Molecular Genetics* R180.

Kaye J et al., 'Dynamic consent: A patient interface for twenty-first century research networks' (2015) 23 *European Journal of Human Genetics* 141.

Kaye J, Bell J, Briceno L, and Mitchell C, 'Biobank Report: United Kingdom' (2016) 44(1) *Journal of Law, Medicine & Ethics* 96–105.

Kazemian L, Pease K and Farrington DP, 'DNA retention policies: The potential contribution of criminal career research' (2011) 8 *European Journal of Criminology* 48.

Kendall M, 'Koh appoints lead counsel in scrum over 23andMe suits' *The American Lawyer* (2014) <americanlawyer.com/id=1202655508972/Koh-Appoints-Lead-Counsel-in-Scrum-Over-23andMe-Suits?slreturn=20140516142508> last accessed 15 May 2014.

Kendall M 'SF judge sides with 23andMe on class claims' *The Recorder* (10 June 2015) <therecorder.com/id=1202729012905?keywords=Marisa+Kendall>

Khanna S and Tosh PK, *A Clinician's Primer on the Role of the Microbiome in Human Health and Disease* (Elsevier 2014).

Khoury M, Rogowski W and Grosse S, 'Challenges of translating genetic tests into clinical and public health practice' (2009) 10 *Nature Reviews Genetics* 489.

Kim NS, 'Contract's adaptation and the online bargain' (2011) 79 *University of Cincinnati Law Review* 1327–70.

Kim NS, *Wrap Contracts: Foundations and Ramifications* (Oxford University Press 2014).

Kim NS, 'The wrap contract morass' (2014) 44(2) *Southwestern University Law Review* 309–25 <https://ssrn.com/abstract=2611815>

Kim NS, *The Fundamentals of Contract Law and Clauses: A Practical Approach* (Edward Elgar 2016).

King RC, Mulligan P and Stansfield W (eds), *A Dictionary of Genetics* (8th edn, Oxford University Press 2013).

Kishore D, 'Test at your own risk: Your genetic report card and the direct-to-consumer duty to secure informed consent' (2009) *Emory Law Journal.*

Klass G, Letsas G and Saprai P (eds), *Philosophical Foundations of Contract Law* (Oxford University Press 2014).

Knoppers B, 'Consent to "personal" genomics and privacy. Direct-to-consumer genetic tests and population genome research challenge traditional notions of privacy and consent' (2010) 11 EMBO Report 416.

Koch V, 'PGTandMe: Social networking-based genetic testing and the evolving research model' (2012) 22 Health Matrix Clevel 33.

Kraft P and Hunter DJ, 'Genetic risk prediction: Are we there yet?' (2009) 360 *New England Journal of Medicine* 1701.

Kraft P et al., 'Beyond odds ratios – communicating disease risk based on genetic profiles' (2009) 10 *Nature Reviews Genetics* 264.

Kramer P and Bressan P, 'Humans as superorganisms: How microbes, viruses, imprinted genes, and other selfish entities shape our behavior' (2015) 10 *Perspectives on Psychological Science* 464.

Kuehn B, 'Inconsistent results, inaccurate claims plague direct-to-consumer gene tests' (2010) 304 *JAMA* 1313.

Kurzweil, '23andMe granted authorization by FDA to market first direct-to-consumer genetic test' (*KurzweilAI*) <kurzweilai.net/23andme-granted-authorization-by-fda-to-market-first-direct-to-consumer-genetic-test> last accessed 23 February 2015.

Kutz G, *Direct-to-Consumer Genetic Tests: Misleading Test Results are Further Complicated by Deceptive Marketing and Other Questionable Practices: Congressional Testimony* (DIANE Publishing 2010).

Lachance CR et al., 'Informational content, literacy demands, and usability of websites offering health-related genetic tests directly to consumers' (2010) 12 *Genetics in Medicine* 304.

Laestadius LI, Rich JR, and Auer PL, 'All your data (effectively) belong to us: Data practices among direct-to-consumer genetic testing firms' (2016) 19 *Genetics in Medicine* 513–20 doi:10.1038/gim.2016.136.

Lanktree MB et al., 'Positive perception of pharmacogenetic testing for psychotropic medications' (2014) 29 *Human psychopharmacology: clinical and experimental* 287.

Laurie G, *Genetic Privacy: A Challenge To Medico-Legal Norms* (reprint edn, Cambridge University Press 2002).

Lawson R, *Exclusion Clauses and Unfair Contract Terms* (11th edn, Thomson Reuters [Professional] UK Limited 2014).

Leachman SA, MacArthur DG, Angrist M, Gray SW, Bradbury AR and Vorhaus DB, 'Direct-to-consumer genetic testing: Personalized medicine in evolution' (2011) American Society of Clinical Oncology 34–40, 36 <https://thepriva cyreport.com/wp-content/uploads/2011/06/ASCO-DTC-Abstract.pdf> last accessed 22 October 2018.

Lee S and Crawley L, 'Research 2.0: Social networking and direct-to-consumer (DTC) genomics' (2009) 9 *American Journal of Bioethics* 35.

Lee SS-J et al., 'Attitudes towards social networking and sharing behaviors among consumers of direct-to-consumer personal genomics' (2013) 3 *Journal of Personalized Medicine* 275.

Lewis NP et al., 'DTC genetic testing companies fail transparency prescriptions' (2011) 30 *New Genetics and Society* 291.

Lindblom A and Robinson P, 'Bioinformatics for human genetics: Promises and challenges' (2011) 32 *Human Mutation* 495.

Liu Y and Pearson YE, 'Direct-to-consumer marketing of predictive medical genetic tests: Assessment of current practices and policy recommendations' (2008) 27 *Journal of Public Policy & Marketing* 131.

Loos M and Luzak J, 'Wanted: A bigger stick. On unfair terms in consumer contracts with online service providers' (2015) 39 *Journal of Consumer Policy* 63–90 <https://doi.org/10.1007/s10603-015-9303-7> last accessed 18 October 2018.

Lynch J and et al., 'Media coverage of direct-to-consumer genetic testing ' (2011) 20 *Journal of Genetic Counseling* 486.

MacLeod R et al., 'Experiences of predictive testing in young people at risk of Huntington's disease, familial cardiomyopathy or hereditary breast and ovarian cancer' (2014) 22 *European Journal of Human Genetics* 396.

Mahon S, 'Impact of direct-to-consumer genetic testing' (2012) 8 *Journal of Oncology Practice* 260.

Mangen A, Walgermo BR and Brønnick K, 'Reading linear texts on paper versus computer screen: Effects on reading comprehension' (2013) 58 *International Journal of Educational Research* 61.

Manwaring K, 'Enforceability of clickwrap and browsewrap terms in Australia: Lessons from the US and the UK' (2011) 5 *Studies in Ethics, Law, and Technology*.

Marchione M, 'Study reveals shortcomings in gene testing; results on estimating disease risk often conflict' Associated Press (27 May 2015).

Marietta C and McGuire AL, 'Direct-to-consumer genetic testing: Is it the practice of medicine?' (2009) 37 *Journal of Law, Medicine & Ethics* 369.

Mason J and Laurie G, *Mason and McCall Smith's Law and Medical Ethics* (8th edn, Oxford University Press 2011).

Mason L, 'Protecting consumers from unfair terms in standard form contracts: The UK approach' (2015) 26 *European Business Law Review* 335.

Mathews R, Hall W and Carter A, 'Direct-to-consumer genetic testing for addiction susceptibility: A premature commercialisation of doubtful validity and value' (2012) 107 *Addiction* 2069.

McDonald AM and Cranor LF, 'The cost of reading privacy policies' (2008) 4 *Journal of Law and Policy for the Information Society* 543–68 <https://kb.osu.edu/bitstream/handle/1811/72839/1/ISJLP_V4N3_543.pdf> last 24 October 2018.

McDonald AM, Reeder RW, Kelley PG, and Cranor LF, 'A comparative study of onlineprivacy policies and formats' (2009) from International Symposium on Privacy Enhancing Technologies Symposium in I Goldberg and MJ Atallah (eds), *Privacy Enhancing Technologies* (Lecture Notes in *Computer Science*, vol 5672 Springer, PETS 2009) <https://link.springer.com/chapter/10.1007/978-3-642-03168-7_3>

McGillivray Kevin, 'Conflicts in the cloud: Contracts and compliance with data protection law in the EU' (2014) 17 *Tulane Journal of Technology and Intellectual Property* 217.

McGinn S and Gut IG, 'DNA sequencing – spanning the generations' (2013) 30 *New Biotechnology* 366.

McGuire A and Burke W, 'Health system implications of direct-to-consumer personal genome testing' (2011) 14 *Public Health Genomics.*

McGuire A et al., 'Social networkers' attitudes toward direct-to-consumer personal genome testing' (2009) 9 *American Journal of Bioethics* 3.

McKendrick E, *Contract law: Text, cases, and materials* (5th edn, Oxford University Press 2012).

McLaughlin H, 'What's in a name: 'Client', 'patient', 'customer', 'consumer', 'expert by experience', 'service user'– what's next?' (2009) 39 *British Journal of Social Work* 1101.

McPherson E, 'Genetic diagnosis and testing in clinical practice' (2006) 4 *Clinical Medicine & Research* 123.

Mello M and Wolf L, 'The Havasupai Indian tribe case – lessons for research involving stored biologic samples' (2010) 363 *New England Journal of Medicine* 204.

Meyer MJ, 'Patients' duties' (1992) 17 *Journal of Medicine and Philosophy* 541.

Meyer U, 'Personalized medicine: A personal view' (2012) 91 *Clinical Pharmacology & Therapeutics* 373.

MHRA, 'New legislation on medical devices' <http://www.mhra.gov.uk/How weregulate/Devices/Legislation/NewLegislationonMedicalDevices/index.htm> 30 May 2014.

Morrison A, 'A research revolution: Genetic testing consumers become research (and privacy) guinea pigs' (2011) 9 *Journal on Telecommunications and High Technology Law* 573.

Motoc IV, 'The international law of genetic discrimination' in Murphy T (ed.), *New Technologies and Human Rights* (Oxford Scholarship Online 2009).

Murray A, *Information technology law: The law and society* (Oxford University Press 2013).

Myers MF, 'Health care providers and direct-to-consumer access and advertising of genetic testing in the United States' (2011) 3(81) *Genome Medicine* 1–13 <https://doi.org/10.1186/gm297> last accessed 20 October 2018.

National Human Genome Research Institute, 'Genome-wide association studies' <genome.gov/20019523> last accessed 9 December 2012.

National Center for Biotechnology Information, 'Genetic Testing Registry' (2012) <https://www.ncbi.nlm.nih.gov/gtr/> last accessed 28 October 2018.

Naveed M et al., 'Privacy and security in the genomic era' (2014) arXiv:1405.1891v3 <https://arxiv.org/abs/1405.1891> last accessed 22 October 2018.

Nordgren A, 'Neither as harmful as feared by critics nor as empowering as promised by providers: Risk information offered direct to consumer by personal genomics companies' (2014) 5(1) *Journal of Community Genetics* 59.

Norwegian Consumer Council, *Consumer Protection in Fitness Wearables* (NCC, November 2016) <http://www.sverigeskonsumenter.se/Documents/Rapporter/Consumer%20protection%20in%20fitness%20wearables.pdf> last accessed 24 October 2018.

Norwegian Consumer Council, *APPFAIL Threats to Consumers in Mobile Apps* (NCC, March 2016) <https://www.forbrukerradet.no/undersokelse/2015/appfail-threats-to-consumers-in-mobile-apps/> last accessed 18 October 2018.

Norwegian Consumer Council, *#WatchOut Analysis of Smartwatches for Children* (NCC, October 2017) <https://fil.forbrukerradet.no/wp-content/uploads/2017/10/watchout-rapport-october-2017.pdf> last accessed 24 October 2018.

Norwegian Consumer Council, *Deceived by Design* (NCC, June 2018) <https://www.forbrukerradet.no/undersokelse/no-undersokelsekategori/deceived-by-design/>

Novy MC, 'Privacy at a price: Direct-to-consumer genetic testing and the need for regulation' (2010) University of Illinois *Journal of Law, Technology and Policy* 157.

Nuffield Council on Bioethics, *The Collection, Linking And Use Of Data In Biomedical Research And Health Care: Ethical Issues* (Nuffield Council on Bioethics, February 2015).

Obar JA and Oeldorf-Hirsch A, 'Clickwrap impact: Quick-join options and ignoring privacy and terms of service policies of social networking services' (2017) in Proceedings of the 8th International Conference on Social Media and Society ACM 8 <https://ssrn.com/abstract=3017277> last accessed 29 July 2018.

Obar JA and Oeldorf-Hirsch A, 'The biggest lie on the Internet: Ignoring the privacy policies and terms of service policies of social networking services' (2018) *Information, Communication & Society* 1–20 <https://doi.org/10.1080/1369118X.2018.1486870> last accessed 22 October 2018.

O'Huallachain M et al., 'Extensive genetic variation in somatic human tissues' (2012) 109 PNAS 18018.

Office of Fair Trading, *OFT Secures Further Improvements To Gyms Contracts* (Office of Fair Trading, Press Release, 2013).

Office of Fair Trading, *Vulnerable Consumer Groups: Quantification And Analysis* (Office of Fair Trading, Research Paper 15, 1998).

Office of the Privacy Commissioner (OPC), *Statement On The Use Of Genetic Test Results By Life And Health Insurance Companies* (OPC, 2014).

Offit K, 'Genomic profiles for disease risk: Predictive or premature?' (2008) 299(11) *JAMA* 1353–55 doi: 10.1001/jama.299.11.1353.

Omri Ben-Shahar, 'The myth of the "opportunity to read" in contract law' (2009) 5(1) *European Review of Contract Law* 1–28.

Online O, '"patient, adj. and n."' in *Oxford English Dictionary* (web edn, Oxford

University Press 2014) <http://www.oed.com/view/Entry/138820?rskey=BIE5 8d&result=1&isAdvanced=false> last accessed 15 June 2014.

Ornstein C, 'Tracking your own health data too closely can make you sick' (National Public Radio, 2015) <npr.org/sections/health-shots/2015/04/06/397848621/ tracking-your-own-health-data-too-closely-can-make-you-sick> last accessed 28 October 2018.

Otlowski M, Taylor S and Bombard Y, 'Genetic discrimination: International perspectives' (2012) 13 *Annual Review of Genomics and Human Genetics* 433.

Pagliery J, 'MasterCard will approve purchases by scanning your face' *CNN Money Cyber-Safe* (1 July 2015) <<https://money.cnn.com/2015/07/01/technology/ mastercard-facial-scan/> last accessed 28 October 2018.

Patenaude AF, 'Commentary: Save the children: Direct-to-consumer test ing of children is premature, even for research' (2011) 36 *Journal of Pediatric Psychology* 1122.

Patsner B, 'New "home brew" predictive genetic tests present significant regulatory problems' (2009) *Houston Journal of Health Law and Policy* 237.

Perton M, 'Read fine print or GameStation may own your soul' *Consumerist* (16 April 2010) <http://consumerist.com/2010/04/16/read-fine-print-or-gamestation- may-own-your-soul/> last accessed 28 October 2018.

Petersen C and DeMuro P, 'Legal and regulatory considerations associated with use of patient-generated health data from social media and mobile health (mHealth) devices' (2015) 6 *Applied Clinical Informatics* 16.

Phillips Andelka M, 'Think before you click: Ordering a genetic test online' (Winter 2015) *The SciTech Lawyer* 11(2) <http://www.americanbar.org/publications/ scitech_lawyer/2015/winter/think_before_you_click_ordering_genetic_test_on line.html>

Phillips Andelka M, 'Think before you click' republished as part of the American Bar Association's 'The Best of ABA Sections' in its *GPSolo* magazine (July/ August, issue 2015) <http://www.americanbar.org/publications/gp_solo/2015/ july-august/science_and_technology_law_think_you_click_ordering_genetic_ test_online.html>

Phillips Andelka M, 'Genomic privacy and direct-to-consumer genetics – Big consumer genetic data – What's in that contract?' ' (2015 IEEE CS Security and Privacy Workshops) (presented at GenoPri'15 [The 2nd Workshop on Genome Privacy and Security] and published as part of IEEE Conference Proceedings 2015) <https://www.computer.org/csdl/proceedings/spw/2015/9933/00/9933a060. pdf> last accessed 23 October 2018.

Phillips Andelka M, 'Take an online DNA test and you could be revealing far more than you realise' *The Conversation* (12 January 2016) <https://theconversation. com/take-an-online-dna-test-and-you-could-be-revealing-far-more-than-you- realise-52734>

Phillips Andelka M, 'Only a click away – DTC genetics for ancestry, health, love . . . and more: A view of the business and regulatory landscape' (2016) 8 *Applied and Translational Genomics* 16–22.

Phillips Andelka M, 'Reading the fine print when buying your genetic self online: Direct-to-consumer genetic testing terms and conditions' (2017) *New Genetics and Society* 36(3) 273–95 <http://dx.doi.org/10.1080/14636778.2017.1352468>

Phillips Andelka M, 'Genetics goes online – privacy in the world of personal genomics' *Privacy Laws and Business International* (October 2018). <https://www.privacylaws.com/Publications/int/PLB_International_Issues/PLB-International-Issue-155/>

Phillips, Andelka M and Finlay T, '"DNA a click away" – Workshop on "agreements" in DTCGT' (Translation in Healthcare – Exploring the Impact of Emerging Technologies, Oxford, 23–5 June 2015).

Pines WL, 'History and perspective on direct-to-consumer promotion' (1999) 54 *Food and Drug Law Journal* 489.

Pirzadeh-Miller S et al., 'Direct-to-consumer genetic testing: Helpful, harmful, or pure entertainment?' (2011) 8 *Community Oncology* 263.

Plaut VC and Bartlett III RP, 'Blind consent? A social psychological investigation of non-readership of click-through agreements' (2012) 36 *Law and Human Behavior* 293.

Pollack A, 'DNA sequencing caught in deluge of data' *New York Times* (30 June 2011) <beacon-center.org/wp-content/uploads/2010/10/NYT113011_DNASeqDelugeData.pdf>

Popovsky M, 'Exaggerated benefits and underestimated harms: The direct-to-market consumer genetic test market and how to manage it going forward' (2010) 8 *Dartmouth Law Journal* 65.

Powell KP et al., 'Educational needs of primary care physicians regarding direct-to-consumer genetic testing' (2012) 21 *Journal of Genetic Counseling* 469.

Powell KP et al., 'Primary care physicians' awareness, experience and opinions of direct-to-consumer genetic testing' (2012) 21 *Journal of Genetic Counseling* 113.

Proffitt A, 'Deals center on self-reported patient data services' (2012) 30 *Nature Biotechnology* 1016.

Radin MJ, *Boilerplate* (Princeton Press 2013).

Ray T, 'Will other states follow NY, Calif., in taking on DTC genetic-testing firms?' <http://www.genomeweb.com/dxpgx/will-other-states-follow-ny-calif-taking-dtc-genetic-testing-firms-0>

Ray T, 'With Decode purchase, Amgen gains genetics expertise, consumers lose DTC testing option' *GenomeWeb* (12 December 2012) <genomeweb.com//node/1163376?hq_e=el&hq_m=1432031&hq_l=1&hq_v=654c94516e> last accessed 12 December 2012.

Rehm HL et al., 'ClinGen – the clinical genome resource' (2015) 372 *New England Journal of Medicine* 2235.

Reidenberg JR, Breaux T, Cranor LF, French B, Grannis A, Graves JT, Liu F, McDonald A, Norton TB and Ramanath R, 'Disagreeable privacy policies: Mismatches between meaning and users' understanding' (2015) 30 *Berkeley Tech LJ* 39 <https://scholarship.law.berkeley.edu/cgi/viewcontent.cgi?referer=https://scholar.google.co.nz/scholar?as_ylo=2015&q=cranor+and+mcdonald&hl=en&as_sdt=0,5&httpsredir=1&article=2053&context=btlj> last accessed 5 April 2019.

Ries NM and Castle D, 'Nutrigenomics and ethics interface: Direct-to-consumer services and commercial aspects' (2008) 12 OMICS *A Journal of Integrative Biology* 245.

Roberts JS and Ostergren J, 'Direct-to-consumer genetic testing and personal genomics services: A review of recent empirical studies' (2013) 1 *Current Genetic Medicine Reports* 182.

Roberts NJ et al., 'The predictive capacity of personal genome sequencing' (2012) 4 *Science Translational Medicine* 133ra58.

Robertson SJ, 'The validity of shrink-wrap licences in Scots Law Beta Computers (Europe) Ltd v. Adobe Systems (Europe) Ltd' *Journal of Information, Law and Technology* <http://www2.warwick.ac.uk/fac/soc/law/elj/jilt/1998_2/robertson/> last accessed 13 August 2015.

Robson M et al., 'American Society of Clinical Oncology policy statement update: Genetic and Genomic Testing for Cancer Susceptibility ' (2010) 28 *Journal of Clinical Oncology* 893.

Rothstein Mark A, 'Epigenetic exceptionalism' (2013) 41 *Journal of Law Medicine & Ethics* 733.

Rubinstein W et al., 'The NIH genetic testing registry: A new, centralized database of genetic tests to enable access to comprehensive information and improve transparency' (2013) 41 *Nucleic Acids Research* D925.

Sampson TR and Mazmanian SK, 'Control of brain development, function, and behavior by the microbiome' (2015) 17 *Cell Host Microbe* 565.

Samuel G, Jordens C and Kerridge I, 'Direct-to-consumer personal genome testing: Ethical and regulatory issues that arise from wanting to "know" your DNA' (2010) 40 *Internal Medicine Journal* 220.

Saukko P, 'State of play in direct-to-consumer genetic testing for lifestyle-related diseases: Market, marketing content, user experiences and regulation' (2013) 72 The Proceedings of the Nutrition Society 53.

Saukko P et al., 'Negotiating the boundary between medicine and consumer culture: Online marketing of nutrigenetic tests' (2010) 70 *Social Science & Medicine* 744.

Saunders R and Ashcroft RE, 'Consumer genetics and addiction susceptibility testing– just what the consumer ordered' (2012) 107 *Addiction* 2075.

Sboner A et al., 'The real cost of sequencing: Higher than you think!' (2011) 12 *Genome Biology* 125.

Schaub F, Balebako R and Cranor LF, 'Designing effective privacy notices and controls' (2017) 21 *IEEE Internet Computing* https://www-computer-org.ezproxy.waikato.ac.nz/csdl/magazine/ic/2017/03/mic2017030070/13rRUwgQpnc> last accessed 5 April 2019

Scherr AE, 'Genetic privacy and the Fourth Amendment: Unregulated surreptitious DNA harvesting' (2012) 47 *Georgia Law Review* 445.

Schlanger S, 'Filling in the cracks: Improving the regulation of direct-to-consumer genetic tests' (2011) 14 *Journal of Health Care Law and Policy* S1.

Schneider G and Dekker C, 'DNA sequencing with nanopores' (2012) 30 *Nature Biotechnology* 326.

Sequeiros J, 'Regulating genetic testing: The relevance of appropriate definitions' in Kristoffersson U, Schmidtke J and Cassiman J (eds), *Quality Issues in Clinical Genetic Services* (Springer 2010).

Sequeiros J et al., 'The wide variation of definitions of genetic testing in international recommendations, guidelines and reports' (2012) 3 *Journal of Community Genetics* 113.

Shanks P, 'Genomic controversy in Iceland: Déja vu all over again' (Center for Genetics and Society, 2014) <http://www.biopoliticaltimes.org/article.php?id=7778> last accessed 30 May 2014.

Shaywitz D, 'Does 23andMe deal mean medical centers are sitting on data worth millions?' *Forbes* (8 January 2015) Pharma & Healthcare <forbes.com/sites/davidshaywitz/2015/01/08/does-23andme-deal-mean-medical-centers-are-sitting-on-data-worth-millions/>

Sigmundsdóttir A, 'Privacy on Ice: This company wants to collect DNA from one-third of Iceland's population' (*Future Tense*, 2014) <http://www.slate.com/articles/technology/future_tense/2014/05/decode_genetics_wants_to_collect_dna_from_one_third_of_icelanders.html> last accessed 9 June 2014.

Simoncelli T, 'Dangerous excursions: The case against expanding forensic DNA databases to innocent persons' (2006) 34 *Journal of Law, Medicine & Ethics* 390.

Slaughter L, 'Genetic Information Non-Discrimination Act' (2013) 50 *Harvard Journal on Legislation* 41.

So H-C et al., 'Risk prediction of complex diseases from family history and known susceptibility loci, with applications for cancer screening' (2011) 88 *American Journal of Human Genetics* 548.

Spector-Bagdady K and Pike ER, 'Consuming genomics: Regulating direct-to-consumer genetic and genomic information' (2014) 92 *Nebraska Law Review* 677.

Ståhl PL and Lundeberg J, 'Toward the single-hour high-quality genome' (2012) 81 *Annual Review of Biochemistry* 359.

Stevens T and Newman S, *Biotech Juggernaut: Hope, Hype, and Hidden Agendas of Entrepreneurial BioScience* (Taylor and Francis 2019).

Storm D, 'MEDJACK: Hackers hijacking medical devices to create backdoors in hospital networks' *Computerworld* (8 June 2015) <computerworld.com/article/2932371/cybercrime-hacking/medjack-hackers-hijacking-medical-devices-to-create-backdoors-in-hospital-networks.html> last accessed 11 August 2015.

Stynen D, 'Revision of Europe's IVD Directive 98/79/EC: Lessons and results from the public consultation document' (*IVD Technology*, 2011) <ivdtechnology.com/article/revision-europe's-ivd-directive-9879ec> last accessed 22 October 2012.

Su P, 'Direct-to-consumer genetic testing: A comprehensive view' (2013) 86 *Yale Journal of Biology and Medicine* 359.

Sunderman SF, 'The need for regulation of direct-to-consumer genetic testing in the United States: Assessing and applying the German policy model' (2013) 12 *Washington University Global Studies Law Review* 357.

Swan M, 'Emerging patient-driven health care models: An examination of health social networks, consumer personalized medicine and quantified self-tracking' (2009) 6 *International Journal of Environmental Research and Public Health* 492.

Tabor HK and Kelley M, 'Challenges in the use of direct-to-consumer personal genome testing in children' (2009) 9 *American Journal of Bioethics* 32.

TallBear K, 'The emergence, politics, and marketplace of Native American DNA1' (2014) *Routledge Handbook of Science, Technology and Society* 21.

Tamir S, 'Direct-to-consumer genetic testing: Ethical-legal perspectives and practical considerations' (2010) 18 *Medical Law Review* 213.

Taylor M, *Genetic Data and The Law: A Critical Perspective on Privacy Protection*, vol. 16 (Cambridge University Press 2012).

Taylor M, 'Problems of practice and principle if centring law reform on the concept of genetic discrimination' (2004) 11 *European Journal of Health Law* 365.

Thomas KH et al., 'Reporting of drug induced depression and fatal and non-fatal suicidal behaviour in the UK from 1998 to 2011' (2014) 15 BMC *Pharmacology and Toxicology* 54.

Thompson D, 'I agreed to what? A call for enforcement of clarity in the presentation of privacy policies' (2012).

Timp Gea, 'Third generation DNA sequencing with a nanopore' in Iqbal S and Bashir R (eds), *Nanopores: Sensing and Fundamental Biological Interactions* (Springer 2011).

Trinidad SB et al., 'Genomic research and wide data sharing: Views of prospective participants' (2010) 12 *Genetics in Medicine* 486.

Trinidad SB et al., 'Genomic research and wide data sharing: Views of prospective participants' (2010) 12 *Genetics in Medicine* 486.

Tuffley D, 'How not to agree to clean public toilets when you accept any online terms and conditions' *The Conversation* (23 July 2017) <https://theconversation.com/how-not-to-agree-to-clean-public-toilets-when-you-accept-any-online-terms-and-conditions-81169> last accessed 18 October 2018.

US Government Accountability Office, *Direct-To-Consumer Genetic Tests: Misleading Test Results Are Further Complicated by Deceptive Marketing and Other Questionable Practice* (GAO-10-847T, 2010).

van den Hoven J et al., 'Privacy and information technology' in Edward N Zalta (ed.), *The Stanford Encyclopedia of Philosophy* (Winter edn, first published 20 November 2014) <https://plato.stanford.edu/archives/win2014/entries/it-privacy/accessed> 10 June 2015 – last accessed 24 October 2018.

Varga O et al., 'Definitions of genetic testing in European legal documents' (2012) 3 *Journal of Community Genetics* 125.

Vermeulen E et al., 'Public attitudes towards preventive genomics and personal interest in genetic testing to prevent disease: A survey study' (2013) *European Journal of Public Health* ckt143.

Visscher P, McEvoy B and Yang J, 'From Galton to GWAS: Quantitative genetics of human height' (2010) 92 *Genetics Research* (Cambridge) 371.

Vorhaus D, 'DNA DTC: The return of direct to consumer whole genome sequencing' *Genomics Law Report* (29 November 2012) <genomicslawreport.com/index.php/2012/11/29/dna-dtc-the-return-of-direct-to-consumer-whole-genome-sequencing/> last accessed 11 December 2012.

Vorhaus D and Contributor G, 'DTC genetic testing and the FDA: Is there an end in sight to the regulatory uncertainty?' (16 June 2011).

Waddington L, 'Reflections on the protection of 'vulnerable' consumers under EU law' (2013) 2 Maastricht Faculty of Law Working Paper 1.

Wagner J et al., 'Tilting at windmills no longer: A data-driven discussion of DTC DNA ancestry tests' (2012) 14 *Genetics in Medicine* 586.

Wagner JK and Weiss KM, 'Attitudes on DNA ancestry tests' (2012) 131 *Human Genetics* 41.

Wallace H, 'The UK national DNA database' (2006) 7 *EMBO Reports* S26.

Wang R et al., *Learning Your Identity and Disease from Research Papers: Information Leaks in Genome Wide Association Study* (ACM 2009).

Ward A, 'Google-backed genetic testing company hires veteran scientist' *Financial Times* (12 March 2015) <ft.com/cms/s/0/ead07e84-c8d8-11e4-bc64-00144 feab7de.html> last accessed 20 August 2015.

Warning Letter from US Food and Drug Administration to 23andMe (22 November 2013) <http://www.fda.gov/iceci/enforcementactions/warningletters/2013/ucm 376296.htm> last accessed 22 October 2018.

Warning Letter from US Food and Drug Administration to Inova Genomics Laboratory (4 April 2019) <https://www.fda.gov/ICECI/EnforcementActions/ WarningLetters/ucm634988.htm?utm_campaign=040419_PR_FDA%20 issues%20warning%20letter%20to%20Inova%20Genomics%20Laboratory& utm_medium=email&utm_source=Eloqua> last accessed 6 April 2019.

Watson L, 'Father who didn't want to pay child maintenance sent another man in his place to give DNA for paternity test' *Mail Online* (5 June 2013) <dailymail. co.uk/news/article-2336469/Father-didnt-want-pay-child-maintenance-sent-man-place-DNA-paternity-test.html> last accessed 25 August 2015.

Wilde A et al., 'Public interest in predictive genetic testing, including direct-to-consumer testing, for susceptibility to major depression: Preliminary findings' (2010) 18 *European Journal of Human Genetics* 47.

Wilde A et al., 'Implications of the use of genetic tests in psychiatry, with a focus on major depressive disorder: A review' (2013) 30 *Depression and Anxiety* 267.

William-Jones B, '"Be ready against cancer, now": Direct-to-consumer advertising for genetic testing' (2006) 25(1) *New Genetics and Society* 89–107.

Williams-Jones B, 'Where there's a web, there's a way: Commercial genetic testing and the Internet' (2003) 6 *Community Genetics* 46.

Womack CA, 'Ethical and epistemic issues in direct-to-consumer drug advertising: Where is patient agency?' (2013) 16 *Medicine, Health Care and Philosophy* 275.

Woodage T, 'Relative futility: Limits to genetic privacy protection because of the inability to prevent disclosure of genetic information by relatives' (2010) 95 *Minnesota Law Review.*

Zawati MnH, Borry P and Howard HC, 'Closure of population biobanks and direct-to-consumer genetic testing companies' (2011) 130 *Human Genetics* 425.

Zettler P, Sherkow J and Greely H, '23andMe, the Food and Drug Administration, and the future of genetic testing' (2014) 174 *JAMA* Internal Medicine 493.

Zimmer C, 'DNA double take' *New York Times* (16 September 2013) <https:// www.nytimes.com/2013/09/17/science/dna-double-take.html> last accessed 28 October 2018.

Zimmern R, 'Issues concerning the evaluation and regulation of predictive genetic testing' (2012) 5 *Journal of Community Genetics* 49–57.

Index